**What others are saying about**

# PLANETS IN THERAPY
## *Predictive Technique and the Art of Counseling*

Seamlessly blending astrology, psychology, and spirituality, this outstanding book offers life-enhancing, transformative ways forward for each of us on our life's journey. I have no doubt that this remarkable work will be enjoyed by astrologers, counselors, teachers, and therapists for many years to come. I couldn't put this book down and struggled to stop reading it at night. It's a generous contribution to the astrological community, a book that's going to help many people. —Margaret Gray, MSW

This book will enrich all readers seeking a grounded, practical astrology. I particularly appreciate Greg's clear and helpful chapter on the astrology of human relationships. This is the best work yet by one of the best writers in the field. Highly recommended. —Ray Grasse, author of *The Waking Dream*

Greg Bogart's book is a must-read for anyone wishing to integrate psychological astrology and spiritual practice. Greg weaves together astrology, meditation, and mysticism in his psychotherapeutic work. His proactive approach to the birth chart as a path of self-empowerment is much needed. I love his willingness to share his own experiences, which makes his work accessible and powerful. Thanks, Greg, for a tour de force manifesto. —Joe Landwehr, author of *Tracking the Soul with an Astrology of Consciousness*

You are going to totally love this book if you are serious about mastering the art of astrology, and if you are interested in how all thinking, both conscious and unconscious, interfaces with planetary alignments. Greg Bogart isn't fooling around. He goes straight into your head so you see yourself more clearly. Finally, if you have a desire to develop a counseling or clinical practice that fuses astrology with in-depth psychological study of human behavior, don't miss this chance for enlightenment. —Michael Lutin, author of *SunShines: The Astrology of Being Happy*

**Planets in Therapy** is Greg Bogart's fully mature work! He presents a wealth of case studies blended with refreshingly honest personal reflections. This book is a valuable addition to astrological literature, and it may well inspire a new generation of psychotherapists whose work will be informed by astrology's archetypal and cyclical wisdom. —Andrea Conlon, astrologer and psychotherapist

I am convinced that astrology is a form of psychology, an enormously helpful technique for understanding life and mind. I am quite happy to see a professional psychotherapist who has investigated and worked with astrology in his counseling, and am sure that in the future we will see many others follow his courageous lead. —Zipporah Dobyns, Ph.D (Review of *Therapeutic Astrology*)

Bogart's approach gives astrologers dignity and professionalism. His book is an important introduction to the marriage of astrology and psychotherapy. Greg Bogart has advanced the cause of a new discipline that seems destined to shape consciousness in the 21st century. —Dell Horoscope (Review of *Therapeutic Astrology*)

Useful and revelatory, this text is a must for your library. Not only is *Planets in Therapy* wide ranging and inclusive of the breadth of astrology but it has a vertical dimension as well, being rooted in a psychological perspective that blossoms with shimmering flowers of spiritual discovery. It is a work of deep soulfulness and wisdom. —Brad Kochunas, M. A., author of *The Astrological Imagination*

# PLANETS IN THERAPY

*Predictive Technique
and the
Art of Counseling*

## GREG BOGART

IBIS PRESS
Lake Worth, FL

Published in 2012 by Ibis Press
A division of Nicolas-Hays, Inc.
P. O. Box 540206
Lake Worth, FL 33454-0206
*www.ibispress.net*

Distributed to the trade by
Red Wheel/Weiser, LLC
65 Parker St. • Ste. 7
Newburyport, MA 01950
*www.redwheelweiser.com*

ISBN 978-0-89254-174-4

Library of Congress Cataloging-in-Publication Data
Available upon request.

Book design and production by Studio 31.
*www.studio31.com*

Printed in the United States of America

# Dedication

This book is dedicated to you,
my friend, the practicing astrologer

The mythical Benedictine Basil Valentine at work
in his alchemical laboratory.

## Books by Greg Bogart

*Astrology and Meditation: The Fearless Contemplation of Change*

*Astrology and Spiritual Awakening*

*Dreamwork and Self-Healing*

*Finding Your Life's Calling*

*The Nine Stages of Spiritual Apprenticeship*

*Therapeutic Astrology: Using the Birth Chart in Psychotherapy and Spiritual Counseling*

# Contents

# Illustrations

Cover: *The King's Bath: Extraction of the White Dove.* Salomon Trismosin, *Splendor Solis*, 1582. © Trustees of the British Library, London.

Frontispiece: *The alchemist Basil Valentine.* Title page from Basil Valentine: *Revelation des mysteres des teintures essentielles des sept metaux* (Paris, 1668).

Photo of Chakrapani Ullal, by the author.

*Musaeum Hermeticum.* Matthaus Merian (1625), from A. E. Waite, *The Hermetic Museum Restored and Enlarged*, London, 1893 (Vol. II, p. 305).

Rembrandt van Rijn, *Faust In His Study.* Victoria and Albert Museum, London. Photo Credit: V & A Images, London/ Art Resource, NY.

Photo of Dane Rudhyar. Photo Credit: Ron Le Blanc. Used with permission of Aurora Press, P.O. Box 573, Santa Fe, NM 87504, www.aurorapress.com. From *The Planetarization of Consciousness*, by Dane Rudhyar.

*Homage to the Sun.* Babylonian cuneiform tablet. © Trustees of the British Museum.

*Planets Mandala.* Da Basilio Valentino, *Azoth*, Frankfort, 1613. Published 1988 by Edizioni Mediterranee, Rome. Used with permission of Edizioni Mediterranee.

*A Wolf Devours the King.* Michael Maier, *Atalanta Fugiens*, Oppenheim, 1618. Reproduced from H. M. E. de Jong, *Michael Maier's Atalanta Fugiens: Sources of an Alchemical Book of Emblems* (York Beach, MN: Nicolas-Hays, 2002).

# Acknowledgments

Warm thanks to my friends and colleagues for all of their support and sustainment: Rick Amaro, Lynn Bell, Robert Blaschke, Ken Bowser, Margaret Cahill, Nick Campion, Cathy Coleman, Andrea Conlon, Sangye Drolma, Robert Forte, Jennifer Freed, Nur Richard Gale, Demetra George, Ray Grasse, Margaret Gray, Dennis Harness, Dan Johnson, David Kesten, Brad Kochunas, Joe Landwehr, Michael Lutin, Tad Mann, Colleen Mauro, Frances McEvoy, Nicki Michaels, Charles Mintz, Shelley Jordan, Barbara Morgan, Bob Mulligan, Glenn Perry, Steve Pincus, Henry Seltzer, Kate Sholly, Richard Smoot, Barbara Somerfield, Elizabeth Spring, Georgia Stathis, Marcia Starck, Richard Tarnas, Tem Tarriktar, Kay Taylor, Jonathan Tenney, Gisele Terry, Chakrapani Ullal, Linea Van Horn, and Stuart Walker. I thank Steven Forrest for his helpful editorial suggestions. I also thank my wife, Diana Syverud, for her steady intuition, humor and discernment.

I'm grateful to Noel Tyl for taking the time to read my work and offering encouragement; to the late Zipporah Dobyns, a trailblazer of psychological astrology, for two lovely conversations in which she shared her wisdom with me; and to Alan Oken, for his kind blessing.

Portions of this book previously appeared in *The Mountain Astrologer, International Astrologer, NCGR Journal, NCGR Memberletter, Astrotherapy Newsletter,* and *Astrological Journal* (U.K.). Most of the writings in this volume originated with presentations at meetings of the International Society for Astrological Research (ISAR), United Astrology Conference (UAC), National Council for Geocosmic Research (NCGR San Francisco, New York, and Boston chapters), Astrological Society of Connecticut, Australian Federation of Astrologers, and San Francisco Astrological Society. It's both a pleasure and an honor to work within these fine organizations to promote this knowledge for the benefit of humanity.

I'm indebted to all of the individuals whose stories are recounted here. Names and identifying details have been altered to preserve their anonymity.

As a writer, it's so meaningful to have found a safe harbor for my work. I'm grateful to Yvonne Paglia, Deborah DeNicola, and James Wasserman of Ibis Press for their enthusiastic support and creative collaboration.

This book was completed in December 2011 under the tidal intensity of a full moon eclipse—a fitting moment to release this work of practical mysticism, which considers how the light of the sky can aid us in our journey on the earth.

*Astrology, a discipline rejected and ridiculed by Newtonian-Cartesian science, can prove of unusual value as a source of information about personality development and transformation. . . . For an approach that sees consciousness as a primary element of the universe that is woven into the very fabric of existence, and that recognizes archetypal structures as something that precedes and determines phenomena in the material world, the function of astrology would appear quite logical.*

STANISLAV GROF[1]

*Astrology provides the best descriptions of character qualities. More than any other field, astrology gives background for the psychology of personality.*

JAMES HILLMAN[2]

*I do not hesitate to take the synchronistic phenomena that underlie astrology seriously. Just as there is an eminently psychological reason for the existence of alchemy, so too in the case of astrology. Nowadays it is no longer interesting to know how far these two fields are aberrations; we should rather investigate the psychological foundations on which they rest.*

CARL JUNG[3]

# Preface

*May our study of astrology enable us to rise above delusion into*
*the higher fields of mind where philosophy transforms the seeker of*
*knowledge and uplifts us into an expanded human consciousness.*

I was raised in a family that taught me to doubt all religion and super-stition, thus my interest and involvement in astrology came as quite a surprise to me. In my early teens I was gripped by a hunger for yoga and spirituality. I visited various yogis and was initiated into Tran-scendental Meditation. I remember browsing in the Samuel Weiser Bookshop in Manhattan and seeing books on astrology, thinking "what a quaint superstition." I remember looking through the books and not being able to make heads or tails of the subject. In 1974 I met Swami Muktananda and began meditating intensely. In 1978, while I was still a college student, I went to India and stayed in Muktananda's Siddha Yoga ashram in Ganeshpuri, north of Bombay. Muktananda's astrologer, Chakrapani Ullal would come visit every week, and one of my roommates told me, "One of the greatest astrologers in the world is here and he is only charging $25. You would be absolutely crazy not to go to see him." So, I mustered up my courage and went over to talk to Chakrapani, who was very intense and somewhat intimidating. He had the most amazing magnetic presence; he seemed very mysteri-ous. He said "You have to come and see me in Bombay. I have no time here. Come after ten days."

I took the train into Bombay, and found a humble hotel room. The trip to his house was an education, a journey into Bombay's steamy urban interior. I showed up at his apartment at the wrong time because the telephones didn't work properly and I thought he said 8 a.m., but he had meant for me to come the previous evening at 8 p.m.. He was in the middle of his morning bath, wrapped in a towel. Then he did his morning puja, waving a candle, chanting quiet Sanskrit prayers to Laxmi, Saraswati, Durga, and Ganesh. There was a customer ahead of me in the waiting room, a very old man wearing a white dhoti. Chakrapani examined the man's planets intently. When he finally called me to sit down at the table with him he began the reading, most of which was not done from the chart. He glanced at the chart for a few minutes but he gave most of the reading with his eyes closed or gazing upward. He told me all about my father and his life, how he'd been injured in the war and had overcome many obstacles in life to become very successful. He told me about my mother and how she was a good writer, but she had much worse vision in her right eye than her left eye, and she had broken her shoulder in an accident recently—all of which was true. He told me my sister was having problems in her love life, but that she would marry within two years. All of this turned out to be spot on. However, none of it seemed like it really came from astrology, but more from Chakrapani's psychic clarity and inner vision. And he said, "You will be an astrologer. You have the qualities of a teacher, a lecturer, a counselor, and an advisor." I thought, "Hmm, that's interesting because I don't know anything about this and I don't even believe in it." I was enthralled by his ability to see the shape of the past, present, and future through astrology and also through an inner vision and expanded awareness that appeared to be the result of his meditation practice. I could feel higher centers opening up just being in his presence. And that was perhaps the biggest lesson: that the power of astrology doesn't come from techniques, but from the clear consciousness, wisdom, and articulate words of the astrologer.

A few years later, I discovered astrology at a time of confusion in my life when I was wandering around in the forests of Oregon and Washington, living in the woods. Astrology found me, and helped me find myself. I learned from people I met along the way, especially the wonderful astrologers of Eugene, Oregon, who assisted me. I was a bit lost and confused then: Transiting Neptune was conjunct my natal Saturn at the time, It was a period of vivid dreams, awakening in nature, and vision quests. Two wise astrologers, Mark McNutt and Susan Dearborn Jackson, taught me about my birth chart and transits.

That's when I started reading books such as Alexander Ruperti's *Cycles of Becoming,* Stephen Arroyo's *Astrology, Karma, and Transformation,* Liz Greene's *Saturn,* Michael Meyer's *Handbook for the Humanistic Astrologer,* and Noel Tyl's books, *The Expanded Pres-*

Chakrapani Ullal

*ent*, and *Analysis and Prediction.* I studied Evangeline Adams, Zip Dobyns, Alan Oken, Tracy Marks. All of these writers were fantastic. I learned that this Neptune transit was, by nature, a period of uncertainty, a transitional time, a time of letting go of certainties. I experienced a deconditioning (Neptune) of all I'd been taught by my parents and my upbringing in New York. I struggled with the values represented by my father (Saturn), an extraverted, highly intellectual business executive who had natal Sun conjunct Jupiter and Saturn. I sat in the woods, recorded my dreams, wrote music, and practiced yoga and meditation. Like Bob Dylan once wrote, "I came in from the wilderness, a creature void of form." But through the study of astrology my life gradually took form, and I began fulfilling the tasks that my birth chart showed me.

As I gazed at my chart and transits, I had glimpses of who I could become. I didn't know how to manifest it yet; I had to go step by step. But I had the beginnings of a dream, a vision for my life, and I trusted that this vision was the seed of my future. I learned that the birth chart needs my conscious involvement to unfold. My vision wasn't just going to happen by itself. I didn't want to just wait out my transits, like bad weather patterns. I realized that it isn't enough to approach astrology in a passive, fatalistic way. We can work creatively with whatever we're given, including our difficult tests and tasks. We can live them consciously. We can respond to each transit and actively unfold its meaning. We anticipate the quality of the moment and act in accordance with it. So during Saturn transits, we work hard. During Neptune transits, we kick back. The rhythmic activity of planetary energies moves us through a series of states—some solid, some liquid, some fiery, some icy cool. Astrology is a creative tool that we can use to evolve ourselves.

In 1981 I met my teacher Andres Takra, from Venezuela. His first lesson to me was this: "Astrology is a sacred and solemn science. It can enlighten you, or it can make you crazy. It can paralyze your free will, or it can make you a bold, successful, evolved human being. It's up to you." All of my work in astrology has essentially been an amplification of Takra's first lesson.[4] Then he asked me, "Why do you want to become an astrologer." I said, "To help people." He said, "That's right. That's the reason to become an astrologer." Some years later I had a student and I asked her the same question, to which she replied, "So I can be a far-out psychic and blow people away with my awesome psychic predictions." I thought that was quite appalling, but it was at least a very honest response reflecting a common assumption many people have—namely that astrology is all about making predictions. The problem is that not everybody is as good at it as Chakrapani is. We can easily get paralyzed or misled by negative or superficial predictions.

But is this what really helps people? If our goal is to be the kind of astrologers who inspire and uplift people, if astrology is to be most helpful, healing, and therapeutic, then we need to clarify our attitudes toward astrological prediction. Tracking transits and progressions, we can use astrology to discern the shape of emerging time. But the real power of astrology goes beyond predicting what will happen. By *anticipating* developmental tasks and responding appropriately, we mold the future. Adding consciousness to the equation changes everything.

## FATALISM AND HUMANISM IN ASTROLOGY

Many people approach astrology with the attitude that everything is fated to happen, predestined by the planets. Many astrologers describe planets as either good or evil, benefic or malefic. In this field we too often hear people saying things like, "Saturn is transiting over your Ascendant, or conjunct your Moon, or square Venus. That's bad. That's difficult. It's a bad time for love, money, career, health, family, children. . . ." Or, "Everything will be better when this Pluto transit is over—in two years!" This is not an empowering approach to astrology.

But our field has come a long way from this fatalistic mentality. In the 1960s and 70s Dane Rudhyar taught the principles of humanistic astrology, which deemphasizes prediction and emphasizes self-awareness, using astrology to guide choices, to become self-actualized, self-determining human beings. In *Person-Centered Astrology*, Rudhyar wrote:

> The purpose of astrology is not to tell a person what will most probably (or some astrologers might say, "inevitably") happen to him at this and that specified time; it is rather to assist him in relating everything that happens, inside even more than outside of him, to the total pattern of his life-development.[5]

Humanistic astrology seeks to understand the *meaning* of events, seeing them as phases within life cycles. For example, we're interested in a Saturn transit as a meaningful phase of life, not as some dreaded malefic influence. Rudhyar elucidated the cyclical structure of time, using the lunation cycle to represent the major phases of evolution. We constantly experience *New Moon* beginnings, *waxing phases* representing the growth of form, *Full Moon* culminations and illuminations, *waning phases* of structural change and reorientation; and the *balsamic phase* of completion, dormancy, and expectancy. This cyclical viewpoint takes the pressure off astrologers, because instead of trying to predict exactly what's going to occur, we can focus on interpreting events and planetary transits as meaningful phases of evolutionary cycles. Rudhyar wrote:

[H]uman experience is essentially cyclic and it unfolds according to structural principles. However varied men's experiences may appear to be, they nevertheless fall within the limits of a series of what might be called "archetypal" meanings. . . . [T]here are only a certain number of basic meanings to be gathered by a human being in his [or her] lifetime, and these meanings can be seen in terms of structural and cyclic sequence. . . . [T]o experience events is one thing; to release from them vital and creative meanings is another. What counts, spiritually speaking, is the harvest of meanings a person is able to gather from these many and varied life experiences. . . . [O]nly those experiences from which meaning has been extracted count spiritually.[6]

Humanistic astrologers aren't passively resigned to what's "fated" to occur. We anticipate developmental tasks, envision possibilities, and make things happen. We discern what actions are required at each moment. Predictive methods enable astrologers to anticipate trends and prepare in advance to meet life's challenges. But it's not just about *predicting*, but also about *acting*, and *responding* to the planets. When transiting Pluto was in my 3rd house conjunct natal Mars, my neighbor's barking dog was keeping me up at all hours of the night and I was getting really angry. Would this just be a situation I'd have to endure? Would it lead to a damaging Pluto-Mars confrontation with my neighbor? Neither was the case. One night at around 1 a.m. I stopped being afraid of Mars and went over in my pajamas and asked the neighbor to please keep the dog indoors at night. That was the last time I had a problem with the dog. I simply had to act, not passively endure the stressful transit due to fear of conflict.

A woman named Sue with Moon-Saturn in Virgo in her 6th house became ill every time transiting Mars, Jupiter, Saturn, or Uranus aspected these Virgo planets, which seemed to be significators of health issues or illness. We worked on helping Sue to become proactive, more conscientious about diet, rest, stress reduction. She began taking herbs, doing yoga, and fasting briefly twice a year. Whenever transits aspected her Moon-Saturn she intensified her health-enhancing practices. Sue transformed her "fate" through anticipation. This is our work: to utilize astrology to better our lives through conscious participation in developmental tasks, not through passive resignation to fate.

## ORIGINS AND OUTLINE OF THIS BOOK

While Neptune was conjunct my natal Saturn I spent the winter of 1980 huddled by a wood stove in a small room in Eugene, Oregon with rain pouring down in cold torrents, reading a pile of astrology books, calculating my first charts for friends. That was 30 years ago. In 1983 I started corresponding with Dane Rudhyar, the visionary astrologer and mystic philosopher. Rudhyar guided me across a crucial threshold as I internally committed to following the spiritual vocation of an astrologer. I was focusing intently on my spiritual studies and inner quest but had not yet established a viable occupation. I also struggled with the fact that on numerous occasions I was ridiculed or scorned by others for my pursuit of metaphysical studies. In one of his letters to me, Rudhyar wrote:

> Yes, being 'in' the world but not 'of' it is very difficult. It is man's supreme power that he can live consistently at more than one or two levels. Polyphonic, counterpunctual living—Caesar and God (say the Gospels). Yet there are periods when singleness of purpose and an all-absorbing focus of vision are required to move safely through the rite of passage. Keep on with your work and do not be impatient if the field of transhuman activity and consciousness seems enveloped in mist. Clarity comes only most gradually, and one has to build means of formulation that emerge out of one's own experiences, indeed out of crises courageously and nobly passed through. May you reach in your own time, and with the help of those of who have gone before you, the "other shore." And may peace, deep peace, be with you.

Rudhyar's message conveys the essence of what astrology means to me: It is an aid in times of transition, and helps me function on many levels simultaneously. It gives me inner peace as I go through various challenges and transformations. And it was clear I needed to do some work on being in the world and deciding how to make a living. Each astrologer works out this issue differently in accordance with the birth chart and one's personal aptitude. I have Cancer Midheaven, ruled by the Moon, and I realized I had an interest in emotional dynamics and counseling. So I studied counseling psychology and began using astrology in my clinical practice. Becoming a psychotherapist during my Saturn return wasn't simply a more viable way of being in the world. It gave me the tools I needed to use astrology in a truly therapeutic manner. And as there weren't many people combining astrology and psychotherapy, I began building my own "means of formulation," describing how I integrate astrology with psychotherapy to assist people in the midst of various complex personal transformations. Eventually I authored a book (published in 1996) called *Therapeutic Astrology: Using the Birth Chart in Psychotherapy and Spiritual Counseling*. This book sold out three printings and went out of print. This present volume was originally conceived as a revised second edition, but it has now become an entirely different book, reflecting my evolution as a practitioner. A few remnants of the original work appear in Part III.

This book outlines a psychological and therapeutic approach to astrology and its predictive methods. We'll consider how astrology's archetypal symbolism and precise time measurements can aid us in emotional healing and creating more resilient and loving relationships. I'll present an approach to therapeutic astrology that has its roots in Jungian psychology and in the humanistic and transpersonal astrology taught by Rudhyar. I'll show how astrology can be utilized for self-guidance and self-transformation; it's the ultimate self-help tool. But I'm also writing here for the practitioner, the professional astrologer, therapist, and counselor, and for anyone who uses astrology to guide their friends, families, and loved ones.

In Part I, after a brief review of basic astrological terms and concepts, I discuss predictive, developmental, archetypal, and therapeutic dimensions of astrology. Then, before exploring therapeutic astrology in more depth, I establish a conceptual basis for the work in Part II, where I contemplate Rudhyar's astrology and philosophy of life, which can serve as a spiritual foundation and touchstone. In Part III, I show how a therapeutic astrologer can apply these principles to do focused, intensive work with clients. I outline the principles of therapeutic astrology, discuss the relevance of astrology for psychotherapists and spiritual guides, and show how to use astrology as a counseling tool. I examine both potentials and contraindications of utilizing astrology therapeutically, and consider how the marriage of astrology and psychology can create a potent new alchemy of self-transformation. I discuss how the symbolism of signs, houses, and planets helps us formulate a multi-level model of human development. I'll demonstrate how astrology can assist us during crises and upheavals, helping us transform during urgent situations of change. I'll show how astrology can counteract depression, revitalizing our mental and emotional health. It is a natural antidepressant, better than Prozac.

Part IV focuses on synastry and relationship counseling. We'll see that astrology can be a useful tool for creating more conscious, vibrant, and intelligent relationships. As I assume this is a goal sought by everyone, I hope readers will find this relevant and nourishing material.

By this time in the book I hope to have demonstrated how it's possible to do some profound work on oneself, and with others, through astrology. In Part V, I offer more specifics on the techniques I use to achieve these results: *transits, secondary progressions,* and *solar arc directions.* This section is presented in a tutorial style and contains detailed examples along with some information about calculations. With these methods in hand it's possible to enter into the chart and its story of development with a sharp and detailed lens, for highly potent astrological analysis. I'll explain how to use transits and progressions with precision and wisdom, for tangible and practical results. Part VI synthesizes archetypal, therapeutic, and relational themes, showing how this knowledge enables us to help each other, to aid people in crisis. The square of Uranus and Pluto in this present decade indicates that we're all at an evolutionary threshold when we need this knowledge to navigate in full alignment with the incoming cosmic forces.

The many case examples presented in the book allow readers to learn from other people's experiences and to identify analogous features of their own birth charts and life stories. You'll read stories of how the healing art of astrology has helped people grapple with real-world problems, including job loss, lawsuits, parenting, muggings, alcoholism, trauma, divorce, illness, anger management, addiction, bereavement, and other forms of human suffering. Each of us needs to transform within our personal condition of woundedness. I've also allowed myself to write autobiographically, and somewhat transparently, sharing stories from different stages of my life. You'll probably find something in these stories that matches something you've experienced, or are going through now. I'll consider this book a success if it activates you, brings your path into clearer focus, and helps you become committed to your own potentials.

# PART ONE
# PSYCHOLOGICAL ASTROLOGY

**Matthaus Merian,** *Musaeum Hermeticum,* **1625.**[7]

Chapter 1

# *Basic Astrology*

Let's begin our journey by defining some basic astrological terms and concepts. A natal chart depicts the positions of the major planets of our solar system at the moment of birth. It represents central character traits, potentials, and steps we need to take to actualize those potentials. The chart contains four central components: *planets*, *signs*, *houses*, and *aspects*. Planets, signs, and houses represent typical, archetypal characters, themes, and situations that each person faces in the course of life. The birth chart also indicates which archetypal structures or themes are emphasized in a person's life. We learn how the potentials depicted in the birth chart come to fruition over time through transits and progressions, the predictive methods of astrology.

## PLANETS

The planets represent personality functions and capacities that we must awaken, express, and embody in order to become complete human beings.

- Sun: our conscious identity, the ego and sense of self, the feeling of unique selfhood; it's the joy, centeredness, and radiance that comes from knowing who you are.
- Moon: our moods, feelings, inner needs, and emotional states.
- Mercury: our way of thinking, learning, and speaking; cognition and communication.
- Venus: our way of relating to others, aesthetic tastes, sense of beauty, and desire for pleasure.
  - Mars: energy, self-assertion, initiative, and our vitality, desires, and sexual drives.

- Jupiter: our goals, aspirations, and quest for a philosophically meaningful existence.
- Saturn: our work to achieve and accomplish, to become stable and secure; focus, responsibility, commitment, and self-discipline.
- Uranus: our urge for freedom and liberation, rebellion against convention and cultural norms; defiant attitude, experimentation, innovation, and a desire to reform society.
- Neptune: our spirituality, imagination, religious faith, dreams, psychic perceptions, mystical experiences; confusion, uncertainty, disorientation, and disability; drugs, alcohol, and addictions.
- Pluto: our experiences of crisis and renewal, endings and beginnings, death and rebirth; emergence into awareness of anything repressed.

Some astrologers also use asteroids and hypothetical, "transNeptunian" planets, as well as midpoints and harmonics. But most astrologers agree that these ten planets are the most important factors, the central archetypes, the central patterns of transformation.

### Conscious and Unconscious Expressions of Planets

Through knowledge of astrology we can shape and transform the expression and manifestation of planetary energies. Rather than trying to precisely predict events, we anticipate the tendency of certain archetypal themes or qualities of experience to occur, in accordance with planetary symbolism. To do this, we need to understand different ways the planets typically manifest so we can evolve our ability to express planetary energies in their most evolved forms.

If a person is relatively unconscious, Mars manifests as aggression, fighting, impatience, selfish demands, injuries, or impulsive actions. But when expressed consciously, Mars symbolizes self-assertiveness, energy, motivation, strength, will. Unconscious Neptune manifests as denial, avoidance, escapism, addiction, naïveté, or spaciness. With more consciousness, Neptune manifests as vision, imagination, surrender, contemplation, stillness, openness, innocence, and spirituality. The Moon can manifest as moodiness, neediness, emotional insecurity, or, more consciously, as tenderness, empathy, sensitivity, caring for others, nurturing, and emotional responsiveness. Unconscious Venus brings attachment to surface appearances, fixation on beauty, fashion, and making a good impression. Conscious expression of Venus enhances our world through artistic or musical expression, pleasing personal aesthetics, care in dress and appearance, and consciousness about relationships. Unconscious Saturn manifests as rigidity, fixation on the mundane, strictly conventional attitudes, workaholism, stodginess, an inability to loosen up. A conscious expression of Saturn takes the form of responsibility, maturity, accomplishment, task orientation, getting things done. Unconscious Sun takes the form of egotism, narcissism, self-centeredness, vanity, pride, while conscious expression of the Sun appears as radiance, self-esteem, creativity, and joy. Unconscious Jupiter manifests as dogmatism, gluttony, laziness, or ungrounded optimism. Conscious Jupiter is expressed as hopefulness, expansion, and planning for the future.

## ZODIACAL SIGNS

Tropical astrology is based on the relationship between Earth and our Sun. Our annual passage around the Sun defines the ecliptic, a circle of 360°. Astrology begins with awareness that we are in constant motion, and that our motion follows the rhythms of the seasons. As planets move through the sky, we measure their positions along the plane of the ecliptic. The ecliptic is divided into twelve sections, each comprising thirty degrees of arc, the *signs of the zodiac.* As each planet passes through these signs, its style of expressing its basic nature (for example: Moon, to feel; Mars, to act) changes. Mars in Taurus, has a different motivation than Mars in Sagittarius. Moon in Aries feels differently and has different emotional needs than Moon in Aquarius.

Each sign represents a set of psychological attitudes, typical experiences, and essential human concerns:

- Aries (ruled by Mars): energy, desire, aggression, and competitiveness; awareness of oneself as an individual; self-centered attitudes.

- Taurus (ruled by Venus): groundedness, ease, material stability, money, possessions, sensuality.
- Gemini (ruled by Mercury): thinking, speaking, learning, curiosity.
- Cancer (ruled by Moon): feelings, memory, home and family; nurturing of self and others; emotional bonding.
- Leo (ruled by Sun): self-expression, play, pride, dignity, the expression of love.
- Virgo (ruled by Mercury): self-improvement, concerns about health, diet, and employment.
- Libra (ruled by Venus): relationship, cooperation, harmony, beauty, and balance; deference to others.
- Scorpio (co-ruled by Pluto and Mars): power, sexuality, sharing of resources; interpersonal conflict, awareness of mortality.
- Sagittarius (ruled by Jupiter): the search for truth, meaning, religious or moral principles; travel and education.
- Capricorn (ruled by Saturn): career, professional goals and achievements, concern with social position and status; conformity to tradition.
- Aquarius (ruled by Uranus): individuation, freedom, rebellion, social and political awareness, involvement with groups, revolution, reform or defiance of tradition.
- Pisces (ruled by Neptune): self-transcendence; expanded consciousness, inner vision, compassion, altruism.

## DISPOSITORSHIP

Each planet is the ruler of one or two signs. This planet has an affinity with that sign and is at home there. This planet is the *dispositor* of that sign and of any other planets placed there. *Dispositorship* refers to planetary rulership of a natal house or planet. The meaning of a transit to a natal planet is shaped by the natal planet's sign and house placement, and its dispositorship (rulership) of a natal house and/or planet. For example, if you have several planets in Libra, Venus is the dispositor of those planets. If a person has Libra rising, Scorpio on the 2nd house cusp and Aries on the 7th cusp, then whenever transits contact Mars, that person's finances and relationships will both be affected because Mars is at home in Scorpio and Aries and is thus the dispositor of the houses of money (2nd house) and relationships (7th house). With Leo on the MC, transits to the natal Sun impact the individual's career. We also consider the dispositorship and the natal house placement of a transiting planet. If Pluto is dispositor of my 10th house then transits of Pluto will always carry a resonance with 10th house career issues. If I have Saturn placed in (or dispositor of) the 4th house natally, Saturn's transits will always carry 4th house ramifications.

| *Sign* | *Dispositor* |
|---|---|
| Aries | Mars |
| Taurus | Venus |
| Gemini | Mercury |
| Cancer | Moon |
| Leo | Sun |
| Virgo | Mercury |
| Libra | Venus |
| Scorpio | Mars and Pluto |
| Sagittarius | Jupiter |
| Capricorn | Saturn |
| Aquarius | Uranus |
| Pisces | Neptune |

## ASPECTS

Planets interrelate with one another as they transit through the sky, forming *aspects*, significant geometric relationships. Two planets together in the sky are in *conjunction*. When they're 180° apart planets are in *opposition*. Two planets 90° apart form a *square*. A 60° aspect is a *sextile*, while an aspect of 120° is a *trine*. Two planets separated by 150° are in a *quincunx* aspect. Two additional aspects, based on division of the circle by eight, are the 45° semi-square and the 135° sesquiquadrate. These are also known as the *octile* and *trioctile*. These are the most important aspects, most likely to visibly impact our lives. These are the aspects I'll mention in this book.[8]

Traditional astrological doctrines stated that trines and sextiles are good, easy, and beneficent, representing talents and harmonious blending of two planetary energies, while the square, opposition, and quincunx are bad, difficult, and malefic in influence. However, trines and sextiles aren't always "good"; squares and oppositions aren't inherently malefic. The conjunction is neutral, its nature being determined by the qualities of the two planets involved. A conjunction represents a need to blend the functioning of two planets so they operate as a single, integrated unit. Some planetary pairs achieve this blending more easily than others. A Venus-Moon conjunction is a gentle, nurturing aspect, while a Mars-Uranus conjunction is a more volatile mixture.

The square, opposition, and quincunx represent stressful, discordant relationships between planets that can create some friction in our life. Thus, they signify psychological and situational conflicts. A man with Jupiter in the 7th house (relationships) square Saturn in the 4th house (family) experienced stress because his parents didn't approve of his friends or his choice of marital partner. A woman with Mercury-Neptune quincunx Saturn was committed to becoming a poet (Mercury-Neptune) yet experienced inner tension because material pressures and her work schedule (Saturn) made it difficult to find time for creative writing.

Aspects such as the square, opposition, and quincunx aren't "bad." These aspects stimulate us to change and to grow. Every chart has some mixture of harmonious aspects and more stressful aspects. No one said growth in consciousness would be easy. Astrology helps us understand our areas of conflict so we can work on them and free up energies that have been bound in conflict. Understanding aspects helps us to achieve internal unity.

All aspects represent a synergistic connection between the planets. I view the specific aspect as less important than the nature of the two planets that are interacting. The planetary pair involved is more important than the specific angle between them.

I occasionally mention *planetary midpoints*, which reveal interplanetary connections not always evident using traditional aspects. The study of midpoints derives from *cosmobiology*, pioneered by Reinhold Ebertin. Cosmobiology is useful for advanced predictive work. Detailed coverage is outside the scope of this book, but I'll discuss midpoints in Chapter 12.[9]

## Houses

Astrology is fundamentally a process of gaining orientation and a sense of direction. Mircea Eliade, the historian of religions, taught that one of the primordial religious acts is to establish the center of the world, the *axis mundi*, and to mark the four directions, to create cosmos from chaos. Astrology applies this principle by marking the four directions at the moment of birth. We calculate the zodiacal degree of the Eastern horizon (the Ascendant); the Western horizon (the Descendant); the point directly overhead (the Midheaven or MC); and the point directly below, opposite the MC (the Anti-Midheaven or IC, the *imum coeli*).

The Ascendant is the point of the self, the individual. It marks our appearance and behaviors that are immediately apparent to others; it describes how we look, act, and perceive ourselves. The Descendant is the point of connection to others; it indicates the kinds of people we are attracted to, and our way of establishing relationships with others. The IC is the point of roots and origins; it represents our connection to the past, our ancestry, nation, or ethnicity. At the IC we feel an urge to establish a foundation through developing a home, family, and sense of place. If the IC represents the root of the plant, then the MC signifies the flower and fruit; it is the point of ambition and achievement. The MC represents primary objectives we hope to accomplish, our social position, and our career. These four angles define four quadrants of the sky, which are then subdivided into twelve areas of the sky—the twelve houses of the birth chart. Through this initial act of defining the four angles and the twelve houses, astrology helps us find orientation and find our center in the midst of constant change.

The houses represent situations, circumstances, and life issues that each person experiences at one time or another:

- House 1: self-image, identity; our own behaviors.
- House 2: survival issues, money, ownership, purchases.

- House 3: thinking, speaking, reading; driving, excursions; siblings and neighbors.
- House 4: family life, parents, memories, emotions; the home or office.
- House 5: self-expression, creativity, recreation, enjoyment, fun, children.
- House 6: health, employment, self-analysis and self-criticism; aunts and uncles; employees and coworkers.
- House 7: relationships, friendship, and marriage; close friends, spouse, and open adversaries.
- House 8: shared financial resources, sex and emotional intimacy; credit and loans; partner's finances.
- House 9: personal beliefs, education, teachers, travel.
- House 10: profession, career, the boss, authority figures, and the dominant parent.
- House 11: social awareness, participation in groups, politics, and professional organizations.
- House 12: solitude, retreat, introspection, altruism, meditation, dreams, fantasy, prayer.

Each house is associated with one of the twelve signs, with which it shares themes in common. For example, the meaning of house 1 shares themes that are related to Aries, the first zodiacal sign. House 5 has much in common with the fifth sign, Leo. House 7 shares themes in common with the seventh sign, Libra. The wheel of astrological houses describes the full spectrum and complexity of our life-world.

## DERIVED HOUSES

The technique of *derived house analysis* enables us to expand the meaning of houses by counting houses not only from the Ascendant but from other houses. For example, the 10th house represents our career, but it's also the 4th house from the partner-7th house and thus represents the spouse's family (your in-laws). The 10th house is also the 6th house from the child-5th so it governs the child's health and employment. The 4th house represents your home and family but it's also the 10$^{th}$ house from the partner-7$^{th}$ and thus the house of the partner's career. The 8$^{th}$ house is the 2$^{nd}$ house from the partner-7$^{th}$ and thus represents the partner's income. It's also the 4$^{th}$ house from the child-5$^{th}$ house, so it signifies the child's housing and housing costs. The 11$^{th}$ house is the 5$^{th}$ house from the partner-7$^{th}$ so it represents the partner's child, or your stepchild. The 11$^{th}$ house is also the 7$^{th}$ house from the child-5$^{th}$ so it represents the child's relationships. The 2$^{nd}$ house is the 10$^{th}$ house from the child-5$^{th}$ so it signifies the child's career. Adding the dimension of derived house analysis to your chart interpretations of can lead to greater interpretive acumen. For example, a woman with transiting Pluto conjunct Sun in Capricorn in the 12$^{th}$ house faced increasing isolation (12$^{th}$ house) during this period due to her husband's protracted illness. The 12$^{th}$ house is the health/6$^{th}$ house from the husband 7$^{th}$ house. She became more deeply committed to her meditation practice and began periods of retreat where she experienced a deep tranquility.

## TRANSITS

Natal planets are placed in various houses of our birth charts, while some houses are empty. However, we experience issues pertaining to all twelve houses because, after birth, the planets continue to transit through the sky. Transits show us what areas of life occupy our attention at a given time. They offer challenges and opportunities for growth and change, and enable us to precisely identify the timing of events. The character of transits is determined by both the transiting planets and the natal planets contacted, as well as the houses involved. Powerful transits of the outer planets, Uranus, Neptune, and Pluto, often indicate major transformations of perspective and behavior. Pluto transits often correspond to traumatic episodes, emergence of repressed feelings or dormant energies and capacities, or experiences of renewal and rebirth. During Neptune transits we experience dissolution of structures, loss of focus, inspiration, or an awakening of our imagination and spirituality. Uranus transits give an urge for freedom, new directions, and rapid change. Saturn transits challenge us to develop maturity, to accept responsibility, and to achieve our goals through sustained, focused effort. Jupiter transits are periods for planning, expansion, and opportunity; these are times when we set goals and perceive new horizons and possibilities. Mars transits are periods for action, initiative, and exertion of energy. Transits of Venus harmonize our lives, making events and relationships flow easily, while Mercury's transits show the current focus of our attention and thinking. The Moon's transits and phases demarcate consistent rhythms of life, our ever-changing moods and circumstances. We'll talk a lot about transits in this book.

## PROGRESSIONS

Astrologers "progress" the birth chart by examining how the birth pattern changes and unfolds over time. While there are numerous ways of progressing the horoscope, the two main methods used are *secondary progressions* and *solar arc directions*. In secondary progressions, we examine the changing positions of the planets in the days immediately after birth. Each day after birth is considered symbolically equivalent to one year of life. The positions of planets on the thirtieth day after birth are considered indicators of our condition in the thirtieth year of life. In secondary progressions, each planet moves at its own intrinsic rate of motion. Since the transiting Moon moves between 11–15° per *day*, the progressed Moon moves 11–15° per *year*; in contrast, the progressed Sun moves between 57' and 61' (minutes) of arc (approximately 1°) per year—corresponding to the transiting Sun's daily motion. The slower, outer planets move only a few minutes of arc per year by secondary progression. In contrast, solar arc directions move the natal planets (and angles) forward at a uniform rate, approximately a degree per year. This rate, the "solar arc," is determined by calculating the distance between the natal Sun and its secondary progressed position. If the Sun has progressed 20° 10' from its natal position, then each planet (and angle) is directed forward by that arc. Progressions and solar arc directions are reliable way of making projections about the course of life, about challenges and opportunities in the past, present, and future.

Transits and progressions allow us to identify the timing and character of crucial events, and we can use these methods for psychological growth and therapeutic benefit. For example, a woman

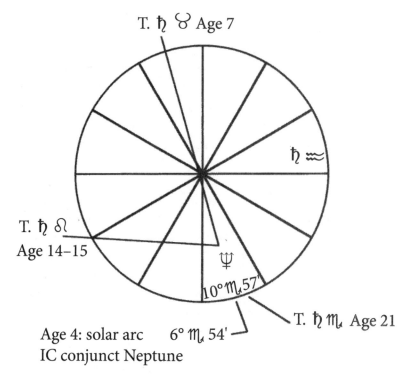

T. ♄ ♉ Age 7

♄ ≈

T. ♄ ♌
Age 14–15

ψ

10° ♏ 57'

T. ♄ ♏ Age 21

Age 4: solar arc    6° ♏ 54'
IC conjunct Neptune

**1. Leslie**

named Leslie had Neptune in her 4th house (family) at 10° Scorpio 57, squaring Saturn (Chart 1). Leslie came from an extended family with rampant alcoholism (Neptune) and both parents physically debilitated. Noting that her IC was 6° Scorpio 54, four degrees away from natal Neptune, I inferred that the sorrows (Neptune) of her family may have been particularly severe at age four, when the solar arc IC reached conjunction with Neptune. At that time, Leslie's mother was hospitalized for an extended period, financial woes were pronounced, and the family situation was unstable and chaotic (Neptune). This astrological observation opened up a fruitful discussion of Leslie's emotional experience at this early stage of life. I also examined later contacts to Neptune, a planet that represents the experience of suffering.

Noting that transiting Saturn was opposite natal Neptune at age seven, I inquired about further problems in family life at this time. Leslie had submerged her own identity in caring for others in her family, especially her disabled mother (Neptune in 4th). At age fourteen, when transiting Saturn in Leo squared Neptune, her father was stricken with a life-threatening illness, her mother became fanatically religious, and Leslie got involved with drugs and alcohol, which she now saw was a way of numbing herself and dissociating from her feelings. These developments closely matched the symbolism of Neptune.

At age twenty-one, while Saturn in Scorpio was conjunct natal Neptune, Leslie had difficulties with housing, living in dilapidated apartments (Neptune in 4th), and feeling lost and estranged from her family. Identifying these crucial periods from the past was the starting point for counseling. But we could look forward too. Noting that Jupiter was about to transit through her 4th house and would soon be conjunct natal Neptune, Leslie expressed her longing for a calm, expansive home, for unconditional emotional acceptance, and for healing and reconciliation with her family. All of this came to pass during the year of this transit. She found a quiet, meditative (Neptune) home in the woods, began to speak with her parents after many years of no contact, and began to feel emotionally centered and satisfied. Leslie experienced peace in nature and in her home environment (4th house), and she stopped her recreational drug use. All of this material came to light in our session simply by examining contacts to one planet, Neptune. We're going to see how powerful astrology can be when we understand each planet, sign, and house and weave their meanings together into a healing psychological narrative, a story of the self in evolution.

Astrology illuminates our unfolding along the dimension of time, and helps us anticipate life's central tasks, themes, memories, and turning points. Psychological astrology is the process of using planetary symbols to gain self-awareness, to focus the counseling process, and to catalyze positive change.

Chapter 2

# Foundations of Psychological Astrology

In the past 100 years, astrology has been transformed by its marriage with psychology. While it was traditionally viewed as an oracular, fortune-telling method, astrology is now recognized as a symbolic language describing our internal dynamics and guiding our evolution of consciousness. Astrology's profound psychological significance has been established through the work of authors such as Dane Rudhyar, Zipporah Dobyns, Noel Tyl, Liz Greene, Donna Cunningham, and Stephen Arroyo. The horoscope can be viewed as a representation of the internal and external life-world of the individual, revealing dominant personality traits, motivations, and conflicts. Astrology's cyclical principles and archetypal symbolism expand our self-awareness, aid in emotional healing, shed light on human relationships, and have a catalytic effect on psychotherapy and personal development.

Psychological astrology is based on the insight that planetary patterns reflect, and organize the cosmos inside us, portraying a series of tasks and initiations that each bear the imprint of specific planetary archetypes. For example, the natal Sun's sign, house and aspects define who we are, the central features of our identity and life path, whereas the natal Moon's sign, house and aspects describes our feelings, moods, and needs—how we feel while trying to actualize our solar essence in this lifetime. The placement of Mercury describes how we think and communicate, whereas Mars describes our capacity for life planning, while Saturn describes how we come to terms with the need to work and fulfill responsibilities, the psychology of social adaptation. By deepening our self-understanding, psychological astrology is a way to develop a more intelligently self-organized personality.

In this chapter, after some introductory comments, I'll discuss *four features of psychological astrology*: the adoption of a developmental perspective, a therapeutic emphasis, the description of mythic-archetypal themes, and a process orientation to chart interpretation.

I'll illustrate these points with case examples and some personal anecdotes.

Our understanding of the entire birth chart has been influenced by psychological concepts. Let's take the houses. We can view each house as a psychological realm. The 1ˢᵗ house is the realm of the persona and self-image. The 2ⁿᵈ house illuminates the psychology of self-esteem and our attitudes about money. The 3ʳᵈ house represents the realm of basic education and learning, our patterns of cognition, and also sibling relationships. The 4ᵗʰ house describes our family systems and dynamics. The 5ᵗʰ house is the realm of generativity, creativity, and self-expression. The 6ᵗʰ house is the realm of health psychology, and the psychology of work, training, and apprentice-ship. The 7ᵗʰ house is the psychological realm of love, projection, and conscious relationship. The 8ᵗʰ house gives us insights into the psychology of sex, intimacy, trauma, or bereavement. The 9ᵗʰ house is the realm of meaning-making and defining a philosophy of life. The 10ᵗʰ house is the realm of vocational psychology, the psychol-ogy of ambition and advancement. The 11ᵗʰ house represents social psychology, and group process. And the 12ᵗʰ house governs the psy-chology of dreams, meditation, and nondual experience. Taken as a totality, the twelve houses define our primary realms of action and agency, a *mandala* of our total life-world. We gradually transform and transition through our experiences in these varied realms.

Astrologers increasingly make use of psychological concepts, theories, and therapeutic methodologies, for example, family sys-tems theory to understand 4ᵗʰ house dynamics. I have been espe-cially influenced in my work by three psychological models: Psy-chosynthesis, Jungian psychology, and existential psychology.

I adapt from Roberto Assagioli's Psychosynthesis the idea that we can use astrology to integrate our various *subpersonalities* rep-resented by planetary archetypes and placements, to illuminate conflicts between them, and to create a sense of internal unity and coherence. I'm also interested in Assagioli's idea of *spiritual psy-chosynthesis*, the process of receiving transformative, reorganizing energies from the higher unconscious, which are expressed and operate through the transpersonal planets, Uranus, Neptune, and

Pluto. Spiritual psychosynthesis is a process of reorganizing the personality around the *transpersonal self*, a silent, tranquil, witnessing awareness that is also a center of will, volition, imagination, and self-determination. We'll apply these principles later in this chapter when we learn a potent technique of self-transformation combining astrology, meditation, and visualization. Our approach here is oriented toward using astrology for what Assagioli calls *self-realization*: the manifestation of spiritual potentials through the embodied individual. This involves the balanced development of the individual's potentials and undergoing a spiritual renewal and rebirth that recenters the personality in this calm, deliberate, intentional consciousness.

Psychological astrologers draw extensively on the work of C. G. Jung, who elucidated the mythic-archetypal characters that populate our waking, conscious life, and our unconscious life in fantasy and dreams. Astrologers note how planetary symbols and events coincide with synchronistic appearances of specific archetypes: Venus, the beautiful, enlivening *anima*; Moon, mother, the nurturing caregiver; Uranus: the trickster; Jupiter, the teacher, sage, priest, philosopher, and guru; Pluto, who appears as the *shadow*, an encounter with evil, a gangster, criminal, dictator, or other scary characters, or in images or acts of violence or cruelty. As an archetypal symbol of transformation, Pluto is Shiva, deity of irrevocable change, awakener of depth power, *kundalini*, regenerative energies of the unconscious. Throughout this book we'll observe how Jung's concept of archetypes provides a new foundation for astrology.

Jung's idea of *individuation* inspired the awareness that astrology is a means to unfold our uniqueness and authenticity as individuals, to be true to who we are. Individuation is a process of coming to terms with our complexity and striving to achieve wholeness by integrating the polarities of the personality—for example, conscious and unconscious (Sun and Moon); feminine and masculine (Venus and Mars), old and young (Saturn and Uranus); practicality and mysticism (Saturn and Neptune); innocence and power (Neptune and Pluto). Astrology describes generic planetary cycles that shape the life cycle for everyone (for example, the Jupiter cycle, Saturn cycle, Uranus cycle), and also portrays the pattern of development for each individual. It fosters the uniqueness of the individual and affirms the unique life story, the unusual paths we follow.

For example, a teacher named Nadia had grown exceedingly bored with her job at the elementary school where she'd taught for many years. Noting that her progressed Sun in Aquarius was moving into opposition with natal Uranus in the 11th house, for several years, I suggested that Nadia explore some new interests related to science and technology. Over the next several years Nadia became a robotics coach; she was immersed in robotics research, science, and technology. Her team of 10–14-year-olds won the National Finals twice, for industrial applications. Progressed Sun opposite Uranus described this phase of Nadia's unique life path.

Psychological astrology aids our individuation—the process of becoming who I truly am, and living my truth and totality. It illuminates how each person's individuation unfolds following archetypal patterns of change. In this example, transformation occurs within the archetypal pattern symbolized by Uranus, the sign of Aquarius, and the 11th house, all of which refer to science, discovery, innovation, and social evolution. In every example cited in this book you'll see the forward movement of the individuation urge. Individuation occurs within the prismatic, crystalline structures defined by the archetypes, which guide the process.

I also approach astrology through the lens of existential psychology, as an aid in confronting four existential realities: death, aloneness, meaninglessness, and responsibility.[10] Astrology's cyclical viewpoint helps us come to terms with the inevitability of death and endings so that we can feel fully alive and make every moment and every transit count. It helps us accept both our existential aloneness (our 1st house) as well as our urge for connectedness to others through the 7th house, aiding us in understanding our relationships. Astrology teaches us to recognize the forces of destiny that act on us, while also showing us ways we can exercise our freedom. Existential philosophy teaches us that our freedom isn't absolute freedom but is *situated freedom*. Within the givens of our situation, as described by the birth chart and transits, we can *respond*, we can make something of it; it's ultimately up to us what we do with our circumstances. We're responsible for what we make of it. Astrology also counteracts the malaise, emptiness, and meaninglessness of our era, and assists us in finding what gives our lives meaning, giving focus to our sense of purpose in existence. The constant forward movement of transiting planets implies directionality, *telos*, specific goals or end states, and invites us to project outcomes through visualization and to gradually accomplish goals in accordance with planetary rhythms. Psychological astrology is also informed by the existential principle of the *will*, which drives our evolution with focus and purpose.

## The Great Ancestors

Now a few brief words about the great ancestors and pioneers of psychological astrology, such as Charles Carter, who delineated the character traits of signs and planetary aspects, and described the Ascendant as a mask a person wears before the world that conceals the true self; Grant Lewi, who explained transits and how to use them productively, especially the Saturn return, and who emphasized action, the exercise of free will, the assertion of the full self within the limitations of our circumstances; Zipporah Dobyns, who developed the astro-alphabet describing the zodiac, signs, and houses as a language of psychological drives; and Noel Tyl, who described the Moon as a symbol of the *reigning need*, and showed that the horoscope has therapeutic and remedial value. In his book, *The Missing Moon*, Tyl portrayed the astrologer as a kind of detective or private eye who studies a client's life and character organization. *Analysis and Prediction* featured case studies illustrating how to synthesize a number of techniques and translate this information in practical terms for the client. In *Holistic Astrology*, Tyl described the relational and sexual profile in the horoscope. His book *Prediction in Astrology* definitively established the technique of solar arc directions as an incomparable tool for identifying crucial moments in human development. All of Tyl's writings show how a counseling astrologer becomes actively involved in the client's development, acting as a life coach and strategist, vocational guide, and spiritual ally.[11]

C. G. Jung studied horoscopes of married couples to understand Sun-Moon contact between charts, and to assess emotional compatibility and the path by which couples embodying opposing traits come to complete one another. Jung's studies foreshadowed work by Stephen Arroyo and Ronald Davison showing the value of astrology as a basis for couples counseling. These explorations inspired my own work as a Marriage and Family Therapist. Jung's work elucidating the archetypes represented by the planets is a central pillar of psychological astrology, which inspired soulful volumes by Liz Greene, Howard Sasportas, Karen Hamaker-Zondag, Melanie Reinhart, Lynn Bell, Erin Sullivan, Bruno and Louise Huber, Richard Tarnas, Glenn Perry, and other luminaries. The writings of these great astropsychologists merit our in-depth study.

Perhaps the most pivotal figure was Dane Rudhyar, who elucidated the transition from event-centered, predictive astrology to person-centered, humanistic astrology, emphasizing meaning and conscious personhood. Rudhyar showed that personal unfoldment occurs according to structural principles, within the time frame of specific cycles such as the lunation cycle, the Saturn cycle, the Uranus cycle. A cyclical perspective teaches us to welcome change and to flow with it creatively. Even our most difficult struggles and crises emanate specific meanings when viewed astrologically.

## EVERY PHASE AND EXPERIENCE IS MEANINGFUL

One of Rudhyar's central contributions is his idea that each phase and each experience is purposeful; even the destructuring, destabilizing periods related to the outer planets have inherent importance and meaning. For example, a 26-year-old woman named Beth had transiting Uranus conjunct natal Venus-Moon and her Descendant (Chart 2). At this time Beth left her boyfriend of seven years and had two brief relationships with men from other countries who returned unexpectedly to their homelands—very Uranian (Venus-Uranus: separations or sudden changes in relationships). Saturn had been transiting through Beth's 12th house of solitude during this period when she felt most alone and abandoned. Now, however, Saturn was beginning its passage over Beth's Virgo Ascendant. She judged and criticized herself harshly for not being partnered or

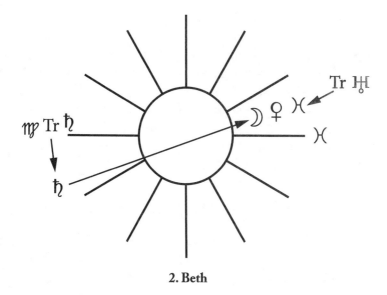

**2. Beth**

married like several of her friends. But the Uranus transit to her 7ᵗʰ
house Moon-Venus indicated this could be a time to explore different relationships, while at the same moment Saturn's transit into
the 1ˢᵗ house suggested a need to focus on developing herself. Beth
felt it was time to acquire some kind of training that would lead to
a better job, to vocational advancement (Saturn in Virgo).

Saturn transiting into the first house often indicates a period
when it's important to be self-reliant and focused on our own self-
definition, self-organization, and self-formation. Here, in Virgo,
Saturn denoted focus on acquiring work-related skills, as well as
changes in diet or health discipline. Saturn in the first house isn't
intrinsically a peak time for relationships. But in this case such an
assessment had to be modified because the 1ˢᵗ house Saturn would
soon oppose Beth's Venus-Moon in the 7ᵗʰ house (along with Uranus conjunct Moon-Venus), which were clearly relationship significators. As Saturn in Virgo went stationary direct, conjunct Beth's
Ascendant, she started nursing school; this was work she felt committed to. She also started going regularly to a yoga class, instilling
new Virgo practice habits. Then she got a phone call from one of
the boyfriends, saying he wanted to return to the United States
to be with her. You could feel the focused ray of transiting Saturn
opposite Venus, beginning to take form.

This example shows that instead of just saying this is a bad time for a relationship, we can emphasize that it's a good time for Beth to focus on herself (Ascendant and 1st house); the 7th house would take care of itself. I wanted her to focus on what *is* happening to her as much as on what *wasn't* happening. That viewpoint helps us avoid the kind of negative language that has a paralyzing effect on people. If you tell someone "your transits are terrible" for relationships, or money, you undermine their capacity to use astrology as a vehicle, and practice, of existential freedom.

## SELF-NARRATIVE AND THE MEANING OF CRISIS EVENTS

Psychological astrology is a practice of giving greater definition to identity by creating a cohesive self-narrative—a story about oneself, and one's personal history and aspirations. Some astrologers interpreting a chart describe a series of events, some positive, some negative, with no connecting threads. The readings often sounds something like this: Saturn is squaring your Sun, that's bad, that's difficult; it's not a good time to have a relationship for two years. But you have Jupiter transiting your MC. That's good." The picture we offer is constantly going up, down, up, down, good, bad, malefic, benefic, with no subtlety or nuance, just a series of disconnected events. I want astrology to be a *tantra*, a connecting, unifying thread, a suture of meaningful experiences that helps us weave the fragments of time and events into a cohesive story, into a self. Astrology increases human intelligence by teaching us to constantly learn from our experience, to make meaning from it, to understand every event as a meaningful phase within cycles of development. This entire perspective derives from Rudhyar's cyclical, person-centered astrology.

This perspective can steady and guide us during periods of crisis. A client named Angela called me during some tumultuous transits: Natally, she had Uranus-Pluto in Virgo in the 1st house opposite Saturn in Pisces in the 7th house. Currently Uranus was conjunct her Saturn and opposite natal Uranus and Pluto (Chart 3). While her husband was on an extended work assignment at sea (7th house Saturn in Pisces) she had an affair with another man—a brief moment

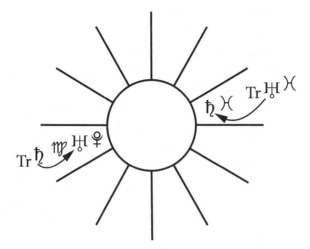

**3. Angela**

of dizzying freedom. But she and her lover became targets of much gossip, disapproval, and rejection by friends and neighbors (Uranus opposite Uranus-Pluto in the 1st house). They were subjected to so much public humiliation that they parted from each other, feeling it was too painful to continue the relationship.

In the end, Angela stayed with her husband (7th house Saturn). These events had a certain intelligibility from the perspective of the symbolism of Saturn opposite Uranus. The experience was organized by archetypal patterns, including the Uranian urge toward freedom, breaking out, defying social convention, and becoming a focus of controversy, and also her decision to stay married, held within Saturn's structures and commitments, which she decided were worth valuing and sustaining.

Would you say Angela's experience was "good" or "bad"? To interpret it in those terms diminishes the complexity of her experience. She wanted the pleasure and excitement of the boyfriend; she didn't regret this experience. She surrendered to it for an exciting and risky moment. But in the end she decided to honor her prior agreements. She did love her husband, but he was gone all the time. Something in their marriage was going to have to change. The change was that she decided to take time away from her job so she could spend time with her husband overseas. This also meant she had to accept the downsizing of her position at work, foregoing a promotion for the foreseeable future and allowing a colleague to advance ahead of her within the company. Angela gave up an opportunity for advancement (Uranus conjunct Saturn) in order to support her husband's work at sea (Saturn in Pisces). For her, this was a good tradeoff.

In my presence Angela closed her eyes and said, "I accept all that I have lost, and that it cannot be helped. Now I feel strangely at peace about it. I'm learning to accept the way things are. I'm just going to go with it." And she took a deep breath and settled into the deep experience of her inner silent being. The crisis of transiting Uranus conjunct Saturn and transiting Saturn conjunct Uranus had shaken her life structures to the core and awakened a deeper interiority, a more conscious spirituality. Angela had to live the tension of opposites, of Saturn opposite Uranus. This transit described several years of hard work to rebuild her marriage and her life, but she survived it and transformed within it. Rather than focusing on the superficial "good" or "bad" quality of events, psychological astrology illuminates the tensions that create spirals of evolution. We take it as a given that there will be stresses, reversals, and mishaps, as there must be in any heroic quest for life's meaning.

Astrology has unique power as medicine for our suffering souls because it helps us view setbacks and sufferings as meaningful lessons and necessary tests. Difficult things do happen. Death, losses, and defeats of the ego are a part of life and can be accepted and courageously endured. For example, when transiting Pluto was conjunct my natal Mars in Sagittarius for several years, I had to deal with intense power struggles in an academic environment (Sagittarius). Several unpleasant encounters left me so upset that one day I lost my temper with my boss for approximately one minute. To keep from being fired, I had to complete a series of anger management classes, which was a humbling experience. During certain transits, each of us can have unruly feelings and experiences that need to be metabolized. It became my task to neutralize some fiery anger that got stirred up and to contain and focus my Mars energies. I had to be strong and develop composure and self-mastery. At this time, I taught with Sagittarian fire and intensity and wrote several books.

Also, when Pluto was conjunct my natal Mars I was injured. I tore a ligament in my foot playing basketball and hobbled around for more than a year. I had to consciously live the Mars moment of pain, swelling, and inflammation. Simultaneously, transiting Chiron entered my 4th house and was conjunct my Capricorn Sun. Chiron is named after the Greek centaur Chiron, who was wounded in the foot and became a symbol of the shaman and the wounded healer. My sore foot and the limp were symptoms of Chiron's wound. So, I tried to receive the injury as an initiation. I couldn't run, but it made me sit still and meditate more. My free will was exercised by how I met the circumstances (the injured foot and intense university politics) that were to some degree beyond my control. Astrology teaches us to go through these experiences with awareness that we are passing through specific planetary tests. Then these Pluto or Mars or Saturn transits become enlightening, transformative processes.

## Process, Not Prediction

Recently, the primary image of the astrologer has been evolving from the traditional roles of prophet, psychic, and oracle, to that of the psychotherapist, life coach, and spiritual guide. What makes astrology therapeutic is the *working-through* of material, facilitating forward movement and tangible changes in behavior and attitudes. We don't just tell people what's going to happen. We focus on *process, not prediction.* We make suggestions for action, and bring inner conflicts into awareness.

A 45-year-old client named Ben (Chart 4) was a devout follower of a guru and a strong meditator, but he was very undeveloped emotionally, both within himself and in the relational realm. He had progressed Moon and Venus in Scorpio conjunct his Descendant, opposite natal Moon on the Ascendant. He was out of touch with his feelings, especially about women, and he had a limited capacity for honest communication.

There was a woman in Ben's life, Christine, a single mother with

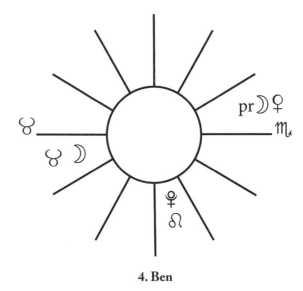

**4. Ben**

two children, who had been cooking meals for him and showing a definite interest in loving and nurturing him. Ben's instinctual response was to reject her. When I pointed out that it seemed to be an important time for a deeper emotional relationship with a woman (Moon), Ben said, "I was thinking of breaking up with her. But you're telling me that I should express my feelings to her more." I said, "That would be a positive step." Ben's natal Moon squared Pluto in Leo in the 4th house; he had a lot of unresolved issues with his mother, a strong mother complex, which caused him to avoid deep emotional entanglement. It was hard for him to tell Christine when he was angry or irritated with her or felt suffocated, and he reacted instead by withdrawing from her. We discussed the importance of telling someone how you feel. This was like a revelation to him. Emotional intelligence was clearly a major focus of Ben's current growth in consciousness.

Therapeutic astrology is process-oriented rather than event-oriented. A young woman named Katya had transiting Uranus conjunct her Pisces Moon in the 7th house (Chart 5). She wanted to know what was happening; she was quite depressed and crying all the time. Katya and her boyfriend were separating. She'd moved to a different apartment (the Moon rules the home), and she wasn't feeling close to her friends. This brought up sadness about the loss

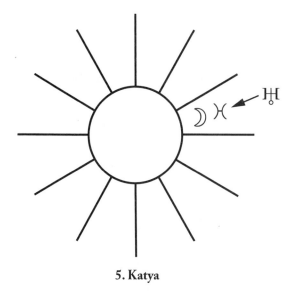

**5. Katya**

of her mother when she was a small child and feelings of being abandoned, both past and present, all of these emotions represented by the Pisces Moon symbolism. I said, "It's okay that you're crying. Bring me your river of tears." We bonded at that moment, and her emotional healing process began.

Awareness of the planetary symbolism helped to make this a workable situation for her. Katya was able to acknowledge her loneliness and hopeless feelings. The transit to the Moon signified her desire to reach out to form new emotional connections, especially with women, and she lived through the transit as a period of emotional transformation and renewal. There was no single crucial event during this period, but she began to change and experience freedom from old emotional patterns.

Katya's birth chart validated her need for close emotional attachment (Moon in the 7th). Part of this was achieved through her connection with me as an empathic figure. I said, "Uranus is moving the furniture around in your 7th house; it's changing the cast of characters right now. If you resist change, you suffer. If you celebrate change, you transform." Later, she told me, "I feel elated! I'm free! It's a good thing my boyfriend and I are breaking up. I'm free of his needs and always considering what he wants first. I can do what I want." She was describing the tendency of her 7th house

Pisces Moon to merge with her partner while submerging her own emotional needs. Katya also began to touch a deep wellspring of instinctual mother energy. She realized that she'd been in a state of emotional fusion with her mother, who suffered from depression. Katya said, "Mom's depression seeped into me on a lunar, unconscious level." Recognizing how she'd been carrying her mother's feelings was profoundly liberating. She began to transform her loneliness into an experience of depth in aloneness.

Therapeutic astrology is not about making definitive statements and predictions, such as predicting that Katya would break up with her boyfriend. That was her choice, not foreordained by the transit. The key point was that she was experiencing changes in her feelings and needs in relationships. Our goal is to serve as catalysts and facilitators of personal transformation. The work should be grounded and lead to tangible and dynamic change. I don't mean to suggest that I never predict for clients. All astrologers predict, to one degree or another, because we anticipate trends and possibilities. I'll discuss precisely how I do this later on. But, for me, it's not just a matter of predicting what's going to happen. Rather, I feel things as they are happening and I become part of what's happening astrologically. I try to understand what's being asked of me during difficult transits. How is this a task? What actions do I need to initiate? My goal isn't just to predict but to discover the meaning, the potential, the emotional quality of each planetary placement, transit, or progression. Instead of being resigned to "what's in the stars," I want to use astrology to transform myself, to understand what action I need to take at any moment.

A process orientation helps us go beyond viewing planetary placements as good or bad. Suppose that you have Uranus in the 7th house. Some astrologers pronounce that, with Uranus placed here, love will always be unstable, or that long-term relationships will be unattainable. In some instances a person with this placement resists relational commitment or attracts partners who are cool, distant, inconsistent, or unreliable. Relationships may be changeable or tumultuous. Or you attract a younger person, someone unusual and quirky, or someone controversial for you to be with. With Uranus here, relationships ask you to grant your beloved the freedom to be uniquely himself or herself. That attitude can make a long-term relationship possible. My father had Uranus in Pisces in the 7th house. He had a 57-year marriage to a very unique, independent woman—my mother, a highly Uranian person who began her career as a labor activist and organizer. Outcomes are far from fixed.

A process orientation involves approaching every transiting or progressed planet with eagerness to learn its lessons. We work with the symbolism and see what we can make of it. We visualize each planet as a part of ourselves. We try to live every archetype. I have a lot of Venus energy in my chart. I'm a musician, not professionally, but I constantly study music and make recordings and share them with my friends. It makes a huge difference to me to complete small artistic performance gestures. This is a living source of joy for me.

## PLANETARY TASKS

Psychological astrologers understand the planets as symbols of inner drives, rather than as forces that strictly determine what happens to us. Instead of reinforcing a sense of powerlessness, we delineate a person's developmental tasks, many of which are generic tasks that everyone experiences. Everyone has Venus tasks of social fulfillment, Mars tasks of expressing initiative and drives. There are tasks of planning and goal-setting at each phase of Jupiter's cycle, and the form-building and form-sustaining tasks of the Saturn cycle. We can map out the maturational tests and turning points in the life cycle—for example, the *early adult transition* in the early twenties during the Saturn square, when we establish our own residence and occupation; the increased commitments and responsibilities of the Saturn return; and so forth.

Psychological astrologers approach transits not as events but as *maturational processes* that we can participate in. Years ago I spoke to Alice, a woman who had been repeatedly institutionalized for schizophrenia since her late teens (Chart 6). She was starting her Saturn return. Her Saturn-Neptune conjunction in the 1st house symbolized problems with maturation and social adaptation in early adulthood. She asked what everyone else asks us: "What is going to happen to me?" I explained the significance of the Saturn

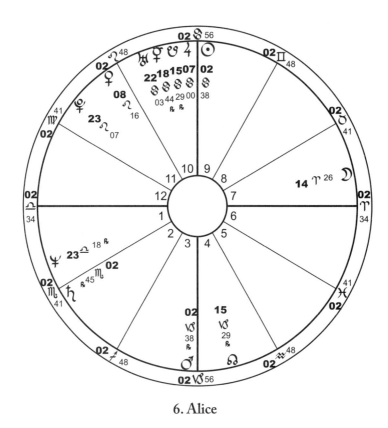

6. Alice

return. I said, "I don't know the future. But I think it's time for you to decide if you can take care of yourself and become an independent adult." I noted that natal Saturn and Neptune were conjunct, so her Saturn return would hopefully be a process of grounding; she needed to take her medication to avoid becoming spacy and delusional (Neptune). Also, religion or spirituality might play some role in giving her faith and strength to resolve her illness. Neptune and her Ascendant were in Libra, opposite her Moon in the 7th house. Maybe, I mused, there was hope for her to find more meaningful relationships (Libra and 7th house) in this next period of her life. Notice that I wasn't predicting. I was delineating themes and possibilities.

Within a year after this conversation Alice was discharged from the hospital, became a born-again Christian, and enrolled in law school, where she met her husband. She stayed on her medication, knowing she needed this to regulate herself. Eventually she was able to become a lawyer, fulfilling the potential of her natal Sun-Jupiter conjunction in Cancer in the 10th house. Here astrology was utilized therapeutically by emphasizing her responsibility for fulfilling the grounding and self-mastering potentials of the Saturn return.

## Positive Evolutionary Language

The language used in interpreting a chart is crucial. In my work I rarely use the terms "malefic" or "afflicted" to describe planetary placements or aspects. For example, a planet in hard aspect to Saturn is usually considered afflicted. I believe this language scares and disempowers us, and our clients. If I say "Your Mars is afflicted," or "You have a weak, debilitated Venus," I'm implying the person is inexorably flawed and can do nothing to change or improve her life. If I'd told Alice, "Your Saturn is afflicted and weakened by its conjunction with Neptune," I'd be implying that she was helpless to change her situation.

## Focus on the Present

In therapeutic astrology, focusing on the present is most helpful. What's happening now? What steps does this client need to take now? How can the person move forward *now*? I like to keep my astrology grounded and practical. I find this more useful than talking about how our problems are caused by something that happened in a past life. And the key to giving useful, practical advice is to follow Saturn's movement through the chart. We can endure anything, any daunting Pluto or Neptune transit, if we keep grounded at the level of Saturn.

## Gifts of Saturn

The key to success in astrology, and in life, is consciousness about the tests of Saturn. Saturn teaches us to stay steady through it all. Obstacles will inevitably appear in our path, but we need to just keep doing our work, stay focused. That's the key to positive evolution during this time when all hell is breaking loose on our planet. I like to hold the attitude that I'm the disciple of Saturn. When I was 25 and transiting Saturn was squaring my Sun I used to go outside and gaze at Saturn in the night sky and absorb its ray. I felt Saturn was my ally, steadying me, guiding me. Since that time, I've rarely had great difficulty with any Saturn transit.

All of us periodically have transits of Saturn. If we're resigned and do nothing, Saturn will crunch us. Our weaknesses will grow more apparent. But if we approach these transits as opportunities to work hard to accomplish specific goals, our effort will pay off, sooner or later.

Many astrologers view Saturn as the "greater malefic," the planet of sorrows, suffering, obstructions, and failures. These astrologers cringe when they see an upcoming Saturn transit and may try to hide out until the "malefic" influence is over. These are people who never accomplish anything. In my opinion, it's not acceptable to just wait around until something "benefic" or easy occurs. Master astrologers aren't afraid of Saturn; they *use* Saturn energy to focus and achieve their goals. Saturn symbolizes our urge to achieve stability and get organized. Saturn shows us where we need to be grounded, make choices and commitments, and handle our responsibilities. We come to understand that Saturn isn't just something that happens to us. It's something *inside* us. Approaching Saturn in this way, it needn't operate as a "malefic" planet.

The natal placement of Saturn—its sign, house, and natal aspects—denotes areas where we face challenges or delays in development. Our first task is to deal with our fears and inhibitions and mature in those areas of life. For instance, if Saturn is in the 2nd house, we may have some stresses around finances that teach us the value of money and what we have to do to get more of it. Over time we could develop a very grounded, practical consciousness about money matters. Wherever Saturn is placed, we face difficulties from youth and immaturity or an unwillingness to face reality; sometimes we confront problems of aging and accepting our limitations.

Each phase of Saturn's transit cycle refers to the themes of its natal position. If you have Saturn in the 2nd house, Saturn's major phases refer to stages in your quest for financial stability. If Saturn is in the 6th house, the Saturn cycle describes stages of your evolution in health, employment, and acquiring skills.

I have Saturn in my 3rd house of speech and communication skills. In childhood at my first Saturn square I had a speech impediment that led to shyness and inhibition at school. By working hard I mastered the speech problem and went on to become a public speaker. In adolescence, during my Saturn opposition, I was disinterested in school (3rd house Saturn) and didn't get good grades. But I enjoyed reading and started to become a good writer. During my Saturn square at age 22, I went on the road (3rd house: travel, being on the move) and wrote extensive journals, poems, and songs. As I prepared for my Saturn return I realized I still needed further education. I studied hard, wrote many papers, earned my master's degree, and taught astrology and yoga classes.

Please, let's stop calling Saturn a malefic planet.[12] Saturn represents accomplishment and mastery that is the result of sustained effort. Saturn teaches us to master the lessons of the earth plane, to persevere, fulfill responsibilities, and achieve our goals. Saturn represents the unending tasks of maturation and the need to develop patience, focus, and persistence. We have to master the task of Saturn in its house. That's where we have work to do. If it's in the 1st house, we have to master our self-doubts and gain confidence in our competency and sense of purpose. If Saturn is in the 11th house, we need to accept the responsibilities of group membership and being part of an organization, helping that organization to fulfill its purpose in fostering change within the collective. With Saturn in the 7th house, we have the tasks of long-term relationships and how to be a responsible partner, how to find someone who is appropriately serious, stable, and saturnine. With Saturn in the 4th house, we learn about the responsibilities of home ownership or making a family environment resilient and workable.

We all have to live within certain structures and limitations. We operate within the limits of our field of life, our occupation, our relationships—all the things that define our life structures. Saturn transits can bring their challenges and adversities, but I believe that these experiences are in some sense intended for us. I try to hold the awareness that "I really need this." Saturn teaches me to be more responsible for what's happening to me, for how my life is unfolding. Through conscious attunement to Saturn, hard work and sustained effort become an integral part of how we shape our lives.

## ASTROLOGY'S DEVELOPMENTAL PERSPECTIVE

Psychological astrology introduces a *developmental perspective*, describing pivotal phases of development, key milestones of a typical life: the first ferocious Mars return during the "terrible twos" period of toddlerhood, a transit marking birth of the will, initiative, and autonomy; the expansive, goal-setting, self-actualizing Jupiter returns at ages 12, 24, 36, 48, 60, 72, and 84; the maturational Saturn transits such as the opposition at ages 14–15; Saturn's waning square at age 21-22; the Saturn return during the Age Thirty Transition; and the waxing, first quarter square of Saturn corresponding to the Settling Down period of the mid thirties. We study the Uranus opposition in the early forties, signifying the urge for reorganizing our life structures, midlife upheaval and awakening, self-liberating choices, the desire to actualize our uniqueness and individuality. We learn that transits of each planet represent opportunities for change within the life cycle. Each is a clear marker of a developmental transition. We can identify predictable, phase-specific challenges of our development.

## EVOLVING OUR EXPRESSION OF THE PLANETS

Our experience of each planet undergoes a process of development, so how we express or embody Saturn or Venus or Mars evolves over time. That's a different attitude than one that implies a planet is just an experience or type of event one is afflicted by. Astrology's developmental orientation emphasizes unfolding the chart and its potentials. To do this, we use the chart to form an assessment of how a person's situation is organized internally. A gay man named Paul (Chart 7) said he'd never had an emotionally significant long-term or even short-term relationship with a man. He had Mars at the MC in Leo, and ruling his 7ᵗʰ house (Aries cusp). Mars in Leo

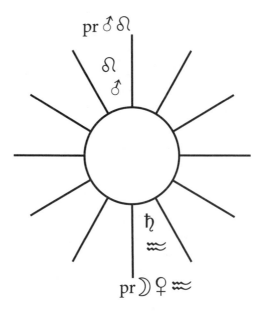

**7. Paul**

opposed Saturn in Aquarius in the 4th house of family. Astropsychologists view the 4th house as the developmental matrix of the
family that sets the foundation for the self. I said, "With Mars in
Leo you long to express the extraverted, creative, sexy, dramatic,
flamboyant side of your personality, but you feel your parents, especially your father, would disapprove. You don't have internal permission to be gay and that's why you haven't allowed yourself to have
a relationship." He started sobbing the moment I said this. I didn't
read that interpretation in a book. I just felt it. I sensed his internal
organization.

Paul said, "My father could never deal with this part of me, so I
shut it down." In my interpretation I avoid the type of astrological
language that might emphasize how Saturn restricts or "afflicts" his
Mars. I want to convey to Paul that he can develop his expression
of Mars energy, that he can live his sexuality more fully. I noted
that an interesting situation was forming in his progressed chart.
Progressed Venus was conjunct the IC, opposite progressed Mars,
which was precisely conjunct the MC. Also, within one month that

the progressed Moon would form a conjunction with progressed Venus. About a month later, Paul met a man and they developed a relationship and moved in together fairly quickly—fulfilling Saturn in Aquarius in the 4ᵗʰ house, and progressed Venus conjunct IC. When the moment is right, things happen smoothly and without struggle. Real change is possible. Transits and progressions help us understand the specific qualities of every time moment, so we can align with it and unfold its possibilities.

## Archetypal Patterns of Transformation

Paul's story illustrates how our development is shaped by the archetypal structures represented by the planets, in this case the union of Venus, the lover, the archetype of beauty, love, and attraction; and Mars, the courageous, sexy hero and warrior, and Saturn, the father, but also a symbol of his own internal authority. Paul needed to develop his inner lover with enough inner Saturn self-control to live the life he chooses for himself. Archetypes are recurrent mythic figures, patterns of transformation, structures within which we grow and develop. But how the archetypes find expression for each person can vary significantly. For example, a man named William became a father while his progressed Sun was squaring Saturn, and transiting Saturn was trine his natal Sun. His development at that time followed that specific pattern of development defined by Saturn as symbol of the father, provider of structure and security.

From a Jungian perspective, each birth chart is an expression, and emanation, of the collective unconscious (also called the *objective psyche*) and is organized by *archetypes*, the universal mythic patterns. Planets are embodiments of the living archetypes. Archetypes represent universal, recurrent human situations and templates of change and transformation. Since Jung's discovery of the archetypes of the collective unconscious, astrology has a new basis. Planetary symbolism can now be linked to timeless mythic themes, characters, and patterns of human experience. Ultimately what we can predict through astrology is the emergence of the archetypes. For example, Pluto represents the archetypal experience of Death-Rebirth. Venus represents the enrapturing Beloved, the Anima. Jupiter is the archetypal Teacher, Sage, Philosopher, and Judge. Asteroid transits manifest goddesses Ceres-Demeter, Juno-Hera, Vesta-Hestia, and Pallas-Athena.

Depth psychology gives astrologers a mythic language that deepens our work, while transits and progressions enable us to precisely anticipate the appearance of the archetypes identified by Jung. Each archetype is a pattern of transformation within the unconscious. For example, contacts to the natal Moon evoke the Mother archetype. Remember Ben, the man with Moon square Pluto who wanted to dump his girlfriend, who was challenged to transform his experience of emotions and of women. The Moon symbolizes the archetypal mother, the womb, gestation, protection, nourishment, the giving and receiving of care and nurturing, need fulfillment or its lack. The natal position of the Moon describes gratifying or ungratifying experiences of trying to get our emotional needs met. The Moon symbolizes our capacity for secure emotional attachments. I'll say more about this in Chapter 7.

A man named Ted has Pisces Moon in the 7ᵗʰ house. His wife Rita complains that Ted constantly needs her to be the nurturing mother. He loves it when she cooks for him, washes his clothes, fusses over his hair; he feels that she really cares about him. This is an example of how in our relationships we constantly call forth from each other our own archetypal potentials. As Ted integrates Rita's lunar nurturance and emotional availability, he feels more tender and nurturing toward her; he develops his expression of his own Moon. Rita has a Moon-Venus-Jupiter conjunction in the 1ˢᵗ house and thus naturally expresses the qualities of a loving, supportive spouse (Chart 8). This is one mark of her identity. Yet Rita resists being his nurturing mother figure, feeling that this conflicts with her desire for independence. She worried that she was too "co-dependent." But the Moon signifies allowing ourselves to be a source of supply for others; it symbolizes the value of our emotional presence for each other. The Moon symbolism helps Rita to accept the pattern of evolution her chart indicates, and that Ted's chart also calls forth. Both charts evoke expression of the lunar archetype—the capacity for nurturing and secure emotional attachment, allowing others to need us and rely on us. Ted's 7ᵗʰ house Moon and

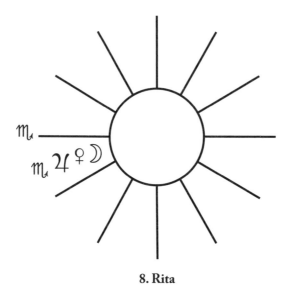

**8. Rita**

Rita's 1ˢᵗ house Moon both highlight this caring, emotionally atten-tive pattern of experience.

Now let's look at a contrasting example (Chart 9). A 42-year-old woman named Gwen has Virgo Ascendant and Uranus-Pluto in Virgo rising and Sun-Moon-Mercury in Aquarius in the 6ᵗʰ house. With her 6ᵗʰ house/Virgo emphasis, Gwen is imprinted by the archetype of the worker. Gwen is a devoted employee of an inter-national technology corporation (Uranus and Aquarius emphasis). Gwen is very attractive, but she remains single, has never been married, and is highly independent. With Uranus and Aquarius as archetypal dominants, her career in the computer industry is the focus of her life, involving her constantly in organizational change and promoting the mission of her company. Corporate life fits her archetypal pattern of development beautifully.

Under transits or progressions involving Neptune, we have experiences of the archetypal Messiah, Savior, or Victim. A man named Don had progressed Sun conjunct Neptune in the 4ᵗʰ house. He had a series of dreams about his deceased father, who had passed away when Don was four. Don dreamed "I am alone in the woods and I'm eating twigs and thorns." This reminded him of Christ with the crown of thorns and it reminded him of how his father, a Chris-tian Scientist, refused medical treatment and had died as a kind

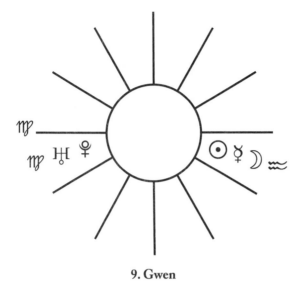

**9. Gwen**

of religious martyr. And just as Jesus on the Cross asked, "Father, why have you forsaken me?" as a child Don had questioned why his father had left this world, leaving him and his mother to fend for themselves. The dream revealed an archetypal core of his experience, which reflected Neptune's symbolism. Neptune is always related to the problem of suffering, in this case the suffering of Don's family (Neptune in the 4th house).

The archetype of the Hero/Heroine or Warrior is often constellated during transits involving Mars. While transiting Pluto squared natal Mars in Pisces, George, a gay man in a long-term relationship, grappled with sex addiction, expressed through a series of anonymous sexual encounters at steamy bathhouses (Mars in Pisces) (Chart 10).

George told me that he had a dream of wild horses breaking out of their corral, running free, with fiery steam flaring from their nostrils. He felt he needed to experience unrestrained libido, and this was symbolized within the unconscious. This is consistent with the Pluto-Mars symbolism. But George felt immense remorse, and feared he had endangered himself and his partner through possible exposure to sexually transmitted diseases. Was it safe to let the horses run wild? Later, George remembered that one of the wild horses in the dream turned into a camel, which he described an

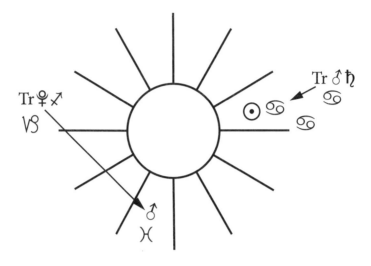

**10. George**

austere animal that can endure dry periods in the desert, representing a part of him that can renounce or delay gratification. The shift from wild horses to a camel reflected a significant internal shift. Planetary transits are constantly translated into symbols within the unconscious, symbols that can release immense energies within us.

Later George dreamed that a man was in the water wrestling with an enormous snake, which was wrapped around his body. This, too, reflects Mars in Pisces: a mythic battle in water. This dream represents the heroic masculine principle grappling with the primitive *instinctual psyche*. In the eternal myth of the Hero, the Hero slays the Dragon, Monster, Gorgon, or Serpent deity through a primordial act of phallic self-assertion. The Babylonian hero Marduk vanquished the dragon Tiamat. In Greek myth, Zeus slays the serpent Typhon. George was enveloped in a regressive union with the energies of the unconscious, with what Jung called the instinctual psyche. One must be able to experience instinctual life force, without being consumed or overwhelmed by it. George was involved in a Plutonian transmutation of his Mars energy. This example shows how astrology illuminates not just *events* but also *patterns of transformation* that tend to occur within each archetype.

## SATURN AS SIGNIFICATOR OF WORK, STRUCTURE, AND ACHIEVEMENT

Let's return to Saturn for a moment. Saturn corresponds to the alchemical *coagulatio*, the solidification of liquids and vapors into material form. It represents coming into form in a specific place and time, becoming fully embodied and grounded, through work, self-discipline and determination. A man named Ralph was trying to start a second career as a schoolteacher during his second Saturn return in the 9th house in Virgo, and while progressed Sun was conjunct natal and progressed Saturn for seven years (Chart 11).

He earned his teaching credential, but was fired from his first several jobs. Managing a classroom was harder than he expected and he was subjected to some fierce criticism of his job performance (Saturn in Virgo). Ralph wanted to quit, and he had fantasies of a more carefree existence. But he had responsibilities, a daughter with expensive medical problems (Virgo), so he had to keep working. Daniel Levinson says that an occupation must be both viable in society and suitable for the self.[13] Ralph found that teaching was neither viable nor suitable for him. He did temp work for several

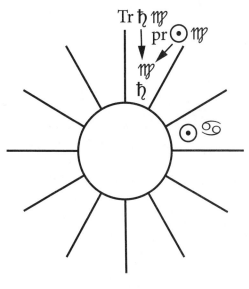

**11. Ralph**

months, and refined his skills (Virgo) in marketing and publishing (9th house Saturn), which was more related to his earlier career, which started during his first Saturn return. The Saturn symbolism illuminated his struggle and his effort towards self-mastery. Most astrologers could predict that this would be a difficult phase. But instead of just telling Ralph "this is a difficult period, and it won't be over for seven years," I explained that Saturn in Virgo is about challenges of occupational advancement, and the process of developing work-related skills.

As Saturn turned direct Ralph got a job offer in the promotion and marketing department of a large health maintenance organization (Saturn in Virgo). Instead of merely enduring the Saturn transit (and Sun-Saturn progression) with grim resignation, he utilized it to find the right job. Astrology contributes to the psychology of success through teaching us persistence in the face of adversity, obstacles, and delays. This example illustrates development within archetypal themes of Saturn, as well as the process orientation favored by astropsychologists. We don't resign ourselves to failure whenever there's a Saturn transit. We try to develop ourselves through focused effort, choice, maturation, and building sustainable structures.

## Astrology, Science, and Human Action

Recognition of archetypal structures as the guiding principle of astrology helps us overcome the criticism that our work is imprecise and not scientifically valid or verifiable. Some skeptics remain unconvinced of astrology's viability as a form of knowledge about human experience. This raises challenges for those of us who seek to validate astrology in our society, to gain respect for our work.

I believe one reason why attempts to prove the validity of astrology through scientific methods consistently fail is that we refer to an outdated approach to science. Modern science has been guided by the philosophy of *logical positivism*, the belief that *knowledge equals certainty* and the view that science is a search for absolute certainty, through knowledge of the regularities of phenomena. Science seeks to predict outcomes and to explain why events occur as they do by postulating repetitions and regularities between events in the world. And science seeks deterministic explanations, which implies the inevitability of actions, causes, and outcomes. So according to this logic, if a person has natal Sun opposite Neptune, or Pluto in the 4$^{th}$ house, then some definite, predictable result must necessarily occur; we should be able to make a definitive statement about what that will mean. Otherwise, astrology isn't valid. And several astrologers looking at the same chart should be able to make the same predictions or draw the same conclusions, otherwise astrology must not be objectively true and valid. But of course this isn't what happens. Pluto in the 4$^{th}$ house or Sun opposite Neptune manifest differently for different people. The outcome of planetary "actions" or causes isn't inevitable. Moreover, the person interpreting the chart influences the meaning elicited from it.

Some would argue that this plurality of outcomes and interpretations invalidates astrology. However, in postmodern, post-positivist science, determinism and absolute certainty aren't the ultimate criteria of knowledge, especially when it comes to understanding human beings. For example, physicists have shown that we may not have any certain knowledge of the physical world; at a subatomic level we can't definitively identify particles as separate entities existing at a specific location. It's more accurate to say that particles show *tendencies to exist* at a particular place and time; uncertainty is part of nature. Also, at a subatomic level, everything is interconnected with everything else. Thus, linear causality and determinism are called into question. This suggests that by preparing in advance for a Pluto or Uranus transit our alignment with the planetary archetype could affect the outcome. In other words, the planet doesn't just act upon us; we also act upon the planet. Also, Heisenberg's Uncertainty Principle showed that all observed phenomena are influenced by the observer, the scientist, and thus there's no pure, unmediated knowledge of an objective reality. If scientists are saying there's no certainty of knowledge about the physical world, then I wonder why astrologers are seen as suspect if we can't make 100% precise predictions of outcomes, or if different astrologers interpret the planets differently.

Rather than seeking absolute certainty, post-positivist thought seeks *understanding*, which is open to different interpretations by different interpreters. We recognize that all knowledge is relative to one's perspective, and that we're always influenced by our beliefs and expectations. One never has pure access to an objective reality. There's a plurality of truths, not absolute certainty. In the human sciences, hermeneutics or *interpretation* is emphasized, making clear the interpreter's biases and interests in the experiment or text to be decoded. According to philosopher Hans Gadamer, interpretation involves dialectic between the interpreter's expectations and the meanings in the text.[14] There's no one correct interpretation. Similarly, in astrology we realize there's no pure, objective reading of a chart; the chart is always open to a plurality of interpretations. No two astrologers read a chart the same way, just as no two musicians play the same piece of music in exactly the same way. Rather than seeking the impossible goal of absolute certainty and predictive accuracy, we can acknowledge that our findings are dependent on the unique conditions of the interpretive moment—which is influenced by what kind of mood the astrologer is in, what transits we're having at the time, and our degree of mastery of what each planet represents. In other words, our ability to interpret a Saturn or Neptune transits depends on our own maturity in facing the challenges these planets tend to present. Our biases as interpreters and our clients' varying levels of consciousness both undermine the determinism often assumed to be implicit in astrology.

But the definitive insights that can help astrologers permanently shed determinism derive from the philosophy of *human action*. As stated by philosopher Charles Taylor, human action isn't caused by prior, antecedent events. People are the agents of their own actions. People can start chains of events in the world and needn't function merely as links in causal chains already started. We're sometimes causes of our own behavior. No prior, antecedent conditions are sufficient to account for the fact that a certain action has been performed. Human action involves *purpose and intention*, the awareness of an action plan. Human actions are autonomous acts of agents, and are teleological (goal-oriented) rather than strictly determined by prior causes. According to Taylor, human action is governed not by causal law but by teleological laws that relate actions to their *intended consequences* rather than to antecedent events.[15] In short, human action is goal oriented, and purposeful.

In this light, we can practice astrology stressing not what *determines* us, but what *pulls* us toward the future, discerning the "intended consequences" of the planets. We can meditate on chart symbols, asking, "What does the universe intend or ask of me now?" Astrology is a special discipline of human action, because it enables us to synchronize our actions to the evolutionary rhythms of the cosmos; it enables us to formulate intentions, and to transform ourselves in accordance with the patterns of the archetypes.

### ASTROLOGY, MEDITATION, AND SYMBOL AMPLIFICATION

Psychological astrology avoids determinism through its *interpretive flexibility*. Instead of ascribing fixed meanings to planets, we work with them, process them, and try to unfold them. We meditate deeply so that we begin to approach each natal and transiting planet as a spiritual practice, a necessary step to wholeness. Most importantly, we adopt *a process orientation to chart interpretation*, rather than static, rigid interpretations that set outcomes in stone—for example, saying that someone with Sun square Pluto always is a control freak, or has obsessive-compulsive disorder; or that all Taureans are stubborn and materialistic; or that whenever Uranus transits to the Moon or the Ascendant, this or that happens. We use astrology as a basis for process work that enables us to develop our potential actively.

There are different techniques for astrological process work. AstroDrama and Barbara Schermer's Astrology Alive are examples of this.[16] My own approach is to combine astrology, meditation, and visualization. In *Astrology and Meditation,* I discussed *symbol amplification*, the practice of contemplating the meaning of our natal planets or current transits and progressions and asking ourselves: What could it mean? How can I unfold the highest potential of this? Just as we understand the meaning of dreams by asking questions and unfolding the meaning of dream images,[17] astrological symbols need to be amplified by imagining possibilities and projecting outcomes. It helps to assume that all planetary symbolism contains instruction for us.

For example, in a quiet, meditative state, consider, what's the potential outcome of this Neptune transit? Maybe everything is on hold. Maybe everything is uncertain, nebulous, and fluid. That's the moment when you need to cultivate serenity, silence, and receptivity. If you're facing a Saturn transit, ask yourself: Where do I need to make a decision or get more focused? You don't have to be the tragic victim of a Saturn transit. Just accept that there's always work to do. As Saturn moves through your chart and activates each planet and house, strive to improve your functioning and expression in those areas. Each transit and each experience is the precise ingredient we need right now to transform ourselves. To the best of our abilities, we become both masters of ourselves and servants of the great work.

Symbol amplification is a way of cutting through our tendency to become scared of astrological events, afraid of what's coming. That's totally natural. We all go through daunting experiences; we all have our heroic challenges. These long Pluto or Neptune or Saturn transits call forth all the courage we've got, but that's what they're for—to test us, strengthen us, and refine us. All transits and progressions describe passages, developmental challenges, and lessons that transform us. If we live through each phase of life with consciousness, at any moment there can be an explosion of light in the heart, a sudden illumination. This illumination can occur each time we open ourselves to the sacred interpretive moment in which everything we need to know is revealed to us.

Process orientation means that everything isn't written in stone; the true meaning of our planets isn't found in an ancient palm leaf or a sacred scripture. We can discover it spontaneously, fresh in the moment, through our own deep meditation, inner work, and visualization. We can practice astrology as a form of meditation and visualization, with a quiet mind, a contemplative attitude.

Begin by opening your breath. Feel your center. Relax your body and quiet your mind. Then draw or visualize your natal chart, and current transits. As you imagine or draw these planets, *feel* them, and ask yourself:

**Rembrandt van Rijn, *Faust In His Study***

*What's the meaning of this natal planet in this sign,
    house, aspect?*
*How can I work with this?*
*Am I living this part of my identity, my totality, my
    potentiality?*
*What's my most important current transit?*
*What parts of my life want to develop now?*
*What are my tasks?*
*What does the universe intend from this?*
*What's the highest outcome or expression of this that I can
    imagine?*

Sit with a quiet mind and envision your next step in working with these planetary energies. Visualize outcomes and possibilities. Rather than relying on what you read in books, find the truth of planetary symbols within yourself, accessing your intuition. Actively shape the meaning of what unfolds. Astrology is a practice of setting your own intention, piloting your ship toward conscious destinations. As you meditate on your chart, form a vision of how your evolution wants to unfold in this moment. Meditative spaciousness and tranquility enable us to understand the deepest lessons of astro-symbolism.

## The Meaning of Events

If astrology's methods are to be most helpful, it's important to avoid superficiality. Humanistic astrologers aren't just concerned with whether events are good or bad. Rather, the goal is to understand how every phase of life is meaningful. Rudhyar said, "Every event is accepted as a necessary phase of the ritual process of existence."[18] We need to go below the surface of events, to the deeper dimension of *meaning*.

When I was 12 years old, I had solar arc Pluto sesquare my Sun (135° aspect), and a secondary progressed Moon-Mars opposition; and on the day of a transiting Moon-Pluto conjunction, I was hit by a car and broke several bones. This event awakened me to the fragility of life (Pluto: emergencies, a brush with death). It was also a classic manifestation of Mars as the planet of mishaps and injuries. But looking more closely at this event I discerned a deeper meaning. Solar arc Jupiter was conjunct my 2nd house cusp, and transiting Jupiter opposed transiting Saturn in Taurus: I won a small financial settlement (2nd house and Taurus: money), which sat in a bank account until I was 21, which aided my development by enabling me to travel around and find myself for an extended period after college. At the time of the accident, transiting Saturn was stationary direct, exactly square my Moon, and solar arc Saturn was exactly semisquare (45°) my Moon: Several nice nurses took good care of me (Moon: women, caregivers, nurturing) until my mother (Moon) arrived at the hospital, and she was especially tender and loving toward me. I grew closer in my relationship with my mother in the days and weeks after this accident. I had a beautiful experience of the mother archetype. All my needs were taken care of. Also, the Moon-Pluto conjunction in Virgo in my 12th house was relevant. This was my first time inside a hospital (12th house) since my birth. In my hours in the emergency room I witnessed many gravely ill or injured individuals. I became aware of the preciousness of life. Events aren't black and white and may have deeper meaning than apparent on the surface. None of this subtlety can be captured by an approach to astrology where we simply say "that is bad," or "this is good." The interpretation of a chart requires attention to the nuances of events, to what Alexander Ruperti calls "the total uniqueness of each moment."[19]

## A LIFE OF SPECIAL MOMENTS

The magic of astrology is that it can transform ordinary moments into extraordinary ones. Fast-forwarding 37 years: The day Saturn entered Virgo I was visiting my now-91-year-old mother, pulling weeds from in between the cracks of her large brick patio. I worked with precision, patience, and increasing skill as I uprooted the weeds. I pulled every single one of them. Then I swept off the bricks. I called my mother outside. It mattered not at all that the weeds would soon shoot up through the cracks once again and that within two weeks the patio would be totally overgrown. We savored the view of the clean patio with immense satisfaction. For a brief moment a form of perfection had been achieved. We may never accomplish anything remarkable or special in life, but at least we can do ordinary, mundane, or mindless tasks with panache and meticulous precision! We try to make each moment a masterpiece.

In this chapter we've discussed the developmental, therapeutic, archetypal, and process emphasis of psychological astrology. We'll revisit these themes in later chapters.

# PART TWO

# HUMANISTIC AND
# TRANSPERSONAL ASTROLOGY

Chapter 3

# Rudhyar's Astrology In Plain Language

Now let's contemplate the work of an astrologer who revolutionized our field, philosopher and metaphysician, Dane Rudhyar. Although Rudhyar passed away in 1985, I believe his message speaks to our deepest needs in contemporary astrology and that we gain immense benefit by studying his work. In this chapter I'll explore some basic principles of Rudhyar's astrology: the lunation cycle and progressed lunation cycle, and planetary transit cycles. I'll discuss Rudhyar's philosophy of *Wholeness* and try to understand what he means by a transpersonal approach to astrology. I'll briefly examine Rudhyar's birth chart, and suggest how Rudhyar's astrology is enhanced by linking it to Buddhism, Jung's depth psychology, and Assagioli's Psychosynthesis. Surveying Rudhyar's work is like hiking on a great mountain; trails lead off in all directions.

## RUDHYAR'S PLACE IN ASTROLOGY

First, let's consider Rudhyar's place in astrology. All the modern masters and Great Ancestors of astrology bring a unique individual quality to their work: Some were technical geniuses such as John Addey and Charles Jayne. Some were great horary and mundane astrologers, such as Barbara Watters, Charles Carter, and Ivy Goldstein-Jacobsen. Ronald Davison and Lois Sargent showed how astrology can help us understand and enhance our human relationships. Alan Leo, Sydney Omarr, and Grant Lewi played an important role in popularizing astrology, as did the great Evangeline Adams, who demonstrated astrology's efficacy to the masses and to wealthy business tycoons, and defended in court her right to practice astrology without harassment. All put their stamp on our field. But more than any of them, Rudhyar was a spiritual teacher. He showed how astrology is a way of life, a spiritual path, a way to the center. With the possible exception of Isabel Hickey, no other astrologer of his generation was as interested in the spirituality of astrology. Rudhyar was modern astrology's greatest visionary. He evoked the most spiritually refined potentials of astrology—not as a way to predict when it's a good time to gamble in Las Vegas, but as a discipline of mind and consciousness, and a method for self-transformation.

There's a commonly held opinion that Rudhyar is a difficult writer. Like any great thinker, his work makes some demands on our intellects. I believe that once we are familiar with his basic themes we can read Rudhyar's books easily. To me, the poetry of his books is eternal. His basic ideas are beautifully stated and easily grasped. His core concept is that evolution is cyclical. Rudhyar's astrology is the study of how our lives unfold in cycles, as structured processes of change.

In *The Practice of Astrology as a Technique of Human Understanding,* Rudhyar said that the purpose of astrology is "to understand the apparent chaos and confusion of [our] life experiences by referring them to ordered patterns of cyclic activity which [we discover] in the sky." [20] The goal of astrology is not to predict events but to identify phases in a person's development.

Astrology is a process of bringing order to experience. Events gain new *meaning* when viewed as moments within cycles. Also, he says, astrology is "threshold knowledge," knowledge that enables us to cross over thresholds, through conscious transitions. It is a means of helping people who are in pain through processes of change, helping them understand what is happening, and what is asked of them.

Rudhyar contrasted event-centered, predictive astrology (the "astrology of information"), with humanistic, "person-centered" astrology, which he also described as the "astrology of meaning." Humanistic astrology helps us become self-aware and self-defining persons. Here the focus of astrology is not, "What is going to happen to me?" But rather, "What can I do to more fully actualize the potentials indicated by my birth chart?" The goal of astrology is not just to predict the future but to *mold* the future through our choices and actions. This perspective was a huge revolution in our field; person-centered astrology means that what happens is *up to us.* Astrology is no longer a matter of fate and destiny; it becomes a discipline emphasizing choice, action, will, and consciousness. As we learn to calibrate our lives with planetary symbols and cycles we develop clear goals, clear timing, and clear intention. I have met many astrologers who say, "What is going to happen to me as a result of this transit?" Instead of "What am I going to *do* with this transit?" The message of Rudhyar's person-centered astrology is that it's up to us what we make of the potentials our charts symbolize. We need to get active with our Mars transits, make plans and set goals during Jupiter transits, and use our Saturn transits to build stable structures in our lives. Rudhyar wrote that the "seed pattern" of a birth-chart

> defines what that organism [or person]... SHOULD be if it fulfills its function in the universal scheme of things, or one might say according to God's Plan. . . . [A]strology does not tell us what will happen, but what would happen should the person act consciously and earnestly according to the celestial instructions represented in code by the birth chart.[21]

The phrase "celestial instructions" is worth remembering, because rather than indicating things that merely happen to us, astrological symbols instruct us in how to act, how to proceed in our lives for maximum accelerated evolution. The study of astrology requires involvement, responsiveness, gauging of opportunities, conscious action.

## ZODIACAL SIGNS: THE PULSE OF LIFE

In *Astrological Signs: The Pulse of Life*, Rudhyar states that astrology is a method for linking the lesser whole and the greater whole, the individual and the collective. This interplay of opposites is implicit in the meaning of the zodiacal signs. He states,

> All astrology is founded upon the zodiac... [,] the symbolization of the cycle of the year. . . . The essential thing about the zodiac . . . is the human experience of change. And for a humanity which

once lived very close to the earth, the series of nature's 'moods' throughout the year was the strongest representation of change.[22]

At any moment, two basic natural forces are active, light and darkness, the Day force and the Night force. The Day force is a personalizing energy, representing individual uniqueness and personality. Night force is an in-gathering of energy, bringing people together in collectives. The twelve signs describe our evolution through phases of individualization (the signs Aries through Virgo) and phases of social integration (Libra through Pisces). The signs represent the pulse of life, the interplay of the individual and the collective. Astrology teaches us to balance these two evolutionary drives, the urge to differentiate identity, and the urge to relate with others, to consciously participate in a greater whole. (See Appendix.)

The zodiacal signs describe our twelve evolutionary assignments. Our task is to move through these varied conditions with consciousness, and to discover a wisdom transcending all changing conditions. Through contemplation of change we find a steady consciousness beyond change—or rather, steadiness in change.

## The Vegetation Cycle

The story of the zodiac is closely related to the metaphor of the seed and the vegetation cycle. The spring signs, Aries, Taurus, Gemini, represent the sprouting of seeds in springtime, the process of plant germination, putting out roots, and growth of branches and foliage. The summer signs, Cancer, Leo, and Virgo, represent the growth of flowers and fruit, with the Virgo symbolic harvest in late summer. During the period of the autumnal signs, Libra, Scorpio and Sagittarius, the plant's leaves wither and fall to the ground, becoming raw humus for future cycles. Seeds are released from the falling fruit, lying dormant in the ground through the winter phase of Capricorn, Aquarius, and Pisces. During the winter signs, when the Night force is in ascendancy, there is anticipation of the future, dormancy and expectancy. These physical and karmic seeds eventually germinate in springtime. This metaphor describes how something sprouts, grows, flowers, bears fruit, releases seed for the future, and withers, until the seed reawakens. Thank you brother Rudhyar for this beautiful teaching, which has so many practical applications in the study of astrology. The metaphor of the seed and the vegetation cycle is the essence of Rudhyar's philosophy of life, for it teaches us to view our lives in the context of cycles, structured changes in the flow of time.

The fact that Rudhyar's astrology is rooted in this most earthy metaphor suggests that the goal of astrology is to understand our own seasons of change—our cycles of birth, growth, fullness, decay, endings, and rebirth. We discern when to begin (however tentatively), when to make sustained effort, and when to bring things to completion. Astrology is rooted in nature and helps us connect to the natural rhythms of life.

## THE LUNATION CYCLE

In his book, *The Lunation Cycle*, Rudhyar showed how the rhythms of life and nature are embodied in the monthly phases of the Sun and Moon. At New Moon, an evolutionary impulse is released. The New Moon represents inceptions, beginnings, an urge to manifest an impulse or desire. This impulse unfolds during the waxing (growing) half of the cycle, which emphasizes *growth of form*, "spontaneous and instinctual action."[23] The First Quarter Moon represents a *crisis in action*, "repudiation of the past," building of new structures or faculties,[24] and meeting obstacles with determination and decisiveness. The Full Moon phase brings full illumination, clarity of purpose, objective awareness of the meaning of this cycle of existence. Rudhyar says that the Full Moon brings "a new vision, a revelation, a sense of fulfillment and renewed purpose."[25] Then, during the waning half of the cycle we experience a reevaluation of structures and a "conscious growth in meaning." The Third Quarter Moon represents reorientation and reevaluation of purpose. Here a "crisis in consciousness" may occur.[26] Our goals, beliefs, and structures are reassessed, and a decay or *dissolution of form* begins, often coinciding with a *growth in awareness*. As the cycle nears completion during the Balsamic phase (the waning crescent Moon), there is a period of waiting in preparation for a new cycle that will commence at the next New Moon. The Balsamic phase is the close of the cycle, and represents release, surrender, letting go of the past, and anticipation of the future.

The lunation cycle symbolizes an eternal cycle of inception, action and momentum, harvest, and reorientation. Following this cycle each month, we tune our actions to the pulsing of the cosmos. We set things in motion at New Moons. We sustain our efforts through the tension of the first quarter and trust that we will reach our time of fullness, the Full Moon climax of the cycle, which arrives with its own inevitability in response to the quality of all our prior actions during the waxing half of the cycle. We learn how every cycle requires change of commitments and priorities. We live consciously through endings, moments of silence, emptiness, waiting. Astrology attunes us to the rhythmical interplay of waxing and waning, action and consciousness, intention and fruition.

The lunation cycle is the core of Rudhyar's astrology. It is the prototype of all planetary cycles—each of which has a symbolic new moon conjunction, first quarter phase, full moon opposition, third quarter square, and balsamic phase. Knowledge of the lunation cycle becomes an ever-flowing fountain of wisdom for astrologers.

## THE PROGRESSED LUNATION CYCLE

One of Rudhyar's great innovations was to apply the rhythm of the monthly lunation cycle to the progressed chart: The progressed lunation cycle. By studying the lunation cycles in the days immediately after birth, we discern a foundational rhythm of our life development.

A basic task for all astrologers is to study the phases of our progressed Sun and Moon. For each major phase, we count how many days after birth have elapsed; this number of days corresponds to the year of life. So a New Moon twenty days after birth indicates a progressed New Moon at age 20, a time of new beginnings. Seven or eight days later there will be a quarter Moon corresponding to a progressed quarter Moon at age 28. And so on with the Full Moon and the third quarter phase. Knowing your current progressed lunar phase is a helpful reference point for understanding phases of life experience, the shape of the life story.

Let me give some personal examples. I was born close to the New Moon, and when I was a teenager I had a progressed Full Moon conjunct my natal Venus. At this stage of my life I was deeply involved in musical studies and performances. I lived the archetype of the musician and felt an intense clarity of purpose. At my progressed third quarter square in my twenties I started playing in nightclubs and on street corners and met obstacles in my attempts to become a professional musician; and thus I began to reevaluate my goals. At this stage I began to study astrology and discovered Rudhyar's work, which made a huge impact on me. This was a period of growth of consciousness, but also a phase of dissolution of form. I didn't know who I was for a while. I experienced breakdown of my former goals and identity, a reevaluation of all I was and hoped to be. The impetus of that cycle was waning.

For several years at the progressed balsamic phase I experienced dormancy, waiting; not much happened externally, but inwardly new goals formed. Then around the time of my progressed New Moon (which trined natal Jupiter) I moved to the Bay Area and taught yoga and astrology classes based on Rudhyar's approach, usually to one or two or three people at a time, you know, really big groups. The New Moon is a time of beginnings, not of fullness. I was reading Rudhyar's books, and writing a lot, and I started graduate school. The cycle began with a focus on education. At my progressed first quarter square I started teaching in universities and I published three books, taking decisive action to fulfill the purpose of this cycle.

I wrote this chapter on Rudhyar during my progressed Full Moon, a culminating phase within the life cycle. The progressed Full Moon is a time of fullness, heightened objectivity. It will happen two or three times in an average lifetime. At the time of this progressed Full Moon I had the opportunity to speak about Rudhyar at the greatest astrological gathering on the planet, the 2002 UAC gathering in Orlando, Florida. Also, my book *Astrology and Meditation* was published, another culminating event. An interesting feature of this progressed full Moon is that it was only then that

I could relinquish my focus on the previous cycle's climactic phase and the idea that I should be a musician. I had a hard time letting go of that central dream and preoccupation of my youth. I realized that I have lived that cycle of my existence, and that now I am in another cycle. With my progressed Full Moon in Virgo in the 12<sup>th</sup> house, this cycle's peak moment asked me to dedicate myself to *moksha* or inner freedom through the spiritual disciplines (Virgo) of yoga, meditation, astrology, and dream analysis (12<sup>th</sup> house). I began to define this clear intention.

Carefully study the phases of your own progressed lunation cycle and try to understand the unfolding of your life in this context. Reflect on the sign, house, and aspects of these progressed lunar phases. It's also illuminating to study the Sabian Symbol for the degree of the progressed New Moon and Full Moon. Understanding the progressed lunation cycle helps us attune to the most basic rhythm of our life and evolution.[27]

## INTERPLANETARY ASPECTS

Rudhyar's philosophy of cycles led to new insights about interplanetary aspects. From this perspective, no aspect, such as a square or opposition, is inherently bad or good. All aspects are necessary moments or phases within a cycle. This approach is greatly needed because many astrologers are still at the stage of understanding where we say, "I have Mars square Uranus or Sun, that's bad, isn't it?" Rudhyar views all aspects as phases of interplanetary relationships. I believe his approach is far superior to traditional approaches that view aspects in a static way, as good or bad. He wrote,

> [A]strology usually considers the angular distance (aspect) between two planets as a thing in itself, as a separate factor unrelated to the cycle of relationship between these two planets. . . . By thus arresting the flow of time the astrologer analyzes death and lets life escape."[28]

In *Astrological Aspects*, Rudhyar describes aspects as phases in a cycle's unfolding. The *conjunction* represents *subjective being* and spontaneous action. The *semi-sextile* and *semi-square* are phases of *focusing* (or reaction); the inertia of the past must be overcome. The *sextile* is the phase of organizing, when environmental opportunities present themselves. The waxing *square* signifies *deciding*—a release from "source"; the faster moving planet is no longer pushed by the power released at the conjunction, but is drawn toward the promise of the Full Moon opposition phase. This is often a moment of decision or cutting away of any influence that would pull one "off the track." This is the moment of acting out the commitment, of severance from past conditioning and subservience to the past. The square is the aspect of individualization. This is the phase of form-building activity, the two planets now being stabilized in relation to one another. The *trine* represents creative expression, outward application. Decisions are made with an aura of pleasant inevitability, or feel as if they have already been made. But patience and perseverance are required. The *sesquiquadrate* is a phase of challenge and of encounter with the "real world" upon one's efforts at expression (trine). The *waxing quincunx* is the phase of *improving*, making adjustments in expression, action, or application. If the opposition is a definite end, then the quincunx is a "last chance"; it manifests as a sense of dissatisfaction. The *opposition* is the phase of *realizing*, objectivity, conscious understanding, and purposeful activity; it signifies a high degree of development of the opposing factors. This is the apex of the cycle, a phase of objectivity, acceptance, and detachment. The *waning quincunx* is the phase of *sharing*, adjusting to the realities of what one can now clearly and objectively see. And the *waning sesquiquadrate* represents disseminating or applying to external reality our vision or understanding. As our attention turns outward, we may experience the shock of the realities of the world into which we are awakening. Now we recognize the need to include others in our point of view.[29]

I won't review Rudhyar's work on aspects in further detail here, but it's explained beautifully in *Astrological Aspects*, and in Bill Tierney's *Dynamics of Aspect Analysis*.[30] The point I wish to make here is that *there are no bad aspects;* all are necessary moments. An opposition between two planets isn't "bad." It's a full moon phase of objective awareness and conscious understanding between those planets.

Each aspect is a necessary moment, a phase of cycles of the planets, each of which performs a specific function in the evolution of our consciousness.

PLANETARY FUNCTIONS AND PLANETARY CYCLES

Now a few words about the planetary functions. The natal Sun represents the potential to develop a particular type of selfhood. And the Sun's purpose is conditioned by the personal planets (Mercury, Venus, and Mars), which express the Sun's light through the functions of mind, heart, and will. In *The Practice of Astrology*, Rudhyar says that "two forces are operating within every whole: one of these is the gravitational pull of its center. The other is the attraction toward the 'greater whole,' . . . the Transcendent."[31] Sun and the inner planets describe our gravitational pull toward a center of conscious solar identity. The social planets, Jupiter and Saturn, link the individual to the group, society, and culture through education, life planning, and social achievement. And the outer planets, Uranus, Neptune, and Pluto, represent our pull further outward toward the galaxy of infinite space and infinite consciousness. Rudhyar calls them "planets of transcendent activity."[32] They are symbols of transpersonal stages of human evolution. A conscious human being lives in the balance between these two tidal movements: the inward tide of ego development and self-awareness; and the outward tide of social relatedness and self-transcendence.

The major "technique" of Rudhyar's astrology is to study two types of transiting cycles: cycles of planetary position, and cycles of interplanetary relationship. Cycles of position are the transiting cycles of each planet with reference to its birth position. We study the monthly lunar transit through the twelve signs; the Sun's yearly cycle; the phases of the two year Mars cycle, which helps us understand changes in how we initiate action and express our vitality; the 12-year Jupiter cycle, our ongoing process of assimilating knowledge and setting goals; the 29-year Saturn cycle, our process of maturing, making choices, working, and sustaining structures; and the 84-year Uranus cycle, which defines stages in the process of individuation. I assume you're familiar with these. We follow the major phases of each planetary cycle—at the very least, the conjunction, square, opposition, and waning square, but also the semisquare, sextile, trine, sesquare, and quincunx. Most importantly, we note the interconnectedness between all phases within each cycle. We view the transit cycle of a planet as a whole, as an organic process of evolution. For example, there's a coherence to our Jupiter cycle, which is hopefully in the direction of expansive planning, goal-setting, optimism about the future. I know a successful investor with natal Jupiter in the 2nd house who makes progress in her financial growth at each major phase of her Jupiter cycle. In my own life, I map out small increments of my progress toward achieving my goals to each phase of my Jupiter cycle.

There's a continuity and inner organization to the flow of time. There's a coherence to our Saturn cycle, which is preferably in the direction of greater stability. If I'm at my Saturn opposition at age 44–45 my life structures should be evolving in accordance with what I set in motion at my Saturn return and sustained through the age 36–37 Saturn square. If these are weaknesses in my life structures I need to address them at each of these phases. At every phase of the Saturn transit cycle we strive to fulfill the responsibilities and commitments suggested by Saturn's natal sign and house position. Maybe if you have Saturn in your 2nd house it's constant attention to finances; or in the 5th house, attention to your kids; or organizational commitments if you have Saturn in the 11th house. Regardless of where natal Saturn is placed, our task is to develop the Saturnian virtues: confidence, patience, responsibility and sustained effort.

PLANETARY PAIRS

Next we examine the interconnecting cycles of the various planetary pairs, which we understand in accordance with the principles of the lunation cycle. We follow the Sun-Moon cycle, the monthly phases of life, traced through signs and houses of the birth chart. I also closely watch the Sun-Mercury cycle, which shows the changing focus of the mind and our attention. Look at your ephemeris and locate the Mercury retrograde periods and Sun-Mercury retrograde conjunctions. Find the sign and house where these fall. Also note where Mercury turns direct. You can plan your calendar around these. If the conjunction is in your 2nd house, reexamine your finances, or spend some time talking things over with your spouse if it falls in the 7th house. With the Sun-Mercury conjunction in the 4th house, focus on projects in the home. Intelligent astrologers make room in their lives for massive learning and rethinking during these periods. Similarly, we study the periodic aspects of Sun-Venus, Sun-Mars, Sun-Jupiter, Mercury-Jupiter, Mars-Saturn, and so forth. We give special attention to the transit cycle of planets that are in close natal aspect, with which we feel a natural resonance. If you have Sun aspecting Neptune in your chart you may be highly attuned to the transiting relationship of those two planets—which define a process of conscious attunement to Spirit. If you have a natal Jupiter-Neptune aspect, follow the ongoing relationship between these planets to understand phases of your quest for spiritual knowledge.

Here I see a connection between Rudhyar and the work of Reinhold Ebertin, who concisely described the meaning of planetary pairs. If there's a quality you want to boost in your life, identify the relevant planetary pair and observe the cyclical relationship of these two planets. If you want to be successful in your work and career, follow the Jupiter-Saturn cycle, the cycle of achievement through strategic action. The Jupiter-Saturn conjunction every twenty years births a new cycle of social ambition, striving, and accomplishment. If you want to understand breakthroughs in scientific paradigms, follow the cycle of Jupiter-Uranus, which marks moments of discovery and innovation in knowledge or theory. Or, if you need to cultivate common sense and thoughtful decision-making, tune into Mercury-Saturn. If you want to be a great writer or scholar or poet, follow the transiting phases of Mercury-Jupiter, Mercury-Uranus, and Mercury-Neptune. If it's love and romance you're looking for, track the cyclical relationship of Venus-Mars, which illuminates the cycles of attraction. To understand changing themes and seasons of relationships, follow the cycles of Venus-Saturn, Venus-Uranus, Venus-Neptune, and Venus-Pluto. These cycles depict themes such as committed love, enduring friendship, and acceptance of human limitations (Venus-Saturn); liberated love and sudden, unexpected attractions (Venus-Uranus); devotion, adoration, and unconditional love (Venus-Neptune); and obsessive love or alchemical sexual love (Venus-Pluto).[33]

We also look at outer planet transit cycles such as Saturn-Uranus, Saturn-Neptune, and Saturn-Pluto, all of which affect the collective climate in which we strive to actualize our purpose. For example, the Uranus-Neptune conjunction in 1993 birthed a new consciousness. If that conjunction activated your chart, you became a participant in planetary consciousness change. Many of us have been defining new spiritual and holistic paradigms, communicating with other dimensions, awakening the third eye, quietly setting the world on fire with the power of astrology.

However, the spiritual and visionary imagination of all we have been trying to birth in our lives since our Uranus-Neptune awakening had to be sustained through the planetary upheaval of the Saturn-Pluto opposition, which brought takeover by the Bush-Cheney clan, the 9-11 attack, mysterious envelopes of anthrax, the pulverizing of Afghanistan with bombs, and renewed violence in the Middle East, Kashmir, and elsewhere. This period also witnessed fierce politics of nuclear waste disposal in Nevada. More recently, the Saturn-Pluto square of 2009-2010 has featured economic contraction and unemployment, the Deepwater Horizon oil spill that sullied the waters of the Gulf Coast, and continuing military conflicts in Iraq, Afghanistan, and Pakistan. Our fragile economic and ecological systems teeter on the edge under the relentless pressures of global warming, over-consumption, and plutocracy, the union of government and money. Nevertheless, the planetary pair of Saturn-Pluto evokes strength and courage under stressful circumstances, the ability to endure and survive, meeting adversity or limitation with courage and steady resolve—again, with consciousness and steadiness in change.

The method of examining interplanetary transit cycles was one of Rudhyar's great technical contributions to our field. Hats off also to Rudhyar's student, Alexander Ruperti, for explaining this technique in *Cycles of Becoming*.[34]

A significant result of studying planetary cycles is that we gradually develop what Rudhyar calls the Mind of Wholeness: the mind that can comprehend each moment as a phase of cycles within cycles. To achieve this heightened consciousness, we need to rigorously study these cycles and how they operate in our lives. Through the study of astrology, we develop a refined intellect able to see each life experience as a phase of some cyclic process. Rudhyar calls this *eonic consciousness*, awareness of the cycle as a whole, in its essential unity.[35] We understand the meanings of all phases of our evolution. Every moment and every experience is seen as a phase of a cycle or evolutionary process. Or, to state this another way: astrology is the totality of experience lived consciously.

### Four Levels of Interpretation

In his magnificent, final astrological book, *The Astrology of Transformation*, Rudhyar stated that there are four levels of interpreting astrology, the biological, socio-cultural, individual, and transpersonal levels. Rudhyar sketched out his understanding of these levels or general contexts of interpretation, but I believe there's still room for fuller expansion and clarification of these ideas. I'm going to present these four levels to you not as linear stages of evolution, but as facets of a mandala of wholeness.

The biological level of astrology refers to areas such as astro-agriculture (coordinating our efforts to grow things in our gardens with planetary cycles), the astrological study of weather patterns and earthquakes, and medical astrology—a subject to which one could devote a lifetime.

The socio-cultural level refers to mundane astrology, the astrology of politics, history and social trends; financial astrology; the astrology of relationships, which illuminates our friendships and romances, business partnerships, marriages and parent-child relationships; and vocational astrology, which helps us understand our optimal path of occupational development. Much of my work with clients is focused on these socio-cultural concerns.

It's important to note that Rudhyar didn't focus a lot on vocational astrology and the sociocultural level. His work came to fruition during the 1960s and 70s, responding to the needs of a youth generation that dropped out of conventional society in pursuit of new alternatives, sexual liberation, vegetarianism, intentional communities, higher consciousness. Rudhyar was especially interested in how astrology elucidates the process of breaking free from social convention. Nevertheless, his description of the sociocultural level clearly implies the value of using astrology to create a life that's socially viable. I believe astrology can help us develop a graceful worldliness where we use planetary cycles for success in action, in business and career planning, in relationships.

The Sabian Symbol for 8° Capricorn reads:

"In a sun-lit home, domesticated birds sing joyously." The wholesome happiness that subservience to the ideals and patterns of a well-established culture brings to those who accept them unreservedly. . . . The power and benefits which a steady and well-integrated culture brings its members. Saturn rules Capricorn; Saturn was the ruler of the Golden Age before he became a symbol of binding limitations. He [or she] who accepts willingly . . . these [cultural] limitations can lead a serene and happy existence, whatever his social status. . . . [H]uman beings can find ENJOYMENT in the roles they are born to play.[36]

In keeping with this Sabian Symbol, let's each embrace this joy in astrology—the joy of finding our place in society and creation, culture and cosmos. We accept the patterns of social existence, going to school, holding jobs or maintaining our businesses. We can be domesticated birds and fulfill the socio-cultural purpose of astrology.

The individual level of chart interpretation is humanistic astrology—the astrology of choice and self-actualization. Here astrology illuminates the psychology of the individual. We use astrology to know ourselves and to define a clear sense of purpose and identity. We develop a sense of existential authenticity, responsibility, and *integrity*—feeling whole and integrated.

Astrology at the individual level is concerned with what Jung called *individuation*, the process of unfolding the wholeness of who we are, which implies striving to live the wholeness of our birth charts. At the sociocultural level we use astrology to help us develop a viable *persona* or social identity. But in Jung's terms, individuation really begins with integrating the shadow. Here we widen the sphere of identity by examining those behaviors, qualities, or emotions that we fear or have aversion toward, frequently projecting these onto others. Integrating the shadow means that we acknowledge buried or rejected parts of ourselves.

I once worked with a client with Sun-Venus-Mars in Scorpio squaring Pluto in the 8th house who was totally sexually repressed. She was very spiritual and holy, hardly ate anything, and wouldn't get close to anyone. She had been living a celibate life in a yoga ashram for years. The issue of sex was highly charged for her. She suffered from depression and an eating disorder. With Pluto square Sun, Venus, Mars, she had been traumatized in childhood and adolescence—timed exactly by transits of Saturn and Uranus to this natal configuration. Sex and desire were associated with pain, domination, and shattered trust. Ultimately, she realized how much she wanted to explore deep intimacy, and she came to understand why this had become so threatening and unacceptable. For her, individuation and wholeness involved facing the possibility that she might be an intensely sexual person. For someone else, integrating the shadow might mean recognizing our unconscious arrogance or hostility toward others. What had been shadow now becomes part of an enlarged sphere of individual identity.

We can approach astrology at the individual level as a form of what Roberto Assagioli called Psychosynthesis, which begins with integrating the many subpersonalities that are denoted by our birth charts. For example, a man with Mars conjunct Ascendant and square Sun had a very willful, selfish, demanding, angry subpersonality. But he also had Pisces Moon, showing a subpersonality that felt lonely, neglected, defeated. He came to understand how he used Mars aggression to compensate for underlying feelings of weakness and inadequacy. Astrology gives us deep insight into our internal psychological dynamics. Rudhyar and Assagioli were great friends and the interface of astrology and Psychosynthesis is an area of study that has yet to be fully articulated.

Another task of astrology on the individual level is to help guide us toward fulfillment in a calling, our life's work, which links individual identity to social needs, *and* to a transpersonal source, so that we feel our actions and our life path are guided by an inner spiritual mandate.[37] We link our definition of self both to our socio-cultural environment and to the ocean of infinite love and source-power from which we emerge. To find a calling you've got to follow your own instructions and fulfill your own potentials. If you have Jupiter rising and planets in Sagittarius maybe education and teaching are a big part of your path. For someone else the calling might be to have children or to pursue success in business, or writing poetry or novels. Maybe our path to fulfillment is through intensive meditation, or through blissful, serene retirement. We decide what we want to dedicate our energy to, and this becomes our source of individual meaning and purpose.

Rudhyar emphasized that becoming a conscious individual inevitably means passing through *tests of severance and deconditioning*. He wrote, "We can truly speak of individuality *only* when a person deliberately severs the myriads of psychic threads attaching him or her to a particular collectivity and culture, and emerges as an at least relatively independent, individual self."[38] We have to free ourselves from the programming we receive from the family, schools, and the media. Rudhyar called this the process of deconditioning. He stressed the need to free oneself from the dominant mentality and preoccupations of one's culture. A painful severance from cultural or family values is often required, usually linked to the planetary symbolism of Uranus.

Under the influence of Uranus we experience turbulence or controversy as we free ourselves from the restrictive viewpoint of the collective and make choices that bring us into conflict with the values of our family or culture—when we pursue a nontraditional career, or leave a stable job or marriage, or follow an unconventional lifestyle. Above all, we seek freedom in all areas of life touched by Uranus: Sun-Uranus: freedom of identity and purpose. Moon-Uranus: freedom from emotional rigidity, freedom of emotional response. Mercury-Uranus: freedom of thought and speech. Venus-Uranus: freedom of affections and aesthetic tastes. Mars-Uranus: freedom of energy and sexuality. Jupiter-Uranus: conceptual freedom, the freedom of discovery. Saturn-Uranus: freedom through responsible reorganization of life structures and social institutions. Neptune-Uranus: freedom of infinite consciousness. At the Uranus level of consciousness, individualized personality becomes a force for collective change and innovation. Uranus also represents exploring the cutting edge of progressive social movements, countercultures, new forms and new paradigms in every field.

With his Aquarius Moon square Uranus in the 11th house Rudhyar was very Uranian, very avant garde, ahead of his time in everything he accomplished. At his Uranus square at age 21, Rudhyar made his own symbolic act of severance, leaving his native France and traveling to America, changing his name, renouncing the whole mentality of European civilization, composing resonant and discordant music conceived totally outside the framework of classical Western harmony. Rudhyar hung out painting in the mountains of New Mexico, acted in Hollywood films, and was involved with multi-media performance art involving music, ballet, theatre, and poetry. Rudhyar wrote, "Uranus *focalizes* the power of the Galaxy... The work of great geniuses ... essentially consists in becoming *focusing agencies* through which what constitutes at any time 'the next step' for humanity becomes visible and fascinating."[39]

Humanistic astrology suggests how we can become self-actualized and liberated individuals. But Rudhyar emphasized that too much focus on individualism can result in isolation, estrangement, alienation, depression, or anti-social attitudes.[40] He taught that individualism is a stage we outgrow as we discover a wider frame of reference. We feel an urge to transcend not only the safe, secure realms of socio-cultural convention but also the limited circumference of individual selfhood. This self-transcending urge is part of the natural movement of wholeness. In *Beyond Individualism*, Rudhyar wrote,

> God is the ... ever-present power of transformation that makes it possible for smaller fields of activity and consciousness to become transformed into ever vaster fields. God is also the power which insures that every release of cosmic and life energy occurs as a unit within which a structural principle operates, maintaining that unit whole and endowing it with consciousness. To operate as a

harmoniously functioning whole; and to transform oneself stage
after stage according to the encompassing rhythm of a Greater
Whole; and to be able to do so consciously through a mysterious
attunement of one's center with the center of the Greater Whole:
this is the meaning and challenge of human existence.[41]

Astrology is the practice of attuning our center with the center of
the Greater Whole through the study of planetary cycles. Astrology
helps us to transform ourselves "stage after stage." And especially
as we resonate to the cycles of the outer planets we may begin a
process that may lead us to a state beyond individual consciousness.
This may be impelled by a vague dissatisfaction, or by Neptunian
experiences of expanded awareness, in which the solid boundaries of ego, objects, and linear time dissolve. We become porous,
transparent to Spirit. And we begin to see our lives as a conscious
spiritual quest, a quest to more fully realize our true spiritual nature.
This evolutionary transition calls for a new approach to astrology—a transpersonal approach, the purpose of which is to guide
us through the stages of awakening to our divine potential. Here
I'm going to briefly discuss the theoretical foundation of transpersonal astrology (the philosophy of Wholeness); its emotional basis
(self-consecration to the whole); and several relevant techniques for
self-transformation (meditation, visualization, and the integration
of archetypal and spiritual qualities). We'll see that transpersonal
astrology is meant to assist us in reaching more advanced stages of
consciousness.

Philosophically, transpersonal astrology is based on an understanding of our existential position as integrated wholes (or individuals) operating within a larger encompassing Whole. In *The
Astrology of Transformation*, Rudhyar said:

> The universe is a hierarchy of wholes, and consciousness inheres
> in every whole. . . . The lesser whole can contact and receive some
> influence, power, or 'blessing' from the next greater whole. For the
> person who is striving to become individualized and to reach ful-
> fillment as an individual, the next greater whole in . . . [which]
> he or she can actually participate may only be his or her com-

munity, nation, or culture. It should eventually be Humanity-
as-a-whole—and by Humanity I mean far more than a chaotic
collection of human beings spread around the globe; I mean a
vast planetary Being that is also in the process of unfolding Its
immense potential of activity and consciousness.[42]

We begin to perceive our individual destinies as connected to the
evolution of Humanity and our planet. Practiced at a transpersonal
level, the purpose of astrology is to help us establish a "vertical relationship" between ourselves and a greater spiritual Reality. Rudhyar
says:

> [V]ertical relationships refer to the direct influence or impact
> (perhaps the 'blessing' or healing power), of a greater Whole upon
> the lesser whole—thus of Humanity (as the planetary Being), or
> of some 'divine hierarchy' upon men and women in need of help
> or inspiration. This directly applies to the transpersonal interpre-
> tation of an astrological birth chart, because in light of it what
> is seen in the chart can be given a new meaning. The . . . chart is
> still understood to represent the starting point of the individual.
> It depicts the convergence . . . of past cycles of activity into a new
> human being, thus his or her karma. But it can also have another
> meaning. It [i.e. the chart] can be seen to represent the mean-
> ing and purpose with which the greater Whole, Humanity, has
> invested this birth—thus the dharma of the new human being.[43]

The awareness that our births are invested with a spiritual purpose
within a larger whole evokes in us a sense of transpersonal meaning
and responsibility. We keenly yearn to know how we may serve the
universe. He continues:

> It is possible for [the individual] to cease acting and thinking as
> a creature of the past and to become a creator of the future–or
> rather to become a focusing agent through whom Humanity (or
> the planetary Being, God), is able to fulfill a particular and limited
> purpose. Such a repolarization is truly the essence of the transper-
> sonal process. . . . Transpersonal astrology is . . . concerned with

the possibility . . . of achieving a state of symbolic 'transparency' enabling the spiritual power that archetypal Man represents to radiate through him or her, and to do so consciously and as an individual form of selfhood.[44]

Astrology guides us through the initiations that transform us into transpersonal individuals, disciples of the Path beyond ego, individuals through whom the power of love and the light of consciousness are expressed. Note the emphasis in this passage on becoming creative, not passive but expressive. We are to bring something to a focus, with conscious intention. Creativity was a major theme in Rudhyar's work, which I've discussed at length elsewhere.[45]

So how do we achieve this state of transparency to the light and power of Spirit? During transits or progressions involving Neptune we experience spiritual transparency and expansion of consciousness through any of the perennial methods: meditation, dreams, prayer, music, dance, and trance. Rudhyar says, "Neptune represents... detachment from every quantitatively measurable object, or from social gains and prestige, demanded of every aspirant to a spiritual condition of existence. Non-possessiveness and compassion characterize that planet, whose symbol is the sea."[46] Rudhyar also viewed Neptune as a symbol of an internal change of heart he called *self-consecration to a greater whole*. He wrote, "At this . . . level, interpenetration has taken the place of separation, and the individual is so totally the servant of the whole that he [or she] has lost all sense of egocentricity."[47] Rudhyar views self-consecration as the emotional, attitudinal shift that makes possible our transition into transpersonal consciousness and activity.

In the moment of self-consecration we quiet down, meditate, offer ourselves, and ask to be shown how we may fulfill the needs of a greater whole, how we may help uplift and heal our world. As we do this, we may feel ourselves tangibly blessed and guided. The power of the Whole becomes accessible, guides us, and begins to act through us. Let's do it right now, each of us. Rudhyar said, "The spiritual life is a life of consecrated selfhood realized in the sacramental performance of every activity."[48]

The significance of Neptunian self-consecration becomes clearer
when we relate it to one of the central practices of Buddhism, the
practice of generating *bodhicitta*, clear mind and pure intention.
Generating *bodhicitta* means that we strive to express enlightened
qualities: friendliness, lovingkindness, equanimity, patience, compassion, mindfulness, and awakeness. We strive to help other sen-
tient beings in all realms of existence. We transform all actions of
body, speech, and mind into positivity and benefit for others. The
presence of Neptune in our birth charts and transits may be viewed
as our potential to awaken *bodhicitta,* to practice the principle of
*sunyata*, no separation or non-ego—particularly through the circumstances of the house in which natal or transiting Neptune is
placed. If Neptune is in the 10th house we try to make our profession or life's work a selfless offering to the universe. If Neptune is in
the 11th house, we dedicate ourselves to a group, community, social
cause, or political movement. If Neptune is in the 2nd house, we
strive to be less selfish and possessive with our money.[49]

Buddhism also teaches us that the Neptunian qualities of spaciousness, tranquility, and loving kindness have to be developed,
trained, actively cultivated through meditation. The enlightened
qualities associated with Neptune can be developed through spiritual practices such as yoga, meditation, and prayer. Neptune represents merging the mind into its source, into the ocean of pure
consciousness. To advance on the transpersonal path, we need to
go beyond astrology to explore deep meditation. We need not only
to understand the cycles of the planets but also to quiet down and
reach a state of deep calm, a calm transcending any particular planetary configuration or life condition—including health, love, success, or even happiness. As Rudhyar wrote in one of his poems, "I
am poised in all destinies."[50]

Now let's return to a passage I cited a moment ago:

The spiritual life is a life of consecrated selfhood realized in the
sacramental performance of every activity. . . . For the individual person, the goal of such an existence is—through the ever-
repeated act of self-consecration to the Whole—the full develop-

ment of the cosmogenic function, with its twin foundations of intuition (holistic mind) and compassion (Christic love).[51]

What does Rudhyar mean when he speaks of the *cosmogenic* function? I think he is saying that we learn to create universes with our thoughts, intentions, and mental images. As we open our breath, surrender the mind, and rest in stillness, we can also form images of desired spiritual qualities or positive outcomes in our life paths. As the Hawaiian Huna teachings say, "The world is what you think it is. Energy goes where attention flows." This process is also described in the final Sabian Symbol, for 30° Pisces:

> A majestic rock formation resembling a face is idealized by a boy who takes it as his ideal of greatness, and as he grows up, begins to look like it. The power of clearly visualized ideals to mold the life of the visualizer. [The symbol refers to] the capacity for self-transformation latent in man. This power can be developed through visualization, when the emotions and the will are poured into the visualized mental image.[52]

Rudhyar is clearly telling us that this is one of the fundamental methods used by initiates for self-transformation. Awakening our Neptune functions, we learn the conscious use of creative imagination. I believe this faculty can be developed powerfully by combining astrology and meditation. Meditating upon our chart symbols, we envision possible outcomes of planetary placements and transits and shape our lives in accordance with their guidance.[53] We strive to embody planetary archetypes. We personalize or incarnate the archetypes. This is another facet of what Jung meant by individuation.

Astrologers study how archetypal structures and mythic themes are constantly enacted in our lives: Moon, the Great Mother, in her various forms; Venus, Aphrodite, the beloved; Mars, Hercules, the hero's quest; Saturn, Kronos, Father Time, the wise old man or woman; Uranus, the trickster; Neptune, mystic or messiah, Tiresias, the blind seer with fully developed inner sight. The topic of mythic, archetypal astrology has been explored by Liz Greene, Melanie

Reinhart, Demetra George, and other luminaries of our field. Here
again astrology aids us in widening our sphere of awareness. Our
personal lives are transpersonalized, lived in the light of timeless,
mythic themes. This is the basis for what Rudhyar called "the astrology of meaning." We individuate the archetypes; we personalize and
incarnate the transcendent structures of the psyche.

Near the end of his life Rudhyar released a booklet called *Beyond
Personhood*, where he explored a similar line of thinking. He wrote:

> The word archetype can be defined generally as a basic and pri-
> mordial form of *organization*.... Theistic religions have produced
> various myths dealing with the creation of a realm of archetypes
> preceding the formation of the material universe.... Spiritual
> Qualities, numbers, and archetypal forms constitute the funda-
> mental trinity of being.... Spiritual Qualities seek concrete, exis-
> tential manifestation through archetypal forms. These forms are
> ... guiding fields pervading all existential wholes, from atoms to
> human beings to galaxies. Every whole has a guiding field.... In
> relation to this "higher Self" or guiding field, individual freedom
> is quite illusory. When the individualized "mind of wholeness"
> apprehends the archetype which is his or her guiding field and
> begins to resonate to the spiritual Quality of his or her innermost
> being..., then individual freedom can only mean choosing the
> best way to actualize this archetype. In this sense, the truly "liber-
> ated" person is consciously and willingly determined by his or her
> archetype. Freedom and determinism merge.... [It is important to
> think of] transpersonal communication ... in terms of the gradual
> *revelation of archetypes*—and primarily of those archetypes which
> it is the individual's destiny (dharma) to actualize in concrete form
> in the substance of daily living.[54]

In transpersonal astrology we consciously attune ourselves to spiritual qualities symbolized by the various signs, planets, and planetary
pairs—for example, the linguistic brilliance of Mercury, the formless, nondual awareness of Neptune, the erotic love and sexual pleasure of Venus-Mars. We try to embody the most evolved qualities
of the zodiacal signs—for example the Libra qualities of harmony

and cooperation; the Leo qualities of radiance, joy, and creativity; Pisces bliss, compassion, serenity, and silence; Sagittarian wisdom, truth, and generosity; Virgo purity and service. Aquarian humor and equality. In so doing, we cultivate the enlightened qualities of awakened human beings. We imagine and invoke the spiritual qualities we are asked to incarnate. Rudhyar continues:

> Human life, once it has reached the level of fully conscious, autonomous, and responsible personhood, should be understood and evaluated as a performance. The quality of a particular person's performance is preconditioned by the temperament of his or her body, the character of his or her personality, and the line of development taken by the process of ego-formation. A time comes, however, when all this conditioning has to face the test of adequacy to the archetype to which the individual is meant fully and irrevocably to attune himself or herself. Before this moment, everything is merely preparation. Then comes the moment of performance, the "hour of truth."[55]

For astrologers, every moment, every act of life becomes "the hour of truth," a conscious performance of the archetypes to which we are meant to fully attune ourselves. We perform the archetype as individuals, as physically embodied beings, within our social context. We avoid any confusing notion that transpersonal evolution involves transcending the ego. Individuality is not transcended, but rather is refined to become a conduit for expression of archetypal and spiritual qualities. The practice of a multilevel astrology elucidates the constant interplay between biological, socio-cultural, individual, and transpersonal dimensions of our evolution, and helps us coordinate our activities in these domains. For example, we see that there's no ultimate separation between individual and socio-cultural levels, for we actualize our individual identity and potentials through social activity and relatedness. The pulse of life always involves dynamic interplay between the individual and collective-social poles of existence. Consciousness is found at the center where these rivers meet. The individual in society is the meeting point of earth and heaven, biology and spirit.

Man is the 'alchemical vessel' in which matter can be transmuted into spirit. . . . The complete process of existence is a two-way process. Spirit descends toward matter as matter rises toward spirit. The individual is the place of meeting, but it is a difficult meeting. The individualized human self seeks to perpetuate itself, believing itself the summit of evolution, the crown of existence. It craves for fulfillment as a separate, unique individual. It clings to what it calls 'my identity.' . . . Eventually the stubborn and proud refusal to admit the existence of . . . what is beyond the individuality and its closed circle of being, must give way to an increasingly open attitude. . . . [Here] the individual opens up to the descent of spiritual, supramental forces, and [begins to discern] the spiritual Source from which the subliminal light and the transcendent power flow.[56]

Ultimately, transpersonal astrology is concerned with the process whereby we become vehicles or channels for the qualities and powers of the divine. For this descent of supramental light and power to flow into us, impediments and impurities need to be removed; we undergo some necessary testing and realignment of the ego. The internal alchemy that transforms us into instruments of infinite love and infinite consciousness is often correlated with transits or progressions involving Pluto. Rudhyar wrote, "Pluto is the power that impels, and most often compels, any living organism and any individual human being to cast aside all that is not its own essential nature—its truth of being."[57] Under the influence of Pluto we experience moments of suffering and catharsis, death and rebirth, a Dark Night of the Soul, or a "karmic confrontation."[58] If Pluto transits the Moon, we may have an emotional upheaval, which has the deeper purpose of clearing old memories and traumas, and liberating our capacity to feel and care deeply. Transits of Pluto to the Sun test our expression of personal power and identity; we may be confronted with negative aspects of our self-expression. When transiting Pluto began to semisquare my natal Sun I found myself acting out some childish arrogance and narcissism. I learned my lesson and reexamined my need for special attention and acknowledgment.

Transits or progressions involving Pluto represent tests of discipleship that expose and purify our deepest motives for action. We have to free ourselves from impurities and obsessions, points of fixation—our lust, greed, and hatred. We become aware of negativity or arrogance in ourselves and others. We encounter violence, abuse of power, betrayals, feuds and resentments. Sometimes we encounter the collective shadow: evil, crime, corruption, greed, racism, sleazy underworlds, dictatorial social trends. We learn sobering lessons about human nature, lessons that teach us about the right use of power, and that may cause to undergo a transformation of character by reexamining our use of power—as individuals and as a collective, a nation. For example, a recent transit of Pluto in Sagittarius conjunct the USA Ascendant brought theft of the 2000 presidential election, advancing globalization, an increasingly toxic environment, revelation of corporate crimes and skullduggery, and the murky intersection of the Bush family, Enron, the Carlye Group, the CIA, and the Bin Laden clan.

It's easy to get caught up in hopelessness, cynicism, and apocalyptic fears. But in his book, *The Sun is Also a Star*, Rudhyar wrote, "At the highest level Pluto serves to focus galactic energies upon mankind *through* individuals ready... to assume a role of destiny."[59] Pluto initiations can empower our actions and prepare us to play our role in humanity's evolution with maximum purity and effectiveness, each in our own way, some as teachers or students, some as astrologers, artists, writers, gardeners, some by having children, others through success in business or science. Whatever our path, we align with the needs of a larger Whole—our family or community, nature, Spirit. We become effective, and unified in our intention.[60] In *Occult Preparations for a New Age*, Rudhyar wrote:

> Courage is the need . . . , the courage to face the awesome darkness of the Night of the Soul in certainty of dawn. . . . [During] the planetary crisis mankind is now experiencing...great personages, some visible but many more invisible, are performing their acts of destiny according to cyclic rhythms. . . . The Age is dark with blatant pride, violence, and greed. Passions are wild. . . . We worship success, comfort, material possessions. Confusion is in every

soul and mind. . . . [N]ations . . . indulge in . . . devastating and
absurd wars. . . . Yet . . . cosmic time moves on toward its fulfillment. Something will be fulfilled. At least the multifarious seeds
of future collective developments will have been sown upon the
Earth. Some individuals will perform their roles of destiny, even
though they falter and stumble in the darkness and against the
powers of darkness. . . . Pluto [is] a cosmic symbol of the Seed. . . .
[I]t represents the power that destroys all superficial glamor and
all illusions. It leaves whatever it touches stark naked. . . but also
strictly and purely what it essentially is. . . . [This] is a period during which many seedmen are living in whom an immense potency
of futurity operates, in whatever field of activity they may perform
their perhaps hidden (occult) task.[61]

And so we return to the beginning: the creative power of the seed.
Rudhyar taught us to become seed men and seed women, dedicated
to our seed visions, spiritual ideals, and visionary projects, seeds that
are origins of new worlds and new futures. As seed men and seed
women we perform our small "acts of destiny," our gestures of healing and enlightening our suffering world, in the face of cultural
crisis and planetary catharsis.[62]

Pluto transits or progressions are turning points in the testing of
our soul, a threshold in evolution. We are either sucked into the vor-
tex of toxic emotions, paranoia, anger, and hostility, or we clear ourselves, discharge past traumas, forgive everyone, bury every hatchet.
When we free the knots of the body and the heart there is a free
flow of energy through every cell and fiber of our being, channeled
to us from the source and center of creation. This may manifest in
a visible way as we begin to exert a positive influence in our world.
We may also receive a stream of blessing and the empowerment of
spiritual or galactic forces.

## THE PLEROMA

Rudhyar taught that at certain stages of the transpersonal way we
become attuned and connected to the Pleroma of illumined beings
and awakened souls. He wrote, "For any human collectivity and for

mankind as a whole... the one sacred goal is the development of the Pleroma of Perfected Human Beings—the omega stage of planetary fulfillment. . . . This is the ultimate goal of the planetary cycle of Man."[63] Here Rudhyar's ideas reflect the doctrines of Theosophy, one of his formative influences. Some people find this side of Rudhyar's work to be somewhat esoteric or perplexing. Nonetheless, because Rudhyar discussed the Pleroma so often in his writings, it's important to try to understand what he meant.

Rudhyar taught that those who take steps along the path of self-consecration and creative emanation become members of a community of illumined souls, which is still in formation. In *Beyond Personhood*, he wrote:

> I have accepted the . . . traditional concept of the existence of a superhuman level of beings. The existence of such beings can be understood . . . if they are seen, in their togetherness, as differentiated, functional aspects of a vast planetary being of [which] the physical globe of the earth is only the physical body. This body includes the biosphere (the realm of life) and is the foundation for a noosphere (a realm of psychic and mental activity). Beyond yet including these spheres is a spiritual sphere of activity which I call the Pleroma. Operating at that level are planetary Pleroma beings who have evolved through and beyond the human stage— and this evolutionary possibility is latent in all human beings, once they have reached the stage of individualized, autonomous, and responsible selfhood free from bondage to both biology and culture. . . . All my activities and writings, at least since the 1920s, have been inspired . . . by this, to me, unquestionable realization: a state of being exists beyond the "human condition," yet it operates through (*trans*) human beings when the latter are open and definitely committed to the possibility of reaching at least the threshold of such a state. . . . [T]here is a level of being beyond personhood and culture. . . . [T]his more-than-human level . . . can be reached through conscious, deliberate, and consistent efforts. . . . [T]hese more-than-individual beings are *planetary beings*. They do not operate at the level of exclusivistic cultures, but in terms of the total being of the earth, thus of humanity-as-a-whole.[64]

Rudhyar is saying that at certain stages of transpersonal evolution we come into contact with agents of superior intelligence, beings who are farther ahead of us, and who reveal to us our next step of evolution—a level of consciousness that is beyond the limitations and biases of our culture, beyond individualism, beyond the human level as we currently know it. Pleroma beings are advanced beings who have transcended the normal boundaries of time and space. They have wider concerns than us, and magnetically influence us, through nonphysical means we cannot understand at our current level of consciousness. They reveal to us that, just as the culmination of the plant kingdom is to feel, and the culmination of the animal kingdom is to think, the culmination of human evolution is to achieve a greater love and inclusivity. Pleroma beings want to communicate with us and to show us how the principles of unity and inclusivity can become operative in our world. As the world goes farther into crisis, we need to imagine such a state and invoke it into being, tuning into this next level of evolution.

Just as the caterpillar sees the butterfly and sees a vision of its future, we glimpse our own future state of evolution through our contact with those adepts or masters who reveal themselves to us, and convey to us their blessings, love, and guidance. Thus, the astrological symbolism of Pluto can also represent the grace and power that comes to us from the plane of the Masters, Buddhas, Siddhas, the awakened ones, who kindle the lamp of our souls. Their unified and illumined Mind is a beacon of light in our time of planetary upheaval. They are always ready to bestow their assistance. Now we turn and receive their transmission. When this contact occurs, a chemical reaction occurs. Some call this *kundalini* awakening, receiving the holy spirit, *shaktipat*—the descent of the power of the divine. There is a notable change in the nervous system, in the energy field of the body's bioelectric system. This numinous, awe-inspiring experience may result from contact with our spiritual guides, both embodied and disembodied. My book, *The Nine Stages of Spiritual Apprenticeship*, describes this process.[65]

## RUDHYAR'S LIGHT AND INFLUENCE

My personal connection with Rudhyar began during a period of confusion and uncertainty in my life. When I was 22 I left New York City and traveled around the West coast with my tent and sleeping bag, doing a kind of vision quest. I began my first studies of astrology. I sat in the woods, wrote down my dreams, and tried to decipher my planetary instructions. I had transiting Neptune conjunct Saturn and transiting Saturn in the 12ᵗʰ house. Rudhyar's writings helped me to make sense of this period of confusion and to allow it fully, trusting that I was being cleared of all past conditioning about what I was supposed to be in the world. To me, the idea that this personal meltdown was a meaningful phase of my existence was a revolutionary insight. I was freed to experience the moment fully in all its uncertainty, and with faith that it would change.

A few years later, when transiting Jupiter-Neptune aspected my natal Mercury, I began corresponding with Rudhyar, and had direct contact with this man of wisdom. Then, while transiting Pluto was exactly conjunct my natal Jupiter, the planet of the sage, I had a dream in which Rudhyar appeared, and a voice said, "This is your guru." I met Rudhyar in person in Palo Alto in March 1985, six months before he passed away, and spoke at a conference celebrating his 90ᵗʰ birthday. On that occasion, Rudhyar gave his final public talk, at the conclusion of which I, and other people present, witnessed something extraordinary: Rudhyar sat up in his chair and began radiating light. His body seemed transfigured and luminous. But perhaps my most significant experience with him was in October 2000.

One night (while transiting Neptune turned stationary direct closely square my natal Neptune), I stayed up late re-reading Rudhyar's book, *Rhythm of Wholeness*. I read this mysterious passage:

Between the symbolic Noon and Sunset of the cycle of being the fundamental goal of evolution is the consummation of the "divine Marriage" of spirit and matter within a human being. In this union of opposites, the all-encompassing meaning of Wholeness is revealed in a moment of Illumination, in a moment of dynamic equilibrium in which the principles of Unity and Multiplicity are of equal strength. The union must be contained within a form that can resist the union's intense "heat" and not be shattered by it. This form is the mind of wholeness—a mind totally filled with the harvest of a long series of life experiences that were spirit oriented yet rooted in the substance of earthly existence. When this mind reaches a perfected state of development, karma is fulfilled. . . . Man is potentially the complete manifestation of Wholeness. To be such a manifestation is man's *dharma*, and the field for such a manifestation has to be given form by the mind of wholeness— the mind illumined by spirit.[66]

The next morning I woke up with this dream: *I was visiting a house. Somebody informed me that Rudhyar had just died, and his body was upstairs. Did I want to see him? I climbed a staircase and entered a room. Rudhyar was lying on a bed on his side, with both arms reaching over his head. His eyes were wide open, gazing into the radiant luminosity of the infinite. He was looking directly into the Light. This image was incredibly vivid, and I was jolted awake by that luminosity.*

Like any dream, I interpret this on many levels, first as a portrayal of Rudhyar's reflection on the eternal Light throughout his life. The "meaning" of the dream is also the *effect* it had on me, which was profound. The dream is what Mircea Eliade calls a *hierophany*, a manifestation of the sacred, the numinous.[67] Rudhyar's eyes are gazing into the luminosity of Being, but also *reveal* that luminosity. The dream was a transmission, bestowing on me the living experience of Rudhyar's Mind of Wholeness, the mind illumined by Spirit. The dream was also my internal reverie on the evolution of a great being's consciousness. It can be interpreted as an intuitive perception of Rudhyar's ultimate liberation into the light of Consciousness, his movement in the after-death *bardo* realms toward the final freedom. His body passes on but the light shines radiantly through his work, his ideas, his life. There was a sense of completion in the dream, as if Rudhyar had consummated his evolutionary journey into the light. As he wrote, "Karma is fulfilled." In the dream I climb upstairs to see him. He has reached a higher level, and my contact with him in the dream raises me into an elevated consciousness.

At the time of this dream I had been drifting away from actively teaching Rudhyar's approach to astrology. The dream felt like potent inner guidance to reconsider his work and its living power. Perhaps some people will find it strange that I relate to Rudhyar as a spiritual guide, but why should I not find a guru who is an astrologer, one who achieved a higher consciousness through his life's reflection on planetary cycles and mysteries? Astrology is the most profoundly integrative and transformative discipline, and astrologers can become spiritually evolved souls. The Mind of Wholeness is not just a philosophical concept but is a direct illumination that can be catalyzed by reflection on planetary cycles and rhythms.

And this brings me back to the Pleroma. Rudhyar is the closest thing to an awakened Pleroma being that I can imagine. The dream suggests to my imagination that Rudhyar has attained membership in this chain of illumined souls. His example teaches us to dedicate ourselves to living whatever karma is implied by our individual birth charts consciously, with an illumined Mind, an awakened Heart, activating all energies necessary to carry out the tasks that our birth charts imply. Rudhyar's life awakens in us an intuition of the possibility of self-transformation. And Rudhyar was a seed man. If he can do it, all of us can do it.

## RUDHYAR'S BIRTH CHART

Rudhyar was born March 23, 1895, 12:42 a.m., Paris, France. His natal Sun was in Aries in the 3$^{rd}$ house: He imprinted his passionate solar identity onto his writing. There was thunder in his words! He had Sun, Moon, Mercury, and north node in his 3$^{rd}$ house, obviously the symbol of a writer. With Chiron conjunct his Midheaven, opposite natal Sun, Rudhyar was a great mentor, teacher, master of many arts, maverick, and wounded healer. With Aquarius Moon square Uranus in the 11$^{th}$ house, he was a genius, way ahead of his time; but he influenced the entire future course of the field of astrology (Uranus in the 11$^{th}$ house). Mars, the ruler of his Aries Sun, is conjunct Neptune and Pluto in Gemini setting right in the

Dane Rudhyar
Natal Chart
March 23, 1895
12:42:00 AM FROT
Paris, France
48N52 / 2E20
Tropical   Koch   Mean Node

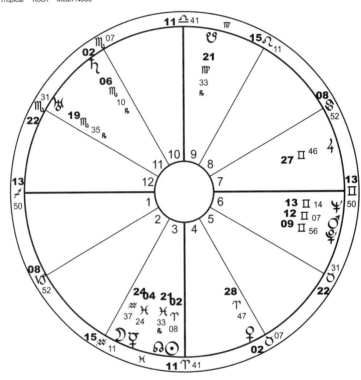

**12. Dane Rudhyar**

Gauqelin foreground of his chart, a symbol of the cosmic power and visionary intelligence that were channeled through his powerful writing, his poetry, his revolutionary approach to astrology.[68] Rudhyar was all about fiery creativity. A brilliant painter and composer, Rudhyar also had Venus, ruler of the 5th house, placed at the 5th house cusp, at the apex of two sextiles, to Moon and to Jupiter. This placement of Venus brought him gifts of refined and unusual artistic tastes and sensibilities. Rudhyar had Saturn, ruler of his 2nd house, in the 11th house, quincunx Sun and quincunx Pluto. He had financial stresses throughout his life, largely due to the obtuseness of the collective, which could hardly appreciate the contribution of this genius. Rudhyar's Ascendant is 13° Sag 50. As I began to write this chapter in the Summer of 2002, the transiting nodes were exactly conjunct his Ascendant/Descendant, and it was during the first pass of transiting Pluto over Rudhyar's Ascendant. I completed this work while Pluto turned stationary direct conjunct his Ascendant, a transit suggesting a resurgence of Rudhyar's seed ideas. It is my hope that Rudhyar's work will become the focus of renewed interest among astrologers who will carry his ideas forward into the future, into the fullness of what Rudhyar—as the avatar of a new type of astrology—envisioned and described.

## Rudhyar's Legacy

Rudhyar's astrology of choice, creativity, and self-transcendence is essential to the future of our field. He taught that instead of approaching astrology primarily as a way to predict events, we can approach it as a means to unify all facets of our existence—individual and collective, active and receptive, male and female, mental and emotional, persona and shadow, worldly and spiritual, human and divine, archetype and embodiment. On the path of astrology we go through the personal tasks and challenges indicated by the birth chart. Then we transcend the chart, becoming universal Man/Woman, living all phases of evolution with consciousness and impeccability.

I view Rudhyar as one of the greatest philosophers of all times because he presented a systematic strategy for expanded consciousness—a practical technology of transformation, through understanding cycles of transiting and progressed planets. There is an elegant simplicity in Rudhyar's approach. Fancy techniques are not required, only understanding of these basic principles about the cyclic nature of life, which apply to all techniques of astrology. Cycle after cycle we grow, like redwood trees spiraling toward the sun.

So how can we sum up the gist of Rudhyar's astrology? At the conclusion of his book, *An Astrological Mandala*, Rudhyar wrote:

To the consciousness that has realized the existence of cycles and is able to shift gears from the profane to the sacred, the whole of living becomes imbued with the magic of eternity. Every event is accepted as a necessary phase of the ritual process of existence radiating at every moment the significance and inner peace that wells out from the security of knowing oneself to be an essential and operative part of a vast cyclic whole. This is the symbolic life. It is also the life of wisdom, for to be wise is to know with unimpeachable knowing that the Whole is fulfilling itself at every moment through and within every act of life, once this life, illumined by nonpossessive love, is rooted in the certainty that order, beauty, rhythmic interplay and the harmony of ever balanced opposites are here and now, indestructibly.[69]

Thank you Rudhyar, for all of your resonant ideas.

# Part Three
# Therapeutic Astrology

*Homage to the Sun.* Babylonian cuneiform tablet[70]

Chapter 4

# *Astrology and Psychotherapy*

Having established an archetypal and cyclical approach to astrology, now let's learn to apply these principles to work with clients. First, let me describe how I came to practice both astrology and psychotherapy. After I had studied astrology for a few years and began to interpret charts for other people, I noticed that I was exploring progressively deeper emotional issues and more intense psychological material. I found that people were entrusting me with the kinds of problems they would ordinarily bring to a psychotherapist. I realized that I lacked the knowledge to skillfully address concerns such as childhood trauma, chronic depression and anxiety disorders, sexual abuse, post-traumatic stress disorder, alcoholism, addictions, and marital discord. I recognized that to deepen my work with others I needed training as a psychotherapist.

I immediately recognized the creative possibilities of combining astrology with psychotherapy and I began using astrology to understand a client's emotional dynamics, relationship patterns, current stressors, and nuances of the counseling process itself. I realized that astrology clarifies the pertinent issues for each person so vividly that it would be a great loss to practice psychotherapy without it. For me, astrology is an essential counseling tool.

I'm frequently asked whether I use astrology with all of my psychotherapy clients or only some of them, and how I go about getting a client's birth information. The answer to the first question is no. In some instances I don't believe it's appropriate to broach the subject of astrology at all. Some people's problems are better addressed through traditional counseling and therapeutic methods. Sometimes I get a client's birth date from an intake form and look up the positions of natal planets in an ephemeris, just for my own information. This usually gives me useful insights. Sometimes I do a one-time chart reading to determine important life themes and use this as a starting point for the counseling process. In other instances, I use the birth chart as an ongoing reference point during the course of therapy.

It's no secret that many psychologists and psychotherapists hold negative views about astrology. Indeed, many people in our scientifically-oriented culture consider astrologers to be charlatans peddling regressive, deterministic, superstitious doctrines. In some isolated instances this description probably holds true; there are indeed people who utilize astrology in this manner. However, our understanding of the astrologer's role has fundamentally changed in recent decades. Traditionally, an astrologer was a psychic who made pronouncements about an individual's destiny. But since the spread of humanistic astrology,[71] we view ourselves more as facilitators helping people transform themselves, stage by stage, using astrology's symbolism to sharpen their capacity for choice to shape their destiny. There's a fundamental difference between the traditional astrology of prophecy or fortune telling and *therapeutic astrology*, which supports and focuses our ability to make choices and create our own futures. Whereas historically astrology may have evoked fear and a sense of helplessness in the face of planetary influences, therapeutic astrology cultivates equanimity, freedom from fear, and the peace of mind that comes from understanding life cycles and our current tasks of development.

Astrology is a useful tool in the practice of depth psychotherapy. There are some types of therapy that focus on symptom reduction through techniques, such as systematic desensitization for the treatment of phobias. But other approaches, known as the depth therapies, address the client's total existential condition in a way that leads to a permanent change in outlook and behavior, renewed energy, and a more clearly defined sense of purpose. There are numerous ingredients that contribute to such life changing therapy: the client's readiness to change; the counselor's empathy, ability to listen, and depth of experience and wisdom; good diagnosis and treatment planning; and a positive therapeutic alliance between counselor and client. All of these factors, among others, make effective therapeutic work possible. My personal testimony is that the responsible use of astrology can also aid us in conducting transformative psychotherapy. The great C. G. Jung knew this; he studied astrology and regularly examined the birth charts of his patients.[72]

Depth psychotherapy isn't just the application of clinical techniques and the dispensing of advice. It's a ministry, an attending upon the soul of the client. Many psychotherapists are aware of how the unconscious leads us forward toward greater integration, revealing our shadows and unlived potentials. Therapists are also aware that every case proceeds differently and no one therapeutic outcome is suitable for everyone. Every person has to walk a different path and to actualize a distinctive set of potentials. Yet many therapists lack a framework that adequately organizes, and deepens, these kinds of perceptions. Astrology provides such a framework, revealing the person's internal dynamics and optimal developmental path. It describes the rhythms of the universe and is a portrait of the intrinsic wholeness of the individual. The birth chart represents an inner blueprint or hidden architecture for each person's unfolding.

Many psychotherapists already use astrology with clients, quietly and behind the scenes. Unfortunately, most of us who do so feel we must hide this interest from public view. It's my hope that recording detailed case studies of therapeutic work informed by planetary symbolism will demonstrate the value of astrology to the practice of psychotherapy.

## USING THE BIRTH CHART IN PSYCHOTHERAPY

In my counseling practice, I have found the birth chart to be a useful reference point for assessment of clients, and for identifying central treatment issues. Astrological symbols can be translated into the language of the therapeutic process, revealing past or present developmental stresses (for example, childhood trauma, financial difficulty, or marital crisis), and indicating needed changes in attitudes and behaviors. In therapeutic astrology we approach the birth chart with a growth-oriented attitude, assuming that every planetary position is purposeful and has positive potentials. We never want to disempower others or induce fear. We avoid reductionistic chart interpretations that will demean clients, injure their hope or self-esteem, fill them with unrealistic expectations, or diminish their sense of open possibility for growth and change.

Approaching astrology with a psychological and therapeutic focus can be valuable for some of the following reasons:

- To identify major themes and repeated areas of emphasis in a person's life.
- To perceive unconscious patterns of thought, feeling, or behavior.
- To gain deeper self-understanding and deeper empathy for self and others.
- To develop an archetypal and cyclical perspective that reveals the essential meaning and purpose of events, including chaotic or painful experiences.
- To facilitate our ability to resolve core life dilemmas and navigate transition periods.
- To identify the kinds of experiences we can expect during a given period of time, as indicated by planetary transits and progressions.
- To help us make choices that are appropriate to the developmental path suggested by the birth chart.
- To understand the meaning and nature of crisis situations.

The principle of cycles shows us that life constantly offers us new cycles, new chances for renewal. As we begin to act with a more conscious sense of purpose, our deepest inner sufferings can diminish. Synchronizing our lives with planetary patterns moves us rapidly forward in our evolution.

To practice therapeutic astrology it's helpful to get training in counseling psychology and counseling skills, developmental theory, and diagnosis. Then we can apply astrology to the problems of couples, to help people suffering from depression and anxiety. To work with a person with prominent placement of Neptune (such as Neptune aspecting the Sun) it's helpful to know something about alcoholism or addiction, and how to recognize patterns of denial. To work with material pertaining to a client's 4th house we need to understand family systems and dynamics. It's also important to gain skill in the art of vocational counseling, one of the areas where astrology can be most helpful.[73]

A woman named Tess, in her mid thirties, had been trying for years to finish college, where she was majoring in film-making and anthropology (after changing her major four times), and struggling to support herself as a gardener. She was depressed and discouraged about the lack of career prospects in her current field of study. Her idealism was foundering on the rocks of poverty. Her chart featured Taurus Midheaven, Mars and Saturn in Taurus in the 9th house, and progressed Moon in Taurus approaching Mars and Saturn. I asked if she had ever considered studying more practical subjects such as accounting, economics, or even international finance and economic development (Taurus and 9th house themes). She was very excited by this idea, and she went to her college advisor and mapped out a new course of study. She signed up to go to school in Mexico for a year to study Spanish, business, and macroeconomics. Later she decided to do graduate work on the economic impact of globalization. Our conversation about the Taurus symbolism of her birth chart was a turning point. It's amazing how the simplest astrology can reveal the most potent insights.

Chapter 5

# Signs and Houses in Therapeutic Astrology

Therapeutic astrology translates planetary symbolism into the language of psychology, personal growth, and therapeutic process. Each birth chart has areas of emphasis that help us understand the person's developmental edge and the likely focus of counseling. We closely examine the house and sign placement of each natal planet, especially Sun, Moon, Saturn, and ruler of the Ascendant, or several planets in the same sign or house. We also pay special attention to planets near the four major angles of the chart.[74]

In this chapter we'll look at the twelve signs and houses as symbols of central psychological needs and therapeutic issues, indicating specific approaches to personal growth or counseling that could be most helpful for this individual. This chapter describes psychological issues and problems associated with the signs and houses, illustrating these with brief examples.

## Aries / 1st House

Aries signifies our instinctual energy and drives, exuberance, spontaneous action, desire, initiative, and motivation. It represents impulse and impulsiveness, acting decisively and assertively, or acting without thinking or considering others. With emphasis on planets in Aries, the person needs to learn to express impulses appropriately.

Mark, a forty-five-year-old man, had Sun in Aries in the 5th house opposite Neptune. He found it difficult to control his daily drinking and wild partying, despite damaging his career and personal relationships. Mark needed to learn impulse control and to have fun and celebrate (Sun in 5th house, the house of play and recreation) without extreme intoxication (Neptune). This man needed to get sober.

Brad, a man with Sun in Aries square Mars, had difficulties stemming from his fierce competitiveness, combativeness, and selfishness, all associated with Aries and its planetary ruler, Mars. He punched holes in walls and bullied his wife. Brad needed to gain insight into the sources of his anger and learn to express his abundant energy more constructively.

In contrast, Hillary had Moon in Aries quincunx Neptune in the 1st house and needed to become more assertive. With Neptune in the 1st, she exhibited innocence and vulnerability, but she'd suppressed the side of her that loved fun and acting on a whim. Her humble, unassuming nature veiled her intense emotional needs and desires (Aries Moon). Hillary realized that she had spent her life in a state of guilt and invisibility, assuming she had no right to ask or wish for anything (Neptune in the 1st house). She'd silenced herself, rarely pursuing her own desires in life. She felt ineffectual and had an external locus of control, feeling that she wasn't really in charge of her life. Hillary's therapy involved learning to be more assertive, discovering what she wanted, becoming less nebulous.

A woman named Tricia had Sun, Mercury, and Mars in Aries in the 8th house. She reported that she began having affairs six months after her marriage, and since then had been in extramarital relationships with numerous sexual partners (Sun conjunct Mars, and 8th house emphasis). She felt entitled to do whatever she wanted, whenever the impulse struck her, without consideration of her husband, who eventually divorced her (8th house). Her impulsiveness, preoccupation with getting her way and lack of empathy, coupled with an unapologetic quest for full sexual alivenesss and authenticity, were variegated expressions of her Aries energy.

The 1st house is concerned with self-awareness and identity formation. Thus, planets placed in the 1st house, either natally or by transit, point to issues concerning self-image, our capacity to define and express our essential identity, rather than just a social mask (persona). Planets in the 1st house represent how we define ourselves and present ourselves. For example, when Venus or Mars are placed in the 1st house, our gender or sexual identity is highlighted. Ted, a man with Mars and Uranus in the 1st house, was an actor and dancer whose exuberant, zany (Uranus) energy electrified film and TV audiences. He claimed to have had dozens of lovers and said that sexual freedom (Mars-Uranus) was central to his identity.

Electra was a thirty-one-year-old woman in the midst of an identity crisis regarding her sexual orientation. Electra had five planets in her 1st house—a Venus-Uranus conjunction in late Cancer and a Sun-Mars-Jupiter conjunction in early Leo. Aptly expressing her unconventional Venus-Uranus conjunction, she was a politically active feminist and lesbian. With Sun conjunct Mars and Jupiter in the 1st house, it was important to be physically strong, to cultivate a muscular physique (Mars), and she tended to be the more dominant, aggressive partner in relationships. During the transit of Saturn square Venus, Electra felt stirrings of her feminine, Venusian side, developing interests in beauty, makeup, and fashion and she noticed that she was feeling very attracted to men. Electra redefined her sexual identity, realizing that she was bisexual. With Venus and Mars in the 1st house, Electra sought a comfortable inner balance of the feminine and masculine sides of herself.[75]

Ahmed grew up in an inner city housing project surrounded by gangs, violence, and crime (Pluto). With Uranus and Pluto conjunct in the 1st house in Virgo, he developed an aura of power and self-mastery (Pluto) that he felt had protected him during a long journey through the underworld of humanity, including a prison term for assault. He emanated a toughness that commanded respect and fear, yet he was armored so deeply that nobody could reach him emotionally. Throughout his life he'd inwardly battled with feelings of persecution and self-hatred (Pluto in 1st), as well as with his desire to incite riots and lead armed uprisings in the streets. He felt that his life's purpose was to become a catalyst of social change and a cultural revolutionary (Uranus). The question was how he could accomplish this goal. Ahmed had Gemini on the Midheaven (career) and natal Sun, Mercury, and Neptune in the 3rd house (writing). He wanted to write films (Neptune rules film), to express his politics and work for social change. Ahmed enrolled in school to study film-making and over several years he established a career in that field.

Taurus / 2nd House

Emphasis in the horoscope on planets in Taurus or the 2nd house (or major transits here) signifies a focus on physical comfort and pleasure, money, satisfying material needs and seeking financial security. Taurus and the 2nd house represent embodiment and groundedness in the physical world. Sensory awareness, bodywork and somatic therapies can enhance our bodily awareness and presence. Here we explore our attitudes regarding money and our feelings of self-worth. A woman with Taurus Sun in the 7th house married a man who earned lots of money in sales. Achieving financial prosperity through marriage was a central evolutionary goal.

A twenty-five-year-old man named Robert came for counseling in a state of anxiety regarding the direction of his life, marital tensions, sexual problems, and financial difficulties. Robert had Sun and Moon in Taurus in the 3rd house, opposing Neptune in Scorpio in the 9th house. In addition, he had Mars in Pisces in the 2nd house. Transiting Saturn was opposite his Sun and Moon and conjunct Neptune. He was on welfare and was confused (Neptune) about how to pay the mortgage for the house he and his wife had purchased with financial assistance from their families. He felt helpless to deal with his problems and spent most of his time getting high (Neptune) and strumming guitars. Expressing his 2nd house Mars in Pisces, he was confused and passive (Pisces) about money and finding employment (2nd house) and lacked the motivation and vitality (Mars) to support himself and his household. Counseling focused on his weak self-confidence and low self-esteem. After some time, Robert began to earn money driving a taxi (Sun-Moon in Taurus in the 3rd house, the house of driving), cut down on his pot smoking, and began to read and write poetry (Neptune opposite Sun-Moon in the 3rd house: reading and writing). Robert eventually returned to college to complete his degree in biology (Taurus), found a good-paying job in the field of water conservation, and published articles on this topic (Neptune, planet of water, in the 9th house: publishing).

## Gemini / 3rd House

Emphasis on Gemini or the 3$^{rd}$ house indicates the importance of speech, language, and a need to address communication problems, self-limiting beliefs, or issues about learning, education, or speech. Cognitive therapy, "reframing" beliefs and perceptions, positive thinking, use of mental imagery, and affirmations can be useful practices for people with planets here. Gemini symbolizes language, storytelling, narrative, literary pursuits. Thus, Gemini and 3$^{rd}$ house planets can be unfolded through writing, reading, recounting stories, and journaling. Robert's 3$^{rd}$ house Sun found expression through writing about water conservation and writing poetry.

Brandon had Gemini rising and Moon, Sun, and Mercury in Gemini in the 1$^{st}$ house. He read many novels and poems and needed constant stimulation and conversation. His wife complained about Brandon's incessant talking, but he was simply expressing his true nature, which was highly verbal.

Don wanted to be a writer but felt blocked and inhibited. His chart presented with Mercury (ruler of Gemini) square Neptune, and Moon in the 3$^{rd}$ house in Pisces (Neptune's sign). One difficulty was that he was trying to write highly structured, academically oriented work, when he was more interested in writing fiction. Once Don tried writing novels and short stories, he flourished and eventually published two books.

Ann was a quiet, shy woman who found it difficult to speak up in social situations. Her Sun was in Cancer in the 3$^{rd}$ house squaring Neptune. She had difficulty verbalizing her feelings (Sun in 3$^{rd}$ house of communication, in Cancer: emotions). I suggested that Ann recount her life story through journal writing and link her feelings and memories (Cancer) to broader universal themes by reading books on mythology and archetypes and practicing dreamwork (Sun square Neptune).

Gemini and the 3$^{rd}$ house represent communication. A woman named Amy with Mercury and Venus in Gemini in the 1$^{st}$ house had a strong need for lively conversation with a partner. She came for couples counseling with her boyfriend Darrel, who had natal Mars and Saturn in the 3$^{rd}$ house. Amy complained that Darrel was taciturn and uncommunicative, never listened to her, and became angry and impatient with Amy's small talk. Darrel needed to improve his communication skills, by learning to make eye contact, to listen attentively, and to respond.

The 3rd house also governs brothers and sisters. Thus, emphasis here can indicate issues related to siblings, as well as neighbors and roommates. Allison, a woman with Mercury-Mars in her 3rd house in Scorpio, experienced conflict (Mars) with her brother over their joint management of family assets (Scorpio). Her brother yelled profanities at her and treated her with contempt and cruelty (Scorpio). With natal Sun in Libra, she was a kind, accommodating person who wanted to get along with others. She felt tongue-tied, intimidated, and unable to cope with her brother. I encouraged Allison to engage this conflict, to stand up for herself and speak forcefully on her own behalf, rather than always backing down to her brother's demands (Mercury-Mars in 3rd). This strategy proved to be helpful as she reclaimed the disowned, unexpressed Mars energy in her chart.

Other manifestations of sibling issues include a man with a Venus-Neptune conjunction in his 3rd house who loved and idealized his brother; and a woman named Jenny, with Moon conjunct Pluto in her 3rd house, who felt terrorized by her roommate, whose hostile, controlling behaviors evoked memories of Jenny's intrusive mother (Moon-Pluto).

Gemini and the 3rd house represent the mind and the internal stream of thought and "self-talk," the mental flow of ideas, concepts, and opinions. Ken had Sun in Libra, square Saturn in the 3rd house. He was a talented, personable artist whom everybody liked. Yet he was full of negative thoughts about himself and his work. He had a very conservative, professionally successful brother (Saturn in Capricorn in the 3rd house) who had made disparaging comments about Ken's artistic career and his poor financial prospects. I introduced Ken to cognitive therapy principles, such as observing negative, self-attacking thoughts, identifying situations that triggered them, and changing these thoughts to be more self-affirming. When Ken changed his thinking, he freed himself from fear of failure and became more serious about pursuing his chosen profession in the arts (Libra Sun).

## Cancer / 4th House

Cancer and the 4<sup>th</sup> house signify feelings, memories, home, and the family of origin. An emphasis here shows a need to explore issues related to childhood, relationships with our families and parents, the presence or absence of emotional sustenance in the family. Our early family dynamics affect our ability to feel emotionally contented in home and family life as adults. 4<sup>th</sup> house emphasis suggests a focus on our emotional needs, and our capacity for self-soothing, self-care, and nurturing of others. We benefit from exploring our family dynamics and emotional memories.

Phyllis had natal Saturn in Cancer on the Midheaven, squaring Moon (ruler of Cancer) and Neptune in her 1<sup>st</sup> house. She came to therapy to address feelings of weakness, insecurity, and low self-esteem. These issues originated with problems in her family of origin (Saturn in Cancer), and an enmeshed relationship with her alcoholic mother (Moon conjunct Neptune: weak boundaries). Mother always acted like a helpless, self-pitying martyr (Neptune) and Phyllis played the role of her placator, caretaker, and enabler. She was a serious, parentified child who suppressed her emotional needs (Moon square Saturn) and took care of everyone else in the family. Phyllis also had traumatic interactions with her father, a tyrannical man who eroded her self-confidence (Neptune-Saturn) by telling her she was stupid and incompetent. Counseling helped Phyllis gain confidence and begin to trust her feelings and intuitions. She could be open, emotionally aware, caring and sensitive to others (Moon-Neptune) without being taken advantage of, without being a doormat for others to walk upon. Saturn in Cancer square Moon-Neptune represented a need to develop stronger emotional limits.

A young Jewish woman named Sara had Sun, Venus, and Saturn in Scorpio, in her 4<sup>th</sup> house, square an Aquarius Moon in the 7<sup>th</sup> house. Her parents, who were orthodox Jews, vehemently disapproved of her previous relationship of five years duration to a man of another race (7<sup>th</sup> house Aquarian Moon squaring her 4<sup>th</sup> house planets). We discussed Sara's difficult relationship with her parents, her anger and resentment (Scorpio) toward them. A memory of sexual abuse by one of her brothers surfaced when transiting Pluto—planet of emergence of repressed material—formed a conjunction to natal Saturn. Natal Mars, co-ruler of Scorpio, was placed in her 3rd house (brothers). Sara's story had a happy ending: As natal Venus and Saturn moved by solar arc direction from the square of natal Moon to a sextile, she was married in a traditional Jewish ceremony with her proud parents in attendance. However, in accordance with the unconventional relational partners signified by her 7th house Aquarius Moon, Sara married a man who was a devout Catholic.

Ellen's natal Moon was in her 1st house, and becoming a mother (Moon) was the milestone event of her life, allowing expression of her lunar, nurturing qualities. She had her first child when transiting Saturn and Uranus in Sagittarius were conjunct natal Moon. She became the Great Mother, the eternal womb, the secure base. Ellen also had Mars and Uranus in Cancer, the sign of home, family, and property. When transiting Uranus in Capricorn opposed Mars-Uranus, her house burned to the ground in a large urban fire (Mars), reducing to ashes years work to create a beautiful home. This resulted in emotional upheaval (Cancer), family reorganization, and a move to a more rural location where she and her husband bought a new home. Here Ellen discovered a deep connection to the land (Cancer) and enjoyed cooking and gardening.

Ann, the woman who couldn't express her emotions, had Saturn and Pluto in her 4th house in Leo. Her father was a physically violent, abusive (Pluto) alcoholic (Sun square Neptune). Now she was depressed (Saturn-Pluto) after separating from her husband. Transiting Saturn in Aquarius was opposing natal Saturn-Pluto. Her marriage repeated the abusive dynamics of her parents' marriage (Pluto, dispositor of Scorpio on the 7th house cusp, in the 4th house). With Saturn-Pluto in the 4th, Ann's quiet demeanor masked suppressed feelings of fury and deep rivers of emotion. She recalled traumatic episodes from her family of origin and her marriage. Facing some unpleasant truths about the family was a necessary step in Ann's road to emotional healing.

## Leo / 5th House

Leo and the 5$^{th}$ house represent our warmth, joy, enthusiasm, and playfulness. Children, play, self-expression, and creativity are central concerns of this sign and house. Zipporah Dobyns associates Leo and the 5$^{th}$ house with the need to love and be loved, to feel our creative power, and to be a shining star that the world will admire.[76] Persons with emphasis here often have commanding personalities with poise and presence. Sometimes they also need to address psychological issues of narcissism, feelings of specialness, superiority, or entitlement, or a tendency to be too easily offended or insulted. With emphasis in Leo or the 5$^{th}$ house, we need means of self-expression, through musical, artistic, or theatrical performance, dance, athletics, or any other fun, recreational activity. Sometimes expressive therapies such as psychodrama, art therapy, or dance therapy, and activities to overcome creative blocks can be helpful. Individuals whose charts highlight Leo or the 5$^{th}$ house need to let the radiance and grandeur of the self shine forth, and to minimize touchiness, self-centeredness, or grandiosity.

Jane, with Sun in Leo in the 1$^{st}$ house opposite Saturn, was a talented actress, but was preoccupied with her beauty and efforts to impress others. Jane's therapy focused on expressing her sunny, flamboyant, dynamic personality without being overly vain, histrionic, and self-absorbed. She worked to overcome a fear of expressing love and putting her heart fully into her relationships (Sun opposite Saturn in 7$^{th}$).

Warren, a man with Moon in Scorpio in his 5$^{th}$ house, was a stand-up comedian who vented his anger by insulting his audience and performing outrageous jokes with lots of sexual themes (Scorpio). Warren needed constant attention and admiration from others, and became hostile if he felt slighted or unappreciated.

Ed had Saturn in the 5$^{th}$ house. During his Saturn return, he experienced depression and anxiety triggered by the birth of his first child. We discussed the fact that he was experiencing an age-appropriate transition (the Saturn return) due to the responsibilities of fatherhood. Ed recalled being restricted from playing as a child, and felt this was the origin of his discomfort about having children. Ed feared that he wouldn't enjoy playing with his child and that his child would reject him. Integrating these realizations, Ed became more comfortable with his new parental role. This example illustrates how the pressures of Saturn transits often enable us to make necessary developmental transitions.

Sally, age thirty-five, sought counseling about an important decision. She and her husband wanted to have children, but she felt her career wouldn't leave her adequate time to devote to parenting. Her chart revealed Mercury, Venus, and Neptune in Scorpio in the 5th house, suggesting that children might be a satisfying addition to her life. Over the next several years, while transiting Saturn squared these planets from Aquarius, she and her husband had two children, who became the source of her deepest fulfillment.

The 5th house also governs gambling and risk-taking. Glen had Saturn in Taurus in the 5th house. He had a compulsive gambling problem and lost large sums of money betting on horse races and football games (5th house: risk-taking, sports and entertainment). When transiting Pluto squared natal Saturn he realized he had financial responsibilities to his children (Saturn in Taurus in the 5th house) and that he was endangering their futures. This realization helped him stop gambling and save his money (Saturn in Taurus).

Joanna worked in a clerical position that she felt was killing her creative spirit. Natal Sun, Venus, and Mars were conjunct in Sagittarius in the 5th house and natal Jupiter and Saturn were in her 6th house. Her real passion was music (Venus). She was a talented musician with a degree in ethnomusicology that she now viewed as completely impractical. She often berated herself for her naiveté in choosing such a college major. During her Saturn return she accepted a full-time job (6th house Saturn) and earned a good salary, yet Joanna felt that an essential part of herself had died. She felt resigned to staying at this job, which at least provided her with some security. But Joanna wasn't expressing her greatest talents, and her misalignment with her true identity was manifesting as sadness and apathy, health problems (Saturn in 6th), and loss of interest in people and relationships. Then, when Saturn in Pisces squared natal Sun, Venus, and Mars, she began to take lessons from a noted musician. He invited her to join his band and go on tour with him. In the blink of an eye, her life changed. She took a risk (5th house) that she never regretted or doubted, seizing this opportunity to perform and to express her true nature. She also got to travel throughout Europe—which, with her three planets in Sagittarius, was very exciting for her. And in keeping with the romantic symbolism of Saturn's transit to natal Venus and Mars, she and the other musician were married after returning from their travels. Joanna found love and full expression of her creativity.

## Virgo / 6th House

Virgo represents our search for refinement, precision, and perfection, the ability to recognize our mistakes and shortcomings and to correct them. A focus on Virgo or the 6th house indicates a sharp, discerning, analytical mind, but also anxiety, nervous tension, a strong inner critic or tendency to criticize others, or a need to develop greater discrimination. Virgo and 6th house emphasis give us an impetus to reflect inwardly, scrutinize ourselves, and implement regimes of self-improvement and purification, such as dietary changes, an exercise routine, or spiritual discipline. Virgo or 6th house emphasis often signifies a focus on health issues and the ways illness can be an opportunity for transformation. Planets here also indicate concerns regarding employment, our work duties, or the need for vocational training.

A man named Jeff, with Sun, Saturn, Mercury, and Moon conjunct in Virgo in the 7th house, came from a family that lost numerous relatives who'd been killed in the Holocaust. He was depressed, plagued by survivor guilt, and suffered from anxiety, phobias, numerous physical complaints verging on hypochondria, and *dysthymia*, an inability to find satisfaction or pleasure in everyday life (Sun-Saturn in Virgo). Jeff was perfectionistic and demanding in personal relationships (7th house planets). Therapy focused on his relationship with his father, who had constantly criticized Jeff, contributing to his self-criticism and inability to tolerate the imperfections of others—all manifestations of Saturn in Virgo.

Clark had a Sun-Pluto conjunction in his 6th house in Leo. He had unpleasant power struggles (Pluto) with his boss and co-workers and had to perform many boring, demeaning tasks at his job

(6th house) that wounded his pride (Leo) and frustrated his desire for self-expression. Counseling addressed the need to transform his attitude toward work, to have fun on the job, and to find ways to express creativity in his work.

Judith had Jupiter in Virgo conjunct her Ascendant and was highly conscientious, a hard worker, employed as an international policy analyst (Jupiter: international relations; Virgo: analysis). She'd suffered from anorexia in her youth, which damaged her health. She was still an obsessively careful and picky eater and needed therapy to address some issues about food, diet, and nutrition.

Libra / 7th House

Planets in Libra or the 7th house indicate a focus on friendship, marriage, and seeking completion through relationships. Emphasis on planets placed in Libra signifies the desire to connect, couple, befriend others, cooperate, defer to others, as well an urge to create beauty or pursue interests in the arts. A social worker with Sun-Venus conjunction in Libra in her 10th house began to cry when I stated that she might have really wanted to become a musician. She decided to pursue her love of music through training in music therapy, which she later reported was effective with her patients.

The 7th house represents our subjective experience of being with other people, and the kinds of friends or spouse we tend to attract. A person with Venus in the 7th attracts people who are friendly, attractive, kind, and pleasant, and relationships tend to be harmonious. With Mars in the 7th house, one attracts a sexy, passionate, physically active, or an irritating, argumentative partner or relationship. With this placement, we may put power in the hands of others, act aggressively, or engage in healthy competition. With Neptune in the 7th, relationship partners can be idealistic, imaginative, spiritually-oriented visionaries, or spaced out, unfocused, dependent, or deceptive individuals.

With Saturn in the 7th, one attracts partners who are dependable, conservative, and older, or more established in the world. Jane (noted earlier) had Saturn in the 7th house opposite her Leo Sun. She was disappointed with her marriage, as her husband felt boring, restrictive, and overly serious. She realized that she'd been searching for a man to support her so she could pursue her career as an actress (Leo Sun). She'd found someone who was capable of taking care of her, but she perceived him as rigid and uptight, like her father. But gradually Jane developed appreciation for this reliable, hardworking man and became more deeply committed to him.

Planets in the 7th house can symbolize unacknowledged facets of the personality that are lived through other people. For example, people with Mars in the 7th house often experience others as attacking or aggressive. The person may disown these qualities, projecting them onto others, failing to see how they provoke angry reactions through their own behaviors.

Clark (discussed earlier) sought counseling after his seven year marriage broke up. He reported poor communication with his wife, and said that she criticized him constantly (Mercury-Saturn in Virgo in the 7th). His response was to become depressed, withdrawn, and emotionally inhibited (Moon in Pisces opposite Saturn). Clark had a history of abandonment and neglect (Pisces). His mother died when he was four years old, leaving him in a state of emotional hunger, emptiness, and loneliness (Moon in Pisces). His father favored his older brother and was stern and verbally expressed his disapproval of Clark (Mercury-Saturn in Virgo). His marital experience was dominated by fear that his emotional needs and longing to be nurtured wouldn't be seen, acknowledged, or satisfied by his spouse (1st house Moon opposing Saturn).

Vernon had natal Mars, Saturn, and Uranus in the 7th house in Gemini. He came to therapy to explore marital difficulties that he said were caused by his wife's insistence on exploring kinky sex (Mars-Uranus) with multiple lovers. In the 7th house our ability to tolerate closeness with another person is tested. Vernon had conflict between his desire for reliable closeness (Saturn in 7th) and his desire for total freedom (Mars-Uranus). He'd attracted a partner who acted out the conflict for him, one whom he could blame for all the problems in their marriage. Vernon began to see that his wife's behaviors reflected his own ambivalence about closeness.

The 7th house also governs the therapeutic alliance, which often parallels or recreates a person's broader patterns of relating with others. Thus, planets in the 7th house may indicate transference issues that need attention in therapy. Planets placed here provide insights into the client's way of experiencing others—as safe or threatening, helpful or demanding, benign or cruel, passive or pushy, stuffy or unpredictable. As planets in the 7th house suggest important relational themes, they can also provide clues about the countertransference that may be evoked in the counselor.

Todd, a man with Mars in his 7th house, made me intensely uncomfortable during our sessions. He often became angry with me, and I often felt irritated and angry with him. Knowledge of his birth chart helped me keep my own feelings in perspective and I explored with Todd how relationships tended to evoke a lot of anger.

A woman named Debbie came for counseling while transiting Saturn was conjunct her natal Sun in Scorpio in the 7th house. She'd been fighting with her boyfriend for several months. Debbie behaved seductively in sessions, wore revealing clothing, and openly discussed sexual fantasies about me. We discussed her tendency to use sexuality as a substitute for genuine intimacy, a means of establishing closeness when she felt insecure, attempting to gain control over others, and trying to energize a depleted sense of self (Sun). Examining the erotic transference was a turning point in Debbie's personal growth.

Scorpio / 8th House

Scorpio represents transformation through the intensities of human interaction and their power dynamics. Emphasis on Scorpio or the 8th house indicates issues regarding sexuality, business relationships, joint financial resources, power, and aggression. A man named Jack with Mars in Scorpio in the 8th house sought therapy because of his violent temper. He was preoccupied with sexual fantasies and practices involving power, domination, and submission.

Scorpio or 8th house planets may indicate that relationships evoke aggression or hostility, intense sexual feelings and energies. There are sometimes issues stemming from interpersonal crisis, divorce, death of a loved one, or a personal brush with death. In some instances, emphasis here indicates a need to address physical trauma or sexual abuse. Scorpio and the 8th house can manifest in rage and ruptures in empathic connections with others. Sex therapy, crisis counseling, Reichian therapy, cathartic methods, rebirthing or holotropic breathwork are appropriate therapeutic modalities to work with Scorpio energy.

Richard, with Sun in Scorpio conjunct his Ascendant square Pluto, often expressed rage and felt that others were persecuting, humiliating, disappointing, and plotting against him. He exhibited resentment, vengeful feelings, hostility, and paranoia. He had many early emotional injuries from childhood that made him angry and highly defended.

Gina, with her Sun, Mercury, Venus, and Jupiter in Pisces in the 8th house, opposite Saturn in the 2nd house, had built a successful business with her husband. But when transiting Saturn and Uranus squared these natal planets from Sagittarius, Gina's husband unexpectedly stole all of their money and ran off to Las Vegas with his secretary. Gina was devastated over their divorce, the loss of her business, and the fact that she was left to raise five children alone (Pisces: abandonment issues). Her husband later declared bankruptcy and refused to pay child support. She had to contend with their joint debts (8th house emphasis) after their breakup. Pisces rules illusions: Gina was stripped of her illusions about her husband, and saw that she'd been in denial (Pisces), failing to see warning signs of his infidelity. She needed to become more practical about earning her own income and handling her finances (Saturn in 2nd house).

Elaine became sexually active during her teens and twenties, while Pluto transited over her 8th house Sun-Mercury-Venus-Neptune in Scorpio. She was the daughter of a strict, puritanical minister and needed to come to terms with the internalized religious judgments she had about expressing her lusty, passionate side.

Scorpio and the 8th house also represent our awareness of death and dying. When transiting Saturn passed through his 8th house, a man named Doug faced the impending death of his father, the first time he'd ever confronted mortality. Reading books on death and dying by Stephen Levine and Elisabeth Kubler-Ross helped Doug understand his grief and fear. This inner work enabled him to help his father die peacefully, surrounded by love and acceptance.

Nicki had Scorpio Sun squaring Mars, Pluto (co-rulers of Scorpio), and Saturn in Leo. At the age of seven, while transiting Saturn was conjunct natal Sun and square Mars, Saturn, and Pluto, her father (Saturn), a severe disciplinarian, beat her after she'd been caught engaging in sexual play at school. Nicki never fully recovered from this incident and had difficulties with sex and emotional intimacy. She was mistrustful and fearful of men and felt they were constantly making unwanted, intrusive advances. When she became intimate with a man intense anger invariably emerged, and she perceived her partners as cruel and vindictive (Mars-Pluto square Sun). Therapy addressed childhood physical trauma and her intense sexual feelings and defenses.

Sagittarius / 9th House

Sagittarius and the 9th house represent the search for truth, meaning, and moral or philosophical values. With planets in Sagittarius or the 9th house, learning, education, teachers or teaching, and definition of our beliefs are central themes. A person whose chart has an emphasis here may grapple with a loss of meaning or a desire to discover a clearly defined philosophy, spiritual doctrine, or religious belief. The individual needs to develop a personal philosophy that imbues life with meaning. One might also be drawn to travel, adventures, and pilgrimages.

Brigit, with Sun-Venus-Mars in Sagittarius, worked in the field of publishing (ruled by Sagittarius) but felt stifled and longed for adventure. Understanding her birthmap affirmed Brigit's desire for travel. She left her job to travel for several years in Asia, where she studied Yoga and Buddhist meditation with several teachers and went on pilgrimages to many sacred sites.

A man with Sun-Mercury in Capricorn in the 9th house opposite Jupiter in Cancer and square Neptune in Libra became a renowned yoga teacher who traveled around the world giving classes and workshops.

Albee, with Mars, Saturn, and Uranus in her 9th house in Gemini, was a highly skilled special education teacher, once described as a "master educator." With these planets in Gemini (language, communication), Albee specialized in working with children with learning disabilities, especially problems with language and speech. She sought counseling to discuss a possible career change, however she eventually decided to continue working in this field, which matched her natal chart symbolism. By training to become a school administrator, she developed her career in education and satisfied her desire for new learning and mental stimulation (Gemini).

Frank's chart indicated that he had the potential to be an intellectual visionary of sorts. With Sun conjunct Neptune in Libra in the 9th house, he had been in graduate school for many years, unable to complete his dissertation in astrophysics. His professors berated him for being a hopeless dreamer and romantic whose interests in cosmology would never draw any research funding or give him any chance of professional advancement. His faculty advisor was trying to direct his studies toward highly detailed technical analysis, which was unsuitable for his Sun-Neptune nature. When he switched advisors, he completed his dissertation, and went on to write a book about cosmology.

A woman named Celeste, who'd always been closed-minded toward religion, metaphysics, and the occult, went on an unexpected journey to Sedona, Arizona when transiting Uranus and Neptune passed into her 9th house. She was exposed to a completely different worldview—including many "new age" ideas that answered her deepest questions about life's meaning. Her twin sister, Celine, had the same transit at the same time; she became a born-again, fundamentalist Christian. Both Celeste and Celine experienced radical shifts in their beliefs and philosophy of life.

## Capricorn / 10th House

Capricorn is the sign concerned with success, achievement, and embodiment of one's beliefs and ideals through work and vocation. For people whose charts emphasize Capricorn or 10th house planets, psychological growth or psychotherapy may focus on career counseling and vocational development, defining ambitions and assessing one's capabilities, and defining occupational goals in relation to social institutions.[77] Our central task is to assume responsibility, gain authority, and pursue our true ambitions.

Nadia, with Sun, Mercury, and Venus in the 10th house, described herself as a workaholic, driven to achieve success, leaving little time for herself. We envisioned how she could live a more balanced life so that amidst the pressures of her career she could make time for art, music, and relationships (Venus).

Zelda sought career counseling because she hated the competitive atmosphere of most offices, had difficulty focusing on tasks she found boring, and longed for a career with more glamour. She'd done psychic readings professionally for some time but she was looking for something a little steadier. Keying on the symbolism of natal Neptune in her 10th house, I asked if she'd ever considered becoming a professional photographer. The idea was appealing to her. She took some classes, and within three years she was doing this work full time.

Elizabeth, a successful corporate marketing executive, had Mars and Pluto conjunct in Leo in her 10th house. While Saturn transited through Leo, an organizational crisis and power struggles (Pluto) within her company caused her to become angry, defensive, and highly stressed out, and she broke out in rashes (Saturn conjunct Mars-Pluto). She faced a challenge to her position from senior managers of her company, who were refusing to give her credit for her work, and trying to force her to transfer to a different division or leave the company altogether. As she became aware of the transiting influence, she was able to remain calm as she prepared her response. She weathered the storm effectively, presenting her grievances to the managers with strength, composure, and dramatic flair, maintaining her dignity (Mars in Leo).

A man named Allan, with Sun in Taurus in the 7th house squaring Saturn in Leo in the 10th house, was married and had three children. He had a high paying job that demanded long hours and much responsibility. Allan longed for escape, scheming of ways he could retire early and live a life of sensual bliss (Taurus) in Hawaii. But he needed to accept that his wife and family depended on his

income (Taurus Sun in 7ᵗʰ house), and to embrace the responsibilities of fatherhood (Sun square Saturn). He was starting to realize
the opportunities for long-range financial security his career offered
him (Saturn square Taurus Sun). This knowledge helped Allan
affirm his life's path and to feel proud of his accomplishments and
commitment to his children (Saturn in Leo).

## Aquarius / 11th House

Aquarius and the 11ᵗʰ house are concerned with awareness of social
issues, response to historical circumstances, and involvement in
efforts toward social change. Aquarius represents a desire to be progressive, to rebel, defy convention, and to explore the cutting edge
of culture, invention, science, and discovery. With an emphasis on
Aquarius or the 11ᵗʰ house, we want to join groups, attend meetings
and conferences, maintain memberships in organizations, establish
a support network, and understand the larger societal context of our
individual problems. We become participants in political change
and social evolution, through our involvement in groups, large and
small organizations, communities, collectives, social change movements, or political activism. Involvement in psychological growth
groups of various kinds are helpful for people with an emphasis
here—for example, group therapy, men's or women's groups, or
Twelve Step meetings.

Liza has Venus and Saturn in Aquarius, quincunx Uranus in
Virgo. She wears colorful clothes, has a unique painting style, and
is involved in a group of artist activists who stage experimental,
multi-media events. She expresses social idealism and a revolutionary spirit (Uranus).

Jill works with corporations and large seminar groups promoting
practical strategies for social change and heightened environmental
consciousness. Natal Saturn and Uranus in the 11ᵗʰ house support
her interest in solar energy, biodynamic gardening, and innovative
solutions to urban housing problems, such as co-housing projects.

Paula, with natal Saturn and Pluto in Leo in the 11ᵗʰ house
opposite the Moon in Aquarius, has been involved in a large spiritual growth movement for over twenty years. In the mid 1980s,

while transiting Saturn and Pluto in Scorpio squared natal Saturn-Pluto, she faced the shadows of the movement as she witnessed serious abuses of power (Pluto) among the group's leadership. She was asked to assume more responsibility within the group as a teacher and administrator. Experiences of strife and power struggles within the organization taught her lessons that enabled her to wield authority (Saturn) wisely and to become a source of positive group leadership.

Brenda was an artist whose illustrations contained themes of interracial equality and harmony, the struggle for human rights, and the gathering of individuals into communities. Her Aquarius Sun was in her 5th house, opposite Jupiter in the 11th. She was an outspoken activist who constantly educated herself (Jupiter) about social issues (11th house).

## Pisces / 12th House

Pisces and the 12th house represent openness, a feeling of connection to everything, a state without boundaries. This sign and house are associated with spiritual growth, mysticism, dreams, imagination, intuition, and psychic awareness. In some cases, planets in Pisces or the 12th house indicate passivity, vulnerability, or lack of focus. A person may feel ineffective, victimized, or powerless. Occasionally, planets placed here are associated with psychopathology, delusions, hallucinations, inflation, loss of discriminative faculties, decompensation (falling apart), or even psychosis and institutionalization. More typically, persons with an emphasis in Pisces or the 12th house need to address alcoholism, addiction, codependency, ACA issues, or feelings of weakness, victimization, abandonment, loneliness, or grief.

Pisces and the 12th house represent a natural movement inward. They signify loosening the tight grip of our rational minds and interiorizing our awareness, spontaneous emergence of unconscious feelings and potentials in dreams, fantasy, and experiences of expanded consciousness. Here we live a "symbolic life," realizing how our personal experiences are archetypal and universal, each carrying inherent spiritual meanings.[78] We connect to mythic material and develop a transpersonal consciousness through dreamwork, active imagination, mandalas, and astrology.[79] Transpersonal therapies, Jungian analysis, shamanic journeys, past-life regression, and meditation are golden roads to follow, into the temple of endless mysteries.

Individuals with a Pisces or 12th house emphasis are likely to be drawn to contemplative practice and periods of solitude and retreat. Denial or avoidance of conflictual material is possible here, which John Welwood termed "spiritual bypassing." Pisces and the 12th house represent transcendence of a limited, ego-centered perspective and the awakening of compassion. With emphasis here we can focus on expressing the spirit of service and loving-kindness in daily life.

Sometimes there are difficult manifestations of a chart emphasizing planets in Pisces or the 12th house. For example, Pierre, a filmmaker, had natal Sun, Mercury, and Saturn in Pisces in the 12th house, opposite Neptune (ruler of Pisces). In the mid 1980s, while transiting Saturn, Uranus, and Neptune squared these natal planets from Sagittarius, Pierre's career hit the skids and he ended up homeless and drug-addicted. Later he was hospitalized after he developed delusional thoughts and hallucinations. He was fortunate to find a psychiatrist who was interested in Pierre's dreams and encouraged him to artistically express his imagination (associated with Pisces, Neptune, and the 12th house), and to let life pour through him. After he'd coped with his addiction and his thought disorder subsided, he was released from the hospital and began to write screenplays again.

Daniel, with Sun-Mercury in Pisces opposite Neptune conjunct his Midheaven, was a chemist for a large pharmaceutical company who had gotten involved in dealing psychedelic drugs. He developed delusions of grandeur, making claims of clairvoyance and enlightenment, promoting himself as a spiritual teacher. He crashed and burned in Reno where he lost all of his money in a card game after he got drunk in a casino. Daniel hocked his car to pay for a few nights in a motel, but he was lost and had no place left to go. Pisces can be a momentary experience of drift, drunkenness, or being lost and without compass. His mother bailed Daniel out and took him back to New York to chill out for a few months (4<sup>th</sup> house Sun: returning home). During this time he began to dedicate himself to regular meditation and let go of using LSD.

A successful psychic named Tracy has Moon, Uranus, and Pluto in Virgo in the 12<sup>th</sup> house, sextile Neptune in the 2<sup>nd</sup> house. She worked to integrate several emotionally intense (Moon-Pluto) past-life memories that emerged in visions during meditation.

After a debilitating accident, Madeline, a woman with Moon and Saturn in the 12<sup>th</sup> house squaring Neptune, suffered from a degenerative physical condition and spent months convalescing, unable to work. Counseling addressed feelings of loneliness and helplessness (12<sup>th</sup> house) brought on by her disability, and assisted her in looking inward for meaning rather than solely to outer activities and achievements.

Frieda, with Sun in Pisces quincunx Neptune in the 12<sup>th</sup> house, had been deeply religious since childhood. She sought counseling during a period when she considered becoming a nun so she could devote herself to a contemplative life. However, her horoscope featured natal Mars in the 7<sup>th</sup> house squaring Venus, signifying her sexual drive and desire for emotional union, companionship, and marriage. Monastic life didn't seem suitable for her. She decided instead to become a Jungian analyst, which satisfied her interest in dreams and mysteries of soul, psyche, and spirit.

Pisces and the 12<sup>th</sup> house symbolize the experience of *liminality*—a condition of transitional uncertainty and dissolution of prior goals, values, or beliefs that is necessary before a reformation of personality can occur. When 12<sup>th</sup> house themes are emphasized natally or by transit (for example, Saturn transiting the 12<sup>th</sup> house) we go through some period of confusion and disorientation, or become preoccupied with dreams and are intensely affected by them. We may feel like spending more time meditating and reading books about spirituality, psychology, and mysticism. There's a tendency toward withdrawal and introspection, turning inward, pulling back from relationships. These can be times of loneliness, aloneness, and important restorative periods. These are crucial periods of inner work, dissolution of identity, a preparation for the birth of a new self. We have to trust this phase of inner exploration, and allow ourselves to immerse in it fully, knowing eventually the period of confusion will end.

Natasha was laid off from work and had to look inward while unemployed for a year as Saturn transited in her 12th house. At the same time she had just gone through a divorce and felt intensely alone. I told her I thought her situation would change in about two months when Saturn would transit over her Libra Ascendant and square natal Venus-Jupiter in the 4th house. Exactly at that time, she received a job offer that provided plenty of money to support her family. She also started dating a man who immediately loved her and her children and wanted to create a blended family (Venus-Jupiter in 4th house). The humbling lesson for Natasha was that she had to witness everything fall apart in her life, her career and her marriage—to let it happen, to wait, and to trust that the 12th house phase of endings and losses would end. This example shows how judicious use of predictive methods such as transits enables a person to endure a crisis period and to understand its meaning and duration. Adopting a cyclical frame of reference, we acknowledge the important developmental transition of Saturn transiting from the 12th house of solitude and isolation to the Ascendant, the point of self-emergence, beginnings, and rebirth. Saturn crossing the Ascendant always represents a new beginning, a restart, a new cycle of conscious personality development. As we tour the wheel of the twelve houses again and again, we go through rhythmic changes that mark the mythopoetry of life.

In this chapter we've noted how the sign and house placements of natal and transiting planets enable us to identify central life themes, stressors, and maturational tasks, providing therapeutic insights that guide and heal.

Chapter 6

# Potentials and Contraindications of Therapeutic Astrology

As we discuss introducing astrology into therapeutic work, it's important to acknowledge the uneasy relationship that exists between the fields of psychology and astrology. Astrology is still considered by most psychologists (and scientists in general) to be one of the last holdouts in modern society of primitive superstition and irrationalism. I understand the skepticism some psychologists feel toward astrology. For was it not the mission of modern science to liberate humanity from fatalistic, deterministic beliefs, rooted in religious traditions, such as those allegedly found in astrology? Science, rationalism, and humanism have tried to free human beings from slavery to the gods and to awaken our capacity to shape the world and our lives through choice, effort, and free will. The repudiation of astrology was part of the rejection of the supernatural and seemed essential to the growth of science, reason, and a more enlightened society.

Psychologists often view astrology with suspicion, believing it to be antithetical to the work of helping people to strengthen their sense of personal efficacy and agency. A common view is that astrology promotes a passive, deterministic attitude in which the locus of control of events is seen as existing outside the person in the planets. To a large extent this view is due to the fact that most of what the public knows as astrology is the Sun sign predictions found at supermarket checkout counters, next to the *National Enquirer*. It's also due to the tendency for astrologers to try to predict specific events instead of emphasizing psychological principles and tendencies.

Another problem is that many astrologers "read" the chart one-sidedly, emphasizing *information* rather than *process*. This approach is disempowering; the astrologer interprets the chart without soliciting any input or feedback from the client. In contrast, therapeutic astrology explores the horoscope's symbolism through dialogue, not a monologue of psychic predictions. A therapeutic astrologer works in a process-oriented, interactive manner, collaboratively constructing interpretations, avoiding pronouncements that sound as if the chart contains predetermined meanings. Dialogue with clients helps us discern their level of consciousness and functioning so we can counsel them effectively. Counteracting the misperception that astrology is fatalistic, therapeutic astrologers emphasizes using our free will to shape the meaning we derive from all planetary placements and transits. Astrology also introduces a mythic perspective, revealing the archetypal nature of people and situations, as discussed in Chapter 2. We show the individual how to cooperate with the patterns and intention of the planets, rather than feeling victimized by them.

Take the example of a man with transiting Saturn entering the 2$^{nd}$ house. A traditional predictive astrologer might state that this indicates impending financial difficulties. A psychological and therapeutic interpretation is that this transit heralds maturation, challenging the man to stabilize his financial situation through concentrated effort. Dialogue about his financial situation can clarify how well he is adapting to the developmental challenges of Saturn, and what might be some sensible ways to approach these problems or issues. The same principle is true with any transit of Saturn. Therapeutic astrology is fully compatible with psychology and rational humanism. It's a practical discipline that helps us make wise choices and enhance our lives.

## ASTROLOGY IS A POSITIVE GROWTH TOOL

It's ironic that while some psychologists complain that astrology disempowers and weakens people's free will, what they often prescribe is endless months and years of therapy and dependency upon the expertise of the therapist. Therapeutic astrology cultivates choice, right timing, and self-understanding. It reveals central psychological themes and issues, suggests paths to growth for the individual, and promotes efficient, focused counseling or psychotherapy.

On the other side, some astrologers view their psychotherapist counterparts with a mixture of envy and disdain, suspicion and admiration. Psychologists and psychotherapists generally earn more money than astrologers and are treated with greater respect in our culture. Some counseling astrologers may decide, as I did, to enter mental health professions (clinical psychology, social work, marriage and family therapy, psychiatry), not only because these are socially and economically viable professions in our society but also to participate in psychotherapy as a life-changing, modern rite of passage, a place where initiation and transformation can occur.[80]

In my vision of the future, therapeutic astrologers—*astropsycho-therapists*—will be culturally sanctioned healers, alongside the psychoanalyst, priest, minister, rabbi, the shaman and traditional medicine man/woman. But to attain that respected status, astrologers need to learn counseling skills and theories of human development. Our astrology becomes more incisive and powerful as we assimilate psychological concepts into our work, such as emotional attunement, attachment, family systems, trauma, dissociation, transference and projection, and the practice of listening to the guidance of dreams. We also need to embark upon a path of self-study exploring core issues such as sexuality, addiction, family dynamics, and personality. This self-knowledge greatly sharpens our work with astrology.

I believe that in the future astrology will routinely be used by psychotherapists. In my opinion, practicing psychotherapy without referring to astrology is like trying to study biology without a microscope, or like climbing Mt. Everest without a map. The birth chart reveals a person's inner life and subjective experience. It offers a precise and individualized roadmap of self-transformation.

## SCIENCE, INITIATORY LANGUAGE, AND SELF-STUDY

What many psychologists and other skeptics don't grasp is that it may not be possible to adequately evaluate astrology strictly as a science. You don't evaluate a poem or a piece of music by the criteria of science, nor should we do so with astrology. I appreciate the efforts some people are making to validate astrology scientifically, but I'm not convinced that astrology is a physical science. Rather, it's a metaphysical, contemplative discipline. Like alchemy, astrology is a Gnostic, esoteric language whose symbols reveal sacred knowledge. It's an initiatory language, best understood through intuition and meditation. It's like the cryptic "twilight language" of Tantrism, which looks like gibberish to non-initiates.[81] We become initiates by reflecting on astrological symbolism and planetary hieroglyphs in a meditative frame of mind. (See "Astrology, Meditation, and Symbol Amplification" in Chapter 2.)

Before trying to practice astrology therapeutically to assist clients, it's important to thoroughly study our own charts through biographical review, examining important life events in relation to astrological symbolism.[82] As we become familiar with, and sensitive to, the characteristic energies of each planet, sign, and house we learn that we can also guide others effectively. Our skill as therapeutic astrologers is directly linked to our own level of consciousness, our own process of self-transformation. Psychological astrologers develop a radiant sense of purpose, identity, and positive self-esteem (Sun). We explore and express our feelings, and become empathic and emotionally available (Moon). We develop curiosity about the world, read widely, and enjoy continuous learning and exchange of ideas (Mercury). We refine our social skills to become friendly, loving people (Venus). We develop energy, enthusiasm, and motivation to pursue our goals; we unfold through our sexuality (Mars). Embodying the intelligence of Jupiter and Saturn, we're hopeful and clear-minded, optimistic and realistic, philosophical, and strategic. We set high goals and work to achieve them. We're concerned with issues of meaning, but also grounded in the real world.

Our evolution also continues beyond Saturn and social adaptation. We feel Uranus's urge toward freedom, to break free from cultural conditioning and social norms, to become individuated and liberated. We respond to Neptune's transcendent tide, rising above illusions, dissipative pursuits, and transient phenomena, cultivating stillness and tranquility through meditation or prayer, drinking eternity, expanding into limitless consciousness, perceiving the omnipresence of the Sacred. And we meet the tests of Pluto, which expose and expel toxins and impurities of the personality, such as resentments, greed, cruelty, or hunger for power over others. As we open to the vibrations of the outer planets, we become bold and free, awakened to the spiritual planes of existence, and purified of selfish, hurtful motivations.[83] Above all, astrologers remain poised and centered in the midst of life's challenges. Because of this self-study and self-transformation, when clients come to see us during crises, we can find the pulse and help them understand what's happening to them.

Astrology is an art of biographical interpretation that involves reinterpreting events in the light of planetary symbols and cycles. Viewed in this context, even a defeat can be accepted as "a necessary phase in the ritual process of existence."[84] In this context, I'd like to recount the following anecdote. I once discussed some professional disappointments with my friend Nick Campion, the noted astrologer and historian. Nick said, "In England we have the tradition of noble failure. We honor and acknowledge the noble failure, the defeat in battle, like Gallipoli. We celebrate the campaigns that failed. These occasions are marked with pomp and ceremony. We honor the defeated warrior, not just the victorious one." I believe that in therapeutic astrology we can heal ourselves by honoring our noble strivings, efforts, and campaigns, both the successful and the unsuccessful ventures. We can achieve self-forgiveness and realize that there's always another cycle, another opportunity to complete the unfinished business of the past. In this way, astrology generates indomitable persistence and determination. There's never any reason to give up.

## A Container for Crisis and Transitions

Astrology helps us guide others through the liminal state—the transition between one way of being and another—by illuminating the meaning of this process, its probable timing, its potential goal or outcome. The birth chart is a container for holding chaotic, turbulent experiences. It can help us make sense out of crises and transitions.

An example of this process occurred with Peter, who had transiting Neptune opposite natal Saturn for a year. At this time Peter lost his job, he was unable to find other work, and his career fell apart. Saturn symbolizes the security of our life structures as well as our career, and Neptune represents erosion, uncertainty, and chaos. Peter felt as if he was on a precipice and the ground was eroding underneath his feet. He asked, "What's happening to me? I feel like I'm going crazy. When is this going to end?" I explained that this present Neptune transit was related to what he was experiencing, and that it was going to last for another few months, so the uncertainty might continue at least that long. I noted that during this period his professional goals would probably change and that achieving security shouldn't be his main priority. With Neptune opposing Saturn, it would be helpful to cultivate faith and serenity and to recognize there'd be some inevitable uncertainties about his work and life structures. However, in a few months Jupiter would transit over his Midheaven, and new goals and plans might emerge at that time. While I wanted to know when Peter's difficulties would end and his life would settle down and stabilize, I also had faith that this difficult period had meaning within the overall unfolding of his life. But a key was to experience this transition consciously.

When we yield, surrender, and allow ourselves to enter Neptune's healing pool we become fluid, liquid, and transparent; and sometimes this allows us to receive a vision of a more idealistic, spiritual life path. During this Neptune transit, Peter began to pray sincerely for the first time, he became concerned with issues of faith, and he enrolled in a program that trained him to do spiritual healing. And right on schedule, when transiting Jupiter passed over his MC, he found another job. Peter came through this passage with a deeper trust in God and the universe and a greatly evolved spiritual consciousness. Moreover, the difficulties he faced during this transit awakened Peter's compassion for everyone. Neptune's visitations can open our eyes to the reality of universal suffering and often stir in us an intention to be healers of suffering. Astrology helped Peter contain his anxiety during this confusing phase of life. What astrology offers us during such a crisis isn't simply reassurance that "everything is going to be okay," but the awareness that we're passing through an intelligent evolutionary process. Astrology shows us a center of calm in the midst of the storm, in the chaos of transformation. Also see the story of Angela with the Saturn-Uranus opposition, in Chapter 2.

## ASTROLOGY, MEANING MAKING, AND CHOICE

Astrology helps us make meaning from our life situations. By strengthening the capacity to make meaning, it contributes to the consolidation of the self, the sense of being a coherent, purposeful agent, one who is able to act. Thirty-nine-year-old Jim had natal Jupiter in the 10th house in Aries and Sun- Mercury in Aquarius in the 9th house. Jim worked a construction job, which he considered menial, and was afraid he might never find a calling, his life's work. I asked Jim (in 1991) what had happened in 1986 when Jupiter transited over his natal Sun-Mercury. Did he have some experience related to teaching or education? (9th house: education; natal Jupiter, planet of the educator, in the 10th house). Jim said, "That's when my dad (a teacher) got sick and I got to fill in for him and teach a few of his classes. He let me substitute for two weeks and I got to be the teacher. That was one of the highest experiences of my life. It was the first time I felt like I knew who I really am."

Saturn was now transiting through Aquarius and conjunct natal Sun-Mercury. Jim had an opportunity to create his identity and work in the world, but he had to build the dream. It wasn't enough to just have the fantasy of being a teacher. He had to work for it, to go through the Saturnian process of going back to college and getting his teaching credential. Having an image of this goal mobilized his efforts to achieve it. Astrology helped Jim evolve from powerlessness to conscious choice.


## CONTRAINDICATIONS OF USING ASTROLOGY

If astrology can be utilized by some people to strengthen their choice-making and meaning-making capacities, we should also recognize that there are people who don't possess the requisite ego strength to use astrology productively or safely. There are some contraindications of using astrology in the context of psychotherapy. One needs to use astrology with wisdom, just as one wouldn't give a five-year-old a chainsaw, or present an unprepared individual with profound Kabbalistic meditations or the secrets of the Tibetan Buddhist Kalachakra.

Some questions I ask myself when considering whether or not to introduce astrology into the counseling situation are the following: Does the client exhibit avoidance, escapism, dissociation, magical thinking, paranoia, or delusions of grandeur? If so, I don't utilize astrology in the therapeutic setting. Other problems arise when there is a tendency toward unrealistic expectations, a tendency to give over responsibility for oneself to the planets, to the chart, or to the therapist-astrologer. For example, a woman named Belle fell in love with a man in a distant city who was married and had six children. It seemed unlikely that he'd leave his wife and children to be with Belle. She asked me, "What do you think he will do?" And I responded, "What are *you* going to do?" I could have done a horary chart to try to predict whether he'd abandon his wife and kids for her, but this didn't seem realistic. It seemed more productive to help Belle face the situation squarely and realize that she'd have to move on with her life and find a relationship partner who was actually available.

Once a woman named Julia came for a chart reading and told me that she suffered from multiple personality disorder (MPD), a serious psychological disorder. Before learning this, I had been noting Julia's Capricorn Sun in the 10th house and describing all of her professional potentials. I was totally taken by surprise when she told me that she'd been raised in a Satanic cult, tortured, sexually abused, and that she'd been diagnosed with MPD. She hadn't been able to hold a job for several years, was on disability, and was in treatment for MPD. Hearing this made me reconsider how to proceed with our session. To examine her chart in-depth we'd need to discuss her natal Mars-Uranus-Pluto conjunction, which I inferred was a symbol of her background of violence and abuse. But Julia wasn't a person with whom I felt I could do this kind of work. She already had a psychotherapist and was only coming to me for a one-time reading. This conjunction of planets was the symbol of highly charged issues about trauma and violence, and I felt it would be unwise to delve too deeply into this material with her. Besides, I lacked training in working with multiple personality disorder and satanic cult abuse. I didn't want to open up more painful material than I was prepared to handle. Moreover, Julia's thinking was so unrealistic that I felt astrology could even be harmful to her. She believed the planets were forces that controlled her life and made things happen to her. She also believed I was "channeling" the chart reading. I wasn't channeling anything; I was exploring planetary symbols.

Therapeutic astrology requires ego strength and a non-magical intelligence that can comprehend the difference between a symbol and reality. Julia related to astrology in a fatalistic, deterministic way. This is a situation where astrology is contraindicated. Julia needed to continue intensive psychotherapy, find employment, and become a functional person. To her credit, she was doing intensive work in therapy and taking steps to help herself. She was also able to understand my reservations about exploring astrology further with her.

Another client for whom I felt astrology was contraindicated was Roger, who had a close T-square between Saturn in Cancer on the Ascendant, Moon in Aries on the Midheaven, and Neptune in Libra at the IC (Chart 12). At the time of consultation, transiting Saturn, Uranus, and Neptune in Capricorn were forming a Grand cross to his Moon, Saturn, and Neptune. Roger was suicidal,

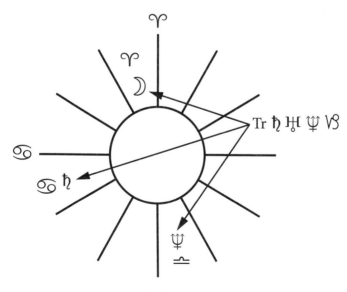

**13. Roger**

depressed, confused, and unable to hold a job. The transiting tension between Saturn and Neptune signified his psychological unraveling and deterioration. While undergoing these strong transits to natal Moon, Roger went through a very emotional time, complicated by the Moon's natal aspects to Saturn and Neptune. The Saturn-Neptune square indicated dissonance between Roger's sensitivity, imagination, and spirituality (Neptune) and the responsibilities of being an adult in the world (Saturn). Roger wanted to be an artist, musician, and mystic but he refused to look for work even though he had no money and was in deep financial trouble. Roger was unable to tolerate strong emotions without panicky feelings of disintegration (Moon-Saturn-Neptune).

Roger was interested in discussing his birth chart, but I felt he used our discussions of astrology to avoid his feelings and pressing, real-life issues. He tended to dissociate, space out, and engage in magical thinking (Neptune). He tried to look at everything in symbolic and mystical terms instead of facing himself and his life realistically. Astrology actually exacerbated Roger's feelings of not being a solid and real person and his tendency to minimize the gravity of his situation. Counseling emphasizing Saturnian groundedness and practicality, and forging a secure therapeutic relationship.

I don't recommend using astrology as a tool for treatment of persons suffering from MPD, bipolar disorder, schizophrenia, borderline personality disorder, or phobias. Here standard psychological treatment methods are preferable. Therapeutic astrology is most appropriate for people who don't exhibit signs of severe psychopathology.

Of course, there are exceptions to this principle. Earlier I mentioned my conversation with Alice, a schizophrenic woman, hospitalized for many years, who showed some interest in her birth chart. I noted that she was approaching her Saturn return. I told Alice she had a choice to make: Could she gather the courage now to come back to the world, to consensus reality, to become autonomous, to care for herself, to leave behind her identity as a sick person, a "mental patient"? I noted that her 10th house Sun-Jupiter was trine to Saturn in her 1st house, and that she had Mars in Capricorn, sextile to Saturn—suggesting her potential to become responsible for herself and capable of ambition. After being released from the hospital, Alice became a born-again Christian and, with the support and assistance of her family and her church, she developed a stronger sense of her strengths and talents. Later Alice got married, began working, finished college, and went to law school. While astrology played an exceptionally small role in her recovery, it pleases me to think our conversation may have helped her, by planting the seed idea that her planets indicated she was capable of getting well.

## Supporting the Individual's Path of Healing and Recovery

Astrology teaches that the path of emotional and relational healing is different for each person. This viewpoint corrects the tendency of therapists to try to get clients to conform to a single model of development or a single goal state, or to follow the same treatment program. Maybe a client's next step runs contrary to our own values or beliefs. Perhaps a client with a Uranus transit chooses to divorce, a decision that could make us uncomfortable if we happen to be opposed to divorce, on philosophical or religious grounds. But divorce might be an appropriate step for that person. Perhaps the client having a Neptune transit decides to leave their job or family to join a religious movement even though we view this decision with suspicion. We should be equally prepared to counsel and support the client with a Saturn transit stressed out from working long hours; the person who abruptly quits a job during a rebellious Uranus transit; someone in a marital or relational crisis during stressful 7th house transits; the client having a 12th house transit who decides to pursue an extended meditation retreat. We support the individual with a Neptune problem who enters a 12-step recovery program. Therapeutic astrologers are open to a variety of decisions and life paths that satisfy the energies and intentions of our planets.

Therapeutic astrology helps us get into alignment with the ever-changing *now*, and with the pathways that fits our unique pattern of development. It highlights the need to use different therapeutic approaches in different cases, and at different times with each client. Therapeutic astrology also assists us in coordinating different levels of evolution.

### ASTROLOGY AND MULTI-LEVEL INITIATION

We're complex people, with many events and processes happening simultaneously in our lives. In each moment, multiple levels of transformation are possible, corresponding to our natal and transiting planets. I call this *multi-level initiation*. We live within multiple narratives, co-existent, interconnected storylines—for example, the narratives of our search for love; our need to work for money; our striving for success; our Neptunian quest for spiritual awakening. In a letter cited earlier, Rudhyar wrote to me: "Polyphonic, counterpunctual living. Caesar and God say the Gospels." Rudhyar was describing our need to live on multiple levels simultaneously, to give equal attention to worldly and spiritual matters. Astrology enables us to coordinate our development in many domains, orchestrating our responsibilities and strivings into a rich, symphonic life. It's a tool for multi-level transformation, illuminating various tasks and levels of evolution that are unfolding for us at any given time.

For example, Dennis, forty-two, had Scorpio Sun in the 1st house, square the Moon in Aquarius in the 4th house (Chart 13). He started therapy when Saturn entered Aquarius and was conjunct natal Moon, square his natal Sun. Transiting Saturn conjunct Moon (planet of feelings, moods, memories) is a classic transit for a period of sadness or depression and the recovery of submerged memories and feelings. This transit often marks a reorganization of a person's emotional life. Dennis told me this dream: *I'm in our family home. I'm six or seven years old and I'm with my mother, and we're cleaning out the closets.* Dennis began to remember what happened in his early childhood and in his family. The Moon and the 4th house are central to the therapeutic process because they're concerned with emotional memory, our family of origin, the family and home situation that shaped us. Dennis remembered what his mother (Moon) looked like, felt like, smelled like, and sounded like when he was a child. He remembered her moods and her sadness, and felt a deep empathy for her.

Dennis' Moon squares his Scorpio Sun. He recalled his precocious sexuality as a youngster, and memories of incest with his older sister surfaced. In several instances he was caught in sexual play with

*Planets Mandala.* Da Basilio Valentino, *Azoth*, Frankfort, 1613[85]

other children, for which he was chastised and humiliated by his father. He had natal Mars conjunct Saturn; he and his father were always enraged with one another. Dennis grew up viewing himself as a bad, naughty, evil child. The message he received from his family was that he wasn't a good kid. He became mischievous and defiant, developing a tough, swaggering persona to defend against the pain of emotional rejection. With Scorpio Sun in the 1st house, his adult identity was organized around sex and aggressive behavior. He'd grown up into an angry man embroiled in a series of disastrous affairs with married women, obsessed with pornography, and filled with self-loathing. Saturn square his natal Sun asked him to recognize that this is who he had become. Scorpio represents our natural urge for emotional and sexual intimacy. But when these needs are thwarted, Scorpio can be expressed as aggression, hostility, or rage.

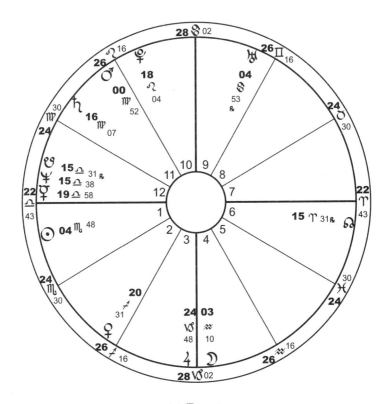

14. Dennis

The person may attack as a form of protection against an underlying insecurity.[86] Dennis tended to become enraged with himself,
turning inward the aggression that had been directed toward him
by his father. Dennis also became hostile when he felt someone
had slighted or insulted him, failing to treat him with respect. His
sensitivity to slights reflected a narcissistic wound—a wound to the
Sun, to his sense of being special and loveable. With Mars conjunct
Saturn in Virgo, Dennis had a critical, perfectionistic streak that
manifested as condescending, abusive behavior toward women; no
woman was ever good enough for him. This mirrored the way he'd
been constantly criticized by his father.

Dennis's Mercury-Neptune conjunction in Libra near his
Ascendant manifested as unrealistic, inflated (Neptune) perceptions of himself. He had grandiose fantasies of becoming a famous

writer, alternating with feelings of worthlessness and a realization that he'd never adequately developed his intellect. As a youth beset by poor self-esteem and conflicted family relationships, he refused to do any schoolwork. He dropped out of high school and had never written a paper, used a typewriter or computer, or developed any work habits or basic Mercury skills. He was articulate and could recite poems beautifully (Mercury-Neptune) from memory; but he was unable to write even a brief business letter because he was paralyzed with fear and anxiety by such tasks. He couldn't organize his thoughts to get any work done. His fantasies of greatness were shattered by the realization that he was a chronic procrastinator and had accomplished very little in his life. He'd never mastered the tasks of the stage Erik Erikson called "industry versus inferiority," when children become industrious and develop a sense of competence by learning skills, completing projects, and overcoming fears of failure. Dennis may have also suffered from attention deficit disorder.[87]

After Saturn moved away from his Moon, transiting Uranus and Neptune squared his Mercury-Neptune, and Dennis began to undergo a spiritual awakening. He became interested in poetry, mythology, and religion, went to a monastery for a retreat, discovered the mystical writings of Thomas Merton, and had an experience of the presence of God (Uranus-Neptune square natal Neptune). This surge of spiritual awareness occurred at the same time as he was assimilating insights about his mother's sadness, family incest, his problems in school, and how all of this had affected his self-esteem. This example illustrates what I mean by multi-level initiation and how astrology helps us understand transformations occurring on many levels simultaneously.

Astrology provides insights about the timing and rhythms of the therapeutic process. When Saturn was conjunct the Moon and square the Sun, core memories emerged, Dennis entered a period of depression and faced disappointments that brought his feelings to the forefront. Dennis was preoccupied with memories from the past (4th house), issues about his mother (Moon), anger (Scorpio Sun) and eventually he recognized how his aggression drove other people away from him.

This intensive period of psychological work reached a turning point when Dennis had this dream: *I'm on my hands and knees potting a cactus plant.* A cactus plant is a prickly plant that can survive in a desert with very little moisture. As he put it, "A cactus finds its juice within its own body." This dream signified living through an arid period of loneliness, and finding purpose and meaning in his own company, in solitude, without being dependent on the excitement of a relationship. Being on his hands and knees signified the discovery of humility. Potting the plant suggested a need for self-care—the ultimate meaning of Saturn conjunct natal Moon. The dream suggested that in a sense Dennis *was* the cactus plant (Scorpio Sun in 1st house). This scorpionic image was a message from his unconscious asking Dennis to come to terms with his prickly, disagreeable personality, and it lent archetypal depth to this moment of self-recognition. This example also illustrates how using astrology and dreams together can be a potent combination.

## Countertransference in Therapeutic Astrology

Therapy always unfolds within an "intersubjective field." A therapist is never entirely neutral and objective, able to perceive the client with unclouded eyes. Through our countertransference, we play a role in creating difficulties and misunderstandings in the therapeutic relationship. We may be uncomfortable with some personal characteristic. Maybe we don't like men or women with Mars in Aries. Or we can't stand Capricorns. Or we have an aversion to Geminis, finding their endless chatter shallow and boring, so that we tune them out and stop listening. Maybe some transit we're going through causes us to be impatient, critical, and judgmental. Therapists learn to recognize their countertransference and their own contribution to the intersubjective field.[88]

Self-study and awareness of how a client's chart and personality interact with our own can help us deepen the relationship. Therapeutic astrology is a demanding growth path for the practitioner, for clients face the same issues we ourselves are grappling with and force us to face our own shadows. In working with Dennis, his critical demeanor often triggered my own defensiveness, sensitivity to criticism, and feelings of inadequacy. During periods when he was very depressed, I had to be mindful of my impatient or hostile responses to him. At other times I began to feel sad and hopeless. One day, while transiting Mars was conjunct my natal Pluto I over-reacted to something Dennis said, becoming irritable and prickly. I immediately knew how this was connected to the Mars-Pluto transit, which helped me to acknowledge my anger rather than blaming it on Dennis. Astrotherapists pay attention to personal transits that may affect our work, for example, transits involving Mars that might trigger anger, or transits to the Moon that can elicit strong emotional reactions within us.

Therapeutic astrologers strive to provide clients with useful information, not excessively technical, arcane jargon. We use predictive methods judiciously, remaining mindful of the language we use to describe planetary influences. We discuss the client's chart interactively rather than prognostically, and practice astrology in a way that empowers the person's capacity for decision-making and choice.

## FUTURE PROSPECTS OF THERAPEUTIC ASTROLOGY

In the future, the use of astrology by psychoterapists will become commonplace. Astrology will take its place alongside meditation, yoga, dreamwork, and breathwork as primary tools of psychology and psychotherapy. Therapists will utilize the birth chart to guide others through the labyrinths of transformation, to facilitate the emergence of liberated men and women, unfolding all of their capacities. In therapeutic astrology we work to free the personality from obstructions and to refine its expression. We address all the major issues: sex, love, and money, work, and family. Living in synchrony with the orderly movement of the planets, we're skillfully carved by the hands of time. The possibilities of using astrology therapeutically promise many new discoveries in the years to come for those of us engaged in this exciting work.

Chapter 7

# Better than Prozac:
# Astrology and Mental Health

Part of astrology's great value to our society derives from its capacity to promote mental health. Depression and anxiety are problems that have reached epidemic proportions in our society. So many people suffer from depressed mood and anxiety—about the future, the economy, our health and environment. Astrology is a potent antidepressant that can help us manage stress and anxiety, maintain our peace of mind, and cut through the suffering of existence with grace, humor, and awareness of cosmic order. Astrology helps us increase our intelligence in navigating change, by aligning with the cycles of nature. Astrology also teaches us to suffer our suffering consciously so it means something to us.[89] I think as a society we'd need less reliance on antidepressant drugs if we could each find meaning in our challenging circumstances, which is one of the great benefits of astrology.

For optimal mental health we need to activate all the *chakras* and states of consciousness associated with the planets, becoming responsive to the developmental tasks each planet represents. Depression and anxiety often result from misalignment with a task or developmental phase, a failure to adapt to an evolutionary challenge or lesson. To me, the most sensible approach to depression is to embrace our entire existential condition with consciousness, wisdom, and equanimity. The antidepressant effect of astrology stems from the way it helps us succeed in fulfilling various tasks and transforming efficiently, with right timing and a positive evolutionary attitude. To survive in these challenging times we have to be complex, intelligent organisms. We have to be enlightened. Astrology will provide the guidance we need, if we will make the effort. The astrological prescription for peak mental health is to realize our total potential by getting in alignment with our natal chart patterns and current transits.

In this chapter, I'll describe more examples of how I use astrology in my psychotherapy practice as part of a holistic approach to the treatment of depression. I'll discuss how each planet influences and supports our psychological health and wellbeing, our development as conscious human beings. We'll consider the relationship between planetary archetypes and cycles and the stages of growth described by developmental psychologists. We'll look at the meaning of planets in the light of various theories of human development, for example Jean Piaget's theory of cognitive development, John Bowlby's attachment theory, and Erik Erikson's lifespan development model. We'll explore how each planet represents a distinctive way of being and specific types of developmental tasks, each necessary to maturation of the personality.

## DEVELOPMENT AND PERSONALITY

Psychologists believe that each person exhibits a set of enduring characteristics known as *personality*. The course of development is influenced by personality traits such as our degree of passivity or activity, introversion or extraversion, dominance or submissiveness, trust or suspicion. The most influential personality model is called Five Factor Theory, which emphasizes five traits: extraversion, neuroticism, openness, agreeableness, and conscientiousness. Research has shown that, regardless of age, gender, or cultural background, people's personality traits fall into patterns around these five personality structures:

- *Neuroticism*: anxiety, angry hostility, depression, impulsivity, self-consciousness, vulnerability.
- *Extraversion*: sociability, interpersonal involvement, warmth, gregariousness, assertiveness, activity, excitement-seeking, positive emotions.
- *Openness*: inquiring intellect, openness to experience and ideas, considering alternatives (it's the opposite of rigidity); fantasy, aesthetics, feelings, actions.
- *Agreeableness*: Trust, straightforwardness, altruism, compliance, modesty.
- *Conscientiousness*: Competence, order, dutifulness, achievement striving, self-discipline, deliberation.

These personality factors are generally stable in adulthood and become increasingly stable with age. Personality changes predictably with age: Conscientiousness, emotional stability and social dominance (a component of extraversion) tend to increase with age, especially in early adulthood. Openness and social vitality (also a component of extraversion) increase in adolescence, then decrease in old age. Ideally, in the course of adulthood we become more agreeable, conscientious, emotionally stable, and socially dominant—and less neurotic. Personality traits define our uniqueness and shape our development in three areas: cultivating relationships; striving and achieving; and maintaining and promoting health. Neuroticism and agreeableness are strong predictors of relationship outcomes. The higher a person is in neuroticism and the lower they are in agreeableness the more likely he or she is to be in conflicted, unsatisfying, or abusive relationships. People high in neuroticism and low in agreeableness express behaviors that are destructive to relationships, especially criticism, contempt, defensiveness, and stonewalling.[90] Traits that make up the factor of conscientiousness (competence, order, dutifulness, self-discipline) are predictors of achievement, occupational attainment, and job performance. These are important traits for completing work effectively, paying attention, striving toward high standards, inhibiting impulsive thoughts and behaviors. People high in conscientiousness are singled out for jobs and promotions. People who aren't conscientious leave demanding, high achievement jobs, because they lack the self-discipline. Recall our earlier discussion of the Gifts of Saturn.

Many personality traits correspond to particular planets. Angry hostility correlates with Mars and Pluto, as in the examples of Brad and Tricia (Chapter 5), and as we'll see in the example of Jason later in this chapter. Impulsivity correlates with Mars. Vulnerability is a trait associated with Neptune; we can be overly vulnerable and sensitive, as we saw in the examples of Hillary, Ann, and Phyllis in Chapter 5. I believe that several planets contribute to openness: Neptune, Uranus, Venus, and Mercury. Saturn correlates with conscientiousness. Extraversion can be correlated with Sun, Jupiter, and Mars. I correlate agreeableness with Venus, Moon, and Neptune. When our relationships are healthier, our minds and hearts are more open. It's a healthier way of being. This all stems from learning to be more agreeable, and less hostile and neurotic.

For example, once I was traveling in Alaska with a group while transiting Mars in Aries was in my 7th house. I started getting angry because other people were making all the decisions about activities. I felt disempowered and that made me grouchy and argumentative. But as I thought about the Mars transit, I realized that it was okay to let other people lead and show initiative. Astrology helped me develop the emotional maturity to defer to the wishes of others without resentment. Being agreeable helped me enjoy my vacation even though I wasn't getting my way. Therapeutic astrology helps us develop a well-rounded personality, by recognizing neurotic traits and cultivating healthier personality traits and behaviors.

The concept of "personality" suggests that the self possesses fixed, enduring characteristics. The astrology of personality suggests a process-oriented view of personality as fluid and ever-changing, and constantly evolving. Personality describes the recurring attitudinal and behavioral patterns that we develop in response to circumstances, which are always changing.

In the astrological study of human development, we assume that human beings grow and change, that we aren't static and fixed. We need to remember this, for many astrologers hold the view that the birth chart depicts traits that are permanently imprinted on us. The birth chart does indicate enduring facets of character, but we can learn to express natal planets in healthier ways as we evolve over time. (See "Evolving our Expression of the Planets" in Chapter 2). Therapeutic astrology is a path to change by enhancing our strengths and recognizing our weaknesses. The impetus for development stems from transits, which represent environmental challenges and opportunities, as well as psychological growth processes. Progressions of the birth chart also show how the imprinted structure of personality symbolized by the birth chart unfolds over time. We'll study this in Chapter 11.

## NATURE, NURTURE, AND THE BIRTH CHART

A perennial question is whether our behaviors and personalities are
determined by innate characteristics or environmental influences.
How much is our growth due to *nature* (maturation), and how
much is it due to *nurture* (learning)? Proponents of behaviorism and
social learning theory view external influences as the major deter-
minants of personality and behavior. Evidence for social learning is
found in the way people's behavior and attitudes can be molded by
conditioning, persuasion, or coercion. Theories of innate psychological traits contend that development is a process of unfolding
characteristics that are latent in the organism. Arguments for innate
personality types include studies suggesting that babies show early
signs of particularity of identity.

Persuasive evidence comes from studies of identical twins separated at birth and raised apart in completely different environments,
which show that as adults the twins seem to be remarkably similar
in appearance, posture, personal habits and preferences. Most psychologists adopt the *interactionist* view that behavior results from
interaction of innate personality with environmental conditions.
Innate, hereditary factors join together with environmental influences to shape our constantly evolving personality.[91] From this perspective, maturation of innate traits and learning of acquired behaviors occur together.

Astrology supports this interactionist view: The birth chart
depicts the interplay of personality and environment. Astrologers
make the claim that what develops over time are latent potentials
that are symbolized by planetary positions at the birth moment.
Our innate capacities mature by learning and by confronting various situations, symbolized by transits. But even if faced with adverse
early conditions, our innate qualities (shown by the birth chart) can
still unfold. Each person develops distinctively both because of our
varied environments and because of our innate potentials. That's
why people with diverse birth charts respond differently to transits.
One person crumbles under the pressures of Mars or Uranus, while
another person responds to the same planet very well.

For example, each of us reacts differently to Saturn transits, such as Saturn's first quarter square at age 21–22, depending on our personality traits and natal chart emphasis. Tim, a young man with natal Sun in Capricorn conjunct Saturn in the 2nd house, was very mature at age 22 and took a full time job at a bank. He was disciplined and conscientious. Reba, an aspiring artist with Sun conjunct Uranus in the 5th house, had difficulty adjusting to the responsibilities of young adulthood during her Saturn square. She couldn't hold a job for more than a month or two. She'd get restless; she had to get out of there. Age 21–22 is simultaneously Saturn's third quarter square to natal Saturn, and the first quarter square of Uranus to natal Uranus. Reba's path was to be much more independent, to live a bohemian life with changeable places, people, and activities. Her life was a constant experiment, but it was hardly stable.

Tim, with his natal emphasis on Saturn and Capricorn, had difficulties a few years later when transiting Uranus was conjunct his Sun. He felt restless with his job, became defiant and got in trouble with his boss several times. But since he hadn't yet evolved an individualized identity, he couldn't envision any viable alternatives to remaining employed at the bank. His lack of openness caused him to suffer from depression while Uranus was conjunct natal Sun-Saturn. Reba, a more Uranian person by nature, thrived during a similar transit (Uranus square Sun), feeling free to create her art and to express her true self. Her innate openness to new experiences was a helpful adaptive trait. The Saturn-dominated person may be rigid and very attached to security and can find the changes demanded by Uranus to be frightening. Astrology supports the view that just as learning and environment clearly affect development, so do innate personality traits.

Our personality makeup determines how we meet developmental tasks and stages. People with a strong Aries or Mars emphasis in their natal charts meet challenges related to intimacy and closeness differently than those whose charts emphasize Venus or the sign of Libra. People with many planets in Libra may be strong in relationship skills and agreeableness, but weaker in self-assertiveness. Astrology contains many implicit insights about personality types. Therapeutic astrology is the art of discerning personality type, strengths, and conflicts.

The ten planets serve as symbols of personality development. Each planet contributes something unique to the evolution of consciousness. Each planet is an archetype, a pathway to transformation and positive mental health. Unfolding each archetype is the antidote to the depression and anxiety of existence.

## Sun: Psychology of the Self

The first key to mental health is to know who we are, to realize and radiate our identity. The most basic astrological description of personality comes from understanding the Sun's signs, each with their characteristic psychology and evolutionary goals. Sun is the central archetype of astrology, the symbol of our evolving sense of self and identity. From early in life, our inborn inner light gradually evolves into a self-concept, a defined sense of our central characteristics, talents, and priorities. Sun symbolizes our desire to be seen, known, and validated as a special, wonderful, talented person. At the very least we want to be treated with respect and dignity. Sun represents this normal, *healthy narcissism*. In childhood we depend on parents and caregivers to provide attentive *mirroring* of our solar identities, which reassures us that we're seen and cherished. This function of supportive reflection from others is signified by the Moon, which symbolizes fulfillment or frustration of our emotional needs.

A primary developmental task is to consciously express the qualities symbolized by our natal Sun. Our Sun sign describes the root energy that we naturally emanate, while Sun's house position describes the area of life in which we try to actualize our essential identity, where we seek to radiate the true light of our individuality. With Sun in the 2nd house: through earning, physical comfort, and acquisitions; Sun in the 11th house: through involvement in groups, organizations, or social activism; in the 9th house: through intellectual pursuits and travel; in the 4th house: through an evolved home, family, and emotional life; in the 7th house: through friendship, love, and marriage; the person's life and identity revolves around relationships with others.

A woman with Sun in the 11ᵗʰ house is a sociologist who studies labor unions and populist social movements.

A man with Sun in the 2ⁿᵈ house is focused on accumulating wealth and achieving financial stability. Another man, with Sun in Taurus (money) in the 1ˢᵗ house (identity), enjoys the security and material comfort that his executive salary affords him.

A woman born in 1904, with Sun in Aquarius in the 11ᵗʰ house, was involved in progressive politics from the 1920s until her death in 1995. This example shows a planet strengthened by its placement in the house corresponding to the Sun Sign—that is, her 11ᵗʰ house Sun is placed in the 11ᵗʰ sign, Aquarius. I consider this one of the most important planetary dignities.

A man with Sun in the 12ᵗʰ house in Virgo spends much time in solitude (12ᵗʰ house) working (Virgo) at home and devoted to disciplined (Virgo) Buddhist meditation practice (12ᵗʰ house).

A man with Aquarius Sun in the 4ᵗʰ house, quincunx Uranus in the 11ᵗʰ house, left his native India to live in the United States. For many years he has resided in an unusual, collectively run household (Aquarius Sun, 4ᵗʰ house). With Sun in the 4ᵗʰ house of domestic arts, he's a talented gourmet cook.

A woman with Sun conjunct Pluto in her 9ᵗʰ house underwent an awakening of religious faith (9ᵗʰ house) as a result of a near-death experience (Pluto).

A man with Sun in Taurus in his 4ᵗʰ house is devoted to gardening and home improvements, and he purchases real estate.

A man with Sun conjunct Venus in Taurus in his 10ᵗʰ house is a professional sculptor (Venus) who has received public recognition (10ᵗʰ house) and financial rewards (Taurus) for his work.

Brigit (discussed in Chapter 5), with Sun in Sagittarius, pursued her dream of traveling abroad and living the life of an adventurer.

For each individual, mental health is maintained by being true to who we are, living our identity with consciousness and radiance. Everything begins with the Sun. Sun represents positive self-esteem, self-respect and self-regard. We need to know who we are, but also to receive some degree of validation, to feel seen for who we are, and to express our essential dignity of being. Beya, a woman with low self-esteem, had a dream while transiting Saturn was conjunct her Sun: *A queen was in her grandmother's garden.* The dream reminded Beya how her grandmother had a humble job as a "sandwich lady" who pushed a lunch cart through an office building. The queen reminded her of dignity, importance, self-respect, not accepting second best, having only the best in life. It reminded her that she was the first woman in her family to go to college and graduate school. The dream invited Beya to move into the world with pride in herself and pride in all the hardworking women who had made possible her own opportunities for advancement. She realized that her grandmother would be so proud of what she was doing with her education and career goals.

## The Sun King or Queen:
### Alchemical Transformations of the Self

To gain a deeper appreciation of the Sun as a developmental path, I find it helpful to refer to the archetypal symbolism of alchemy. An intriguing area of C. G. Jung's research was his study of alchemy, that branch of the esoteric wisdom in which transformations of physical matter serve as metaphors for stages of psychological transformation. Many alchemists were also astrologers, including Dr. Jung. And I believe that conscious astrologers can become modern-day alchemists. Here I'm going to sketch out some speculative ideas about the relationship between astrology, alchemy, and the psychology of the evolving self, focusing on the symbol of the Sun. For just as alchemists sought to transform base metals into gold, the goal of astrologers is to become a Sun, a conscious center.

In my work I focus on helping the client develop a cohesive sense of self, to evolve the Sun. I don't believe in premature attempts to transcend the ego. We have to individuate, to unfold the self. Heinz Kohut's psychoanalytic theory of Self Psychology is useful for understanding solar psychology.[92] According to Kohut, we develop a cohesive self by receiving from our lunar caregivers and attachment figures (mother, father, friend, lover) the nutrient of *mirroring*, which makes us feel seen, validated, and special. A parent affirms a child through responsiveness and acknowledgement of the child's thoughts, feelings, and personhood. Mirroring affirms us, builds self-esteem, and gives us confidence to express our talents and emanate solar warmth and radiance. It enables us to develop healthy narcissism, a sunny feeling of being lovable and special, a bright star. In contrast, if we're starved of mirroring and validation, we become depressed, empty, deflated. The example of Dennis in Chapter 6 illustrates this. When Saturn squared his Sun, Dennis realized he didn't have positive memories of being mirrored, affirmed, or loved by his parents. The frustration of these natural needs led to rage, rebelliousness, depression, and low levels of achievement in school and career. All of this stemmed from injuries or delays in developing a cohesive solar identity.

The inner emptiness of the unmirrored self becomes the root cause of many symptomatic behaviors, such as addictions, and compulsive gambling, stealing, eating, or risk-taking, all of which can be understood as attempts to energize a depleted sense of self. In Chapter 2, I noted the example of George, whose sexually compulsive behavior intensified while transiting Pluto was square natal Mars (Chart 10). At that time, transiting Mars and Saturn were conjunct his Cancer Sun in the 7th house. His boyfriend Jack had been drinking too much and flirting with other men at parties, causing George to feel depressed, wounded, and undesirable. He felt neglected, unappreciated, insulted, devalued, narcissistically injured. These feelings contributed to his desire to have unsafe sex with strangers. Transiting Mars and Saturn conjunct his Cancer Sun stirred a fiery desire and emotional neediness, which expressed an underlying evolutionary urge to share emotional comfort and nurturance (Cancer).

If our solar narcissism is wounded, we may develop an unhealthy sense of *entitlement*, and a constant need for attention or to be seen as special. These are negative expressions of the Sun: excessive pride, self-importance, grandiosity. George convinced himself he was entitled to have secretive encounters because he was insulted that Jack wasn't paying sufficient attention to him.

Sun signifies our healthy strivings to be seen, to externalize our individuality, according to the Sun's house, sign, and aspects. By identifying the potentials suggested by our Sun's placement, we can affirm and reinvigorate the self. A man named Tim had Sun-

Mercury-Venus in Leo in his 3$^{rd}$ house. Tim wrote a self-published book, but had a lot of wounded pride about his unrecognized talents as a writer. While transiting Neptune opposed his Sun, Tim dreamed about the movie star Denzel Washington. Celebrities represent the solar principle of radiance and successfully expressing and externalizing one's identity. Denzel reminded Tim of his desire for recognition. The Sun also signifies *self-validation*, enjoying who we are. Tim's dream of being a famous writer hasn't been fulfilled, but he still has lots of fun with his writing, and he invests himself in this work because it gives him enjoyment to do so. The Sun is what lights us up. We find fulfillment and take pride in achieving our personal goals. That is the way of the Sun. Sun symbolizes pride in myself, in what I create, in what I am—joy in being myself.

The Sun is related to the royal archetype of the King or Queen, representing the fullness of identity and individuality. We saw this earlier in Beya's dream about a Queen. King and Queen were central symbols in medieval alchemical texts, whose pictorial images often depicted the King and Queen in various conditions to portray stages in the evolution of the self. Now I'm going to relate the unfolding of the solar self to a series of alchemical operations, symbolized by Sun's aspects to various planets. In some alchemical images, a King and Queen meet, embrace, and make love. This corresponds to the symbolism of Sun-Moon, the union of conscious and unconscious, masculine and feminine, active and receptive consciousness. This union of the King and Queen also relates to the aspects of Sun-Venus, signifying attraction and relatedness of the self. We're stirred by the Beloved, experiencing pleasure, connectedness, and mutual responsiveness. We treat ourselves and each other with respect and honor.

Sometimes the King is portrayed majestically seated on his throne, which I relate to Sun-Jupiter symbolism. Under Sun-Jupiter contacts (by natal aspect, transit, or progression) we emanate warmth, generosity, pride in self, and a hopeful outlook, and find opportunities for positive projection of the self into the world. Once, when transiting Jupiter opposed my Sun, I dreamed that the actor Jack Nicholson walked up to me, gave me a fantastic smile, and shook my hand. To me, Jack Nicholson represents positive self-

*A Wolf Devours the King.* Michael Maier, *Atalanta Fugiens,* 1618

esteem and capacity to relate well to others. This dream encounter awakened a sense of my own capacity for warmth, relatedness, and successful extraversion.

Other alchemical pictures portray the old King, who symbolizes the dominant, ruling attitude of consciousness. In one of these pictures, a ravenous wolf devours the old King. Edward Edinger comments, "the ego has been devoured by hungry desirousness. The wolf in turn is fed to the fire. But wolf=desire and desire=fire. Thus desirousness consumes itself."[93]

In the background of this picture the king is portrayed being reborn from the fire, suggesting that passion and desire resurrect the King. At times we're transformed by rousing our fiery Mars drives and motivation. This image depicts the alchemical *calcinatio*, in which a substance is heated until reduced to ashes. Interpreted psychologically, *calcinatio* refers to burning up and consuming fiery emotions, desires, and urges for power. *Calcinatio* generally occurs during transits or progressions involving Mars. Think of George grappling with fiery horses of desire while Pluto squared natal

*Drowning King.* M. Maier, *Atalanta Fugiens,* Oppenheim, 1618

Mars. Later in this chapter I'll discuss an example of a man whose Sun-Mars conjunction brought fiery rage and a serious anger management problem.

At other times, the solar self is transformed through water. In alchemical images, the King is often portrayed as drowning, or bathing in a pool of water with a white dove hovering over his head. Edward Edinger interprets the dove as a messenger of the transpersonal Self, which guides us and provides a spiritual impetus to action. In the New Testament the dove heralds the Annunciation of the Holy Ghost, a descent of peace, guidance, and blessing, a moment of divine intervention and disclosure. The white dove is also a symbol of the Greek goddess Aphrodite, mother of all desires, and thus represents the kindling of "an ardent desire."[94] According to Edinger, individuation is set off by an ardent desire, which is also an annunciation of the Holy Spirit, "the assignment of a difficult task," which becomes an opus, a project impelled by something greater than the ego.[95] We awaken to a larger sense of our life purpose.

*The King's Bath: Extraction of the White Dove.*
Trismosin, *Splendor Solis*, 1582

The picture of the King in the Bath from the *Splendor Solis* portrays the moment of spiritual realization. When we quiet ourselves in any moment of meditation, prayer, or quiet contemplation, when we yield and inwardly surrender, we experience a current of light, a descent of the supramental consciousness, or feel a mysterious guiding presence. In this image, a kneeling man with a bellows stokes a fire underneath the water of the king's bath, representing the fiery *tapasya*, the effort and exertion that heats up the process of soaking

and dissolving ego boundaries and imperious attitudes. This fan-
ning of the flames reminds me that the Mars element is always
present to some degree, insofar as I need to constantly exercise my
will, channel and refocus my anger and energy, and strive to increase
my emotional aliveness. The kneeling man also signifies an attitude
of humility. Cultivating the right balance of intention, awakened
vitality, and deep oceanic stillness, we encounter the invisible guru,
the pleroma, the divine splendor. The Sufis call this *pir*, the angel
Khidr, the spirit of guidance.[96]

The drowning and bathing motif in alchemy refer to the *solutio*,
the alchemical bath, the melting down of base metals, which I relate
to Neptune, especially Sun-Neptune aspects. Under these contacts
we experience watery initiations, spiritual baptism and purification,
an immersion in the unconscious through dreams and fantasy, or
illumination in a state of faith, openness, and receptivity. We experience confusing meltdowns, grandiose fantasies, or receive spiritual
blessings, or all of these at the same time. When Neptune was conjunct my natal Sun I was living in the woods surrounded by beautiful trees, birds, and raccoons. It was a period of intensive meditation
and creativity as I spent an entire year crafting my book, *The Nine
Stages of Spiritual Apprenticeship*, an idealistic, spiritual book about
initiation and discipleship under the guidance of spiritual teachers.
Gripped by the idea that I was writing a very important work, I
may have gotten carried away in my expectations, printed far too
many copies, and lost a good deal of money. I experienced the Neptunian alchemical bath, full of visions and grace. I also "took a bath"
financially. During Neptune-Sun transits or progressions we may
experience some inflation or grandiosity, some unrealistic attitudes
and self-delusions. A touch of inflation isn't always a bad thing as
it is a normal part of the creative process to fill up with energy and
enthusiasm.[97] We feel inspiration and a sense of connection to the
spirit in body, mind, and action. I wouldn't trade the experience I
had completing that book for anything. I'd stay up all night writing
and meditating while a family of four raccoons sat on a tree branch
outside my window keeping me company, watching me working
at my desk. It was a magical time of mysticism and reflection. I'd
go outside under the silver moon and midnight sky and hear owls

gently hooting and felt healed and illumined. There was a flow of blessing from nature and from within my own being as I experienced a living meditation that flowed into creative expression. I fulfilled what I felt to be an inner mandate and stretched myself to evolve a deeper spiritual understanding. Under Neptune-Sun contacts we can awaken inner psychic faculties, have inspiring visions, and dream big dreams. Regardless of the outcome, we can be at peace knowing we're offering ourselves as instruments for a task, a work. And that's the moment when the white dove comes.

After the bath we need to find solid ground. In another image from the *Splendor Solis* the drowning old King calls out for help to his son, the young King, who stands on land. The old King appears to be drowning in the background, but he is reborn as the regal Young King, who is crowned and robed, representing the ennobling and validation of our identity and self-worth. According to Edinger "the old ruling principle, which has undergone *solutio*, is calling out to be coagulated again in a new, regenerated form."[98] The *coagulatio* stage of alchemy refers to the solidification of liquids and vapors into material form, and represents coming into form in a specific place and time, becoming fully embodied, grounded, and practical. I relate this process to Sun-Saturn aspects, which denote building self-esteem through work, self-discipline, determination, gaining credentials or seniority.

My next example is a 27-year-old man named Ted. I had previously done consultations for Ted's father, Neil, who had Sun-Venus in Taurus, made a fortune in tech stocks, and retired at age 50. His son Ted dropped out of college at 19 and went into technology sales, expecting to become a tycoon like his father. Ted had Sun-Mercury-Mars in Capricorn, and Saturn conjunct Moon in Leo in the 2nd house: He was focused on career, ambitions, money, and material success. Early in Ted's career the sky was the limit, his earnings soared in 2000 when Jupiter and Saturn in Taurus were conjunct natal Jupiter in the 11th house. The industry (11th house) he worked in was very profitable; life was abundant and full. But by 2004 the wheel of time had turned. Ted's progressed Full Moon in Leo was exactly conjunct natal and progressed Saturn. His progressed Sun and Moon both aspected Saturn precisely. Although

Ted was working long hours, his earnings that year were one third of his former income. He was learning tough Saturnian lessons, facing limits, and focusing on survival and bare essentials, rather than a life of luxury. This was the reality he had to come to grips with now. Two years earlier, when solar arc Saturn was conjunct his IC, Ted bought a house, so he was responsible for a monthly mortgage payment. He longed to travel and enjoy the good life. But he had to keep working, to sustain the life he'd created. Ted was experiencing the alchemical *coagulatio*, coming into form in a particular location, in the new contracted economy of Silicon Valley.

Under progressed Full Moon conjunct Saturn, Ted realized he must work to survive. His chart suggested that even if for the time being his lifestyle was modest, he could find fulfillment through friendships and relationships (Sun-Mercury-Mars in the 7th house). Ted wanted to get married (Sun in the 7th house) and have children (Moon-Saturn in Leo). The progressed Full Moon conjunct Saturn awakened in him the archetype of the Father. I asked him to view his current challenges as tests forging a strong character that would enable him to endure all adversities and sustain a family. Astrology enables us to transform a difficult, painful situation into one that's felt to be meaningful, purposeful, and even necessary.

Ted had natal Sun in Capricorn square Pluto in Libra. While transiting Saturn in Cancer opposed natal Sun and squared Pluto, Ted experienced challenges to his sense of specialness or entitlement. A part of him believed that earning a lot of money would be easy. Meanwhile, some of his better-educated friends (Capricorn planets in the 7th house) were advancing professionally and earning more money. He felt sad and humbled by this. During transits or progressions involving the symbolism of Sun-Pluto, we often experience defeats of the ego, narcissistic injuries, challenges that wound our sense of specialness and greatness.

Astrology helped Ted meet these challenges with maturity, and unfold his potential. Soon after his progressed Full Moon, Ted became engaged and then was married. Saturn, activated by his progressed Full Moon, is dispositor of Sun-Mercury-Mars in Capricorn in the 7th house of marriage. During his Saturn return, Ted established a career in a financial services field (Moon-Saturn in 2nd house), started earning money, and had children within two years. Astrology was helpful to Ted, because it showed him that even though he was experiencing a painful period, Saturn's transit to his Sun was a meaningful phase of defining his identity and objectives as a professional (Capricorn) and husband (7th house). Transits and progressions to the Sun are crucial stages in the development of a defined identity and confident self-expression.

## Moon: Seeking a Secure Base

The Moon is a key factor in mental health, representing our feelings and emotional life, our capacities for empathy, caring, self-sooth-ing, and nurturing of self and others. The Moon is the symbol of emotional maturation, experiencing a full spectrum of emotions: fear, anger, sadness, surprise, disgust, embarrassment, empathy, envy, bliss, joy, exultation. Certain lunar conditions manifest as "flat affect," being expressionless, unfeeling or extremely detached, or insensitive to the feelings of others. Stressful natal aspects to the Moon are often seen in the charts of people who have suffered emotional trauma or deprivation and feel depressed, insecure, or distressed. Transits to the Moon are opportunities to attend to these emotional wounds.

The Moon symbolizes the mother, a figure of enormous impor-tance for everyone. We look to the natal Moon to understand the emotional connection between mother (or the primary caretaker) and child, and the kind of "holding environment" she provided for the child.[99] By internalizing the mother's soothing, comforting, nur-turing presence, a child gains a feeling of trust, safety, and security. John Bowlby calls this the *secure base*, an internal feeling of emo-tional safety and satisfaction. D. W. Winnicott taught that compe-tent parents or caregivers provide an "average expectable environ-ment," a physical and emotional climate that's reasonably attentive to the child's needs, while also providing inevitable frustrations of some of the child's desires. The Moon's placement in the birth chart can alert us to the possibility of disturbances in the mother-infant bond, such as a neglectful, smothering, or harshly punitive relationship. Our goal in examining this relationship isn't to blame the mother for all of the child's problems; nor is the actual person of the mother always accurately described by the child's natal Moon position or aspects. What's described is our subjective experience of relating with mother, which results in a feeling of emotional security or insecurity.

## LUNAR ASPECTS

Moon's natal aspects inform us about the mothering we experienced in childhood, and our prevailing emotional state in adulthood. A person whose Moon is strongly aspected to Mercury may be nervous, high strung, highly communicative and talkative, and these qualities may have been evident in the relationship with the primary caretaker. Moon-Venus aspects signify a nurturing, satisfying relationship with mother, and a serene, loving, joyous emotional essence; emotional needs are well satisfied and one's affectionate feelings are expressed with calm demeanor and through tender physical touch. A person with harmonious aspects of Moon and Mars can be courageous, daring, energetic, and enterprising, but one whose Moon aspects Mars by conjunction, square, opposition, or quincunx is often emotionally excitable, reactive, irritable, or volatile. The mood is a little testy. There can be a heated or irritable emotional connection between parent and child, between self and other. With Moon-Mars aspects we express our needs actively, or express anger because basic emotional needs aren't being met. Moon-Mars aspects are a spontaneous expression of feelings and needs.

Moon-Jupiter aspects denote a patient, encouraging mother, or our own kind, nurturing feelings. This aspect promotes a positive, optimistic emotional demeanor. Moon-Jupiter aspects can also represent exaggerated emotional responses and voracious emotional needs. People with Moon in aspect to Saturn often need to feel responsible and productive, and they're often very serious, hard working, and highly competent. The person with a Moon-Saturn hard aspect may have experienced maternal care as stern, restrictive, or rejecting, and sometimes these aspects are linked to sadness or depressed moods in adulthood. With these aspects, we need to learn the art of savoring the sweet sadness of existence. We can even touch feelings that are painful and learn to tolerate them, to integrate our feelings; in these ways Moon-Saturn promotes emotional strength and maturation.

With contacts of Moon-Uranus, mother may be distant, detached, or inconsistent, or a very independent person who nurtured the uniqueness and individuality of her children. Moon-Uranus individuals sometimes are detached from their feelings, or fiercely guard their freedom and independence. Mother may have been a little chilly. When the Moon aspects Neptune, boundaries between mother and child are fused, indicating either mutual devotion of mother and child, or an enmeshed relationship in which the child was encouraged to rescue a parent who was passive, weak, or irresponsible (for example, Phyllis in Chapter 5). When the Moon aspects Pluto, the emotional relationship with mother or other caregivers is usually deep and intense. In some cases, mother may be controlling, spiteful, or intrusive, a domineering presence. With Moon-Pluto aspects we have to feel our emotional agonies and work them through to completion. We feel something deeply, then it's done. Or, we hold onto a feeling and experience a buildup of resentment.

## You and Your Mother: The First Relationship

Study your natal Moon and its aspects. How does your Moon position relate to your earliest experiences of attachment? Did your basic needs get fulfilled? What about now? Do you feel emotionally contented and satisfied, or empty and unsatisfied? Study the relationship between your chart and your mother's chart. Even if you don't know mother's birth time, use her solar chart and place her natal planets on top of your chart. What aspects are formed between your charts? How do her planets interact with yours? We'll cover principles of synastry in Chapter 8.

My natal Sun is conjunct Moon. I'm very close to my mother and she has played an essential role in forming my solar identity. But my Moon is quincunx Pluto and mom has always been a somewhat bossy, controlling person. Moon is also square Neptune; for years she was a heavy drinker. My Moon is opposite Uranus, and

I experienced my mother as chilly, standoffish, and uncomfortable with physical affection. In her natal chart, a Neptune-south node conjunction in the 12th house signifies her excessive alcohol intake, and Sun conjunct Pluto indicates a powerful, dominating personality.

My mother has Sun-Pluto conjunction in Cancer and Mars in Virgo conjunct the Ascendant. She is tough, aggressive, willful, controlling (Sun-Pluto), and highly critical (Mars in Virgo). She is one determined individual. With Venus conjunct Saturn, she's not very demonstrative of affection. But her marriage lasted 57 years (Venus-Saturn: long-term love). With Mars in Virgo, she's obsessed with neatness. This has been a source of problems for me since I have natal Sun in the 4th house square Neptune, and I used to be quite messy around the house. I've improved our relationship by learning to adapt to her chart. When I'm around her I try to be very neat. I pick up my clothes and put them away. When I cook in her kitchen I clean up surfaces and wash the dishes *before* I sit down to eat, because she's so obsessed with cleanliness that she becomes distressed by any clutter, even if it's only for a few minutes. Quite honestly, it's less stressful for me to accommodate her needs than to hold on to my need to be laid back and sloppy. Now make your own honest assessment of your relationship with your mother.

## THE MOON, OBJECT RELATIONS, AND PATTERNS OF ATTACHMENT

I view the Moon as the symbol of our earliest experiences of attachment with mother or primary caregivers. In the language of psychoanalytic *object relations* theory, Moon symbolizes the quality of our early "object relationships"—the experience of caregivers (and other people in general) as either warm, responsive, nurturing, comforting, and gratifying, or as cold, unresponsive, hostile, and rejecting. Moon represents the quality of the early "holding environment" we experienced, the extent to which needs were fulfilled or frustrated. This becomes a template for future interpersonal attachment and relationships.

My work is influenced by John Bowlby's Attachment Theory.[100] I view the Moon's aspects in terms of secure or insecure attachment style in childhood and adulthood. Attachment refers to the fact that one of our earliest instinctual needs is to be securely held and comforted, and to maintain proximity to caregivers. These basic needs, when thwarted, become the source of enduring emotional distress. Natal aspects of the Moon to Sun, Venus, and Jupiter generally show a secure attachment with a reliable mother or caregiver, which is reflected in a feeling of safety and well-being. Stressful lunar aspects to Mars can show an irritable or volatile mother-infant bond. Moon-Pluto aspects often show the conflicted patterns of what Bowlby called *insecure-ambivalent attachment* with its alternating cycles of intense hostility and desperate clinging to others. This can manifest in stormy, tumultuous relationships in which one is often flooded with rage. In contrast, Moon-Uranus aspects can denote *insecure-avoidant attachment* with its characteristic coolness, aloofness, and unavailability. Avoidant, counter-dependent behavior is used to preserve a tenuous attachment because we fear our needs, or our attempts to achieve greater closeness, will drive away the attachment figure. This can make it difficult to form or maintain emotional attachments to others. Moon-Neptune aspects can manifest as feelings of merger or fusion with mother or caregiver, a poorly attuned caregiver who is oblivious to the child's needs; or the child may feel compelled to rescue the mother or caregiver. In adulthood these patterns of attachment are reenacted as characteristic styles of relating to others.

## The Moon and Emotional Maturation

Transits or progressions to the natal Moon stir up memories and emotions. We become more conscious of our feelings and needs. The Moon is a key to our mental health because it depicts our mood and our longing for fulfillment of our basic needs for comfort, food, holding, and emotional attachment. Transits to the Moon evoke feelings, sensitivity, moodiness, and charged memories. During Saturn-Moon transits, our mood is often serious or sad; we might even suffer from *dysthymia*, a chronic depressed mood that makes it hard to enjoy daily life. Uranus-Moon transits awaken a restless urge for change and freedom, and breaking out of ruts. Neptune transits to the Moon evoke feelings of helplessness, confusion, uncertainty, or self-pity, or of empathy and compassion. Pluto transits to the Moon are an emotional catharsis and release, dredging up painful feelings, resentments, or desire for emotional closure and completion. During most transits to the Moon, we encounter some difficult emotions, face issues about food, and become aware of whether or not our basic needs are being satisfied.

A woman named Terra had transiting Saturn square Moon in Gemini. She suffered from dysthymia, a chronic, low-grade depression that made it hard to enjoy daily living. She lived alone, and was eating nothing but junk food. She was unhappy about her job where she had numerous unspoken grievances that she suffered silently. Therapy revealed that her depressed mood was rooted in early life experience: Her mother became ill after giving birth, and Terra and her mother were separated for over a month. They never really bonded. Her natal Pluto and north node were conjunct her ascendant, the point of birth. The crisis surrounding her birth instilled in her an unconscious guilt, a belief that she shouldn't have been born, that she'd caused her mother's suffering. The Pluto-Ascendant symbolism was very helpful in focusing her awareness of this core belief. Also, she'd lost touch with her children after a bitter divorce and had lost her maternal role. She never fully recovered from this. Now she wasn't eating well or taking care of herself. She was living out of boxes in a dirty, cluttered apartment. Transiting Saturn in Virgo square Moon portrayed a series of tasks to transform her emotional reality. She came to therapy and did some intensive inner work, focusing on lunar tasks. She cleaned her apartment. She learned about nutrition, eliminated junk food and coffee, started cooking more nourishing meals, and learned to be a better mother to herself. Astrology supported her mental health by clarifying her feelings, and presenting definite tasks of development: emotional reconciliation, healing the mother wound, and learning self-care.

Memories, feelings, and insecurities stimulated during transits to the Moon will center around matters connected with the Moon's house position—for example, friendships and relationships if Moon is in the 7th; career and professional responsibilities if Moon is in the 10th; a desire for travel or learning if Moon is placed in the 9th;

political concerns and involvements with groups or political organizations with Moon in the 11ᵗʰ house.

Some years ago transiting Saturn was conjunct my natal Moon.
This transit is often associated with periods of sadness, depressed
mood, regrets about the past, or problems related to the mother.
While some of that did come to pass, this transit was one of the most
important periods of emotional growth for me. Externally, this was
a demanding year of professional development. I have Cancer on
the Midheaven, thus Moon rules my profession as a counselor and
emotional support person. My work as a psychotherapist demanded
a lot of emotional maturation and ongoing training. Being a man of
feelings didn't always come easily to me. I'm a somewhat intellectu-
ally-centered person and a bit cool, detached, and impersonal. My
natal Moon opposes Uranus. During Saturn's transit to my Moon
I was presented with some painful lessons about my tendency to
be emotionally distant and remote. As Saturn fine-tuned my lunar
nature, I developed a new capacity to welcome, and be with, other
people's feelings. Developing greater concern, empathy, and sensitivity toward others, and becoming a nurturing container for their
feelings, was a major step forward for me.

The Moon represents personal memories and rules our emotional complexes. Transiting Saturn conjunct my Moon triggered
many feelings associated with family since my natal Moon is in the
4ᵗʰ house. I became aware that I needed to resolve some issues with
my parents, both of whom retired during this period. Our family
relationships grew warmer, more accepting and supportive.

While Saturn was conjunct my Moon (which rules the stomach), I had problems with food and digestion, both governed by
the Moon. I mysteriously lost the ability to cook, and everything
I prepared tasted like sawdust. Food became less appealing and
I often debated whether or not to eat. I was also bothered by a
mild ulcer, and recognized that my digestion was being disturbed
by unexpressed emotions. I saw that my problems with food and
cooking stemmed from a desire for someone to take care of me, and
resentment that no one would do so. I became aware of my needy,
childish side. I didn't feel taken care of by my girfriend and was
grumpy because I felt she didn't nurture me sufficiently. I realized

that I needed to stop waiting for someone else to be my mother. As Saturn neared its final conjunction to Moon, I knew I faced a choice—to continue being moody and resentful, or to nurture and feed myself.

When Saturn turned direct and approached my natal Moon for the third time I was very emotional for several days, crying, feeling sad and afraid. I was like a cranky, whiny child. On the day when Saturn was conjunct natal Moon for the final time, I found myself calmly witnessing my emotions. I realized that *I am not my emotions.* I was reminded of the sage Ramana Maharshi, who taught meditative self-inquiry in which we inquire, Who am I?, recognizing that the Self (our true identity) is not the body, thoughts, or emotions. The Self is pure consciousness, silent witness of feelings, thoughts, and sensory perceptions. I felt myself settling into the witness consciousness and a condition of tranquility, fullness, and spaciousness. I felt emotionally centered. I wasn't trying to control or repress my emotions, but I became inwardly steady and serene, less affected by fluctuating moods. I felt compassion for myself and began talking to myself lovingly. I discovered that I had an "internal mother" who could soothe and reassure me.

Transits to the natal Moon are processes of emotional transformation, opportunities to process feelings and memories, to identify our needs. These are times to reorganize our core emotional structures, to find our secure base, our sources of comfort, times to care for the home and create a nurturing environment in which to grow. People in the states of upheaval that lead them to seek counseling often are experiencing significant transits or progressions to the natal Moon. We work with the Moon to enhance our emotional health. We saw this in the examples of Ben in Chapter 2, and Dennis in Chapter 6.

## MERCURY: DEPLOYING ATTENTION EFFECTIVELY

Now we turn to a completely different archetypal pattern of transformation, a different way of being that shifts us from *feeling* to *thinking.* Mercury is important to mental health in the sense that we need adequate stimulation, learning, a chance to formulate and express our ideas and opinions.

Wayne, a man with Sun-Mercury in Gemini conjunct his Gemini Ascendant, was bored to tears at work and was drowning his depression in beer. Transiting Uranus in Pisces and Saturn in Virgo were squaring natal Sun-Mercury. Wayne's depressed mood lifted when he took a writing workshop and began reading fiction and carrying around a notebook and sitting in cafes writing descriptions of people and places. He changed his whole mindset and developed new interests. Absorbing the ray of Saturn, Wayne started to get more focused on his writing, and stopped binge drinking. I'll return to Wayne later in this chapter.

Mercury symbolizes learning, thinking, communicating, and formulating opinions and ideas. Its natal placement indicates an area of life that occupies our thoughts and where our attention is often focused. A woman with Mercury conjunct Saturn in the 2nd house manages her company's $17 million yearly budget and is constantly weighing options for personal finances and investments. A man with Mercury in the 4th house thinks about his family all the time. A woman with Mercury in her 1st house is a professional speaker and writer who often speaks and writes about herself (1st house). A man with Mercury conjunct Uranus in his 11th house is a computer scientist and journalist who writes incisive commentaries on politics and social issues.

Mercury's sign placement shows our mental attitude and way of thinking. For example, Mercury in Taurus is pragmatic, down to earth, and unhurried, thinks about how things work, and thinks about money, while Mercury in Sagittarius meets the world in lofty conceptual, philosophical terms, measuring experience against beliefs and ideals. Mercury in Libra weighs its ideas and opinions against the views of others, and thinks about relationships. Mercury in Scorpio is probing, searching for hidden facts and secret motivations. Placed in Capricorn, Mercury organizes ideas for achievement and success.

Mercury is the planetary symbol of cognitive development, as described by Piaget, who studied how we develop progressively more advanced forms of thinking.[101] During early childhood we form categories of objects and phenomena. We try to fit new experiences into existing categories or mental constructs through a process Piaget calls *assimilation*. When assimilation is no longer effective—when there's too much disconfirming evidence to support our present perceptions of an object, person, or situation—we must suspend our mental schemas and reshape them. Piaget called the process of changing our perceptions of the world *accommodation*. Through accommodation, we shift and adjust our mental constructs to better match reality and to perceive the world more accurately. Transits to Mercury challenge us to accommodate, to change our perceptions. Saturn transits to Mercury require accommodation to reality, becoming more sensible and organized in our thinking. Uranus transits to natal Mercury stir innovative thinking, and unexpected, inventive ideas.

Stressful aspects of Mercury (especially to Saturn, Uranus, and Neptune) are sometimes seen in the charts of people who suffered from learning disorders, speech pathologies, attention deficit disorder, or other problems in cognitive development. A woman with Mercury conjunct Uranus was severely dyslexic as a child and had problems with speech, grammar, writing, and mathematics. As an adult she made significant progress in overcoming these problems, especially when transiting Saturn opposed natal Mercury-Uranus. She also began to read new genres of literature such as books about political science (Uranus). This was a fascinating period of learning for her.

A woman named Lenore, with Mercury in Pisces in the 5th house, was diagnosed as autistic as a child and institutionalized for several months; but it turned out she wasn't really autistic. She grew up to become a talented poetess. She wasn't a highly intellectual person, yet her mind was clear and serene and her voice was hypnotic (Pisces), which enhanced the public's reception of her poetry readings (5th house Mercury). Many of her poetic images emerged in dreams or during quiet meditation, when her mind was free of agitation and rational thought. These are beautiful expressions of Mercury in Pisces.

While astrology isn't a treatment for learning and speech disorders, its perspectives can sometimes help us view a learning problem in a different light. The parents of an adolescent consulted me about their son, Jeremy, who was diagnosed with attention deficit hyperactivity disorder (ADHD). Jeremy had natal Mercury and Sun in

Gemini (Mercury's sign) quincunx Uranus in Scorpio and opposite Neptune in Sagittarius. He had a very active fantasy life (Neptune) and a talent for science and computers (Uranus). His mind was quick and restless, and he had difficulty adapting to the slow pace of the classroom and traditional instruction. When transiting Pluto was conjunct natal Uranus and quincunx Mercury, and transiting Saturn was square natal Mercury, Jeremy began to act strangely in school—defiantly disregarding rules and refusing to do his homework, which bored him. His doctor wanted to prescribe Ritalin, a drug commonly used in cases of ADHD, which can have side effects such as rashes, chest pain, headache, dizziness, and loss of appetite. I asked his parents if they'd consider looking for a school that provided a non-conventional (Uranus) learning environment and accelerated curriculum. They found such a school and Jeremy thrived there, without need for medication.

## Piaget's Stages of Cognition

Piaget's stages of cognitive development can be viewed astrologically as the process of activating the spectral potentials of Mercury. In the *sensorimotor stage*, a child is aware only of immediate sensations, experimenting with objects and observing how they react to his or her actions. At the end of the first year the child attains *object permanence*, the realization that a hidden object still exists even though it's not visible or immediately present. The child develops a rudimentary ability to imagine or predict the results of actions. During the *preoperational stage* (from 18 to 24 months to 7 years), thinking becomes conceptual and symbolic. A child acquires mental images, concepts, and words and learns to talk and think about objects and events. The child learns that words are symbols that make it possible to talk and think about absent objects or persons, or about past or future events. The child is egocentric, incapable of imagining how things look from another perspective. But a gradual *decentration* of perspective occurs as the child learns to view the world from the perspective of others. Ages seven to twelve are the stage of *concrete operations*. More competent thought develops, including counting, classifying, and reversing procedures mentally.

The child learns that external events have causes outside himself and is better able to imagine how things look from another perspective, how others think and feel.

From an astrological perspective, maturation involves numerous decentrations of awareness as each planetary function awakens. For example, Venus makes us aware of the presence of others—their beauty, their values. Our relationships constantly ask us to overcome our egocentrism; we'll spell this out in Chapter 8. Jupiter awakens us to the broader sphere of philosophy, morality, or religious doctrines. Saturn makes us aware of social institutions and the need to adapt to them. Mercury's function is to learn to think and perceive multi-perspectivally.

During adolescence, Piaget says, we're in the stage of *formal operations*. We learn to think about abstract relationships such as ratio and probability, to comprehend algebra, to engage in scientific thought, to formulate hypotheses, devise theories and examine possibilities, probabilities, and improbabilities, and reflect on the future, justice, and values.

## JUPITER AND MORAL REASONING

Cognition (Mercury) becomes more advanced and sophisticated as we develop conceptual knowledge through education and assimilation of our culture's values (Jupiter). Jupiter, the planet of philosophy, truth, theory, intellectual growth, and cultivation of a broadened worldview, is associated with the capacity to think abstractly, which is central to the evolution of moral reasoning. Lawrence Kohlberg contended that moral intelligence evolves through six stages, with two preconventional stages reflecting the egocentric attitudes of children, two conventional stages reflecting internalization of cultural norms and role expectations, and two postconventional stages with more advanced conceptualization of moral problems.[102]

- Stage One is *naive moral realism*: we determine what is right or wrong by following rules and avoiding punishment. This is also known as obedience and punishment orientation (*How can I avoid punishment?*).

- Stage Two is *pragmatic moralism*: action is based on the desire to maximize our own reward or benefit, and to minimize any negative consequences to ourselves. This is the stage of self-interest orientation (*What's in it for me?*).
- Stage Three is *socially shared moralism*: we base moral decisions on anticipation of what other people would think, and whether they would approve or disapprove. This stage of morality emphasizes interpersonal accord and conformity (*The good boy/ good girl attitude*).
- Stage Four is *social system morality*: actions are based on a sense of duty and fear of formal dishonor, not just disapproval. This is known as the authority and social-order maintaining orientation (*Law and order morality*).
- Stage Five is a phase of *human rights and social welfare morality* or rational morality: we base our moral decisions on the values and rights that we believe ought to exist in a moral society. This is a social contract orientation (*How would this accord with or violate the universal social contract?*).
- Stage Six is universal morality and ethical principles: our actions and choices are determined by values such as equity, fairness, and concern about maintaining our personal moral convictions, even if it involves breaking the rules. At this stage moral decisions are based on universal ethical principles (*Principled conscience*).

To understand Jupiter as a symbol of these stages of moral development, let's consider the example of Ruth, a woman in her early sixties, with natal Jupiter and Mars in Virgo conjunct the Ascendant, squaring her Sun in Gemini. Ruth sought counseling because she was having trouble accepting her daughter's values and lifestyle. Ruth was a devout Catholic who closely followed the moral doctrines of the Church. She felt that God would punish her daughter, Ann, for not attending church, drifting away from the faith, and "living in sin" with her boyfriend out of wedlock. She was concerned about what her friends and neighbors would think and say. They were all members of the same congregation, and in their small town gossip traveled quickly and mercilessly. Ruth warned Ann of the disapproval and scorn to which they'd both be subjected unless Ann changed her ways, returned to the Church, and married her boyfriend. Ruth especially feared that if Ann became pregnant she might even be excommunicated. In Ruth's mind, Ann's relationship was bad because others would disapprove or because she might be punished for it.

During a year when transiting Saturn opposed natal Jupiter, Ruth underwent a transformation of her moral sensibilities. First, she began to listen to Ann's reasons for not wanting to get married at that time. She decided that if Ann and her boyfriend loved each other, wanted to live together, but didn't want to legally formalize their union that was their business, and that the Church should keep its nose out of their private lives. This was the first time she'd ever questioned Church doctrine. She also became interested in a progressive movement within Christianity known as liberation theology, in which religious doctrines support struggles of political liberation. Ruth became a fighter (Mars) for social justice (Jupiter) and human rights, actively lobbying for reform within her Church. Ruth's Sun, which squared Jupiter and Mars natally, ruled her 11th house of political awareness and activism. This story illustrates a movement toward more mature, individualized moral principles as Ruth became more broadly educated and informed.

Jupiter contributes to our mental health because it symbolizes our desire for expansion, growth, new goals, and a more cultured, educated perspective. The lack of opportunity for growth and learning can contribute to depression and hopelessness. A woman with Jupiter in her 9th house (education) opposite the Sun went back to school in her mid thirties after transiting Uranus squared natal Jupiter. She became keenly interested in philosophy, law, and ethics. She also traveled outside the United States for the first time, which expanded her perspective.

Natal and transiting aspects between Mercury and Jupiter are significators of education and learning. Jupiter lends conceptual, philosophical, intellectual depth to Mercury's thinking and search for information. Piaget's theory implies that abstract, rational, logical thinking (formal operations) is the most advanced stage of cognitive development. However, there are many post-formal modes of thinking—including imagistic, extrasensory, intuitive, and mystical forms of perception—which are likely to develop when outer planets influence Mercury. Uranus aspects to Mercury awaken the spirit of discovery, originality, and innovation in ideas. Neptune's aspects to Mercury awaken imaginative thinking, poetic writing, interest in metaphysics, symbols, myths, and religion. Attunement between Mercury and Uranus, Neptune, and Pluto leads us to stages of mental development far beyond those described by Piaget. Some of the better-known post-formal forms of cognition include:

- *Crystallized Intelligence*: Knowledge dependent on education and experience; the set of skills and bits of knowledge we learn growing up in a given culture; verbal comprehension and vocabulary; the ability to reason about real-life problems; technical skills learned for a job and practical skills (balancing a checkbook, making change, finding items in the grocery story).
- *Fluid Intelligence*: the ability to form concepts, reason abstractly, and apply material to new situations; drawing inferences, analogies, solving problems, understanding relationships between concepts; abilities required for adaptation to new situations, for which prior education or learning provides little advantage.
- *Existential Intelligence*: intuition, thinking about ultimate matters and philosophy.
- *Naturalistic Intelligence*: understanding of nature, and biophilia, a love of nature, an organismic resonance with nature.
- *Dialectical Thinking*: For every viewpoint there's an opposing viewpoint and these two can be considered simultaneously.
- *Visualization*: which can be used in healing through imagery, and in performance rehearsal.
- *Nondual, Mystical Cognition*: transpersonal or superconscient awareness as described by Buddhism, yoga psychology and parapsychology.
- *Mythic-Archetypal Intelligence:* taught by Jung, Joseph Campbell, James Hillman, and in my book, *Dreamwork and Self-Healing*.

In the course of life we're constantly engaged in acquiring and exercising these various forms of intelligence, especially during transits involving Mercury. Evolving ever-more complex thinking is a key to mental and emotional health.

## The Cycle of Mercury

To maintain spiritual and mental health, we need to keep learning and evolving our minds to make productive use of our time, and to make progress with projects requiring attention and thinking, such as studying and writing papers, reports, or other creative writing, and to counteract boredom. We can improve our mental acuity and clarity by coordinating our activities with the transit cycle of Mercury. While many astrologers know how the Moon's cycle defines the rhythms of life, very few recognize the importance of Mercury's cycle.

Mercury governs thinking, speaking, communicating, writing, decision-making, and information-gathering. Through conscious attunement to Mercury, we function efficiently, recognize when to focus on reading, writing, and research projects, and when it's best to patiently wait for new ideas, insights, and solutions to emerge—periods of what I call *diffuse awareness*. The Mercury cycle helps us plan activities requiring focused thinking, especially involving writing or thinking. Knowledge of the Mercury cycle can help us to overcome writer's block or difficulties with studies and work more efficiently.

I'd like to dispel the commonly held but fallacious notion that periods when Mercury is retrograde are "bad" or "difficult" and that no decisions should be made at such times. The main problem I experience during Mercury retrograde is a tendency to lose things! I believe Mercury's retrograde periods can be productive periods of thinking and rethinking. We increase our mental acuity and efficiency by living in accordance with all phases of Mercury's cycle, including its retrograde periods.

I've found that Mercury operates in four major modes, which I call investigative, discriminative, illuminative, and diffuse intelligence. These four modes of mental activity correspond to the zodiac signs Gemini, Virgo (the two signs in which Mercury is at home), Sagittarius, and Pisces (the signs opposite Mercury's domicile).

- *Investigative Intelligence* (corresponding to Gemini) is concerned with data-gathering and getting the information necessary to answer a question.
- *Illuminative Intelligence* (corresponding to Sagittarius) is concerned with discovering meaning in the information gathered, and elucidating a theory, concept, or belief.
- *Discriminative Intelligence* (corresponding to Virgo) analyzes this solution or concept and tests its adequacy with discernment and precision.
- *Diffuse Intelligence* (corresponding to Pisces) is mental activity in which we go beyond concepts, theories, and critical thinking, and allow our minds to be unfocused and undirected, accessing intuition, fantasy, and imagination.

Regardless of which zodiacal sign it is passing through, Mercury continually alternates between these four modes of functioning during the different phases of its relationship to the Sun (as observed from Earth).

The cycle of the Sun and Mercury repeats several times per year. The most important phases of the cycle occur when Mercury is conjunct the Sun or when it changes direction—turning stationary retrograde or stationary direct. Traditionally, periods when Mercury was conjunct the Sun were considered inauspicious since Mercury was said to be combust the Sun, its powers of thinking and reasoning occluded and diminished by its proximity to the Sun. While it's true that at these times life can be extremely hectic and speedy, this is also a time to make creative breakthroughs in thinking.

Mercury can be in two kinds of conjunction with the Sun—the "inferior conjunction," occurring while Mercury is retrograde, and the "superior conjunction," which occurs when Mercury is direct in motion. Open up your ephemeris and look for the next time Mercury goes retrograde. Then, find the days when Mercury and the Sun occupy the same degree; this is the inferior conjunction.

From the time when Mercury, while still direct in motion, slows down in the sky and turns retrograde, some unresolved issue or problem begins to occupy our attention. This can be viewed as the symbolic "12$^{th}$ house" or ending phase of the previous Sun-

Mercury cycle. During the days after Mercury turns retrograde, we begin searching for a solution to this problem. As Mercury turns retrograde, life seems busier, and one often feels more worry and tension. Know that a solution or clarification will emerge at the right moment. Now is the time to think about the issue, research it, gather new information, reading, and make provisional notes. At this stage, don't try to organize your thoughts into a coherent or definitive decision, statement, or piece of writing. Simply try to get things moving and get the ideas flowing. This is the period of *reflective intelligence* or thinking. For students or writers, this is the time to read, take notes, and jot down ideas, not to try to create a finished project.

At the time of the Sun–Mercury inferior conjunction, our minds become clearer and full of ideas. I call this the period of *illuminative* intelligence, because this is when flashes of insight or new solutions to problems emerge into consciousness. It's the symbolic New Moon of a new Sun–Mercury cycle. We can contain the intensity of this period by focusing on mercurial tasks: thinking, writing, taking care of the small details of life, gathering information, and trying to shape our ideas into a clearer, more lustrous form. At this period, I find that I can write, think, and communicate more clearly and efficiently than at any other time.

The sign and house placement of the Sun–Mercury inferior conjunction indicates the area of life requiring attention and the kind of thinking or writing or communication style that would be most appropriate now. During a Sun–Mercury conjunction in the 4th house, it's time to put more energy into decisions affecting your housing, domestic environment, garden, or communication with your family. In the 9th house, Sun–Mercury seeks expression through intellectual activity, a search for truth and meaning through study or travel. A Sun-Mercury conjunction in the 3rd house is a time for reading, writing, driving, or being on the road and going on short excursions, going from place to place. With the conjunction in the 10th house, professional demands require focus and new insight.

At the inferior conjunction, mental powers are at their peak. It's common to be incredibly busy and preoccupied with our own affairs. This is because Mercury's influence is so strong at this time that all of our "mental circuits" feel highly active. However, this isn't to say that everything will be resolved or completed at this time. The period between the inferior Sun–Mercury conjunction and Mercury's turning stationary direct is a time for re-evaluating, reconsidering, and reviewing all decisions or lines of thinking or analysis that emerged at the inferior conjunction. I call this the period of *discriminative* intelligence, because now we can edit, revise, and reshape our work into a structure that's appropriate for the task at hand. This is the time to bring a piece of writing, research, or a decision to a conclusion and to shape it into its clearest form of expression.

When Mercury catches up with the Sun again and makes the superior conjunction, the Sun–Mercury cycle reaches its symbolic Full Moon phase. Now, one presumably sees the results of the new way of thinking or the decision reached during the inferior conjunction. However, new questions, problems, and decisions will inevitably emerge when Mercury turns retrograde again and a new cycle of mental activity begins. Attention to the cycle of Mercury assists us in learning, thinking, refining opinions, and expressing our ideas. This process never ceases. As Mercury transits through the sky, there's always something new and interesting to learn.

## MERCURY AND COGNITIVE THERAPY

To achieve mental health we need to examine and reorganize unhealthy patterns of thinking. Cognitive therapy is a process of examining our thoughts to understand unhealthy patterns of cognition, such as overgeneralizing, catastrophizing, or erroneous perceptions. Malu, a depressed woman who had transiting Saturn in Virgo square her Mercury in Gemini, arrived early in the morning for a doctor's appointment and saw her doctor in the parking lot. He didn't say hello to her. She went into a tailspin of hopeless thoughts, thinking to herself "He doesn't like me, nobody likes me. No one would ever want to be close to me. I'm so horrible. . . ." I said, "Is it possible that you don't know why he didn't say hello. He might have just been in a really bad traffic jam and be all frazzled. He might have had an argument with his wife on his cell phone while in the car. He might be bracing himself to see a lot of clients scheduled back to back all day. He might have a splitting headache. So you don't really know if he didn't speak to you for one of those reasons, instead of all those things you believe." I told her I had recently seen a bumper sticker that read, "Don't believe everything you think!" Examining Malu's negative thoughts and self-limiting beliefs was a basis for improved mental health.

## Venus and Mars: The Rhythms and Vitality of Relationships

Venus is another key to mental health, because it represents our need for social fulfillment, good company, good music, art, and beauty. If our relationships aren't working, astrology can help us figure out how to make them work better. One man learned to relate to his ex-wife better when transiting Uranus squared his natal Venus in the 8th house. He started to speak and relate to her more openly about their financial obligations and agreements.

Venus, planet of love, symbolizes how we interact, what kinds of people we find attractive, how we relate to others, the quality of love we express and receive in relationships. Natal Venus' placement and early transits to Venus help us understand childhood issues related to learning to play with other children. Studying transits involving Venus during adolescence helps us understand how we adapted to the social challenges that teenagers experience. For example, one man had difficulties at ages fourteen and fifteen when transiting Saturn opposed his natal Venus-Saturn conjunction. He was socially awkward and preoccupied with his clothes, hair, and physical appearance. He recalled an experience of rejection and romantic disappointment, but also an affectionate relationship that led to several months of dating. Significant natal aspects or transits involving Venus focus attention on our social life and relationships.

John, a 54-year-old man, was experiencing hopelessness and despair about love. He feared it would never happen, that he'd never find someone to love. He told me a dream: *I'm living in an apartment with a married couple, and my room is a little cubbyhole in the wall overlooking their room.* This dream portrayed John's isolation. He was living as a voyeur, witnessing other people match up and

form couples while he remained alone. John had natal Venus at 17°
Leo and Mars also in Leo. As soon as Pluto reached 2° Capricorn (135° from Venus) he started dating for the first time in many
years. Astrology helped give John a vision of what was possible. His
Venus-Mars in Leo portrayed him as a passionate, creative, demonstrative, loving person. It showed that learning to express his love
in a relationship was an essential task of his development. What
made him depressed was hopelessness. Astrology gave him hope. It
gave him a picture of his essence, the true self, the man he always
believed he could be. Discovering that person in therapy was the
start of a new period of life for him. John didn't immediately find
his true love, but he did start dating consistently, and for John this
was significant progress. Astrology counteracts depression by giving
us courage and clarity about tasks, even those that are difficult for
us. It provides an image of potential outcomes to give us faith in our
ability to grow and develop.

Many people who seek guidance from astrologers have pressing
questions about their relationships. Will they ever find a partner?
Should they trade in their sweetheart for someone new? Why does
the person they once loved seem so intolerable now? Sometimes
relationships are our joyous refuge, and at other times a difficult
entanglement. We complain about our parents, lovers, or children,
and often feel they must have been sent to us by mistake. But there's
an evolutionary intelligence at work within our relationships that
can be discerned astrologically.

Some people use astrology to bolster their fantasies of finding
an ideal relationship or the perfect lover. We give up on partners
with whom our composite charts don't seem propitious, or with
whom we share problematic inter-chart aspects. One man told me
that he dumped his girlfriend because they had "incompatible Sun
signs." We find it difficult to live with someone passing through
the emotional crisis and catharsis of transiting Pluto conjunct the
natal Moon. Surely this hysterical person couldn't be our soul mate!
Astrology teaches us how our relationships reflect and manifest the
archetypal energies of the planets. It helps us understand, and value,
our relationships.

A woman named Shanti had Neptune in Scorpio on the Ascendant, opposite Sun-Venus in Taurus in the 7th house. She was a very spiritual lady but she kept getting involved with men who were materialistic and weren't interested in spirituality. She expressed doubt about whether her current boyfriend could be "the one" because he wasn't interested in meditating with her. She was very depressed about this and said the same scenario had repeated in her past several relationships, all of which she had broken off. I told Shanti that her Taurus planets in the 7th house seemed to indicate that her evolutionary path was to form a relationship with someone whose attitude is more concrete, focused on the material, financial, and sensual realms—a grounded, steady guy capable of relaxed sensuous enjoyment and contentment in the present time. She needed this to balance out her etheric nature and lofty spirituality, with all of its longing and disillusionment with the material realm (Taurus Sun opposite Neptune). This simple statement allowed Shanti to take a breath, relax, and inwardly accept this relationship, to realize that it could actually nurture her and help her develop her own Taurean potentials.

Astrology illuminates the complexity of relationships, the maturity and patience they require. It assists us in working through difficult facets of our relationships. It helps us know when to come together, when to hold together through tough times, when to travel different paths. It helps single people understand when they're more likely to meet someone new, or when it's best to keep a low profile and attend to other concerns.

A woman named Cammie was in a depressed mood, discouraged about her prospects of finding a partner. She had natal Venus and Mars in Gemini in the 8th house and Aries Sun in the 7th house. I told her there was a stronger likelihood she'd become involved in a relationship in early 2005 (about one year in the future), when transiting Uranus in Pisces squared Venus-Mars, and when the transiting north node would be conjunct her Sun in the 7th house. Also, transiting Saturn would square her 7th house Sun, activating Cammie's potential to unfold herself through relationship. Here the prediction was made in general terms, emphasizing possibilities and hope. It came to pass exactly this way.

The degree of our fulfillment or frustration in the domain of romantic love affects our mental health, so this is certainly a realm where the wisdom of astrology can benefit our well-being. The evolution of the social, Venusian self is closely connected with Mars, symbol of our vital-instinctual energy. In childhood, Mars energy is usually sublimated into motor development, physical education, and competitive pursuits, whereas in adolescence Mars begins to be expressed sexually. Significant focus on Mars in the birth chart can indicate that sexuality is a focal point of our personal growth.[103]

Natal aspects of Venus and Mars are especially important. When aspecting Venus, Mars ignites Venus's sociability and the person is often outgoing, popular, and able to attract friends and romantic partners. Mars intensifies Venus's warmth, thus the blending of these two energies manifests as affection and passion. Venus-Mars aspects provide the needed chemistry for romantic love. Occasionally, if natal Venus and Mars are in a square, quincunx or opposition, a person may experience conflict between friendship and sexual intimacy. One could be sexually attracted to someone who is only interested in friendship; or sexual drives might overpower the capacity to form a variety of relationships, some of which aren't sexual.

The transiting conjunctions of Venus and Mars are times of chemical attraction. I met my wife Diana in 1983 during a Venus-Mars conjunction on her Ascendant. Also, transits to a natal Venus-Mars aspect, or to the Venus-Mars midpoint can spark passionate, sexual, and romantic love. Love (Venus) and sex (Mars) converge, generating an enlivening eros. Passionate relationships often occur when transiting planets such as Mars, Jupiter, Uranus, or Pluto form aspects to natal Venus, or contact the Venus-Mars midpoint (especially when these transiting planets turn stationary retrograde or direct). These contacts often time precisely the period when we feel attracted to someone.

It's important to understand that this moment in a relationship always passes, so we need to focus on other areas of life. After the transit to Venus or Mars (or the Venus-Mars midpoint) is over, we might experience some big Saturn transit. Now we (or our beloved) might be preoccupied with career, money, aging, or creating more stability in life. We might be physically or emotionally stressed, focused on vocational tasks, or in the throes of major decisions, and much less interested in sex. The good news is that the passionate feeling periodically comes back. I often counsel people who are depressed and disappointed about their relationships not being passionate or sexual enough. Understanding, accepting, and flowing with the rhythms of nature is essential for our mental health.

Relationships follow cycles, cycles of passion. Couples tend to feel more amorous during transiting aspects of Venus-Mars, Venus-Pluto, Sun-Mars, Mars-Jupiter, or Mars-Uranus, as well as lunar aspects to Venus and Mars. Transiting Mars-Pluto aspects often correspond to intense passions that occasionally spill over into anger or resentments. When such configurations aren't occurring, trying to force sex can feel strained and awkward; it just doesn't flow in a natural, effortless way. Instead of simply abandoning a relationship at this point, we can use astrological knowledge to trust that the tender and amorous moment will arrive again, following the tidal movements of nature. We learn to travel through life with another person allowing our passions to ebb and flow, to come and go like the tides coming in and the tides going out, never being attached to one experience at the expense of another. This single insight can change your life—once you accept that you don't have to feel depressed and resentful during periods when great sex isn't happening. We realize something else is happening, and that's what we need to attend to.

Astrology helps us understand the seasons of relationships and to live through life's changes together with courage, humor, and faith. Partners can gain understanding of what's happening for each them individually by studying their current transits. We allow various aspects of the relationship to evolve. Maybe it's time to put more energy into the garden, cooking, children, practicing yoga, or pursuing separate interests and projects. A key to healthy relationships is to discern how each individual is unfolding, what transits each person is going through, to cooperate with what needs to occur for each person.

Ralph was a twenty-eight-year-old man whose previously gentle and compliant girlfriend, Lauren, now had transiting Pluto conjunct her natal Mars. Lauren was learning to express anger and be less accommodating, even though this made Ralph uncomfortable. Knowing that Lauren needed this awakening helped Ralph celebrate the emergence of her strength and assertiveness, rather than being threatened by it and trying to suppress it.

## Venus-Uranus and Venus-Saturn Aspects

Bruce had a Venus-Uranus conjunction in Gemini. Uranus is the symbol of freedom and experimentation. Uranus aspecting Venus can indicate distancing oneself from others, or an inconsistent way of expressing love, hot and cold. Love and attractions surge suddenly and with great excitement, but don't always endure. Bruce had difficulty sustaining relationships for more than a few weeks. When he met women he emanated aloofness, an air of cool indifference.

Venus-Uranus people need independence and freedom in relationships. People with strong Venus-Saturn aspects seek more structured and steady relationships, with serious commitment. Saturn is a positive planet for relationship if you desire stability, continuity, and trust. One woman complained that transiting Saturn was about to square her natal Venus and wondered if she'd break up with her boyfriend. I suggested that this would be a good time to express to her partner her desire for greater commitment, stability, and permanence in their relationship. I told her that Saturn is the planet of conscious choice. They ended up getting married during that transit.

## Venus-Saturn-Neptune Conjunction

Anna, a woman named with Venus, Saturn, and Neptune conjunct in Libra, told me that her relationships have been the major focus of her life. With Neptune conjunct Venus, she sought perfection in love, and had a romantic ideal that had never been fulfilled. Saturn conjunct Venus symbolized how Anna's romantic illusions were always challenged by the reality of another person. One relationship after another ended in disappointment. She always attracted either stern, rigid, stuck-up men (Saturn types), or dysfunctional, alcoholic, or drug-addicted poets (the Neptunians). Where was her shining prince? Meditating together on this conjunction, we imagined how Anna could experience the healthy sides of both Saturn and Neptune, in one person. She made up her mind that she needed a man of spirit, kindness, and imagination who was also stable and reliable. She warmed up to the idea of commitment in a relationship, and in her next relationship she became more able to tolerate her boyfriend's imperfections—his bad jokes, depressed moods, his confusion and disillusionment. Anna sought to balance her Neptunian idealism with the maturity of Saturn, which teaches us to live with both the limitations and the endearing qualities of real people.

## Sun-Venus Conjunction and Saturn in the 7ᵗʰ House

Peter had Sun-Venus conjunct in Aries, sextile Mars in Gemini in the 1ˢᵗ house, and Saturn in Sagittarius in his 7ᵗʰ house, opposing Mars and trine Venus. Peter's striking good lucks (Sun-Venus) got him lots of attention from women, and in his youth he was very sexually active and promiscuous (1ˢᵗ house Mars). But as he entered adulthood he discovered that his life path involved expressing his Mars energy within the containing structure of stable, long-term relationships (Mars sextile Venus, opposite Saturn in the 7ᵗʰ). At the beginning of his 7ᵗʰ house Saturn return, Peter was seeing a woman but started to panic about her desire for commitment, and he tried to bail out of the relationship. But during Saturn's retrograde conjunction to natal Saturn, Peter learned that she was pregnant. By the third pass of Saturn over natal Saturn they were married, and this marriage has been the center of Peter's life for over two decades.

## Sun-Venus Conjunction and Uranus in the 7ᵗʰ House

Contrast Peter's story with that of Seri, who has a natal Venus-Sun conjunction in Aries, and Uranus in Cancer conjunct her Descendant. Like many people with Sun conjunct Venus, Seri was an attractive, affectionate person. But her 7ᵗʰ house Uranus symbolized turbulence in relationships and fear of being tied down. Some people with Uranus in the 7ᵗʰ house experience discomfort with too much closeness, find it difficult to have conventional relationships, or feel restless and discontented with enduring commitments. Long-term relationships are possible, if their partners give them plenty of freedom, regular time alone, their own room, or the freedom to have other friends.

At birth, Seri's conjunction of Venus-Sun was wide. Now they'd moved by secondary progression into a conjunction lasting seven years; she was currently in the fourth year of this. During a progressed conjunction of Venus-Sun, one is likely to experience an active period of romance, possibly even marriage. However, when assessing transits or progressions we must always refer back to the birth chart; and Seri's Uranus in the 7th suggested the possibility of instability or experimentation in love. Seri told me that during the past four years she'd been married and divorced five times! Because of Uranus's 7th house placement, she didn't want to commit to anyone for very long. Seri was concerned that other people were judging her and that I would judge her too. She knew that she had many unresolved issues about relationships and intimacy, and she felt there was something disturbing about her love life. But she didn't *want* to settle down into a conventional marriage with one person. This was a keenly felt truth of her being.

Several therapists and counselors had attempted to impress upon Seri the importance of Saturnian values of marital commitment, fidelity, and longevity. I approached her situation differently, recognizing that the god Uranus was asking to be honored and appeased through Seri's search for freedom within the relational domain. Something inside her demanded permission to be free, to experience different lovers, without commitment. She continued in this way for several months, until she finally grew tired of this constant experimentation, and decided she was ready for something different. Soon thereafter, she met a brainy scientist with wild, frizzy orange hair, a perfect avatar of Uranus. They evolved an open relationship in which they gave each other freedom to explore connections with other people. They were very happy together with this polyamorous arrangement.

Astrology clarifies what kinds of relationships truly suit us. Seri realized she wasn't a failure because she didn't stay married to anybody. She accepted that she wanted freedom in love, to experience excitement and change and unusual people and connections. Once she accepted this about herself, her experience changed. All of us need to find relationships that are in line with our own birth patterns.

## TRANSITS AND PHASES OF RELATIONSHIPS

Astrology teaches us to move through changing periods and phases of relationships. We can see when transits (for example Mars transits) are likely to trigger little arguments, and thus we can keep these in perspective, rather than allowing them to fan into huge infernos of discord that tear people apart. We learn to avoid overreactions during some brief transit that will be over quickly. And we learn to follow the rhythms of nature and of desire, not trying to generate sexual fireworks at times when the energy simply is not there—during a low-energy waning Moon or some arduous Saturn transit that's occupying us.

Transits to Venus, or through the 7th house, show the quality of our relationships at a given time, the kind of person we relate to, and changes in relationship goals or needs. Mercury passing through the 7th (or contacts Venus) stimulates communication, good conversation, a talk with a friend. With Venus we share some pleasant aesthetic or social experience. When Mars passes through the 7th, we have relationships with assertive, aggressive, demanding people, experience more sexual vitality, or pass through some interpersonal conflicts and frictions. Transiting Jupiter in the 7th denotes an urge for shared learning and adventure. Saturn's transits through the 7th house (or aspects to Venus) brings serious, significant relationships, sometimes with someone older, more established, or interested in commitment; we face relational challenges and tests. When Uranus transits the 7th house we change a relationship, break up, experience a period of more distance and independence, meet new and unusual partners, or explore unconventional partnerships. During Neptune transits we're drawn to spiritually-oriented people, and spiritual, devotional love. During Pluto transits to Venus, or in the 7th house,

our relationships stir erotic passion, obsessive lust, jealousy, possessiveness, or feelings of betrayal.

## THERAPEUTIC ASTROLOGY IN A CASE OF ANGER MANAGEMENT

Mars is another key to mental health because it represents our need
for activity, sexuality, exertion, use of the body, and right expression
of the will. Jason was referred to me for therapy focusing on anger
management. He had an Aries Moon, Sun partile square Pluto, a
Mars-Jupiter conjunction, and a wide conjunction of Sun-Mars.
Jason was an extremely belligerent man who had been in many fist
fights and screaming arguments. He had angry outbursts at work
and couldn't get along with his coworkers. Since childhood he'd gotten into violent fights and angry confrontations. His Aries Moon
seemed to express though poor impulse control and a vehement
temper. He was rude, unyielding, and never backed down from a
fight. Jason also had a tight Saturn-Neptune conjunction in Libra.
His father was an alcoholic, and so was Jason (Saturn-Neptune). He
drank lots of beer and smoked weed incessantly. He avoided taking
responsibility and was in trouble with the IRS and the Department
of Motor Vehicles. His avoidant behavior was a problematic expression of his Saturn-Neptune conjunction. He needed to deal with
his substance abuse issues and stop avoiding reality.

Jason did some significant work in therapy, and was able to change
himself and change his life. For the first time, he was able to speak
to his ex-wife in a civil manner, without being belligerent, and she
responded by writing him a check for $75,000 she owed him. He got
instant feedback that expressing his Mars energy differently could
greatly improve his relationships and his life. He learned to transmute
his negativity and hostility, which stemmed from early trauma and
repeated encounters with violence (Sun square Pluto). He learned
that destructive anger corrodes or destroys our precious human relationships. He was afraid that if he didn't fight he'd be viewed as weak;
his Saturn-Neptune represents this fear of weakness.

Speaking about his fears evoked in Jason a lot of sadness
about his father, who drank to mute his frustration about lack of

economic opportunity. He said, "When I get angry there's a devil in me. I don't know how to confront people without hurting them." Astrology affirmed his strong Mars-Aries-Pluto personality type, the fact that he was, by nature, a fighting spirit. And it showed that the way forward was to transform his aggression and reach a deeper feeling level. Therapy helped him transform his life by changing his behaviors, his demeanor, and his actions.

When there were setbacks, they almost always correlated with transits involving Mars, times during which Jason felt seething resentment and had angry outbursts. For example, during a Mars-Sun conjunction he had an altercation with his ex-wife's new boyfriend. He had to repeat the lesson that childishly acting out his aggression destroyed, rather than strengthened, his web of emotional connections. After this, he took steps to straighten out his legal problems, made amends with several friends and family members, and defused several tense altercations that could have turned into nasty fights. He decreased his neurotic traits of angry hostility and explosiveness, and increased his agreeableness and warmth. There was a palpable and positive change in Jason's character.

## Therapeutic Astrology in a Case of Major Depression

The next example combines the symbolism of Venus and Mars with Neptune, Moon, and Saturn. Walter was a recovering alcoholic and heroin addict who started using drugs when he was 15. His Sun was in Scorpio in the 11th house and Venus-Mars-Neptune were conjunct in Scorpio in the 12th house (Chart 14). With Pisces on the 4th house cusp, and its ruler, Neptune, conjunct Mars, his mother was a prostitute and drug addict who had four children with four different men, all of whom beat her up and abandoned her. There was no father, no man in the household. Mars-Neptune's rulership of his 4th house denoted severe parental neglect and absence. Walter had a natal Moon-Saturn conjunction in Aquarius and suffered from major depression, for which he'd been hospitalized several times, while transiting Neptune was conjunct his Moon-Saturn. He felt sad about his mother's suffering and her difficult life. But mother

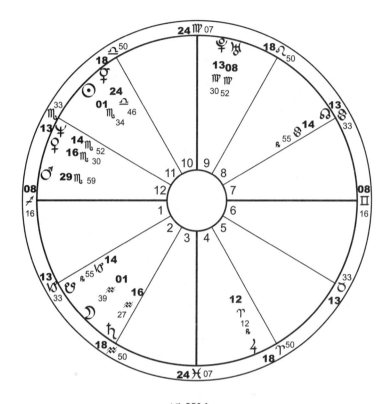

15. Walter

was also a big disappointment to him. He described her as being constantly high on cocaine and speed, neglectful, never nurturing.

Walter's Venus-Mars-Neptune in the 12th house fueled years of out-control, addictive binges and desperate fixes. Mars-Neptune aspects are sometimes seen in cases of addiction and alcoholism, although many people can express the Mars-Neptune desire for ecstasy and expansion of consciousness in less disruptive ways. Typically Walter would retreat with a girlfriend to a hotel room for days of sex, heavy drinking, and heroin stupor. With his 11th house Sun, he spent years doing drugs and drinking with groups of people. He had a strong yearning for an experience of group initiation, belonging, and membership. For a while he was a member of the Hell's

Angels. Now, however, he was finding meaning and comfort in his regular attendance at AA meetings.

With his 5$^{th}$ house Jupiter, and his Venus-Mars-Neptune conjunction, Walter was a warm, affable, and outgoing person, extraverted, and very popular. But with his 12$^{th}$ house planets, he periodically withdrew into solitude, shame, and inner desolation. As soon as a woman became emotionally involved with him and sought to form an attachment, he rejected her, breaking up after buying her some expensive jewelry, to assuage his guilt. Then he'd withdraw into a lonely, depressed, regressed state (12$^{th}$ house) and he wouldn't get out of bed to go to work. His 12$^{th}$ house planets denoted a need for solitude, as well as an unrealized spiritual urge or potential. Something in him was striving toward a deeper interior life. I taught him meditation, dreamwork, and basic astrology. He did his 12 Step program and prayed and contemplated the will of his higher power.

Astrology helps us understand our inner polarities and helps us balance the opposing forces within us, which I consider a key to mental health. Walter learned that he can't always be outgoing and gregarious. He needs solitude and time alone, even within a passionate relationship. But that doesn't mean he has to destroy his relationships whenever he wants to be alone. With natal Pluto conjunct MC, Walter was a successful salesman and business entrepreneur who made a great deal of money. Pluto conjunct MC also described his anger at his absent father, and his self-destructive bent. For him, heroin addiction was an expression of a death wish, a longing for oblivion and the end of pain. With Uranus conjunct his MC, Walter was very independent and rebellious and sometimes didn't show up for work. This caused him major problems when transiting Saturn was conjunct his natal Uranus in Virgo. He stayed home and missed work so many times his boss finally chewed him out and he almost lost his job. This was a sobering moment that marked a turning point, timed precisely by the Saturn-Uranus transit, which showed a tension between work and freedom, between structure and discipline and the urge for change and anti-structure. Walter was forced to change his work habits in a hurry, to save his job. It was a crisis that made him take his work more seriously; he began to do his job more diligently (Saturn in Virgo). He became more conscientious, more punctual and self-disciplined. Astrology was an effective aid in the treatment of Walter's depression.

### SATURN AND URANUS: MATURATION AND FREEDOM

Saturn is one of the most important planetary influences on our mental health and the course of our lives. Saturn is often associated with depression, but this effect is accentuated when a person isn't responding to the developmental challenges Saturn poses. Saturn can also be a source of satisfaction that gives our lives steady focus and stability. Saturn symbolizes maturation, the process of establishing an occupation, settling down, finding a place in society, meeting the requirements of survival in the material world. To understand this process we study the major phases of Saturn's transit cycle, and Saturn's transits to other planets.

Saturnian maturation unfolds in constant counterpoint with the search for personal freedom and individuality, symbolized by Uranus. Wherever Uranus is located (natally or by transit) we experience freedom or an agitation for change, an urge to experiment and innovate, or to be unconventional. The individual attuned to Uranus challenges social norms and conceptions, defying tradition, seeking independence. The interplay between Saturn and Uranus represents the process of balancing our quest for personal authenticity with our acceptance of adult responsibilities.

Saturn also represents fears and inhibitions, and its natal position (by sign, house, and aspects) often indicates areas where we experience problems, failures, and disappointments early in life. For example, a person with Saturn in the 7th house may have experienced problematic relationships. A person with Saturn in the 4th may have struggles with parents or responsibilities to the family. Saturn compels us to confront difficult tasks and situations repeatedly until we master them, developing stability and confidence.

## Saturn and the Father

Saturn is the archetypal father and represents order and discipline, the need to assume responsibility and conform to social standards. Aspects to Saturn often reveal information about a person's relationship with the father. When Saturn forms supportive aspects (such as trine or sextile) to natal planets, the father tends to be a reliable, consistent figure who fortifies the child's sense of capability, confidence, and ambition. Stressful Saturn aspects can signify problems related to the father. For example, with Sun-Saturn hard aspects (such as conjunction, square and opposition) issues with the father can affect our self-confidence or instill a strong impetus to work hard to prove ourselves and demonstrate our competency, seeking to win the father's approval; we may need to overcome shyness, inhibition, or self-doubt. Stressful aspects between Saturn and Mars can represent a tense, discordant relationship with the father. Recall Dennis (Chapter 6) with his Mars-Saturn conjunction. Those Mars-Saturn people who overcome their sense of frustration and anger may develop powerful drives and ambitions and become successful, commanding people, carrying big power, inner authority, and strength of will.

With stressful aspects of Saturn-Neptune, the father may have been absent, weak, unreliable, or a great disappointment. Some people with these aspects struggle to gain confidence in their capacity to cope with the pressures of being in the world.

Lawrence, who was in his forties, suffered from chronic depression and was struggling with issues of material survival. Lawrence had natal Saturn conjunct Neptune in the 6th house in Libra, and natal Sun conjunct Venus. Although he was a gifted, self-taught artist (Sun-Venus, Saturn in Libra), he'd never learned to earn a livelihood through his art and was barely hanging on financially. He enrolled in art school to learn professional skills that would help him find a job (Saturn in 6th). However, the discipline of learning the techniques of his trade brought up insecurities, panic, and a sense of incompetence (Saturn-Neptune). He felt judged by his teachers, who were never satisfied with the quality of his work (6th house Saturn). He took their criticisms particularly hard because they reminded him of the constant berating he received from his father, an alcoholic (Saturn: the father, conjunct Neptune: alcoholism) who abandoned the family when Lawrence was fourteen—when transiting Saturn opposed natal Saturn-Neptune.

With Saturn in his 6th house, Lawrence was obsessed with his failings and shortcomings. As he worked to learn the craft of an artist he tended to fall apart, becoming confused, distraught, and unable to work. Lawrence needed to develop his Saturn function, the toughness that would enable him to contain Neptune's sensitivity. I taught him breathing and body awareness to center himself so he wouldn't fall apart whenever faced with challenge or adversity, so he would feel less fragile. I encouraged him and expressed trust in his capacity to succeed. He practiced positive thinking to override his feelings of weakness and helplessness (Saturn conjunct Neptune). He came to see himself as a beautiful, sensitive man and began to provide inner support to himself with compassion.

## Saturn and Mature Adaptation

We can understand Saturn as a symbol of what George Vaillant calls *mature adaptation*.[104] Vaillant studied various forms of adaptation, the defense mechanisms we use to deal with stress and anxiety. As Freud showed, many of our defenses involve self-deception or distortion of reality: We forget things that make us uncomfortable (repression), or we remember things in a way that's less unpleasant (distortion); we justify doing things we shouldn't do (rationalization); or we project onto others our unacceptable feelings instead of acknowledging them in ourselves. According to Vaillant, some defense mechanisms are more adaptive than others. Inaction, daydreaming, complaining and rejecting help are less effective ways of coping than taking action, expressing initiative, and seeking support and assistance from others. Engaging in denial and disavowal of problems is less than adaptive than facing reality and acknowledging what is happening. Having a distorted, inflated self-image and puffing up in a state of omnipotence is maladaptive, as is a negative distortion of reality where we become excessively self-deprecating and see ourselves as "all bad"; accepting both our strengths and limitations is a mature coping mechanism. Repression—expelling thoughts and wishes from awareness—is less adaptive than consciously acknowledging our thoughts and wishes. And selfishness is considered less adaptive than altruism; helping others is a "high adaptive" level of coping. According to Vaillant, adults' defense mechanisms must mature if they're to cope effectively with the slings and arrows of life and to be successful in life. Many of the maladaptive strategies of distortion and self-deception can be understood astrologically as expressions of Neptune, while adaptive strategies reflect the realistic, pragmatic, and effective consciousness we associate with Saturn. Note how emergence of compassionate altruism reflects a positive integration of Neptune's ray, resolving many of its neurotic and dysfunctional expressions, and contributing to evolution of the personality.

## THE INTERPLAY OF SATURN AND URANUS CYCLES: KEY PHASES OF DEVELOPMENT

Astrology counteracts depression and aids mature adaptation to the extent that we embrace the challenges of Saturn at each major phase of its transit cycle. More than any other planet, Saturn affects our mental health and personality development over time insofar as we reap the results of our self-discipline and conscientious effort. Saturn represents work, striving for achievement, bringing projects to completion, organizing ourselves to attain goals and ambitions. We have opportunities to master these capacities at the pivotal moments of Saturn's transit cycle, many of which dovetail precisely with tasks and phases described by Erik Erikson's theory of lifespan development.[105]

Erikson described how we go through a series of psychological passages at different stages of life. Infancy involves a struggle of *trust versus mistrust*, in which an infant, through receiving the mother's (and father's) loving care, soothing, and protection, develops an enduring sense of trust in the world. In the second year of life, a child is in the stage of *autonomy and shame* or self-doubt, which should result in will power, independence, free choice, and self-control. During play age we experience the stage of *initiative versus guilt*, which ideally results in a sense of purpose and goal-directedness.

During school age (6–10 years) children are in the phase of *industry versus inferiority*, successful resolution of which brings a sense of skill, competency, focus, and productivity. Crucial milestone events usually occur at transiting Saturn's first quarter square (ages 7–8), when school-age children confront limits, learn the consequences of their actions, and face punishment or rewards from parents and teachers.

I have Saturn in the 3rd house (school, speech), and when I was in the second grade my teacher, Mrs. Zilboorg, made me stand in the corner one day as a punishment for talking out of turn. She stopped me in my tracks and made me gain self-control so I wouldn't blurt things out without thinking. Early stresses or failures during this Saturn square (usually in areas of life signified by Saturn's house, sign, and major aspects) may dominate personality development for some time to come, in the form of complexes. Saturn in the 7th house (or aspecting Venus) can result in complexes of rejection and lack of social acceptance. Saturn in the 4th house (or Saturn-Moon aspects) may result in mother complexes. Saturn in the 8th house (or aspecting Pluto) may emerge as complexes related to sex, trauma, or violence. Problems or fears arising at this time need to be addressed during subsequent phases of the Saturn cycle. In some cases they aren't resolved until the Saturn return, or even later.

During the Saturn opposition at ages 14–15, adolescents grapple with *identity versus role confusion*, sorting through attitudes and behavioral prescriptions encouraged by the family and peer group to achieve a defined sense of self, clarifying our central interests and values. We experience tension between our desire to conform to the expectations and attitudes of our family and society and the need to express *non*-conformity by adhering to the values and attitudes of our peer group. This tension is symbolized by the fact that, during the Saturn opposition, transiting Uranus sextiles its birth position. Adolescents strive to define their uniqueness and freedom from social conventions and traditions, and often engage in the rebellious, defiant, and predictably unpredictable behaviors (Uranus) we expect from teenagers. During Saturn's opposition we can achieve a sense of discipline, personal competency, and self-confidence, and we have to make decisions such as whether or not to finish high school, or find a job, or go to college. We apply ourselves with heightened focus to goals such as getting good grades and demonstrating our sense of responsibility. To make matters more complicated, during adolescence Neptune semi-sextiles its birth position and we experience heightened fantasy life (daydreaming), drug and alcohol use, early spiritual awakening, or intense religiosity.

Early adulthood, Erikson says, is the period of *intimacy versus isolation*, the goal of which is to develop loving relationships, friendships, and affiliations. Daniel Levinson called this period the *early adult transition*, which is focused on four tasks: forming a dream (a vision for one's life), developing an occupation, pursuing mentor relationships, and forming a marriage or secure emotional union.

At ages 21–22 we simultaneously experience major phases in the cycles of Saturn and Uranus. Saturn reaches its third quarter (waning) square while Uranus reaches its waxing square to its natal position. This is a period of creating an initial, provisional adult life-structure, living within the structures imposed by jobs, relationships, and new responsibilities. Due to the transit of Uranus square Uranus, people strive at this time to achieve emancipation (Uranus) from parental control and to find their own life paths, which may not conform to the expectations of parents and society (Saturn). We strive to fit in, adapt, and survive in the world (Saturn) while evolving our individuality and uniqueness (Uranus). This is a moment when the interplay of Saturn and Uranus can help us balance the need for both *adaptation* and *freedom*. Indeed, the open-minded, experimental intelligence of Uranus aids our mature adaptation through our willingness to try new things, consider new ideas, and be willing to be surprised.

Many young adults are well attuned to Saturn and focus on starting a career, completing their education, starting families, and finding a place in the world. However, the influence of Uranus is always present, even if not consciously acknowledged, bringing a restless urge to explore options and alternatives. Those responding strongly to Uranus may try to remain free from responsibilities and structures, choosing to work part-time or pursuing unusual jobs and lifestyles. During my Uranus square I became an astrologer, a Uranian life path, which elicited shock and controversy among my family and friends. At this stage some people search for alternative identities and resist being absorbed into the mainstream culture, and are energized to unfold their youthful freedom and idealism. A man with a natal conjunction of Sun-Jupiter-Uranus and the Moon's north node in Sagittarius became an internationally renowned computer scientist and mathematician in his early twenties, at his waxing Uranus square. He was highly sought after for his brilliant, original ideas and publications.

During the Saturn return between ages 28–30 we approach life more seriously, choosing a direction, pursuing occupational training and advancement, developing a career or starting a family. Levinson calls this the Age Thirty Transition.[106] This is a time to make formative decisions, striving to create a more stable life while remaining committed to our individual paths. For example, a man named Rupert spent most of his twenties working part-time in a bakery, playing the flute, and learning various healing arts. At the age of twenty-nine he became aware that all of his clothes were full of holes and his musical career wasn't progressing, yet he consistently got rave reviews from his friends for his impromptu bodywork sessions. During his Saturn return, Rupert took out student loans and enrolled in chiropractic school, which enabled him to develop a profession in line with his interests in healing and that provided the financial security to keep pursuing music.

The Saturn return is a time to make choices and commitments that give our lives focus and stability and allow us to function effectively within our culture and social group.[107] Because Uranus has reached the trine to its birth position at age 28, our uniqueness can now begin to manifest. Rudhyar wrote about the significance of this age, calling age 28 the *second birth*, to be followed by a *third birth* in late middle age:

> What is noticeable is a kind of wave pattern of development which is based upon a 7-year and a 14-year rhythm. The 7-year cycle in human life has been known to ancient civilizations. . . . Fourteen is usually considered . . . as the time of puberty. At twenty-one, a

boy or girl definitely "comes of age". . . . Then comes the twenty-
eighth birthday. . . . [S]ince Uranus was discovered . . . we have
now a new archetype—a theoretical pattern—for a human life,
as Uranus's cycle of revolution . . . is almost exactly 84 years. . . .
Eighty-Four is 12 x 7. . . . This twelvefold zodiac subdivides itself
very significantly into three 28-year periods. . . . [I]n my book
"New Mansions for New Men," I spoke of these three periods as
the first, second, and third births—i.e., birth as a physical organism determined by parental heredity and developing biologically,
then psychically, within a particular social and cultural environment . . . ; then rebirth as an individual, asserting. . . his or her
self in an individualized manner in order to fulfill a more or less
unique destiny; lastly, a possible final readjustment of this individuality by means of which a more mature, more mellowed, wiser
participation in social affairs is made possible. This means that
there are two fundamental turning points in this 84 year theoretical pattern of development—around 28 and around 56. . . .
[T]here are two great turning points . . . when you can *reorient
and transform* your character and the nature of your capacity for
human relationships. You can "see" yourself inherently; as a result,
you can also meet others in a new way. You can do that between
the ages of 27 and 30; you can do it once more between the ages
of 56 and 60. . . . One should also realize that Jupiter and Saturn at
30 are in an aspect opposed to . . . their natal aspect. If, for instance,
they were conjunct at birth, at around 30 they must be in opposition. This is significant because in the second great turning point
of individual development, they will be, at about 59, in the same
relative position as at birth—and what is more, at about the same
zodiacal places. . . . [W]hen a person is about 28, the positions of
the Moon's nodes in the zodiac are inverted in comparison to their
natal positions. Around 28 to 30, a definite inversion occurs in the
relationship between Jupiter and Saturn and similarly with regard
to the moon's natal position. On the other hand, the progressed
Moon ends its first complete cycle . . . and Saturn has also returned
to it natal place.[108]

The convergence of these interconnected planetary phases between ages 28–30 make this a pivotal phase in the life cycle. Those who don't make wise decisions or commitments during the Saturn return may drift without direction into their thirties and are more likely to suffer from depressed mood and anxiety, because they're aware their lives aren't stable and they're not progressing and advancing. Sometimes we need to undergo a major adjustment at Saturn's waxing square to its birth position at age 36, a time when we begin to seek more lasting life structures (job, home, relationship), and begin to be aware of our aging, witnessing the aging or death of parents. Levinson calls this the *settling down* period, marked by tasks of advancement, self-determination, and progression along a timetable.[109]

During the period of ages 40–45, the cycles of Saturn and Uranus interconnect again. Saturn opposes its birth position, while Uranus opposes its natal position. During the Saturn opposition we may experience fulfillment and advancement, or frustration, setbacks, or dissatisfaction in our work or relationships. We may well be on the way toward actualizing our dreams. Yet this is also a time of reevaluation, weighing our goals and ambitions against the expectations of our family, our peer group, our society.

In midlife, our central issues are generativity, caring, and concern for others in the work and family spheres in the context of changes associated with aging. Erikson saw middle adulthood as a phase of *generativity versus stagnation*. We seek to express caring for others, nurture children, our creations, and our legacy, and try to make a contribution for future generations. We try to create something so that in the end our life will mean something. Midlife adults are linked to the welfare of others, children, parents, coworkers, family, and friends. The story of midlife is one of peaks and valleys, emphasizing the need to balance multiple roles and manage the conflicts that arise. Impetus for change is strong. Accident, loss, or illness can lead to a major restructuring of time and a reassessment of our priorities. Often changes are precipitated by "wake-up calls," which trigger a new appreciation for life.[110] For Walter (Chart 14), nearly losing his job during his Uranus opposition was a wake-up call that led to needed changes. Walter's depression in part reflected boredom and self-preoccupation and a lack of generativity. He had no children, but also no creativity, no spark of aliveness or sense of legacy.

The Uranus opposition generates an urgency for change and a tension between our obligations to existing structures and our desire to radically change directions. This is often a period of boredom, restlessness, or nostalgia for lost youth. We reappraise our commitments and life structures, sometimes resulting in career changes, divorces or separations, and other crises. Our mental health at this time hinges on feeling free and youthful, and committed to moving in a new direction to more fully unfold our creativity and uniqueness. There is a realignment of our biomagnetic field. All kinds of new energies are moving through us and we have to receive and allow this to move us differently, activating all dormant potentials. Wayne, discussed earlier, quit binge drinking and became a writer at his Uranus opposition. He felt an urgency in his writing quest, a need to actualize the potentials of his Sun-Mercury in Gemini. We keenly feel the imperative of individuation during the Uranus opposition.

The ages from 44 to 59, between the second Saturn opposition and the second Saturn return, can be a time of stability and enduring accomplishments. However, if the gap between our ideals and the reality of our life is too great, we may give up in defeat and resignation to living according to the collective norm.[111] We have to come to terms with the realities of the life we have created, accepting both our strengths and limitations.

At Saturn's third quarter square at age 50–51 we may experience fulfillment, or a crisis as children grow up and move away, as childbearing years end, or if our physical vitality has diminished. This period is dominated by responsibilities to job, family, and our life's work, and trying to make a positive social contribution; or one may feel defeated by a lack of advancement or meaningful accomplishment. As this is a waning square, it's a time of reevaluation in the spheres of occupation, business ventures, home, friendships, group memberships, or creative activities. It's important that our actions are strategic and that we build structures within which we can grow older. People who consistently fail to focus, make choices, and build life structures during these various phases of Saturn's cycle are more likely to suffer from anxiety or depression.

The period between 56–60, during the second Saturn return and the waning trine of Uranus, is potentially a time of productivity and creativity. Rudhyar called this the second "great turning point . . . when you can *reorient and transform* your character."[112] Sometimes the second Saturn return marks increased authority, achievement, recognition in society, or stature and prominence in one's field. It can be a period of strength, accomplishment, and responsibility. Others become aware of fatigue and the limits of advancement, and look forward to retirement. Marcia Starck notes, "Health issues related to Saturn often occur; we may have problems with teeth . . . , bones, or joints."[113] We become aware of growing older and search for a frame of reference and source of meaning that transcends our individual life story, accomplishments, and identity. For some people, it's time to retire from the world of ambitions and striving and to devote oneself to meditation and spirituality. Regardless of our plans for retirement, it is good to take more time for contemplation, play, or artistic expression. At age 60 we have our fifth Jupiter return, which can bring relaxation, benefits accrued, release, and adventure.[114]

After the second Saturn return, aging becomes a central focus of attention. The challenge is to experience physical decline, retirement, and the illness or death of spouse and friends with equanimity and wisdom. The Saturn square of age 65–66 is a time to work to fulfill our remaining goals, and to adjust to either increase or decrease in our responsibilities. "For those who retire from a profession, this time can also elicit depression unless they find new activities that interest them."[115] The Saturn opposition at ages 73–74 can mark a climax—reconciliation with our lives and with others, or feelings of anguish or failure.

As we consider later life stages it's helpful to consider three facets of aging that have been emphasized in research: disengagement, activity, continuity. *Disengagement theory* emphasizes the need for disengagement from some of our social roles and responsibilities as we accept that resources need to be made available to younger adults. From this perspective, successful aging entails competently disengaging from roles in the workplace, family, and community, and doing so in good spirits.[116] With this one may develop an inner-world orientation, an increased interiority. My father, Leo, had a hard time stepping back from his career as a sociologist and kept working through his late seventies. At age 81, during his waning Saturn square, he told me this dream: "*I am in a city at night. All the windows are painted with brightly colored shutters. The streets are empty. Nobody knows me.*" The brightly colored window shutters reminded him of his extraverted personality, his love of parties and social life in the big city. But the empty streets and his anonymity represented his feelings about retiring, disengaging from his work, and letting junior colleagues carry on the enterprise without him. This dream can be viewed as a kind of internal self-initiation into old age, into a deeper interiority.[117]

A contrasting viewpoint is found in *activity theory*, which contends that older people's sense of life satisfaction is greater when the individual's activity level is higher, when they continue activities pursued in middle age for as long as possible.[118] Older people have the same psychological and social needs as midlife adults; they desire social interaction, and when they become isolated it's often not voluntary but most often results from society's withdrawal from older people. Research studies have identified how aging is influenced by both individual factors (nutrition, exercise, active engagement with life, avoiding high risk behaviors such as smoking and alcohol abuse) and social variables (poverty, isolation). My mother, Agnes, is a shining example of the validity of activity theory. Currently 95 years old, she lives independently, walks and exercises in a fitness room every day, reads the newspaper and keeps current, volunteers weekly helping people craft their resumes, and her mental faculties are completely intact. She has survived her third Saturn Return, her Uranus Return, and her Pluto opposition. Her resilience is a testimony to the validity of *continuity theory*, which contends that, in the face of the inevitable changes of aging, it's desirable to maintain a continuity of identity and lifestyle, to whatever extent possible.[119] We should continue to follow the pattern of life and experience indicated in our birth charts and in our late life transits, as these can guide us to the end of our days.

Those who live wakefully until the Uranus Return at age 84 and the third Saturn return at ages 88–90, have the potential to become wise elders, carrying the memories and values of prior generations and the distilled lessons of their lifetime. Starck writes, "The Uranus return at age 84 signifies the full cycle of individuation. By this time, one has acquired life's wisdom, has few emotional attachments, and is ready to pass onto another plane."[120]

## Uranus: The Space Beyond Saturn

At any age, Uranus awakens an urge for freedom, independence, unconventional beliefs, and controversial pursuits. Uranus enlivens our interest in cutting edge trends, social movements, and scientific innovations that are emerging within the collective and that may influence the future, contributing to societal betterment and cultural evolution. Uranus can impact our mental health if rebellious attitudes and irresponsible behaviors create discord or controversy. Uranus is a catalyst challenging us to becoming free individuals, to break free from the dominant views and mindset of the collective. We envision political liberation and freedom from oppression, or discover new systems and technologies to solve problems and serve human and planetary needs. The Uranian individual can be an artistic or literary genius who defines a new and unique style, or a person applying progressive values to social activism, raising a child, or earning a livelihood independently through self-employment. Finding this individual ingredient is a key to mental health; without it we feel bored, oppressed, and contracted.

Uranus beckons us to explore the free space out beyond Saturn—the freedom to create new structures, new social roles, new paradigms. Uranus is freedom from cultural conditioning. Of course, when we respond to Uranus there's always a chance we'll experience exile, ridicule, or controversy. Yet it's exhilarating to take risks, challenge assumptions, and display our inventiveness.

While transiting Uranus squared his natal Sun, Dr. Jackson, a respected physician, was faced with a dilemma. He developed interests in herbal medicine, homeopathy, and other alternative forms of treatment. His colleagues urged him to "return to reality" and stop entertaining these "preposterous" ideas. If nothing else, they advised, he should protect his reputation by not associating himself publicly with "kooks," "quacks," and "fringe elements." Although his new medical practices were shocking to his colleagues, Dr. Jackson was true to himself and continued pursuing these interests. He challenged the inflexible mindset and doctrines of his profession and spoke up at meetings and conferences about the need to reform Western medicine to include a more holistic perspective. These actions generated much controversy and he got a certain amount of attention, which can happen during transits to the Sun; we get seen, noticed. Dr. Jackson felt excitement because he knew he was part of a trend that would eventually transform society and medicine. He was an active participant in professional associations, practiced medicine responsibly, and demonstrated his results in a scientifically sound manner. As a result, some of his colleagues began to listen to him and to incorporate some of his views and findings. Responding to Uranus, we don't simply adapt to the world, we act believing that we can *transform* the world.

Occasionally Uranus manifests as manic excitement. One young woman with Moon-Uranus conjunct her Ascendant in Sagittarius experienced problems at age 21 when transiting Uranus reached its first quarter square to Moon-Uranus. While traveling abroad (Sagittarius), she exhibited bizarre behaviors, stopped sleeping and eating, and began speaking nonstop. She got in trouble when she started taking off all her clothes in public, which drew unwanted attention and controversy to her. Her subjective experience was that she felt free for the first time, liberated from her parents, excited to be on her own for the first time. She was eventually hospitalized, medicated, and diagnosed with bipolar disorder. Her behavior had become quite unpredictable.

Another woman who suffered from bipolar disorder had natal Moon-Uranus-Pluto in Virgo in the 12th house, opposite Saturn in Pisces. In 2009–2010, transiting Uranus in Pisces was conjunct natal Saturn, and transiting Saturn in Virgo was conjunct natal Moon-Uranus-Pluto. She had immense creativity and political fervor that she tried to express through her work (Uranus-Pluto in Virgo). However, at this time her life was disrupted by a manic episode that caused her to spiral out of control so that she needed to be hospitalized (12$^{th}$ house planets, Saturn in Pisces). She had to retreat from her work for a period of recuperation while the manic excitement calmed down. Of course, most people don't respond to Uranus in this way. Nonetheless, we should be aware that Uranus is a high energy, high intensity force that can generate a restlessness and speedy intensity that can sometimes be disruptive. For optimal mental health we need to respond consciously to the outer planets, which can at times be forces of instability and change.

## Individuation and Crisis

Sometimes individuation causes a crisis. A man from Portugal named Juan had the Sun in the 11$^{th}$ house at 20° Aries, conjunct Venus. At the age of twenty-five, while transiting Uranus and Neptune were squaring his natal Sun, Juan became aware that he was gay. This transformation of identity became the focus of his life, and it entailed a conscious embrace of the feminine side of his self-experience (Sun-Venus conjunction). Juan faced the challenge of expressing his identity in a conservative, traditional, Catholic society that hasn't gone through the liberalization of attitudes about sexuality that has occurred in the United States. It entailed an act of rebellion (Uranus) against cultural norms and religious prohibitions, and an act of self-offering (Neptune). Juan knew there was going to be a painful price to pay for his decision, and that, in a sense, he was offering himself up as a sacrifice. He felt a strong identification with Christ and his conscious acceptance of suffering (Neptune).

During this transit to his Sun, the pressure built up for Juan to come out to his friends and family about his sexual orientation. He viewed this as a transpersonal act in that he knew this step would impact not only his family, but also, to a small degree, his culture as a whole. The 11$^{th}$ house is the domain of social awareness, our perception of the historical moment and our place in it. Juan's self-proclamation was also an act of dedication to a larger social movement of liberation encouraging everyone to be free to be whoever they are. Juan experienced terror and excitement, crying, swaying, and ecstasy. After coming out to his family, Juan reported a release of tension, accompanied by trembling, exhilaration, and a peaceful feeling of divine protection. Juan's awakening combined Uranian liberation of values and lifestyle, and a Neptunian experience of suffering and redemption.

## NEPTUNE AND PLUTO:
### SELF-TRANSCENDENCE, INITIATION, AND REBIRTH

Uranus represents the beginning of transition beyond ego. The individual is electrified by the power of the universe and the spirit of change, inspired by the universal mind to invent, reform, innovate and individuate. With Neptune we transcend the limitations of ego-centered awareness and experience a limitless consciousness.

Astrology serves our evolution in many areas of life, for example, our quest for secure emotional attachment (Moon), and for fulfillment through love, sex, and relationships (Venus and Mars). It helps us sharpen our cognitive functions so our minds operate with peak acuity (Mercury). It helps us to achieve stability within the social order (Saturn) and to liberate and express our individuality (Uranus). Interwoven with these varied tasks is the yearning for transcendence, for the peace that comes from experiences that are timeless, ecstatic, sacred, or mystical. These realizations pursue us and fascinate us during Neptune visitations.

Neptune is a planet of extremes, highs and lows, agony and ecstasy. It symbolizes watery initiations that require surrender, trust, letting go. Things may fall apart or be at a complete standstill in our lives. Always a test of faith in the unknown is involved. In the end, if all goes well, we receive a blessing, a rain of peace. Under the ray of Neptune, we feel ourselves dissolving, or losing control, or feel that we have no boundaries. Or we experience inspiration, grace, vision, intuition, imagination, expansion of consciousness, and mystical dreams. Those who practice meditation may touch a deep stillness, a state of breathless serenity, pure consciousness, inner silence, eternal Being, radiant awareness. Neptune represents positive spirituality that enhances our health and wellbeing. It represents the pure and innocent experience of non-ordinary states of consciousness, deep meditation and *samadhi* states, out-of-body journeys, telepathy and precognition, dream lucidity and radiance, visionary journeys induced through various methods, past life memories, experiences of clairvoyance, telepathy, and other psychic phenomena; channeling, awakening of *chakras* and *kundalini* energy, states of communion with plants, animals, and transhuman beings. It awakens the experience of nondual consciousness in its changeless tranquility. Neptune awakens an urge to pursue practices that awaken higher perceptual and energetic potentials: yoga, pranayama, shamanism, ecstatic dance, devotional practices, chanting and toning, and visualization. Neptune symbolizes movement into the realms of spiritual liberation and illumination described by mystics and seers.

Neptune can also manifest symptomatically as dependency, difficulties coping with the material world, absorption in fantasies, delusions, and hallucinations, or peculiar ideation. Neptune sometimes evokes confusion, disorientation, delusional thinking, depressed states of hopelessness, defeat, resignation, helplessness, victimization, passivity, addiction, withdrawal, or inability to function. Some people will exhibit symptoms of weakness, devitalization, or loss of focus at the time of transits or progressions involving Neptune.

## NEPTUNE AND LOCUS OF CONTROL

To understand the developmental challenges associated with Neptune, it's helpful to consider the concept of *locus of control*. An external locus of control is the belief that what's happening to us is governed by external forces. An internal locus of control is the belief that what's happening is governed by our own efforts and skills, indicating a feeling of control over events. Our locus of control affects our behavior. People with an internal locus of control tend to get higher grades in school, take better care of themselves, and are generally more successful. Those with external locus of control are more prone to "learned helplessness," a feeling of hopelessness, passivity, and inability to cope with their problems. Learned helplessness is the belief that nothing we do matters or helps our situation. It's closely associated with depression, which is often rooted in a feeling that we can't influence circumstances. This is a Neptune problem. Neptune can paralyze our sense of motivation (Mars) and effectiveness (Saturn), making us feel helpless and out of control. While Neptune passed over his natal Saturn, Roger (Chart 12) was confused, uncertain about his direction, and unable to make decisions about a job or career path. In other instances, such as the case of Walter discussed earlier, an emphasis on Neptune in the natal chart can represent a struggle with addictions and alcoholism.

Many people associate astrology with an external locus of control, the view that our success and failure is due solely to fate and planetary influence, rather than to our own actions. I believe astrology can help us overcome learned helplessness and develop a more internal locus of control. We learn that in a certain sense the planets are inside us, representing parts of ourselves, and that the entire drama of development is taking place within our own psyches. Neptune signifies awareness of forces larger than the ego, accepting the impermanence of things, and openness to the spiritual order of existence. But this is a conscious act, different from weakness or paralysis of the will.

## NEPTUNE, SURRENDER, AND SPIRITUALITY

Neptune awakens faith, trust, innocence, surrender to the will of the Great Spirit, the unfolding of the Tao, the natural way of things. While Neptune was opposite her Sun, a woman named Vicki lost her concentration and felt she couldn't focus on her clerical job and eventually quit to dedicate herself to a new career as a spiritual healer and educator. Despite the precarious financial situation this decision caused, she felt compelled to do it, as if commanded by a higher Law, the truth of her being. While it seemed impractical (Neptune), Vicki felt guided from within to pursue this work, which she felt would be of service to others. Over time, this new life path worked out beautifully. The oceanic tides of Neptune wash some things in our lives out to sea, into nothingness, yet in their wake everything is fresh and clean.

Stacey, a woman with transiting Neptune conjunct her Descendant, was depressed because her marriage was disintegrating. She and her husband, Brent, were drifting apart, avoiding conflict (Neptune), and their relationship lacked true intimacy. Stacey thought of leaving him, but her will wasn't strong enough to do it. She only desired that whatever happen be for the highest good of both of them and of all beings. I suggested that she try to meditate for a few minutes each day. One day while sitting in quiet contemplation she perceived that there was no fundamental difference between Brent and herself; they were, in essence, one being. She came to realize that under the vibration of this Neptune transit it was okay that there wasn't much sexual passion in the marriage; there was calm, stillness, a feeling of their cells merging as they walked holding hands or slept next to one another. After this, Stacey allowed herself to surrender inwardly to the marriage, devoted herself to Brent, and felt that they were achieving a state of deeper union, Neptune's greatest gift.

During Neptune transits we may experience visions, dreams, or intuitions that guide and inspire us. A woman named Sunam had her natal Sun at 20° Capricorn in the 5th house. In 1993, while transiting Neptune and Uranus were conjunct her Sun, she began to have visions of the future and of her past lives. She received inner guidance from various saints and spiritual masters, and began to channel information. Sunam believed she'd been chosen for a unique spiritual mission. She met with a psychiatrist, who thought she was experiencing hallucinations and delusions of grandeur. But Sunam's work with astrology helped her understand the situation differently. Reflecting on Uranus-Neptune conjunct natal Sun, she felt this was a moment to consciously receive an infusion of spiritual energy. Sunam needed to avoid delusion and grandiosity; but neither did she wish to close the gates on these psychic perceptions and spiritual insights. She dedicated herself to daily meditation and felt gratitude for the knowledge she was receiving. Later, with humility and a sense of humor about what she was undertaking, she began to teach others what she was learning through her inner awakening.

Some traditional psychologists and psychiatrists view the altered states of consciousness of Neptune to be pathological, regressive, or delusional. The astrological perspective is that there are stages in development when we go beyond the quest for achievement and social status, beyond Saturn, beyond Venus and the search for love. When we receive Neptune's vibrational influence we may feel drawn into expansive states of consciousness and begin perceiving other realities. Neptune also signifies awakening of dormant forces of the unconscious, especially as expressed in dreams.[121]

## C. G. Jung's Crisis and Renewal

One of the most inspiring examples of consciousness transformation mediated by the combined influence of the outer planets is the story of C. G. Jung's upheavals and awakening. While Uranus in Aquarius transited over his Ascendant, opposite his Sun-Uranus in Leo, and transiting Neptune was conjunct his Descendant and natal Sun, Jung entered the period of his "confrontation with the collective unconscious."[122] He was flooded with visions, prophetic and disturbing dreams, and psychic, paranormal phenomena. His fantasies and interior life became so intense that he felt compelled to withdraw into solitude, giving his unconscious mind free rein through drawing, painting, dreamwork, mythological studies, sculpting, and building with stones. He experienced visitations of an ancient Gnostic spiritual teacher named Philemon, and in January 1916 he penned "Seven Sermons to the Dead" through a process of channeling or automatic writing.[123] This was when Jung began creating the Red Book, a revelatory, visionary, mystical text.

This period of psychological crisis was preceded by the crucial transits of 1907–08 when psychoanalysis was birthed through the collaboration of Freud and Jung, during a major outer planet phase—the opposition of Uranus in Capricorn and Neptune in Cancer. Uranus and Neptune were directly aligned with Jung's Venus-Mercury in Cancer, in the 6th house—realm of training and apprenticeship. Jung employed techniques of Freudian psychoanalysis as well as the Word Association Test, an intuitive and effective diagnostic tool. Jung related to Freud as his mentor, conducting an active and stimulating correspondence with him (Mercury and Venus) and also during this time Jung worked as a psychiatrist at the Burgholzi asylum, under the supervision of Dr. Eugen Bleuler.

C. G. Jung
Natal Chart
July 26, 1875
7:32:00 PM SZOT
Kesswil, Switzerland
47N36 / 9E20
Tropical   Koch   Mean Node

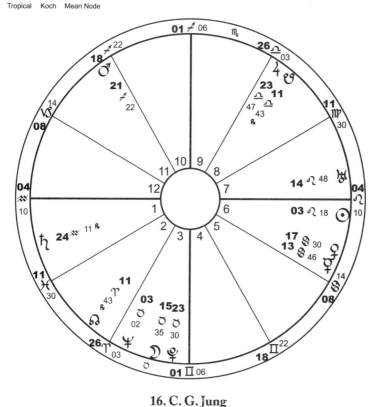

16. C. G. Jung

Bleuler was Switzerland's most prominent psychiatrist, widely known for his writings on "schizophrenia," a term he coined. Bleuler showed unusual devotion to his patients. A bachelor, he lived in the hospital and spent all his time with the patients, involved in their physical treatment, organizing work therapy, and achieving close emotional contact with each patient. He thus attained a unique understanding of mentally ill patients and their inner life, attempting to make sense of the supposedly "senseless" utterings and delusions of schizophrenics. Bleuler conceived the primary symptoms of schizophrenia to be a loosening of the tension of associations, in a manner similar to what happens in dreams or daydreams. He used treatments that sometimes produced miraculous effects, sometimes resorting to early discharge of apparently severely ill patients, or a sudden, unexpected transfer to another ward; or he assigned a responsibility to the patient. He organized a system of work therapy and arranged the leisure time of his patients and the functioning of a human community in the mental hospital.[124] Jung was trained in Bleuler's compassionate approach to mental illness under the transit of Neptune conjunct Mercury. At the same time Jung was experiencing his own loosening of associations as his unconscious life of dreams and fantasies became highly charged and the state of his own mental health became questionable for a time. Throughout all this, genius was unleashed through his original theories and writings while Uranus awakened natal Mercury.

While Uranus opposed Venus and Mercury in the 6th house Jung experienced many stimulating, changeable, and controversial relationships with patients, coworkers, trainees, and research assistants. During this period he conducted an unorthodox psychoanalytic treatment of Otto Gross, a prominent German psychoanalyst, who had been committed by his family to the Burgholzi to undergo treatment for his mental disorder, drug addiction, and strange ideation, which focused on his advocacy for polygamy. The work was unorthodox in that Jung and Gross stayed in a room together for up to twelve hours at a time analyzing each other's dreams, in a kind of mutual psychoanalysis.[125] There was a certain manic excitement in the conversation between the two men and Jung would soon confess to Freud the conflicts stemming from his own polygamous desires. This was also the time of Jung's brief involvement with Sabina Speilrein, a young patient who became his research assistant, became romantically smitten with Jung, and was obsessed with fantasies of bearing Jung's love child. This little *imbroglio* would strain his relationship with Freud, as well as his marriage.

During 1911–12, while transiting Saturn was conjunct Pluto in the 3rd house, Jung's mind was illuminated through his reading and studies of Gnosticism and alchemy. I believe Pluto also influences Jung's 4th house, as it's in the 4th sign from the Ascendant and in the 4th house from the perspective of equal house system and whole sign houses. While Saturn transited Pluto, Jung delved into his family genealogy and ancestral heritage, and experienced marital discord and domestic upset, echoing the estrangement of Jung's own parents during his childhood (Pluto in 4<sup>th</sup> house: the family). Saturn conjunct natal Pluto is a transit that often evokes the archetype of the shadow, the encounter with a difficult or hidden side of others, and of ourselves. At this time, Jung experienced Freud as increasingly rigid and dictatorial, and felt stifled under the oppression of the tyrannical father. He encountered Freud's controlling, patriarchal traits, his unwillingness to yield an inch to Jung in their theoretical disagreements, and Freud's somewhat paranoid obsession with the idea that Jung harbored a death wish toward him. Freud and Jung were becoming increasingly uncomfortable with each other.

While Uranus opposed his Sun, Jung experienced many problems in his relationship with Freud due to Jung's interests in religion, mythology, paranormal realities, and synchronistic phenomena. Jung also had doubts about Freud's theory of sexuality, believing that sexuality was not the only expression, or goal, of the libido. In his view, the unconscious psyche sought wholeness through a union of opposites and had a spiritual, centering, ordering tendency, which he called the Self—evident in dream images of a divine child, jewel, cross, mandala, a Christ or Buddha figure, or other numinous symbolism that Jung considered equivalent to personal "God images."

Jung's questioning of the primacy of sexuality and his immersion in mythology, religion, and esoteric philosophies were anathema to Freud, who decisively rejected and disdained Jung's innovations, and broke off their correspondence in early 1913. When Uranus conjoined Jung's Ascendant and opposed Sun-Uranus the separation and breaking of ties was irrevocable. In the year or two after 1913, Jung's whole center of gravity shifted and he was on his own in the Uranian free space of self-discovery and identity reconstruction.

During 1913–14, as Saturn transited through Gemini and his 5<sup>th</sup> house, Jung retired from teaching, resigned his positions in the international psychoanalytic movement, and took time off. It wasn't exactly a vacation, but he allowed himself to play like a child and became very involved in his writing (Gemini) and creativity (5th house). Inwardly Jung felt somewhat unhinged and disoriented. With his professional life and his psyche in chaos, he was in deep waters, beginning a five-year phase that has been called a "creative illness" and a "breakdown."[126]

From August 1915 to October 1916, Neptune was conjunct his Sun and Descendant. He entered a period of dissolution of identity, and fluid boundaries between the ego and the deep unconscious. Jung had a dream of a "monstrous flood" descending upon Europe, visions of "the whole sea turned to blood," and recurring dreams of "an arctic cold wave" causing death and desolation—vivid premonitions of the outbreak of World War I.[127] At times he felt that he was on the edge of a psychosis. Yet he consciously surrendered to the inward-moving flow of imagery and symbolism that flooded him during Neptune's high tide. He yielded to the unconscious and wherever it would lead him. His intensive inner work through dream interpretation, painting, sculpting, writing, and wide-ranging studies culminated in the formulation of the core ideas of analytical psychology, such as the relations between the ego and the unconscious, individuation, the psychological types, and the archetypes or "dominants" of the collective unconscious, such as the great mother, hero, divine child, wise old man, anima, trickster, persona, shadow, and wounded healer.[128] Jung's story illustrates the meaning of the Uranus opposition as a phase of awakening and self-liberation, and of Neptune conjunct the Sun as a spiritualizing of identity and entry into the archetypal dimension. These events led Jung to drink from the well of the unconscious, whose fountain would fully quench his thirst.

## NOTES ON A VISIT TO JUNG'S RED BOOK

In 2009 I had the opportunity to visit the Rubin Museum in New York to view the Red Book of C. G. Jung, which was on public display for the first time. This book's inception was the period of illuminating, numinous, and highly charged visionary experiences and dreams in the years after 1913, lasting until approximately 1918.

Jung was at a low point after severing his ties to Freud and the psychoanalytic movement in which he'd been a prominent participant, Freud's heir apparent and favorite son. As noted earlier, Jung was having his Uranus opposition: Transiting Uranus opposite natal Sun-Uranus in Leo. Jung asserted his independence and autonomy, breaking away from Freud and the Freudian paradigm, becoming a free thinker and promethean figure whose discoveries and innovations merging depth psychology, religion, comparative mythology, and alchemy would forever alter the consciousness of humanity.

Jung also had transiting Neptune conjunct his Descendant and natal Sun-Uranus in Leo, a transit signifying inner awakening, a flood of material from the unconscious, highly active dream life, fantasies, and psychic premonitions, and Jung's intensified study of mythology, alchemy, astrology, and Gnosticism. This Neptunian period was characterized by introversion and uncertainty caused by erosion of friendships and professional alliances (Neptune in 7th house). Former colleagues became rivals and enemies; his 7th house alliances were totally overturned. Jung was highly controversial and he was shunned and scorned by the Freudians. Many of Freud's followers and Jung's former colleagues (for example, Karl Abraham) viewed Jung as peculiar, egotistical, and arrogant (Sun-Uranus in Leo). For his part, Jung probably felt that Freud and his other adversaries were themselves quite arrogant and unruly. Following the break with Freud, Jung embarked upon an inner journey that ultimately allowed him to find a deep center and unfold his unique identity and creativity (Sun in Leo).

During this transit to his 7th house Sun-Uranus, Jung's marriage was in some disarray, largely due to the fact that Jung was engaging in emotional and erotic discourse with Toni Wolff, his *anima* muse, as well as with his wise and steady wife, Emma.[129] These relationships ultimately flowered in mutual devotion during Neptune's transit in his 7th house. I consider Emma Jung a highly inspiring personality. She remained devoted to her husband while he appeared to go completely off the deep end, preoccupied with channeling spirits of deceased Gnostic gurus, studying myth, alchemy, and astrology. He was in love with another woman. But instead of going into a complete emotional snit, Emma embodied Uranian openness and adaptability, and the purest Leo loyalty and dignity. She was ultimately able to accept Toni Wolff as a friend, ally, and family member. Emma's love made it possible for Carl to individuate through an unconventional marriage and approach to love (Uranus in his 7ᵗʰ house). As he entered stormy seas, Emma and Toni accompanied Jung to the edge of his sanity into the radiant experiences that inspired all of his mature theories and ideas.

The exhibition at the Rubin featured reproductions of some of Jung's paintings and mandalas, along with a series of line drawings that served as preparation and models for the more elaborate mandala paintings that appeared in the Red Book. I observed the evolution of the imagery and symbolism of these pictures. What was most noteworthy was how the pictures began with two distinct features: In the center, a series of shapes that looked like flower petals, which gradually increased in complexity of organization, showing an evolving internal order within the ego or conscious personality. In each drawing, above the central petal-like structures was a star, drawn at first very simply, depicted in one picture as a fish, then evolving in subsequent pictures into a much more complex and organized center of light and intelligence, depictions of the Self, the internal center of order and wholeness, encompassing the opposites and polarities of the personality.

These pictures remind me of the Rosarium images of medieval alchemy portraying a star hovering above the figures of the King and Queen, representing the transpersonal element or transpersonal Self. Jung's subsequent paintings depicted a line of contact between the star and the central lotus petals of the ego, showing lines of connection between above and below, heaven and earth, in a process Edinger called establishment of the ego-Self axis.[130] As this axis between ego and the unconscious is strengthened and elaborated in *The Red Book* mandalas, it begins to grow more charged and intense, adding a horizontal dimension forming a cross as a central feature of the mandalas, signifying the tension of opposites within the personality. This process later blossomed in a painting with Christlike imagery of crosses, with several characters clearly undergoing states of inner spiritual and emotional agony—personal crucifixions. Note how this symbolism reflects, and expresses, the Neptune transit.

**C. G. Jung,** *Vision of 1914*

These paintings culminated in one of the most striking vision-ary paintings in *The Red Book*, in which Jung depicted scenes of a city in somber earth tones, with details of sailboats, smokestacks spewing smoke, and soldiers with rifles engaged in target practice and populating walled towers—in short, a modern city engaged in industrial production, commerce, and the machinery and strategy of war. Above all this, a little man called Phanes, the divine child, symbol of the emergent Self, sits with a huge cross mandala over his head surrounded by a shimmering kaleidoscope of multi-colored light exploding into expansive radiance. The painting depicts an explosion of fire that Jung saw as a premonition of the outbreak of World War I. This is Jung's apocalyptic vision of impending vio-lence and destruction. This was also Jung's vision of himself, his own awakening, and of awakening humanity. It is intensely resonant to this very moment. 1914 was also the year of a transiting Pluto-Saturn conjunction in Jung's 5ᵗʰ house. This painting gives expression to the immense power implied by the symbolism of Pluto-Saturn. Jung was also experiencing the transit of Pluto at 1° Cancer, semisquare natal Moon, intensifying his emotional experience of the volcanic, turbulent and transformative powers emerging from within the collective unconscious, as well as marking this period as a crisis of death and rebirth.

Jung's heroic, mystic journey culminated while transiting Neptune was conjunct his Sun. Jung's Red Book is a reminder that each of us can experience this axis, this connection to the higher Self, the center of inner light. We may be going through some personal ordeal but we can find meaning in it. At the moment of alienation, the star of the Self shines. In the time of darkness, brightness radiates. We can energize and potentiate the axis that connects us to the light of the Self, the guide, guru, sheikh, the inner messiah, the part of us that is already whole and perfected.

### Pluto as a Symbol of Initiation

Jung's story illustrates an initiatory process occurring under the combined influence of the outer planets. Now let's look more closely at Pluto's role in our personal evolution. Neptune and Pluto work in tandem to bring about a recentering and repolarizing of consciousness, in which we're pulled forward and transformed by the magnetism of the center. If Neptune represents revelation of the light, then Pluto is a revelation that comes from confronting the shadow, the underworld of life. Neptune is the spiritual vision of unity, enlightenment, and universal compassion. Pluto is the ordeal that tests and purifies us, exposing imperfections such as self-centered intentions and motivations.

Neptune shows us glimpses of perfection and awakens visions and high ideals; yet it leaves large corners of our personalities unseen and unperfected. Pluto counteracts Neptune's tendency to be in denial, showing us the things inside us that hinder us from attaining our highest potentials. Pluto uncovers what Buddhism calls *the three poisons* of greed, hatred, and delusion, which obscure our natural clarity and openness—the serenity, vision, openness, tranquility, and universal concern that Neptune symbolizes—our intrinsic Buddha nature. Pluto is an internal reorganizing energy. Also, Pluto rules fixation; it shows us where our consciousness is fixated so that we can free ourselves. It reveals our obsession with power, wealth, or an object of desire; it can evoke possessive jealousy. By bringing this material into the light of consciousness, Pluto refines and uplifts our character.

Isabel Hickey wrote that Pluto is the catalyst of a process through which the person becomes "the servant of the real Self and take[s] its proper place as a channel through which the power of the Essential Being can flow. . . . Pluto is the death of the separated self." It teaches us "to die to the self and be born to a Self." It asks us "to be willing to be nothing on a personal level," to awaken humility, and to use our will appropriately. She observes that, "Every seed must be buried in the darkness of the Earth before it can break out of its shell and come up into light." Thus, Pluto's influence tends to bring extremes of light and dark—construction or destruction; illumination or obsession; wisdom or struggle. Hickey notes that it's often through painful experiences that we're able to grow into the light.[131]

Pluto is the planetary symbol of reintegration, metamorphosis, radical shifts in consciousness, and experiences of rebirth. Its goal is self-mastery and increase in our personal power and effectiveness. When transiting Pluto opposed her Sun, a young woman left her parent's home for the first time to go to college and shed her old identity as a cynical, alienated teenager, becoming a hopeful, energetic woman with an active social life and well defined career goals. When transiting Pluto squared his natal Sun, a lawyer began to make more money than ever before and won a highly publicized case in which he faced down a corrupt politician. This example illustrates how sometimes Pluto asks us to confront corruption or criminal activities.

In October 1995, transiting Mars and Pluto were conjunct. Within that week my house was burglarized, my neighbor's car was vandalized, another neighbor was robbed at gunpoint, and another neighbor was involved in an incident of domestic violence. A major forest fire devastated a large area of the beautiful park at Point Reyes in Marin County, California. These are typical Plutonian events: crime, trauma, violation of personal boundaries, and destructive acts of nature. Also, my septic tank exploded all over the front yard; Pluto rules sewage, return of the repressed, and breakdown of structures that are no longer working.

Developmentally, Pluto refers to the way the individual responds to the tragedies that are an inevitable feature of history and human existence. It rules bigotry and racism. Under the influence of Pluto we may experience historical events that are manifestations of ancient hatreds and feuds spanning centuries—for example, the animosity between Jews and Arabs, or between Sunni and Shiite Muslims.

Pluto strongly influenced my father, who is one of the generation of soldiers that fought the battles of World War II, most of whom were born between 1915 and 1925 and had natal Pluto placed in the early degrees of Cancer. My father's Pluto was at 10° Cancer. In 1945, at the conclusion of the war, transiting Saturn was in early Cancer, passing over natal Pluto and that of his entire generation. His perspective was radically and irrevocably changed as the horrors and atrocities of Nazi genocide and mass incinerations were uncovered, and the world witnessed the devastating nuclear bombing of Japan. Through confrontations with cruelty, brutality, fascist politics, and violations of human rights, Pluto teaches us appreciation for our freedom and the preciousness of life. However, some situations associated with Pluto are capable of evoking lasting bitterness, malice, and mistrust, feelings that can become toxic to us if they aren't purged and cleansed.

Pluto initiations confront us with the choice between hatred and love; between seeking power over others, and joining with others in unity and shared commitment. Responding to Neptune we may be selfless, loving, and forgiving. But during some tests of Pluto we face situations where it's difficult to love and forgive, where it's easy to feel wounded and angry. These situations evoke our primitive instinct to react according to the law of the jungle: fight or flight, eat or be eaten, an eye for an eye. Pluto shows us what happens when we meet life on these terms: mutual destruction, rage and despair, seething resentment, death in life. It offers opportunities to respond according to a higher law: Neptune's compassion, the ability to let go and forgive.

Sometimes Pluto's tests involve painful events—deaths and bereavement, being mistreated by another person, material setbacks, or loss of reputation. A woman with Pluto in the 2nd house in Cancer was swindled out of money in a real estate deal, when transiting Saturn opposed natal Pluto. When transiting Pluto passed over the Ascendant of a man named Benjamin, several close friends and relatives died within a ten-month period. Such Plutonian situations are part of our human existence. Although we may hope for Neptunian light, visions, and inner journeys, sometimes Pluto's ordeals squash our egos definitively. So be it. These wounds can occupy us for many years. There are certain events that we don't get over quickly. At the same time Pluto is the planet of renewal and rebirth. We can survive suffering and losses if we trust the natural law that life is ever-renewing—the defining principle of astrological cycles.

Bert and Devi, a couple in their early forties, came to see me while Bert was undergoing chemotherapy treatment for cancer. Since they were born within a year of each other, both had transiting Pluto in Scorpio square natal Pluto in Leo, and transiting Saturn in Aquarius opposite natal Pluto. Bert also had solar arc Pluto conjunct natal Saturn, and Devi's progressed Sun was square natal Pluto. Bert was fighting for his life and Devi was facing the possible loss of her husband. This was the first time something of this magnitude had happened to them. Neither of them had ever suffered a major illness or faced the death of anyone close to them. Bert began to see the futility of his strivings for power and status through his corporate career.

Their unexpected encounter with illness and possible death forced them to completely reevaluate their lives. At first, they both just wanted to ventilate all of their bitterness that life had dealt them such a cruel blow. However, the potential finality of the situation forced Bert to consider all the ways he'd never truly lived fully. Several major changes resulted from this. Bert began to exercise regularly and enthusiastically. He and Devi decided to go on an extended trip to Europe and another in Hawaii. They realized that they had to live *now*, while there was still time. They took up yoga and began to taste inner freedom. They healed some long-simmering disputes in their relationship that had been a source of discord and mistrust.

Miraculously, Bert's cancer went into remission, after the Pluto transits had passed. Confronting death and its finality awakened him to the impermanence of life and the need to drink it to the fullest. While we may not understand the *cause* of such unfathomable events, we always have the power to respond with courage and to welcome the transformative possibilities of every crisis.

A woman named Marissa, who had natal Pluto in the 10<sup>th</sup> house and transiting Pluto conjunct her Scorpio Sun. At this time, Gwen was pressured to accept a demotion during a hostile corporate takeover and major reorganization of her company. Marissa fiercely fought the takeover, then ended up taking a position with a competing company that offered her a salary increase. Pluto's initiations teach us toughness to navigate skillfully in the world of power. Pluto is reptilian; it is the consciousness of a survivor.

Through Pluto we gain an awareness of how power operates in society, especially through the agencies of government, banks, corporations and other influential interest groups. When the progressed Sun was opposite his natal Pluto in the 11<sup>th</sup> house, a man went through a transformation of his social perspective (11<sup>th</sup> house Pluto) as he participated in a class action lawsuit against a large corporation that had released toxic pollutants into the atmosphere. He was angry and cynical about the corporation's lack of social responsibility and their efforts to avoid paying for their actions—even to the point of trying to destroy the reputation of key witnesses in the case. In the end, this experience led him into an affiliation with an influential political organization (Pluto in 11<sup>th</sup>).

Plutonian misuses of power aren't limited only to large-scale abuses, but also result from confrontations with the hurtful, wrongful actions of individuals—for example through experiences of betrayal. A dentist was reported to the state licensing Board by an employee after a casual conversation in which the dentist mentioned that he occasionally smoked pot; solar arc Mars was conjunct his natal Pluto. While transiting Pluto squared her natal Venus, a woman discovered that her boyfriend had slept with her best friend. A woman went to court after her husband beat her, when transiting Pluto passed over her Descendant. A man who stood to inherit a considerable amount of money from his mother was shocked when his uncle challenged her Will in court, leading to a protracted legal battle. Transiting Saturn was opposite natal Pluto in his 6th house, which, by derived house analysis, is the 3rd house from the mother-4th house, and thus governs the mother's sibling.

One lesson of Pluto is that, as we witness some of the terrible actions people are capable of, we recognize that these are our own shadows—that all of us are capable of deluded actions. We see the hidden side our own personalities, our mean, abusive, or arrogant tendencies, our obsessions and compulsive behaviors. By facing our own unconscious, not only do we become more self-aware, we also become less eager to demonize others and to see them as inherently inferior. Pluto teaches us about the karmic law of action and reaction—that if we hurt others we ourselves are hurt. Showing us the effects of unethical, or injurious actions, Pluto can strengthen our resolve to use our powers and capacities properly, reverently, free of the desire to do harm. Pluto also teaches us that we can't afford to be naive, that sometimes we must fight for what's right.

### Pluto and a Lawsuit

For many years a businessman named Doug had been in partnership with William, a man whose work habits were considerably different than his own. William took ten to twelve weeks of vacation every year, and worked part-time hours. Doug took no more than two weeks off every year and worked ten hour days, sometimes six days a week. Yet the two men evenly split the profits from their business. Eventually, Doug made the decision to stop dividing the proceeds equally, as William obviously didn't do an equal share of work. Subsequently, William sold his half of the business. Now, six years later, William was suing Doug and his wife Patricia for fraud and embezzlement. He was trying to extract a large amount of money from them, dragging them through a lengthy trial, in which Doug and Patricia were forced to submit for review all of their financial records—a hellish ordeal. They felt they were being sued unjustly, and that William was trying to ruin their lives for no good reason other than greed and malice. They had already spent over $50,000 in lawyer's fees.

At the time, Patricia had transiting Uranus opposite her natal conjunction of Pluto and Moon in Cancer in her 7$^{th}$ house (the house of "open enemies"). These events were disturbing the emotional equilibrium of their marriage, and both of them were understandably upset, edgy, in a turbulent emotional state, fearing that they were in danger of losing their home (Pluto conjunct Moon in Cancer) and all that they had worked for. During this protracted marital crisis (7$^{th}$ house Pluto), Patricia and Doug felt that, no matter what happened with this lawsuit, they still had each other. Nothing except death itself could take away their love. They became more deeply committed to each other's wellbeing, sticking together through the toughest period of their lives. That is the nature of Pluto; it takes us to an edge and we have to abide there, open to how the emergency is going to resolve itself: death or life, bitterness or closure.

Doug had transiting Pluto opposite natal Venus in Taurus in the 7$^{th}$ house. The lawsuit threatened their marital finances (Taurus, 7$^{th}$ house), and brought them into conflict over money with an old friend who was now an adversary; the 7$^{th}$ house also governs open enemies or rivals. In addition, Doug had natal Sun in Aries square Pluto in Cancer, and both of these planets were being closely aspected by transiting Uranus in Capricorn. During this Uranus-Pluto contact, Doug encountered an unscrupulous person who was trying to exploit his financial success. With Neptune near his Midheaven, Doug was a spiritual man who did volunteer work with substance abusers and dying people. He didn't understand what he'd done to deserve this predicament. A devout Christian committed to love, compassion, and nonviolence, he struggled with anger and bitter, vengeful feelings that were stirred inside of him by William's lawsuit.

While originally Patricia and Doug sought astrological counsel for predictions of the outcome of the lawsuit, I focused on trying to understand the meaning and purpose of these events as a form of spiritual testing and initiation. The Pluto transits they were both experiencing forced them to confront the shadow side of humanity, evident in another person's desire to willingly injure them. We meditated together on the Pluto symbolism and energy, and we all concluded that the goal of this process was for them to face evil without becoming evil themselves, and to defend themselves fiercely without succumbing to hatred. They had ample justification for feeling bitter and resentful, yet they aspired to a higher ideal than to hate. Plutonian encounters with the collective shadow mark the end of innocence and the potentially the birth of power and wisdom.

Doug and Patricia examined their own actions and motivations and felt genuine remorse for past actions that were hurtful or unjust. They meant no harm to William and wished only to resolve their differences. Later they settled the case out of court, for a large but not devastating sum. They lost a great deal financially and in terms of emotional stress and drain of time and energy. But they gained greater appreciation for their good life and a deeper emotional connection. They'd confronted a situation that tested their capacity to love.

Pluto's lesson is that, having perceived the divisive effects of hatred, we can act in the world with the right motivation, free of the desire to control or injure others; we can be powerful without being power hungry. Pluto confronts us with the violence and cruelty of both nature and humanity, so that we become free of violence and cruelty. Pluto liberates us from these poisons so that we might become truly human.

## PLUTO IN THE DALAI LAMA'S CHART

In some instances Pluto challenges us to confront injustice and bring the truth into the light of day. The chart of the Dalai Lama shows Pluto conjunct the Ascendant and south lunar node and widely conjunct the Sun.[132] He has peacefully opposed and protested against the Chinese invasion and occupation of Tibet since 1959, bringing human rights abuses (murder, rape, torture) and the destruction of temples and monasteries—monuments of a price-

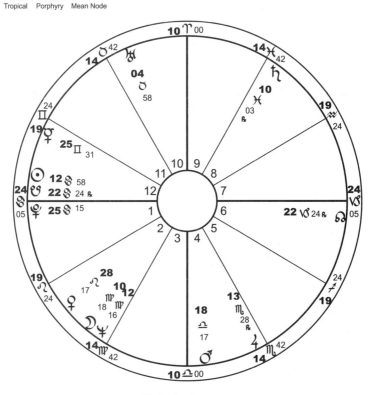

Dalai Lama
Natal Chart
July 6, 1935
6:00:00 AM 7E
Tangster, Tibet
36N32 / 101E12
Tropical   Porphyry   Mean Node

**17. Dalai Lama**

less cultural tradition—to the world's attention. Yet he has done so without advocating violence and without losing sight of the essential humanity of the Chinese. I'm always amazed at how free of malice, bitterness, and hatred he is, even though his entire life has been dominated by the violent subjugation and exile of his people.

The Dalai Lama also has Moon closely conjunct Neptune, symbolizing his great compassion, his selfless dedication to the service of his people, and his living embodiment of the ideal of Buddhahood. He is a religious teacher (Saturn in Pisces on 9th house cusp), a political leader and activist (Uranus in 10th), and a monk dedicated to his spiritual practices (Sun in 12th). With Sun in a Grand Trine with Jupiter and the 9th house Saturn, he is a man of wisdom, moral strength, and spiritual authority. The development of evolved personality traits often emerges out of the worst of circumstances and the most difficult tests.

## A Process Approach to Pluto

A process orientation is especially important in approaching a planet such as Pluto, which has such a wide range of expressions and manifestations. Pluto governs death and rebirth, endings and renewal, losses or terminations of our involvement with people, places, or institutions. Pluto represents completion, finality, and closure. Pluto can represent an area of fixation or obsession, as well as the process of releasing this fixation so we experience an unimpeded flow of energy.

Sometimes Pluto manifests as an encounter with negativity, or ruthless people driven by power urges. A lawyer with transiting Saturn conjunct Pluto in Leo in the 10th house experienced a professional rise to power, yet she was also confronted with a controlling boss and unscrupulous competitors. She felt she was in a rat's nest of vicious politics and power plays. At the same time she was working with force, focus, and intensity.

Plutonian situations are opportunities to release resentments and root out hatred, bigotry, racism, sexism. At times we encounter the criminal element in society. A woman named Dana was mugged when transiting Pluto formed a quincunx to her natal Sun in Taurus. She was shocked to learn firsthand what some desperate people do to get some money. Another woman was stalked by her ex-lover when solar arc Pluto was conjunct her Descendant. She took him to court for a restraining order and the judge rebuked the guy in court.

Sometimes when Pluto is active, death is a central theme. Astrology promotes mental health by aiding us in coping with death and bereavement, and accepting our emotional losses. Astrology helps us accept what is. A woman named Wanda consulted me after her husband died at age 57. Transiting Pluto was stationary direct, conjunct her natal Mars in the 12th house (which is the 6th house from the spouse 7<sup>th</sup> house, thus the house of the husband's health). Wanda's progressed Sun was squaring Pluto in the 8<sup>th</sup> house; and transiting Saturn was conjunct natal Pluto. Sometimes we're presented with the lesson that Death Is. It's just a fact of life. We need to consciously experience and honor the death stages, the breakdown of forms, the terminations of life structures, the shedding of old skin, the pruning of dead branches, the recognition of dead-end roads that don't lead anywhere. We view death and endings with the eye of wisdom that knows "this has to be."

But Pluto has other meanings and doesn't always involve a literal death. A man with progressed Sun conjunct Pluto in his 8<sup>th</sup> house was very concerned that someone was going to die. What actually happened was that he experienced business losses and interpersonal disagreements about money, credit problems, and difficulties collecting money owed to him by others. He also had a degrading sexual experience that left him feeling ashamed, and this transformed and refocused his attitude toward sexuality. This was how he visited Pluto's underworld.

In some instances Pluto manifests on physical levels as toxicity, infectious diseases such as flu, viruses, infections, staph. Pluto is also the principle of elimination. In cooperation with this archetype we can undertake cleansing diets, detoxification, cessation of old habits and harmful addictions. Pluto can also spur a spontaneous purge. During a transiting Mars-Pluto conjunction in Sagittarius I experienced an impressive incident of food poisoning. Mars-Pluto manifested in my becoming violently ill while dining at the swankiest restaurant in town. I had actually been poisoned six hours earlier at lunch in an Indian restaurant. I knew from the first bite that the spinach tasted spoiled, but I ate it anyway. The spiritual lesson here is that we need to listen to those immediate intuitions we have about those first bites of a toxic situation or toxic relationship. Most of the time we seem to follow an unconscious compulsion to enter into it even more fully, to get the full taste of the experience—like a moth drawn to the flame. Pluto compels us to complete our karma. The presence of consciousness doesn't always mean that we avoid passing through the unpleasant experience. So there I was in the full throes of the food poisoning episode thinking about Mars-Pluto.

It helped ease my mind and made me willing to surrender to the process. That transit felt like a wave rolling through me.

## A PLUTO TRANSIT DURING A FAMILY CRISIS

Here's another story of a Plutonian crisis. A young woman named Tanya had transiting Pluto conjunct the IC and transiting Neptune quincunx natal Saturn in Virgo. She became disillusioned with her father (Saturn), a prominent professor who was exposed as being corrupt, lecherous, and a petty dictator. The whole family was embarrassed by revelations of an affair with one of his students. Tanya became depressed and began drinking heavily for a few months and eating junk food. She dropped out of college, stopped working, and moved back in with her mother. Astrology helped her understand the meaning of the family crisis. She was upset by how her mother was being treated (Pluto conjunct IC). There was lots of anger, resentment, and negativity in her family. Simultaneously, her progressed Moon in Pisces was opposite natal Saturn, and her solar arc Moon was conjunct her Descendant. She moved back home, took care of her mom, and regrouped. She became more nurturing and emotionally connected to her mother. She prepared to leave the nest again and moved away to a distant city to return to school. Pluto conjunct IC signified the painful process of exposing family secrets. It marked a period of exile from home, the end of childhood, and beginning a new life in a new place. Astrology helped Tanya find meaning in this family crisis, and provided a helpful sense of timing to guide her next steps forward.

## PLUTO AND THE TRANSMUTATION OF SUFFERING

A man named Lewis had the Sun in the 12th house at 25° Scorpio. While transiting Pluto was conjunct his Sun and while transiting Saturn in Aquarius squared his Sun, he was diagnosed with cancer. Lewis has been a dedicated Buddhist practitioner for many years. For those consciously pursuing spiritual growth, the 12th house represents retreat, meditation, and striving for enlightenment. Lewis recognized that he had a choice: He could sink into feelings of victimization, self-pity, and hopelessness, or he could transmute this confrontation with death (Pluto conjunct Scorpio Sun) into an occasion for self-transcendence—a higher expression of the 12th house.

Lewis went through an ego death experience, feeling that he was surrendering to the way of the universe. As he came to terms with his illness, Lewis became more dedicated to service, and was willing to let go of his personal identity, even his body if necessary. Lewis was committed to being a healer in the world, through working with troubled adolescents in a hospital setting (12th house: institutions, and selfless service). A great power began to arise in Lewis through his meditation practices and was expressed through him in this work.

A predictive astrologer might have looked at Lewis's Pluto-Sun transit and said, "It's going to be a really heavy time, a bad year. This is an inauspicious transit. You might even die." This interpretation would have missed the transformative potential of this life crisis. Lewis believed that, through his cancer, he was confronting some ancestral karma. Through this illness, he felt that he was being given the chance to release all of his hatred and aggression. "Something hideous grows within the minds and hearts of everyone," he said, "and it has taken form in my body now as this cancer. I could become angry and resentful about the cancer, but I choose to use this as an opportunity to develop a universal heart, no matter what happens to my physical body." Pluto represents *transmutation*. Lewis transmuted his illness, becoming a modern Bodhisattva, a man of true heart and compassion. It is now 20 years later, and Lewis is still alive, still working to help others, still practicing the Buddha's way. His story demonstrates that it's possible to use any planetary placement or transit, however difficult, as a path to spiritual awakening.

## An Ordeal Involving Neptune, Saturn, and Pluto

I'll conclude this section with another personal anecdote, this time regarding a most intense test and initiation that occurred under the combined influences of Neptune, Saturn, and Pluto. Neptune is an archetypal pattern of transformation through experiences of suffering, impermanence, and non-solidity. A few years ago, transiting Neptune was quincunx my MC, and I experienced some job insecurities. I have natal Saturn in Sagittarius, so part of my career is in counselor education, as a professor of counseling psychology. I was recruited for a teaching job at a school, only to have the job offer challenged because student activists argued that the school hadn't conducted a nationwide search for the position. They wanted a more diverse pool of applicants to be given a chance to apply for this job. I was also criticized for not being knowledgeable about racism and diversity issues. As a result, I received only a short-term contract and I lost my healthcare benefits.

This ordeal occurred as Saturn was entering Virgo and was part of the Virgo worker experience. At this time, transiting Saturn was conjunct natal Pluto in Virgo in my 11th house. Intense, subterranean politics were at play in the workplace (Virgo); contentious, Plutonian forces were erupting within the group. I was caught in the middle of a larger political struggle occurring within the institution. I didn't do anything wrong, nor did I blame anyone. It just happened. Sometimes we're pinned to our fate and just have to accept that *this is what is*. During Neptune transits we have to surrender to situations that aren't entirely in our control. With Neptune quincunx MC, I was reminded of the truth of impermanence, that there's no ultimate stability. At first I felt victimized, but I tried not to indulge in self-pity. I viewed the situation as a test and tried to learn from it. I continued teaching part-time and waited a year to reapply for the job.

Neptune teaches us to bear our sorrows and sufferings, transcend our clinging to security, and to surrender, to trust what is and what will be. It's the symbol of inner serenity and spiritual faith. It helped me immensely to know about Neptune, and Pluto, and Saturn in Virgo so I could remain conscious while going through the ordeal. Indeed, I felt illuminated by the experience. Through astrology we find refuge in the eternal consciousness and love pulsating through every moment. This experience opened my eyes to the suffering of displaced workers, people without health insurance. I took some training about racism, and learned about racial microaggressions, micro-invalidations, and micro-insults—derogatory, dismissive, or insulting messages directed unconsciously by whites toward people of color.[133] I gained new skills in facilitating group process around diversity (Pluto in the 11th house: the organization, the group).

A year later, as Saturn turned stationary direct on the degree of my natal Pluto I reapplied for the job and interviewed for it, but again I wasn't hired for the fulltime position because the school was committed to hiring someone from a more diverse background. I had to step back from some of my teaching and accept a smaller role in the department. Transiting Saturn conjunct Pluto in the 11th house transformed my position within an organization, where I had to yield to larger forces. I refocused my attention on working as a psychotherapist in a managed care environment (Saturn conjunct natal Pluto in Virgo in the 11th house), seeing clients referred by insurance companies. I worked with the Pluto energy, and faced some things that made me very uncomfortable. Astrology is a tool for our development. It doesn't just describe events that happen to us.

During this time, I read Sri Aurobindo's commentary on the *Bhagavad Gita*, a text that describes a path of transformation through work and fighting the battle of being in the world.

> This Yoga can only arrive at its success by devoting, by consecrating, by giving up the whole self to the Divine. . . . [T]he Liberator is within us, but it is not our mind, nor our intelligence, nor our personal will—they are only instruments. It is the Lord in whom . . . we have utterly to take refuge. And for that we must first make him the object of our whole being and keep in soul-contact with him. This is the sense of the phrase "he must sit firm in Yoga, wholly given up to Me"(*Gita*, II.61). . . . [T]hen, free from reactions, the senses will be delivered from the affections of liking and disliking, escape the duality of positive and negative desire, and calm, peace, clearness, happy tranquility, *atmaprasada*, will settle upon the man. That clear tranquility is the source of the soul's felicity; all grief begins to lose its power of touching the tranquil soul. . . . It is this calm, desireless, griefless fixity of the buddhi in

self-poise and self-knowledge to which the Gita gives the name of Samadhi.... "He has no personal hopes, does not seize on things as his personal possessions.... He who is satisfied with whatever gain comes to him, who has passed beyond the dualities, is jealous of none, is equal in failure and success, he is not bound even when he acts" (IV.21–22).... The immutable Brahman is there in the spirit's skies above this troubled lower nature of the dualities, untouched by either its virtue or by its sin, accepting neither our sense of sin or self-righteousness, untouched by its joy and its sorrow, indifferent to our joy in success and our grief in failure, master of all, supreme, all-pervading, ... calm, strong, pure, equal in all things.... "He who can bear here in the body the velocity of wrath and desire is the Yogin, the happy man.... When one has conquered one's self and attained to the calm of a perfect self-mastery and self-possession, then is the supreme self in a man founded and poised... in cold and heat, pleasure and pain as well as in honour and dishonour.... He who desires nothing, is pure, skillful in all actions, indifferent to whatever comes, not pained or afflicted by any result or happening, who has given up all initiation of action, he ... is dear to Me. He who neither desires the pleasure or rejoices at its touch nor abhors the unpleasant and sorrows at its touch, who has abolished the distinction between fortunate and unfortunate happenings ..., he is dear to me" (V.23, and VI.7).[134]

The fierce truth expressed in these passages could not be denied and helped me view these Plutonian events as a spiritual test, asking me to step outside the viewpoint of the ego into the higher Self, the witness consciousness, which was detached and untouched by my grief and self-pity, my self-righteous anger. Following these teachings, I tried to generate a spirit of detachment, renunciation, and self-offering, abiding in a "griefless fixity," allowing myself to be satisfied with whatever happened, with failure or success, honor or dishonor. The job was not to be seized upon as my personal possession. Through my experiences during Saturn conjunct natal Pluto, I felt that God was cutting the knot of the ego, my attachment to security and the idea of advancement. Pluto cut through my attachments to my professor role, salary, and health insurance, and invited me into

*Winged Figure Kneeling with Tree of Life.*
Babylonian cuneiform tablet

a calm self-possession, clarity and tranquility—the *atmaprasada*. In the end I felt contented with the outcome and trusted that it was the will of the universe that things turned out this way. The end result has been a greater commitment to my true work as a therapist, astrologer, and writer. As Hazrat Inayat Khan once said, "A worldly loss often turns into a spiritual gain."[135]

What's also astonishing is that in that moment of suffering my teacher Swami Muktananda appeared to me, twice, in dreams. After this job hiring decision went against me, I was feeling very hurt and misunderstood. I dreamed:

> *I was in an apartment with Swami Muktananda and offered him a*
> *container of mixed nuts. He grabbed them from me. I asked, "Would*

*you like me to prepare you something for lunch?" He said no, he just wanted his own stash of nuts. I saw his face, his body, his detachment, and his freedom beyond form, beyond the world.*

My teacher appeared to me at my absolute worst moment, at the low point of my life. Offering to feed him was offering to feed the part of myself that is unconditioned by form, by success and failure. This dream reminded me that my real existence is outside the play of the world, outside academia. It reconnected me to an inward moving stream of consciousness. In this dream, Muktananda appeared to me as the *avadhut*, radically free and detached, transcending ego consciousness and worldly concerns, and seeing him felt like an invitation to join him in this freedom, in this state of unconditioned awareness.

A year later, I led a seven-day retreat for this school, doing some of my best teaching ever, but I was also feeling somewhat stirred-up about my unsettled position within this organization. I crossed an internal threshold one day where I felt that I no longer cared what anyone thought about me. I was teaching from a wilder, freer, more spontaneous place than I'd ever touched before. That night Muktananda appeared again in a dream:

*Swami Muktananda was sitting right next to me. He put his forehead right up against mine. He was talking to me very quietly and intimately. He said he was leaving on a trip to India. I couldn't understand everything he said, but he silently conveyed the current of his blessing, his approval, his interest in me. He smiled and closed his eyes ecstatically. I felt all lit up and felt waves of energy running through my body.*

This dream was a wave of bliss, a ripple through silence and eternity, a mind-to-mind transmission. Muktananda was literally in my face. The Teacher cannot be much closer than this. I was face to face with the fire of the Real.

Aurobindo's Gita teachings and these initiatic dreams inspired me to transform through the tests of Saturn conjunct natal Pluto. Astrology supports our mental health by helping us find meaning in our most difficult circumstances, in our darkest hour.

To fulfill this meaning consciously is to evolve. After the storm, illumination.

## The Healing Moment

Astrology helps us embrace the beautiful, transient moments that touch us and heal us. Some months after the events just described, I went out on the beach at Amagansett one morning in August at around 5:30 a.m. to watch the warm Leo sunrise. No one was around, only some quiet gulls flapping and swooping over the open water, and little sand pipers skittering along the beach. This opened my heart. I needed that healing moment. It brightened up my being, seeing the sun's purple-orange orb and the silver Moon in Taurus still sparkling in the blue morning sky. The whole domain of nature was lit up with vibrant color and luminescence. Inwardly I felt how a long night of darkness and upheaval transforms into illuminated sunrise, a fresh dawn of possibility.

In the next chapter, we'll discuss how astrology supports our mental health and satisfaction in life by increasing our relational intelligence.

# PART FOUR

# SYNASTRY

*Microcosmos Hyponchondriacus*, 17th century[136]

Chapter 8

# *Synastry, Conscious Relationship, and Couples Counseling*

One of astrology's great contributions to society is the light it sheds on our human relationships. Astrology generates insights that can enhance, heal, and sustain our relationships, enabling us to interact and live with other people more joyously, with greater tolerance and humor. In this chapter we consider relationship symbolism of the natal chart, and synastry, the process of comparing two charts and their interactions. Planetary contacts between charts depict the cross-fertilization of individual potentials, and understanding these supports our transformation through relationship issues, conflicts, and challenges.

Astrology is especially helpful in the practice of couples counseling. In my work as a Marriage and Family Therapist, I've found that astrology is an effective tool for understanding a couple's dynamics, conflict areas, and stress points. Its precise insights can enhance communication not only in romantic relationships but also in parent-child relationships, business partnerships, friendships, and relationships with our rivals and adversaries.

Astrology helps us adapt to changing periods and phases of relationships, and to develop a sense of humor. Astrology teaches patience and acceptance of another person's character, just as it helps us understand and accept ourselves. This isn't about finding the perfect relationship. Astrology doesn't tell us whether or not we should be in a relationship with somebody. It helps us consciously relate to that person, if we choose to do so. It's up to us what we make of the inter-chart energies. People show up in our lives when we're ready to encounter a particular energy or archetype indicated by our natal and transiting planets. For example, when undergoing Pluto transits, some powerful, intense, bossy, controlling, or mean person often appears in our lives. We may encounter some unscrupulous, power-hungry person. Similarly, during Neptune transits we may have relationships with Neptunian people. A woman with

Neptune in the 7th house had a dysfunctional, mixed-up, space-case boyfriend; yet he was also peaceful, compassionate, and poetic, a sensitive and high-minded soul. He embodied her natal Neptune. She loved him despite his shortcomings.

## RELATIONSHIP SYMBOLISM OF THE NATAL PLANETS

Each natal planet refers to qualities we need for fulfilling relationships:

- Sun: joyfulness, playfulness, warmth; a clear sense of identity; consciously emanating the light of who you are.
- Moon: emotional sensitivity, empathy; capacity for secure attachment, tenderness and nurturing.
- Mercury: communication skills, sharing of ideas, ability to make conversation.
- Venus: touch, sensuality, compatible tastes, material comfort, cooperation, tact, ability to accommodate the needs of others.
- Mars: anger, assertiveness, passion, sexual drive, anger management and conflict resolution skills.
- Jupiter: patience, generosity, kindness, tolerance; planning and goal-setting, interest in learning, travel, and adventures.
- Saturn: reliability, trustworthiness, commitment, ability to sustain stable life structures such as a job, home, or family; having good boundaries.
- Uranus: spontaneity, excitement, zaniness, individuality, idiosyncrasies, adaptability to change, independence, but also separations and distancing.
- Neptune: inner peace and tranquility, selflessness, intuition, spirituality; telepathy, dependency; ability to meet another person in a space beyond form, beyond separateness.
- Pluto: intensity, power struggles, negativity, need for control, and transformation by letting go of hostility, hatred, resentment, and aggression.

## PLANETS IN THE 7ᵀᴴ HOUSE

To understand our orientation to relationships, we study the aspects of Venus and natal planets in the 7ᵗʰ house. Planets ruling the sign on the 7ᵗʰ house cusp or placed in the 7ᵗʰ house describe how we seek wholeness and completion through friendships and love unions. If you have Moon or Jupiter or Mercury or Pluto or Uranus in your 7ᵗʰ house you'll tend to attract relationships with people who exhibit characteristics of these planetary archetypes. Jupiter is a kind, generous, or learned person. Saturn: a serious or older person, someone reliable. Mercury: a talkative person, good conversationalist. Moon is a nurturing, emotionally sensitive friend or partner. Pluto: an intense person who is sometimes controlling, powerful, or a little hostile. The same insights apply to Venus aspecting each of these planets.

Let's focus for a moment on several examples involving natal Mars in the 7ᵗʰ house. Brian, a man with Mercury and Mars in Virgo in the 7ᵗʰ house, felt constantly criticized by his wife. Brian needed to learn to stand up for himself, and as he did so their quarreling and bickering (Mercury-Mars) was transformed into more clear, precise (Virgo) communication. They rediscovered the art of conversation, renewing shared interests in health, nutrition, and the healing arts (Virgo).

Ruth, a woman with Mars in Scorpio in the 7ᵗʰ house, had three consecutive relationships with men involved with military service and police occupations. She kept ending relationships because she thought she should be with a more intellectual type of man. She had Sun-Jupiter conjunct in her 1ˢᵗ house, and she herself had an intellectual, thinking orientation. But with Mars in the 7ᵗʰ, in her love life she kept meeting the warrior-hero archetype. She later got back together with her most recent boyfriend, who was a police officer. She said our conversation reminded her of how she liked his potent sexuality, and how he made her feel safe and protected. She said, "I'm glad I stopped rejecting him." They were very happy together. The laws of wholeness often lead us to mate with our psychological opposite. Astrologers try to own the whole chart as a representation of our vast potentials. That includes seeing the people we attract as part of our own potentials. This makes us especially willing to take responsibility for the mood and character of our relationships.

Alice, a woman with Mars in Scorpio in the 7th house, square Pluto in Leo in the 4th, kept getting into relationships with arrogant, selfish men who dominated her. She projected her force and power onto them and suppressed the strong, angry part of herself because she feared being perceived as bitchy. Alice wasn't owning her Mars energy but kept meeting it in her relationships with men who bullied her. This repeated the dynamics of her relationship with her father, who was a bossy, enraged, and physically abusive individual. Planets in the 4th describe family dynamics and relationships. Alice began to claim her Mars, becoming more willful and assertive with her current boyfriend. She stopped suppressing aggression and anger and felt more liberated and energized.

Vicki, a woman with Mars-Saturn in Aries in the 7th house, kept getting in relationships with men who she said were self-centered, demanding, and inconsiderate. Mars-Saturn in the 7th house made me wonder about her relationship with her father. I said, "I can imagine that you might have felt declawed, defanged, like you were never allowed to be difficult and demanding. Maybe you need to show your claws a little, and allow yourself to be a little difficult." Vicki later told me this insight helped her feel more connected to her vitality.

Mars isn't just a malefic planet that sends nasty people and contentious events to attack you. It's also an internal principle of motivation and drive. A man named Bruce has Mars in Leo in the 7th house and his wife Alice is a fiery woman with a reddish complexion who is incredibly dynamic, creative, intense, powerful, and she's often angry at Bruce. His Mars is conjunct Alice's Ascendant and her Mars is conjunct his Ascendant. Sometimes they argue, but their relationship is also highly active and creative. They run a thriving construction business together. They prod and motivate each other. They make Mars work.

Earlier I mentioned a woman named Jane with Saturn in her 7th house. Jane lived with Allan, an accomplished, reliable Capricorn man. Jane had Sun in Leo and wanted to have fun. She bemoaned Allan's lack of spontaneity and playfulness. She was bored and felt that Allan was dull. I asked Jane to embody the Leo joy and sense of fun she was seeking, to let Allan be himself, and to appreciate his consistency and steadiness. He could be serious Saturn. She could be the sunny Leo. Astrology teaches that sometimes what you want from a partner is what you need to be yourself. Don't expect your partner to be what *you* need to be.

## ACCEPTANCE

Astrology teaches acceptance. We can learn to appreciate all types of people: Pisces/Neptunian mystics and space cases; competitive, feisty Aries/Martian people; Sagittarius/Jupiterian types who love to teach, lecture, pontificate, or regale you with travel stories; artistic, graceful Libra/Venusian types. Talkative Gemini/Mercurial types. Intense, sexy, volatile Scorpio/Pluto types. Nurturing, sensitive Cancer/Lunar types.

Astrology illuminates people's character and teaches us to accept the idiosyncratic, sometimes exasperating qualities of our friends and loved ones. It shows us who this other person is, and *needs* to be. I live with a woman who has three planets in Virgo. She is neat, detail-oriented, and often stressed out. I have Neptune in the 1st house and tend to be messy, laid back, disorganized. I have to accept that she can be tense and high strung. That's not going to change, nor is the situation helped by telling her to "Just relax." Knowing this about her and her chart, I don't have to fixate on the idea that she ought to change and be different. This is how she is! But I'm free to change, to adapt to, and be influenced by, her way of being. John Gottman's research has shown that the willingness to be influenced by one another is a key to successful spousal relationships, whereas criticism, contempt, defensiveness, and stonewalling corrode relationships.[137]

Relationships work better when you aren't attached to your own chart, your own way of being. Relationships ask us to view the world from another person's perspective. You can accept the other person's chart as part of your own life—like your second chart. Being married to Diana I become an honorary Virgo. I try to straighten up around the house. Since this isn't part of my natal makeup these behaviors don't come naturally to me, but I attempt to mold my behaviors to conform to this archetype. It doesn't diminish me to do this to make her happy. Relationships ask us to expand outside the comfortable range of our own typology. I need this woman with Virgo energy because it balances me and helps me grow. We seek out relationships with our opposite so we can become whole. This is what synastry is all about.

## OPPOSITES ATTRACT: JUNG'S TYPOLOGY AND SYNASTRY

Opposites attract. In relationships we seek what we don't have, and we're balanced by the other person. A practical, grounded sensate type balances out an imaginative, reflective, creative intuitive type. Introverts and extraverts bring balance to one another.

Jung distinguished between extraversion and introversion, two general available directions of the psychic energy or libido: outward into the world or inward toward one's own psychic process. Our goal is to have a balance between introversion and extraversion. There are certain houses that are notably introverted, especially the 4th and 12th houses. Certain houses are more extraverted, for example, the 5th, 7th, and 10th houses.

Jung identified four functions of consciousness, thinking, feeling, sensation and intuition. Two of these are "rational functions," involving evaluations and making judgments (thinking and feeling) in terms of true/false (*thinking*) and pleasant/unpleasant (*feeling*). The other two are "irrational functions" (sensation and intuition) that circumvent reason. *Sensation* is direct sensing of reality (perception) while *intuition* is perception guided by the unconscious, through hunches, intuitive intelligence, or spiritual, unitive perception.

One or more of these functions usually predominates. We have some degree of balance between functions, but usually one function is noticeably weak or absent, our inferior function. Have you ever met someone with a noticeable absence of feeling? Here the inferior function is feeling. Another person might be caring, emotionally present, imaginative, and perceptive, but can't think straight. Here thinking is the inferior function. I tend to be up in my head, exercising my imagination, and feeling-oriented as well, but I'm not very sensate, perceptive, or present-centered. Sensation is my inferior function. My sensate presence is weak and needs to be developed. Or take the example of a very Saturnian, grounded, down-to-earth person who thinks and perceives clearly and who might be very emotional as well, but is obtuse, lacking imagination, a sense of future possibilities, or ability to access inner hunches or spiritual perception. Here intuition is the inferior function.[138]

Jung's insights are of great practical value to couples. We're often attracted to someone who is opposite in type to ourselves, and carries our weak or inferior function. A key to conscious relationship through synastry is to notice the play of opposite types in a relationship. For example, a woman with Moon conjunct Jupiter and Uranus in Cancer has six children, and many grandchildren. She is a very nurturing, giving mother. Her husband has Sun, Mercury, and Saturn conjunct in Sagittarius and is much more intellectual and analytical. In another couple, the man has Sun square Neptune and is a very introverted, spiritual, intuitive type, while his wife has Sun conjunct Saturn in Capricorn and is a very grounded, practical sensation type. These types of oppositions and polarities comprise a whole, a totality.

Superimposing one person's chart over another creates an alchemical *conunctio*, a union of opposites. Edward Edinger described the *conunctio* as the creation of consciousness through the union of opposites.[139] Relationships and astrology are both alchemical experiences—means to transform our substance. But if you're not willing to be flexible, and change the process won't work. One woman said to me about her partner, "I can't stand how different he is from me. I won't tolerate these obnoxious traits in a man. I refuse to compromise." But intolerance is an impediment in love. No one can sustain a relationship if they are uncompromising. Here is the wisdom of Saturn in Libra in a nutshell.

Kristine, a woman with Neptune in Libra in the 8th house is married to Sam, a man with Sun, Moon, Venus, and Jupiter in Libra in his 8th house, conjunct her natal Neptune. Sam is an artist whose dreams of success never panned out. He's financially dependent on Kristine and he is now retired, while she continues to work. His 8th house planets in Libra are conjunct Kristine's Neptune in the 8th house of shared finances. While his artistic projects have never been commercially successful, these works of art do enhance the world. Kristine adores Sam and willingly supports him. She believes in his talent and his work as an artist. His Mars in Libra exactly trines her Venus-Mars in Aquarius. They have great physical and relational chemistry. She loves him even though he never makes any money. That's not the most important thing for Kristine; for someone else it might be intolerable. We're willing to overlook a great deal for the sake of love. Love extends tolerance and grows in the soil of tolerance. A Hawaiian Huna teaching states, "To love is to be happy with." From one perspective, Neptune in the 8th house can represent suffering through a spouse's financial dependency or incompetence. Or, as in this case, it can mean that we surrender to a situation where we consciously accept the fluidity of our boundaries. That surrender to one another makes Kristine and Sam one of the most passionate, sexy couples I know.

## The Moon in Synastry

Two people who have a relationship of some kind have connections between their charts. Their energies "lock in" and they get involved in an exchange or interaction. We seldom connect with people whose charts don't connect to ours. Even if we try to get to know them or become romantic, it doesn't work out. We're like ships passing in the night. There's no spark, no karma, no energy between us. Synastry is the art of discerning the quality of that energetic exchange.

The Moon is the central point of connection. When someone's Moon contacts your chart you feel an emotional resonance with that person. If someone's Moon is conjunct one of your angles, or aspects your Sun, you feel a strong emotional affinity, you feel connected in the belly. You care about each other. There is tenderness and nurturing between you. Person B receives comfort and soothing from the Moon person. Some of our strongest emotional connections occur when our Moon is in aspect to the other person's Moon, especially in conjunction.

Inter-chart aspects involving the Moon indicate the emotional tone or mood of a relationship, how it viscerally feels to be together, and signify our emotional resonance with another person. Aspects to your natal Moon from someone else's planets describe how you feel around that person: Moon-Sun: a sense of emotional unity and affinity. Moon-Mercury: you feel talkative, stimulated, or nervous around that person. Moon-Venus: love, affection, tenderness. Moon-Mars: you feel energized or the relationship arouses anger, irritability, impatience. Moon-Jupiter: hope, kindness, generosity, nurturing, encouragement. Moon-Saturn: sadness; emotional disappointment; feeling that one's needs are rejected; taking responsibility for each other's feelings. Moon-Neptune: empathy, compassion, intuition, psychic attunement. Moon-Pluto: trust and mistrust, having an intense emotional impact on one another.

With Moon-Uranus contacts between charts, note the exciting but inconsistent or distant feel of the relationship; you repel each other a bit. There may be an enlivening connection but you need some space from that person too. Of course, it also helps to understand your natal moon's aspects, where similar themes may be expressed. I have natal Moon opposite Uranus and I have a tendency to be emotionally distant and aloof. I've had to learn to counteract that. Or if you have natal Moon in a stressful aspect to Saturn you may bring to all of your relationships an underlying sadness or feeling of emotional rejection or disappointment.

## The Sun in Synastry

Inter-chart aspects of the Sun are also important. Aspects of someone else's planets to our own Sun signify the extent to which we feel seen and validated by that person, as we are, in our essential personhood. If the aspects are supportive, the other person "gets" us, validates our essential identity Otherwise we feel unseen, disliked, or misunderstood. When I was growing up I was tormented for several years at summer camp by a boy who used to call me names and slander me viciously. Later we went to the same college and I learned his birth date. His Mars exactly squared my Sun, apt symbolism for a relationship with a rival, adversary, or competitor. In contrast, a man whose Jupiter is conjunct my natal Sun has been a supportive colleague of mine for over 20 years. Inter-chart aspects involving the Sun are pivotal in relationship analysis.

## THE SUN'S HOUSE PLACEMENT IN SYNASTRY

The house where another person's Sun falls in your chart signifies a major theme in the relationship. If the other person's Sun falls in your

House I: That person validates you, illuminates your identity, makes you feel good about you, acknowledges you, helps you see yourself more clearly.

Sun in House II: The relationships may emphasize financial matters, or require you to focus on earning money and providing material sustenance.

Sun in House III: There's an emphasis on conversation, travel and transportation, shared ideas, and literary interests.

Sun in House IV: Focus on domestic tasks, home life, property, house projects.

Sun in House V: Fun, play, creativity, or partying are keynotes of this relationship, or children play a significant role.

Sun in House VI: You share interests in work, health matters, diet, nutrition, and achieving optimal health. This person is in your life to help you improve yourself, but you may have to overcome the feeling that you are constantly being criticized.

Sun in House VII: The other person makes you feel complete. There's a natural affinity between the two natives.

Sun in House VIII: The relationship strongly focuses on sex, money, shared assets, investments, and joint purchases or business ventures.

Sun in House IX: The relationship is focused on learning, travel, intellectual interests. The Sun person is a teacher to the 9th house person.

Sun in House X: The relationship, and the Sun person, support actualization of the 10th house person's life objectives and career goals. The Sun is a catalyst to the 10th house person's success.

Sun in House XI: The relationship focuses on friendship, community, and group membership. The Sun person connects the 11<sup>th</sup> house person to a wider circle of friends, and raises awareness of politics and social issues.

Sun in House XII: The relationship has a focus on spirituality, mysticism, and the inner life. The Sun person reveals to the 12<sup>th</sup> house person greater awareness of the dynamics of karma and the play of spiritual mystery in existence.

## MERCURY

If Mercury contacts an angle, luminary, or lunar node of the other chart, the two people communicate actively, and have a lot to talk about. The Mercury person provides stimulating ideas to the other. Aspects of Mercury show how two individuals communicate with each other, whether they have a meeting of minds. Mercury-Mercury aspects between charts are very important, showing mental affinity and active exchange of ideas. Mercury-Neptune aspects indicate shared interests in spiritual matters, dreams, fantasies, metaphysics, astrology. In some cases there may be confused communication, miscommunication, dishonesty (especially with Mercury square Neptune) or telepathic communication. Mercury-Saturn aspects highlight practical decisions, strategy, making choices. In some cases of stressful Mercury-Saturn aspects there are blocks in communication; one partner may be terse, uncommunicative, or verbally shuts down. Mercury-Venus aspects denote shared interests and tastes, listening, tact and diplomacy. Mercury-Mars aspects between charts denote quarrel, debate, arguing, sarcasm, wit. Mercury-Jupiter inter-aspects suggest shared interests in learning, travel, planning, and intelligent discussion. Inter-aspects of Mercury-Uranus highlight exciting new ideas, new conceptions, discovering new interests, talking about the political domain. Mercury-Pluto aspects signify investigation, persuasion, influencing each other's opinions. Mercury-Sun aspects show shared ideas, sense of purpose, mental attunement.

## VENUS

If chart A's Venus contacts an angle, luminary, or lunar node of chart B there's a loving feeling of warmth and affection, and it may also be a pleasingly sensual relationship. The two feel abiding affection for each other. My Venus is conjunct the natal Sun of one of my best friends. We've been friends from our first meeting in 1982 and have played music together for years.

Aspects between Venus in both charts indicate whether the two people have compatible tastes and aesthetics. A woman who had Venus in Cancer was very into "kitchy" old antiques, and collecting things that had sentimental value to her, but these items were annoying to her boyfriend, who had Venus in Aquarius and had more progressive, futuristic tastes. She didn't like the wild looking colorful clothes he wore. They liked totally different types of music: She was into country and folk music, and he liked acid jazz and electronica. They didn't like listening to music together. They were aesthetically incompatible.

One of the most important interplanetary contacts between charts are those involving Venus and Mars, planets of love and passion, eros and sexual desire. When these planets are well aligned, two people can have easy physical compatibility. Let's briefly look at the meaning of one person's Venus aspecting planets in another person's chart. Venus-Mars: eros, sexual attraction, pleasure and friendship. Venus-Jupiter: enjoyment of wealth, luxury, and pleasant, artistic surroundings. Venus-Saturn: trust, commitment, relational longevity, mature and platonic friendship. Venus-Uranus: independence, ambivalence, distant, standoffish behaviors, need for space or periodic separations. Venus-Neptune: devotion, adoration, unconditional love. Venus-Pluto: deep erotic fascination, possessiveness, jealousy; sometimes themes of love and betrayal.

## MARS

If chart A's Mars contacts an angle, luminary, or lunar node of chart B, then B will feel that A is aggressive, impatient, irritable, angry, selfish, or demanding. The relationship may feature some anger, stress, irritation, and discord. Hey, welcome to the club! But on the other hand, the Mars person provides energetic stimulus, motivation, and impetus for action to person B.

Mars governs sex, but also fighting, quarrels, and irritability. A good relationship allows some expression of anger, and doesn't suppress a good argument that needs to happen. We need to engage with Mars and learn to disagree and work things through to completion so both people feel they've been heard and can understand the other person's position. You've got to be able to deal with Mars without falling apart or breaking up, or slugging each other. Anger and irritation can scorch the fields of love and emotional attachment, so learning to manage anger and conflict is an essential skill for successful human relationships. Understanding stressful dynamics in relationships is an important benefit of synastry.

In my opinion, many relationships end in breakups, separation, or divorce because people don't know how to handle Mars energy. Ted, a man with natal Mars in Taurus in the 7th house, kept breaking up with women whenever anger emerged. When transiting Jupiter-Saturn were conjunct in Taurus, conjunct natal Mars, he met a woman, things were going great, but they broke up as soon as anger began to flare up. With Mars in the 7th house, how could he have a relationship without some conflict and disagreement? Impossible! I told him, "You'll never settle down with anybody unless you learn to handle conflict and anger in relationships."

Inter-chart aspects involving Mars can energize a relationship or create heat and friction that makes relationship immensely uncomfortable. Mars-Mercury: energetic communication; debate, quarrel, sarcasm; Mars-Jupiter: energized relational plans and goals. Shared drive for growth, learning, adventure, enterprise; Mars-Saturn: focused application of will; the expression of sexual drives may be intense, forceful, or constrained; Mars-Uranus: flare-ups of anger, irritability, excitement, orgasm, a powerful release of energy; Mars-Neptune: strong fantasy life; attunement to subtleties of sexual energy; Mars-Pluto: sexuality linked to issues of power, domination, anger, jealousy, or resentment.

Inter-chart aspects of Mars (especially the square, opposition, and quincunx) often signify stressful dynamics in relationships. I consider these a *given*. But we can try to understand the conflicts, disagreements, and clashing styles that cause discord. In most couples, discordant planetary aspects are balanced out by harmonious aspects that draw two people together despite their disagreements. I'll return to this in the case example below.

## Transits: Phases of Relationships

Transits through the 7th house or to natal Venus shed light on current dynamics in friendships, business alliances, or marriage. Mars transits to Venus or in the 7th house spark heightened energy, sexuality, or some friction and discordance in relationships. When Jupiter transits Venus or the 7th house you connect with helpful, generous, educated people; relationships and social life improve. Transiting Saturn aspecting Venus, or in the 7th house, indicates it's time to settle down with somebody, make a deeper commitment, or face adversities in relationships with a mature attitude; we experience tests of friendship; we might once and for all confront our fears about fully accepting a life-partner. When Neptune transits Venus or the 7th house we feel up in the air or undecided about a relationship; there may be patterns of denial or avoidance; a partner or spouse may be dependent, spacy, or ungrounded. Transiting Pluto aspecting Venus or passing though the 7th house often symbolizes a time of relationships with powerful, magnetic people, or relationships featuring jealousy, mistrust, vindictiveness, or power struggles.

A man named Chris was happily living with a woman named Trina when transiting Pluto entered his 7th house. Then his father died, and his elderly mother needed care and attention. Chris wanted to move Mom into the house with him and Pam. His experience was that Trina suddenly changed, becoming cold, mean, resentful, and rejecting. They separated. I felt sad about that because I believe the relationship might have survived had they been able to work with the archetypal dynamics involved. Many relationships can go to a much deeper place if we're willing to tolerate, or even embrace, the negativity and shadow that comes up in all of us at times.

Transits help us understand, what does this period of relationship (or lack of relationship) feel like? A basic method is to follow the Moon's daily transits, its zodiacal sign and phase (i.e., new Moon, 1/4 Moon, Full Moon, 3/4 Moon), but also the Moon's aspects to other transiting planets—especially the conjunction, opposition, and square. For example, days of Moon-Mercury aspects are times to talk or read together, to share ideas, or to be on the move. During Moon-Venus aspects we experience emotional comfort, harmony, ease, love, and tenderness. During Moon-Mars aspects we experience moodiness, anger, or irritability; being direct and blunt with each other; moments of tactless egotism; asserting our wishes and desires; erotic fire. Moon-Jupiter: kindness, generosity, travel, learning, adventures. Moon-Saturn: focus on responsibilities, time management, attention to everyday tasks and chores; washing the car, paying bills, buying groceries, doing laundry. Moon-Uranus: periods of emotional distancing and detachment; greater need for "space" from one another; moments of humor and incongruity; awareness of breaking news from the social-political sphere or realms of scientific discovery. Moon-Neptune: emotional fusion; avoidance, spacing out watching movies or TV; spending time together in silence and contemplation, meditation and prayer, quiet time in nature. Moon-Pluto: deep emotional catharsis, uncovering of deep hidden truths; processing old resentments and disagreements and working them through. We allow changing cycles of states and experiences.

We can apply the same principles to periods when the *secondary progressed* Moon forms aspects to natal planets. These periods mark momentous emotional experiences. Note the effects of the progressed Moon's conjunctions and oppositions to your natal planets and configurations—for example, progressed Moon setting off a T-square, rectangular formation, Grand Trine, or Yod (Finger of God) pattern.

Transits and progressions show changing phases and seasons of relationships. For example, during Mars-Uranus aspects we experience fierce anger or catch fire in bed. During Mercury-Saturn aspects we ponder decisions and mull over the facts. Mars-Jupiter aspects generate vigor, enterprise, and adventure. During any major Saturn transit partners or spouses face decisions or adversities together, persevere through difficult times, create stability and plan together for security, and exhibit reliability and maturity. During major transits of Uranus we should be open to change and adaptable to the unexpected. A woman with transiting Neptune conjunct Saturn in Aquarius in the 7th house was shaken when her husband lost his job unexpectedly and went through a lengthy period of uncertainty. But knowledge of the transit gave them both courage and faith as they went through this period. They both began to meditate and adopted an enlightened spiritual viewpoint.

Studying transits helps us understand phases of relationships. At times all relationships pass through rough waters. A woman named Beth with Pluto in the 2nd house (in late Leo) opposite Mars in the 8th (late Aquarius), had a difficult time in 1993 when transiting Saturn was conjunct her natal Mars and Pluto. Her husband's business failed, they got involved in some shady real estate deals, lost a lot of money, and were facing big tax problems. The 8th house rules marital finances, thus her husband's business income, and taxation. Issues of debt and marital finances dominated their lives during this period. Also, transiting Uranus and Neptune began passing over her Descendant. Her husband began drinking heavily, stopped working, and let his life spiral out of control. When we make a commitment to someone, we have to work with the other person's natal planets and transits, which become a new set of influences on our lives.

## Transforming Relationship Challenges

I once spoke to a woman named Nora after a two-month period when the progressed Moon was conjunct Uranus in her 8th house, the house of shared finances. She wanted to leave her husband. They were in the middle of a real estate deal, and there were some disagreements about money, sex, and lack of intimacy. I told Nora, "This is not a warm and fuzzy moment. Uranus feels chilly, like you want to separate and be independent. But this, by itself, is not an enduring trend—the progressed Moon is already separating from Uranus. Is it worth letting go of your marriage over some financial squabbles? Let this moment be what it is. The progressed contact in Gemini has stirred your creative thinking about your 8th house, your shared assets and investments." She thought hard about that. If we can help save one marriage through such a rudimentary insight about the progressed Moon, then our practice of astrology is powerful, and its immense therapeutic value is self-validating.

Then I said: "You have Mars in Aries in the 7th house opposite Venus in Libra. You've always been the conciliatory peacemaker. You also have to accept your husband's dynamic and assertive energy. Sometimes it feels like he's pushy. Can you see that engaging with his energy has made you stronger? Does it really diminish you if Mars sometimes gets his way? Would your relationship change if you could be more accepting of his initiative?" She conceded that, without him, she never would've made all these changes. She said, "I've been failing to see how beautiful and noble he is. I project my Mars onto him and let him take the initiative, and then I get angry at him for it." She accepted this challenge to change her way of relating. A Hawaiian Huna teaching states, "To love is to be happy with." Learning to be happy with other people is one of the fantastic things astrology can teach us.

## A Case Example Comparing Two Relationships

Brian, who married twice, is a very spiritual guy who has struggled to live with other people. He has Sun conjunct Uranus in Cancer, square Neptune in Libra. With Cancer Sun and Saturn in Scorpio in the 4th house he has a longing for family but he comes from a family with a lot of aggression and unpleasantness. Domestic life has always been fraught with anger. His Sun-Mars quincunx shows his potential for discordant anger, seething resentment, and emotional outbursts. Sun-Uranus also shows his eccentricities, and his 12th house Sun is very introverted, emotionally sensitive and touchy. He withdraws in the face of anger but is then inwardly consumed by it.

Brian's first wife "Ann," was 14 years older than Brian. She had Moon in Sagittarius in her 7th house closely conjunct Brian's Mars in Sagittarius. This 7th house Moon was a defining symbol of the relationship. She wanted a nurturing relationship and she wanted to nurture him. They lived in India, Kashmir, and Nepal and had many travel adventures together (Sagittarius). They were both good cooks and loved to prepare exotic meals for each other. But Brian's

Mars conjunct Ann's 7$^{th}$ house Moon brought irritation, anger, and constant quarreling. The marriage was emotionally volatile, moody, and touchy. Brian's Mars was opposite Ann's Venus in Gemini, which brought sexual attraction, but this gradually withered in the heat of their fiery arguments so that eventually they were left with a platonic friendship. Brian's Mars excited Ann's love (her Venus) but also evoked angry feelings (Moon-Mars) that made it hard for them to live together. Moreover, her Mars in Leo was exactly conjunct his Ascendant. It seemed she was always angry at him. Ann's Jupiter in Taurus was conjunct Brian's Midheaven. This Jupiter contact also symbolizes their extensive travels and their involvement in scholarship and international projects and business ventures. She was his teacher. Her Jupiter also trined Brian's Venus, indicating friendship and an emphasis on art and beauty in their relationship; they imported and sold Indian and Kashmiri art. His Moon was conjunct her south node in the 11$^{th}$ house. They were connected through involvement in a spiritual community (11$^{th}$ house). Her south node conjunct his Moon signifies that they were connected by a strong, caring emotional tie. But they didn't handle Mars energy (anger) well, and that was what made the difference. Ultimately they divorced and remained close friends. Sadly, Ann died of breast cancer when Pluto passed over her Descendant and conjunct her Moon, a few years after her divorce from Brian.

Now let's examine the synastry for Brian's second marriage. Brian met his second wife, Jenna, online. She lived on another continent. He traveled half way around the world to meet her, and they married after a one-week courtship. Jenna has Venus-Moon in Taurus conjunct his Midheaven. It was love at first sight. He enjoyed her physical beauty and felt her warm affection. Her Sun is closely conjunct his Moon, one of the strongest inter-chart contacts. Her Saturn and south node in Aquarius are conjunct Brian's Descendant, indicating that he took her seriously, and her presence in his life greatly increased his sense of responsibility. Brian had been having problems with drinking too much and not working, but the relationship with Jenna forced him to get his act together, to go out to work, and ultimately to become a father and a husband.

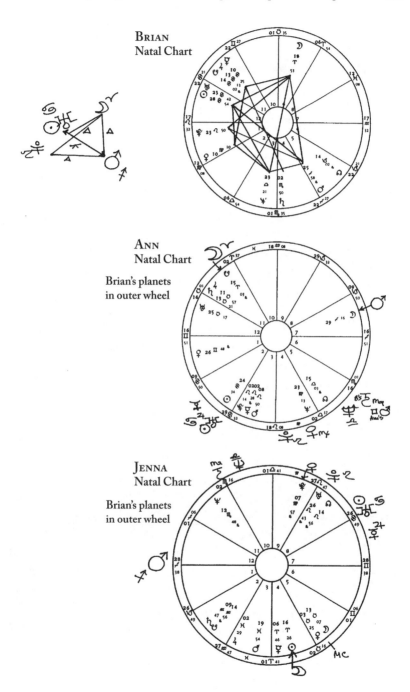

**18. Brian, Ann, and Jenna**

Jenna's Mars in Pisces squares his Mars in Sagittarius, indicating discord and clashes of will. Here's what Lois Sargent says about these Mars-Mars synastry aspects:

> Mars opposite or square Mars: There is some conflict of individual wills and desires, subtle if not openly expressed. There is a tendency at times to interfere with or obstruct each other's work. Disputes arise when differences cannot be adjusted. . . . There is usually some friction or hostility and in the square, vindictiveness is aroused unless individuals are in command of their emotional natures. These Mars aspects do not bring out the best in individual dispositions, so one or both must use much self-control to adjust this. These are very difficult aspects to work with in a close association unless there is much mutual tolerance as shown by other aspects. In marriage they can cause tensions, since the desire natures conflict; or, if they are in agreement, the individuals will not want what they want at the same time. In business or work association there will be differences in technical methods. Cooperation is difficult to achieve. It comes usually at the cost of one submitting to the other, in which case the submitting one will have to fight inner resentments.[140]

This interpersonal stress became particularly intense when transiting Pluto was conjunct Brian's Mars and square Jenna's Mars. They had bitter conflicts about money and sex, he became fixated on pornography, and there were two domestic violence incidents in which Jenna punched Brian.

Jenna's Pluto is conjunct his Venus; at first they had a deep sexual relationship but she became jealous and possessive and felt that he was still in love with his first wife, Ann (while she was still alive), which led to outbursts of jealous rage; again, his natal Mars-Sun quincunx was fully activated by transiting Pluto. They separated for a year. Once the Pluto transit was finished, their tempers cooled down and they got back together. Brian's Mars is square Jenna's Mars and conjunct her Sagittarius Ascendant; he motivated her to pursue further education. Mars-square Mars is always a need for two strong-willed people to fire each other up; clashes must be transformed into the energy to prod and change each other. Brian had gone from an angry family to an angry marriage with Ann, to an even more angry marriage with Jenna. Brian's Mercury-Jupiter is in Jenna's 7<sup>th</sup> house. They have a great intellectual connection and long conversations. His Moon is conjunct her Moon in the 4<sup>th</sup> house; he fulfills her sense of family. Jenna's Moon is in Taurus in the 5<sup>th</sup> house, symbol of her motherhood, and her Sun is in Aries in the 4<sup>th</sup> house. Jenna's Sun is conjunct Brian's Moon in the 9<sup>th</sup> house. Jenna is from another country and she fulfils his interest in other cultures, and for travel. She affirms Brian as a teacher, scholar, and writer (Sag. Moon in 9<sup>th</sup> house).

The real difference in his second marriage is that Brian receives Jenna's Venus-Moon energy; she is his loving, beautiful wife. By taming the fires within him and becoming more emotionally accessible Brian's life has been enhanced. His family is now reunited. He has made peace with his 4<sup>th</sup> house Saturn, the responsibilities that bind him and make his life whole.

All relationships require intense love, effort, commitment, patience, persistence, humor, and the wisdom to live through an infinite variety of conditions represented by the natal and transiting planetary patterns of both people in the relationship. Undoubtedly we are in a time of turbulence with Uranus square Pluto for the next five years and beyond. How we fare during this time will be largely determined by the quality, depth, and pliancy of our relationships. The wisdom of astrology can help each of us create more beautiful and resilient relationships.

# PART FIVE
# PREDICTIVE ASTROLOGY

Chapter 9

# *Introduction to Predictive Astrology*

Astrologers use reliable and time-tested methods to make their deductions. We can't predict exactly what will happen at a given time, because planetary symbols can manifest in many different ways, depending on our attitude, responsiveness, and level of consciousness. What we can discern are the structural outlines and major themes or tendencies operative at a given moment of time. This knowledge allows us to make realistic and helpful predictions about the unfolding shape of time.

To help us transform challenges into the finely woven threads of a conscious life, we need a clear understanding of astrology's time-measuring techniques. Rudhyar wrote:

> Astrology does not predict "events" but only phases in a person's development. Every individual develops along lines which are first of all "generic. . . . [I]t can be fairly certain that the known order of normal phases of human development will be approximately experienced by the client in as much as he is a human being; and this gives the astrologer a basis for prediction. Yet no astrologer should stop there. He should seek to define and understand the "individual equation" in his client—which means, the way the client does, and can be expected to react to the basic turning points of his life as an individual. This can only be done by considering the birth-chart and its time development as a whole. The individual is the whole-man, the integral person. And no one can determine in advance the actions and reactions of an integral person who has become truly individualized; for such a person has become free, within the limits of his generic structures. Astrology can define the limits, but it can only suggest the freedom. Every moment of the life of an individual is a composite of both these factors.[141]

In this chapter I'll discuss three techniques of modern predictive astrology, and how you can apply them to your own life. I won't

cover all the available methods, but the ones I have found most useful and reliable:

- *Transits*: tracking the continuous motion of planets through the
  sky.
- *Secondary progressions*, measuring the unfolding of the birth chart
  by examining planetary movements in the days after birth,
  viewing one day after birth as symbolically equivalent to one
  year of life.
- *Solar arc directions*: directing all natal planets and angles forward approximately one degree per year of life—the distance
  between natal Sun and the progressed Sun.

I won't discuss the important topics of solar returns, horary
astrology, and mundane prediction. Also, there are several additional predictive methods not covered here that I feel are well worth
studying, for example *tertiary progressions*, which view one day after
birth as equivalent to one lunar month (27.5 days) of life; and *minor
progressions*, where one lunar return (i.e., one month) after birth is
considered symbolically equivalent to one year of life. Minor progressed planets move around quickly so they're fun and exciting to
work with. [142]

The most basic astrological symbolism can be used for prediction. Natal, transiting, or progressed planets in a particular sign
evoke characteristic themes that can be a starting point. Here are a
few brief keywords:

♈ : assertiveness, anger, egocentrism.
♉ : money, comfort, purchases, ownership.
♊ : words, language, speaking and writing, communication, reading, travel and mobility.
♋ : home, family, real estate, moods, emotions, memories.
♌ : fun, play, joy, self-expression, pride, performance, creativity,
  children.
♍ : work, health, training, analysis, criticism, self-improvement,
  dissatisfaction.
♎ : love, friendship, marriage, harmony, cooperation.

♏ : sex, intimacy, power, control, jealousy, discord, death-rebirth.

♐ : education, distance travel, teachers, knowledge, ethics, beliefs, religion, philosophy.

♑ : career, ambition, achievement, status, social position, conservative values.

♒ : politics, groups, membership, change, revolution, innovation, progressive values.

♓ : spirituality, surrender, helplessness, mystery, dreams, sleep, the unknown.

## PREDICTION AND ANTICIPATION

It's important not to fall into the belief that everything is predestined by the planets. Prediction and anticipation shouldn't be an excuse for passivity. However, the core belief shared by all astrologers is that there are *patterns of experience* indicated by planetary movements. The purpose of predictive astrology isn't to know exactly what's going to happen. That's unrealistic. Our goal is to discern the inner pattern of our life experience, seeing it as unfolding in accordance within the symphonic celestial order.

We have free will in molding our responses to transits and progressions. Yet free will isn't absolute. There are unexpected acts of God, manifestations of fate, occurrences that seem destined, not consciously chosen. For example, Pluto often manifests as an encounter with forces beyond our control, or as the intervention of a higher power. When transiting Pluto was conjunct my Ascendant, at age 20, I had a near-death experience after contracting typhoid fever in India. As I lay for five days in a hospital bed I realized what a thin line there was between life and death. Pluto brought a moment of awakening. Astrologers are fascinated with decoding the celestial indicators of events, but our attitude and actions also affect the course of events.

Psychological astrologers believe that we influence the level at which planetary symbols can manifest. We always have *choice* about how we respond to the planets and our circumstances. Thus, when we speak of astrological prediction we aren't suggesting that we're powerless. The study of predictive astrology should make us more active and involved in how we create our destiny, not passively resigned to what is fated. Humanistic astrologers study transits to anticipate trends and developmental tasks and to guide our choices and actions. We experience the planets as internal principles, not as deities that strictly determine our destiny. Instead of remaining stuck in a fatalistic, doom and gloom attitude, we can use astrology to envision possibilities. This is the foundation of my approach to the study of prediction. Instead of thinking that events are predestined, we determine what actions and responses are required of us at each stage of evolution. To the extent that we anticipate trends and prepare ourselves in advance to meet life's challenges, we're intelligently practicing predictive astrology. But I reiterate it's not only about *predicting*, but also about *acting*.

## Looking Backward, Looking Forward

Astrologers anticipate upcoming tasks and trends using transits and progressions. We begin by looking backward into the past, studying events that have already occurred and finding correlations with natal patterns, transits, and progressions. In this way we learn to assess the possible outcomes of future transits and progressions. We look backward into the past before trying to look forward into the future. We study our own charts to see how we've responded to past planetary contacts. We also study life histories, to see how a person's natal structures, transits, and progressions have manifested. By studying past events we anticipate the outcome of future transits and progressions; we can predict.

While reading through the next several chapters, begin to identify central transits and progressions you've experienced and what happened at those crucial moments. Identify core events that mark the major milestones of your life: love, marriage, divorce, births, deaths; accidents, injuries, and illnesses; successes and failures; voyages and homecomings. Locate the transits and progressions that symbolize these events. Also study multiple contacts to the same natal planetary configurations. For example, note the effects of several outer planet transits to your natal Sun, Moon, or other planets. Notice themes emerging that reflect the birth chart symbolism.

For example, my father had Pluto in Cancer in the 12<sup>th</sup> house. Transiting Saturn was conjunct natal Pluto near the end of World War II, at which time he was seriously injured and spent several months recuperating in a hospital (12<sup>th</sup> house). 58 years later (two Saturn cycles), Saturn returned to conjunction with natal Pluto in the 12<sup>th</sup> house. I was fully aware of this transit and watched with awe when, like clockwork, he was hospitalized again, this time with an infection (Pluto). Astrological patterns and experiences repeat. In both instances, a force apparently beyond his conscious control forced a retreat from the front lines of his life and a period of time turned inward (Pluto in 12<sup>th</sup> house).

By studying how your chart has responded in the past to transits you can predict what may unfold during future or upcoming transits, because you'll understand how your planets express themselves, how they tend to manifest. Before making predictions about the future I assess how major transits and progressions have already manifested in a person's life. If transiting Uranus is about to aspect a natal planet, I assess prior transits of outer planets (especially Saturn) to the same natal planet. In this way, I assess the person's level of consciousness and ability to express the major themes indicated by the horoscope. Prediction isn't magic. It's the result of careful analysis of the chart and thoughtful deductions.

Making mistakes is also part of the process of learning to be an astrologer. We may misjudge certain astrological symbolism, underestimating or overestimating its influence. You don't have to be perfect at this. Becoming a great astrologer is a learning process, a lifetime apprenticeship. Hopefully it's a very fun and interesting process that challenges us to anticipate trends more and more skillfully. We gain proficiency in prediction by testing our expectations of results against our observations of what actually unfolds. With practice, we feel how the planets operate more precisely and accurately. Aligning with the planets, we begin to act in ways that enhance the evolutionary potentials shown by transits and progressions. We learn to co-creatively participate in our evolution. This is why astrology is such a valuable tool in helping us become extraordinary human beings.

Chapter 10

# *Transits*

The study of planetary transits is the central technique of astrological prediction. Following the ongoing motion of planets through the zodiacal signs and the houses of our birth charts, and forming aspects to natal planets (and angles) allows us to observe correlations to major life trends. During transits a particular quality of experience is dominant: Venus: peace, love, and harmony. Mars: anger, energy, momentum, initiative, or desire. Jupiter: goal-setting, aspirations, adventurousness, planning, and optimism; growth, ease, and opportunity. Saturn: serious attitude, hard work, decision, commitment, practicality. Uranus: change, restlessness, originality. Neptune: unfocusing, uncertainty, idealism, dreams and visions. Pluto: turning points, endings and new beginnings.

There's no definitive statement one can make about any transit. The interpretations I offer here don't come from books I've read; they're not the law. They're simply what I've observed. I want you to make your own observations, follow your own intuition, and reach your own conclusions. What I want you to grasp in your own way is the exquisite poetry of transits, their beautiful rhythms, which are steady and reliable, and descriptive of each moment's poignant meaning.

To anticipate the outcome of a transit, study how a natal planet (or angle) has responded in the past to transits. Remember that you're not the passive victim of transits. But it's up to you to turn it into an active process. If transiting Uranus is square your Sun, examine where your Sun is placed, and what past transits you've had to your Sun. For example, what happened when Saturn aspected your Sun by conjunction, square, or opposition?

I treat the conjunction, square, opposition, semisquare and sesquiquadrate aspects of transiting planets equally. All of these aspects are dynamic activations of the natal planet. The major difference is that with the conjunction only one house is involved. But if, for example, transiting Jupiter is square or opposite the Sun, then in our interpretation we need to consider both the natal Sun's house placement and transiting Jupiter's current house position.

## TRANSITS AND CRISIS

Transits symbolize processes of behavioral and attitudinal growth and change. Some of these changes are challenging and require reassessment of our assumptions, commitments, and behaviors. Some of these challenges are so intense that while experiencing the transit we feel that we're in crisis. Astrology can enable us to identify the nature of the crisis, its meaning and purpose, what it asks of us, and its probable length. Transits to natal Moon can involve an emotional crisis or realization. Transits to Mercury may involve a crisis in our way of thinking or communicating. Transits to Venus can denote a crisis in our way of relating to others, a change or upheaval in a relationship, or a crisis involving money. Transits to Mars signify a crisis involving the necessity of taking action, expressing initiative, anger, or self-assertiveness; or there can be a crisis involving our expression of sexual drives and desires. Transits to Jupiter may indicate a crisis involving clarifying our beliefs or philosophy of life, or formulating plans and life objectives. Transits to Saturn may involve a crisis involving our commitments, life structures, and work. Saturn teaches patience, perseverance, and commitment; everything in life takes time. Transits to Uranus can evoke a crisis stemming from our need to be true to ourselves, to individuate, to innovate. Transits to natal Neptune may denote a crisis involving our faith in unseen powers and intentions of the Spirit.

Consider this teaching from Alexander Ruperti:

WHAT IS A CRISIS? Cycles are measurements of change. In order for any purpose to be realized, change must take place, and change . . . involves crises. . . . A crisis, however, is not a terrible calamity. It derives from the Greek word krino, "to *decide*," and means simply *a time for decision*[,] . . . a turning point—that which precedes change. In order to avoid a crisis one would have to avoid change itself, an obvious impossibility. . . . [T]o humanistically oriented astrologers, crises are not external events, even though external events may precipitate them or condition their development. Crises . . . are . . . opportunities for growth. . . . Some of these turning-points are biological (such as adolescence and menopause) and are met at specific ages, while others are individual and may occur at any time. . . . An astrologer can deduce the timing and nature of potential future crises from the transits and progressions. If one expects a specific type of change . . . he or she can prepare to meet it *consciously and with open eyes,* and may gain more from it in terms of personal maturity and spiritual unfoldment. Such knowledge may also help one to avoid overly rash or hasty decisions. Also, the sense of despair which often arises in the midst of a crisis can be dispelled by the astrologer's ability to predict the cycle's end. Foreknowledge can also have negative effects, however. The anticipation of an impending crisis very often induces fear and anxiety. . . . Ideally this negative approach should be less likely . . . since its aim is spiritual development rather than materialistic enrichment or comfort. The humanistic astrologer should know, moreover, that crises are not isolated events, but phases of individual growth. He should interpret them with reference to the smaller or greater cycles within which they occur—as phases of these cycles. . . . Humanistic astrology will therefore be able to bring a sense of direction, orientation and purposefulness to every crisis. The ability to envision what could and should develop in the future . . . even while one is in the midst of a chaotic current situation is not aided by most astrological textbooks. It must be learned by facing experiences in terms of the fourth dimension of time . . . by seeing the whole cycle in every living moment and by approaching that present moment in a clear and conscious manner. Although humanistic astrology can greatly assist in the understanding of future crises, this approach may be even more valuable in understanding those crises which have already occurred. Such hindsight is the best preparation for . . . meeting the crises of growth yet to come.[143]

## STUDYING TRANSITS IN THE EPHEMERIS

To study transits properly it's useful to utilize a planetary ephemeris. Some people read the newspaper or magazines to keep up with the news. Investors and stock traders read the stock reports. Astrologers study the ephemeris. These days, however, our computer software programs do all the necessary calculations and print out beautiful charts, so why do we need the ephemeris? Computers can significantly aid us and are essential, but there's no way one can become a competent astrologer, much less a masterful one, without studying the ephemeris. When you see a computer printout of a chart you see something *static*. When you read the ephemeris you observe the ongoing motion of planets; you observe something *alive and dynamic*, the living process of the sky, the fluid, ever-changing pattern of the planets. By reading the ephemeris you observe the unfolding planetary pattern as an ever-evolving story that you can feel, anticipate, and participate in.

Studying the ephemeris enables us to feel the length of time a transit will be influencing us. For example, a friend of mine once had a very difficult week at work where a coworker criticized his work to their mutual boss, and made a grab for power on a major project. The coworker exuded hostility, negativity, and paranoia. At the time, transiting Sun and Pluto were conjunct for a few days in my friend's 6ᵗʰ house. He called me and asked if I thought he should look for another job. As this was such a brief transit I was confident the crisis would pass quickly, as soon as the transit ended. That was exactly what happened. With Sun-Pluto in the 6ᵗʰ house, my friend had to pass through a brief unpleasant encounter with an unscrupulous person in the workplace.

## TRANSITS OF THE SUN, MOON, AND INNER PLANETS

Look at the ephemeris for this year. Look at the column of the Sun. Note the transiting Sun spending a month in each of the zodiacal signs. For that month we attempt to realize the evolutionary goals of that sign.

Observe when the transiting Sun will be conjunct or opposite your natal Sun, Moon, and other personal planets, your Ascendant and MC, and any prominent natal configurations. Those days will place notable emphasis on experiences and events signified by those planets or angles. For example, when transiting Sun is conjunct Mercury you may find that on that day you're drawn to reading, learning, talking, or traveling from place to place. When transiting Sun is aspecting Venus you focus on friendship, love, or the arts. Days when transiting Sun is conjunct or opposite Saturn emphasize work, focus, responsibilities. Next, study the Sun in relation to other transiting planets. Note when it's conjunct, opposite, or square the other planets. Interpret the transit as a strong emphasis on that planetary archetype for several days. The transiting Sun is an important influence that should be tracked constantly.

Recently the transiting Sun was conjunct Neptune for a week. It rained steadily for eight straight days. People I encountered were sorrowful, lost, confused, feeling helpless, weak, or victimized by their circumstances. It was a time of collective suffering as the stock market fell dramatically. During this Sun-Neptune conjunction I was immersed in studies of dreams, hermetic philosophy, alchemy, and astrology. I was flooded with intuitive insights and felt inner access to formless realms of spirit. Knowledge of the transiting aspects allows conscious responsiveness and expression of each potential.

During a transiting Sun-Mars square I felt a surge of physical energy, played several competitive games of basketball with a friend, and was injured when he lowered his shoulder and plowed into me. This collision threw my neck of out of alignment and I had to go to the chiropractor. Mars often manifests as a clash, a scrape or cut, an injury. I was in a testy mood after this incident.

Now look at the Moon in the ephemeris. Note how the Moon changes signs every couple of days. For the next month, watch the transiting Moon passing through the twelve signs and notice any subtle correlation between the Moon sign and the focus of that day:

• Aries Moon: assertiveness, selfish attitude, feisty mood, aggression, impulsiveness.

- Taurus Moon: focus on money, comfort, sensual enjoyment, purchases.
- Moon in Gemini: talkative mood, more communicative, curious, reading, literary interests.
- Moon in Cancer: fluctuating mood, focus on emotions, home, family, memories.
- Moon in Leo: joyous mood, having fun, relaxing, creativity.
- Moon in Virgo: anxious mood, worry, concern with work, health, order and cleanliness, self-improvement.
- Moon in Libra: outgoing, sociable, friendly mood, accommodating others.
- Moon in Scorpio: sexy or mischievous mood, passion and intensity; issues in partnership about power, sex, and money.
- Moon in Sagittarius: adventurous mood, planning, expansive, philosophical reflection.
- Moon in Capricorn: serious mood, task oriented, getting down to business.
- Moon in Aquarius: rebellious, defiant, zany mood, unpredictable events, interest in groups, politics, social issues, breaking news.
- Moon in Pisces: spacey mood, laid back, sleepy, at peace, unfocused, feeling alone, helpless, or victimized; spiritual mood and longings.

Observe the Moon sign changes for one month. Then observe it for the month after that, and the month after that. Study this forever. Watch the transiting Moon! Transiting Moon passing over natal planets can be felt mildly. Closely observe the Moon's transiting conjunctions and oppositions with other transiting planets.

Observe monthly contacts of the transiting Moon by conjunction, opposition, and square with all the other transiting planets. Days when the Moon is conjunct Mercury are very busy, focused on details, documents, communication, errands, writing, ideas. When the Moon is conjunct Venus, it's time to focus on people, relationships, art, music, beauty, clothing, and appearance. When Moon is conjunct Mars there's more anger, annoyance, impatience, hostility, and sexual energy. Moon-Jupiter days focus on learning, education, patience, kindness, generosity, trust, hopeful attitude. Moon-Saturn days are highly focused, task-oriented; we have to stay on schedule, bring order to our lives, and follow through to finish and accomplish things. When the Moon is conjunct Uranus, expect the unexpected; we feel an urge to freedom. Moon-Neptune days are good times to space out, meditate, study astrology, sleep, read fiction and spiritual literature. Moon-Pluto days often see eruption of deep emotions, or something buried resurfaces; emotional upsets and realizations.

The transiting Moon always describes the mood of the moment, the emotional quality of that day, and it acts as a trigger for other planetary transits. For example, in the fall of 2003 transiting Mars and Uranus were conjunct in early Pisces. The effects of that explosive Mars-Uranus conjunction were felt most powerfully on those days when the Moon was also in Pisces, conjunct Mars and Uranus. The occupation of Iraq was in full swing, as was the active and violent resistance to it. Moon acts as a trigger, like the second hand of a clock. Many events are timed precisely by the transiting Moon. Think of my earlier example of the Moon-Pluto conjunction in Virgo on the day when I was hit by a car.

Pay attention to the lunation cycle, the ongoing relationship of the Sun and Moon. Energy builds from New Moon to Full Moon, and begins to dissipate from Full Moon through the end of the lunation. Study the section on "The Lunation Cycle" in Chapter 3. If you've never studied Rudhyar's book, *The Lunation Cycle*, read it now.

Look at the ephemeris and find the next several New Moons and the next Full Moons. Track these lunation phases by sign, house, and aspects. The house of the New Moon shows an area where we may observe notable developments over the course of the month. The New Moon is the time to initiate some new cycle of activity in that house. Things develop and come to a climax in that realm of life around the time of the Full Moon. Then we reassess during the waning phases of the lunation until we prepare to meet the challenges of the next New Moon, the next new cycle in a different house, a different realm of life. Examine any major aspects formed by the New Moon or Full Moon to other natal and transiting planets—especially as lunations trigger other aspects forming in the sky.

Pay special attention to New Moons and Full Moons that occur within about 10° of the Moon's nodes—the solar and lunar eclipses. Eclipses can be very potent if they contact our natal planets or angles. The effect of the eclipse is felt for 6–12 months afterwards. Watch any transits over the eclipse point, including subsequent lunations and especially transiting Mars, Jupiter, Saturn, or Uranus. These transits trigger the eclipse point powerfully. But the eclipse, in and of itself, can have a potent effect if it closely contacts natal planets or angles. One famous example is the assassination of John F. Kennedy on November 22, 1963. The preceding solar eclipse was on July 20, 1963 at 27° Cancer 24, closely conjunct JFK's natal Saturn in the 10th house at 27° Cancer 10. This eclipse conjunct Saturn signified the ultimate tragedy in subsequent months.

Once I had a solar eclipse conjunct my natal Saturn in the 3rd house of driving and motor vehicles. On that day I was peacefully driving my old Honda station wagon when it suddenly died from a blown head gasket. R.I.P., sweet jalopy. But the deeper meaning of the event was that I was truly ready for a better car. For financial reasons, I'd been hesitant to move forward with a new vehicle until events forced me to do so. Another eclipse occurred in Gemini in my 9th house, conjunct transiting Saturn in my 9th house, and opposite my natal Saturn in Sagittarius. In other words, in the height of my transiting Saturn opposition there was also an eclipse contacting both natal and transiting Saturn. Clearly this was a significant eclipse. Would it indicate tragedy, difficulty, or adversity? I had an extremely demanding schedule of teaching over the next several months after the eclipse, indeed for the next year. I was offered additional work teaching at a second university and was intensely focused on a writing project. It was a focused, constructive, Saturnian period of hard work. The lesson here is not to accept traditional negative, fearful interpretations of Saturn, or any other planet.

Now look at Mercury in the ephemeris. Transits of Mercury show the current focus of our minds, and show what we're thinking about. Track the retrograde periods of transiting Mercury and the conjunctions of Mercury and the Sun, noting their house and sign placement. You can make use of these transits to rethink the issues related to those signs and houses. (See "The Cycle of Mercury" in

PLANETS IN THERAPY

Chapter 7). Mercury's transits to natal planets are also significant. We're involved in thinking about the matters connected to that planet. I closely watch Mercury's conjunction or opposition to other transiting planets: Mercury-Mars: argument, debate, verbal repartee, sarcasm. Mercury-Jupiter: learning, reading, education. Mercury-Saturn: practical thinking, strategy, decision-making. Mercury-Uranus: exposure to new ideas, hatching original thoughts; interest in science, innovation, discoveries, social issues and politics. Mercury-Neptune: interest in fiction, fantasy, myth, religion, dreams, astrology, mysticism, spirituality. Mercury-Pluto: research, investigation, persuasive expression of opinions. Attunement to the transits of Mercury brings increased intelligence and mental clarity to the conscious astrologer.

Transits of Venus denote peace and harmony in the realm of life where Venus is transiting. I watch Venus transits in aspect to other transiting planets, showing changing qualities of relational experience. Venus-Mercury: a good conversation, pleasant verbal expression. Venus-Mars: harmonious sexual experiences; heightened artistic or musical expression. Venus-Jupiter: relating to cultured, refined people; enjoyment of luxury, comforts, wealth. Venus-Saturn: stresses in relationship, issues of trust, loyalty, and commitment in relationships; longevity of friendships; financial stress, savings, conservative attitude toward money and spending. Venus-Uranus: Independence, distancing, or freedom in relationships, sudden attractions, connecting to unusual people, groups of diverse individuals. Venus-Neptune: Devotion, adoration, compassionate love. Venus-Pluto: obsessions, fixations, and possessiveness in love; deeply erotic relationships; in some instances these aspects are associated with jealousy, affairs, and betrayals in love. Follow in the ephemeris as you watch Venus approaching conjunction and opposition with other transiting planets. Observe how you relate to others on those days.

Now study the movements of Mars in the ephemeris. Mars transits the entire chart in two years, acting as a potent catalyst of any natal planet or other transiting planet it contacts. Many major events occur during Mars transits. Mars can manifest as the planet of discord, conflict, or injury, or we can also consciously relate to

Mars as our capacity for action, initiative, drive, and motivation. Transits of Mars may correspond to stresses, conflicts, anger, or mishaps, but if we anticipate Mars transits we can use the energy of this planet as an impetus to action.

Once I saw transiting Mars approaching an extended stay in Capricorn in my 4th house (home, property, domestic matters). I got several projects underway in the garden and began sanding my front steps to prepare them for refinishing. This involved a lot of physical exertion (Mars). I did lots of house cleaning, too. "Predicting" the effect of a Mars transit enables us to make good use the planetary energy. The transit becomes a process I'm involved with, not just something that happens to me.

Study the current house placement of Mars. This is a place where we're active, applying our energy, getting motivated. Especially watch periods when Mars is retrograde; this is often a stress period in that house, a time when we may face conflicts, disagreements, mishaps, impatience, or the abrasive effect of hasty or impulsive actions. When Mars is retrograde in the 2nd house we may have expenses and expenditures. Retrograde Mars in the 4th house often marks family or domestic stress, discord; or something in the home breaks and needs repair. Mars retrograde in the 8th house may denote stress and conflict in relationships regarding money, sex, and power. Mars retrograde in the 6th house may manifest as some stress around health issues, or in the workplace. During Mars transits we need to deal with the stress and pressures that suddenly mount. Being informed about the Mars transit helps us keep cool under pressure.

While Venus transits tend to be soft, Mars transits pack more of a wallop. One woman had transiting Mars in Pisces conjunct her Descendant and opposite natal Saturn in Virgo on the Ascendant. For a few days she experienced health upset (Saturn in Virgo), employment stress, feeling fatigued (Saturn), and anger toward her boss (Saturn: authority figures), whom she felt was pushy and demanding (Mars conjunct Descendant). She was stressed by her boss's demands. She felt anxious and dissatisfied, and considered quitting her job (Mars opposite Saturn in Virgo). I recommended that she wait until after the transit was complete before making that decision. Mars transits such as this are not catastrophic, but they're not always pleasant either. However, the aggravation usually only lasts a few days, so we needn't make a mountain out of an anthill. The annoyance often passes quickly.

Also study contacts of transiting Mars with other transiting planets. Once a Mars-Pluto conjunction formed in Sagittarius. Big storms were brewing at my school (Sagittarius) with a problematic student who couldn't control her anger (Mars-Pluto). She was eventually asked to leave our program. It wasn't pretty. Sometimes Mars transits bring a little heat!

## Transits Through the Twelve Houses

Before discussing transits of the slower-moving planets let's examine the general effect of transiting planets moving through the natal houses. All transits can be understood partly through reflecting on the house a planet is transiting through. Transiting planets moving through houses of the birth chart tend to awaken new awareness of the issues related to that house. The same is true of progressed planets, such as the progressed Moon moving through a house.

Transits through the 1$^{st}$ house evoke issues about my identity, my appearance, the way I behave, the impression I make on others, the image I project. These transits focus on my self, my desires, who I want to be at this time. Also, the Ascendant and 1$^{st}$ house govern the body. If Saturn is passing through my 1$^{st}$ house I might want to straighten up my appearance, or exhibit a more serious or professional demeanor; also, I tend to feel more tired from hard work and responsibilities. In contrast, if Uranus is transiting my 1$^{st}$ house I may wish to radically change my appearance or deliberately project a more independent, rebellious, colorful, or unconventional image or demeanor. I may be somewhat high strung. When Jupiter transits the first house, I might experience weight gain, improved self-image, feeling better about myself. Transiting Venus in the 1$^{st}$ house is a great time of the year to get your hair done or buy some new clothes to enhance and beautify your persona. When Mars transits in the 1$^{st}$ house I'm more feisty, assertive, energetic, and motivated.

Transits through the 2<sup></sup> house evoke issues about my finances, my need to work, my wish to own or acquire something to enhance my pleasure or comfort. With transiting Saturn in the 2nd house I need to work hard to survive, to slowly save money, to develop a more mature and practical attitude about money. With transiting Neptune in the 2nd house I might make poor financial decisions, or be unattached to material possessions, or make generous charitable donations to others. We don't hold onto money.

Transits through the 3rd house evoke interest in learning, reading, acquiring information, traveling, and being mobile, issues about cars and transportation. Transits in the 3rd house may also bring greater awareness of siblings, neighbors or others contacts in daily life. For example, transiting Mars in the 3rd house: stress about car or transportation, arduous journey, friction with siblings, neighbors, or roommates. Jupiter in the 3rd house: enjoyment of travel, excursions; educational reading; better communication skills. Uranus in the 3rd house: being exposed to new ideas, new learning, new interests, new verbal expression; change in one's mode of travel or transportation.

Transits through the 4th house evoke issues about my home and family, and my desire for emotional closeness with family members. These transits bring greater attention to my actual living situation (whether enjoying it or changing it), domestic activities, the office, and the need to invest energy into home improvement projects.

Transits through the 5th house evoke my desire for fun, play, recreation, and self-expression; or these are periods to give more attention to children. These transits may correspond to more outgoing periods of enjoying entertainment, hobbies, dating, dancing, or performing. The behavior of children, or quality of interaction with children, changes with 5th house transits. When transiting Mars is in the 5th house, children are more physically active, willful, and prone to tantrums or selfish demands. With Mercury in the 5th, children are more talkative, alert, perceptive. Jupiter in the 5th often denotes growth in a child's intelligence, understanding, moral character. When Saturn transits the 5th, children face challenges, fears, obstacles, grow more responsible and mature, and learn discipline. Uranus in the 5th: children act zany, funny, unpredictable, defiant, unique. Neptune in the 5th house: a child may seem sleepy, unfocused, or inattentive, lives in a fantasy, make-believe world, or seems physically weak or lethargic, or emotionally dependent; or the child may show signs of heightened imagination, intuition, or spirituality.

Transits through the 6th house focus my awareness on needed changes in health, habits, diet, or improvement of work skills. There may be changes related to the job or workplace environment. While transiting Mars was retrograde in her 6th house for several months, a woman made great efforts to improve her health and lost 25 pounds through regular exercise.

Transits through the 7th house shed light on current relationship dynamics, in friendships, business, or marriage. For example, when transiting Saturn is in the 7th house we may settle down with somebody, make a deeper commitment, or we face difficulties and adversity in relationships. This period demands maturation in relationships. Periods when Mars transits in the 7th house correspond to times of heightened energy, sexual desire, or friction and discord in relationships. Transiting Jupiter in the 7th house often denotes meeting new friends, contacts with helpful, generous, educated people; improvements in relationships and social life. When Neptune transits the 7th house we may feel up in the air or undecided about a relationship. We may be in an ambiguous interpersonal situation. There may be patterns of denial or avoidance in a relationship; or a friend, partner, or spouse may be dependent, spacey, or ungrounded. Transiting Pluto in the 7th house may symbolize relationships with powerful, magnetic people, or relationships in which jealousy, mistrust, vindictiveness, or power dynamics predominate.

Transits through the 8th house evoke issues and concerns about trust, intimacy, sex, money, and power in relationships; issues about credit, debt, shared assets or purchases may also be involved.

Transits in the 9th house correspond to periods of greater interest in travel, education, expanding one's horizons, seeking truth, or clarification of our moral, spiritual, or philosophical principles.

10th house transits correspond to periods of focus on career, position, status, authority, and ability to meet professional or occupational goals.

11th house transits bring more involvement in groups, organizations, social activism, gathering together, networking, attending meetings or group meetings. The quality of this involvement changes depending on the transiting planet involved. Saturn in the 11th: organizational responsibilities. Uranus in the 11th: affiliating with an unusual group, or new kinds of people or associates, or involvement in a political movement for social change. Neptune in the 11th house: more interest in spiritual growth in groups, or groups focused on healing addictions.

12th house transits can enhance one's inner life through greater focus on spirituality, meditation, mysticism, astrology, metaphysics. These may also be periods of more solitude, inwardness, isolation, or feeling of invisibility.

This general framework can be applied to understanding transits of any planet through the houses of the birth chart.

## JUPITER TRANSITS

Jupiter strengthens, amplifies, or magnifies the expression of any planet it contacts. Jupiter transits to Venus expand our sociability, artistic expression, our ability to connect to others and project our talents in a graceful, pleasing way. Jupiter-Mars contacts increase vitality, motivation, and initiative. Jupiter-Mercury contacts increase the clarity of our mental concentration on learning tasks, readings, writing, or clear communication. Jupiter transits to Saturn show increased focus on achieving goals and solidifying commitments and life structures. Jupiter transits to Neptune amplify our interests in spirituality, meditation, mysticism, or dreams. Occasionally, if a person hasn't found a spiritual path or isn't attuned to the guidance of the unconscious, these transits can increase a sense of confusion, helplessness, or victimization.

Jupiter transits bring opportunities for growth, expansion, and improvement in whatever area of life it is transiting. Here's a brief tour of Jupiter through the houses:

1st House: improved self-image and projection of personality; more hopeful outlook, planning and goal-setting.
2nd House: improved income and enjoyment of material comforts.
3rd House: improved learning, mental acuity, and access to infor-

mation; greater mobility, improved communication, speech, or writing skills.

4$^{th}$ House: improved living situation and family relationships; bigger or improved home or office.

5$^{th}$ House: improved ability to relax, play, enjoy, engage in hobbies; growth and expansion of children, creative activities.

6$^{th}$ House: improved skills, work situation, and relations with co-workers; improved health through better diet, exercise.

7$^{th}$ House: improved social life, friendships, and relationships.

8$^{th}$ House: improved marital finances, partner's income increases; access to loans and financial assistance from spouse, family, or financial institutions.

9$^{th}$ House: improved educational and travel opportunities; improved outlook cultivated by learning, study, travel.

10$^{th}$ House: improved career opportunities, reputation, and job standing; new professional goals.

11$^{th}$ House: improved involvement in groups, organizations, politics, professional associations.

12$^{th}$ House: improved spiritual life, enjoyment of solitude, understanding of metaphysics and spiritual doctrine; increased dream activity.

Jupiter's movement through each house uplifts and improves our involvement in that house, provided we act upon opportunities. Jupiter transits can correspond to periods in which things fall into place naturally. But if we remain inert nothing much will happen. Jupiter can also be the planet of laziness and false hopes. Jupiter transits bring opportunities, but these moments pass quickly—unless Jupiter goes retrograde. Watch the four phases of the Jupiter cycle: the Jupiter return, Jupiter's waxing and waning squares and opposition to its natal position.

Study the past several Jupiter transit cycles. What happened when Jupiter was conjunct, square, or opposite your Sun, Moon, and other natal planets? What happened as transiting Jupiter passed through the houses of your birth chart? Note how you experienced periods of growth, improvement, or planning in the areas of life indicated.

## Saturn Transits

Both Saturn's natal position and transiting Saturn's current position should be considered carefully in the interpretation of any horoscope. Find natal Saturn's house position, which indicates areas where we face some difficulties and obstacles in life, especially in youth. Saturn's house shows where we have to overcome problems and fears, and develop structures:

- Natal Saturn in the 1st house: regarding self-image and identity.
- Saturn in the 2nd house: regarding money and survival, the ability to support oneself and attain material security.
- Saturn in the 3rd house: regarding one's intelligence, the ability to communicate, speak, or write one's ideas and opinions; also issues about driving and transportation.
- Saturn in the 4th house: regarding family, home, parents, and one's emotional life.
- Saturn in the 5th house: regarding creativity, performing, the ability to play and have fun, and regarding children.
- Saturn in the 6th house: regarding health and employment.
- Saturn in the 7th house: regarding friendship, love, and relationships.
- Saturn in the 8th house: regarding sex and intimacy, and sharing of resources in relationships.
- Saturn in the 9th house: regarding travel, education, religion, truth.
- Saturn in the 10th house: regarding career, ambitions, status, social position.
- Saturn in the 11th house: regarding politics, social issues, groups, organizations, meetings.
- Saturn in the 12th house: regarding solitude, isolation, spirituality, mysticism.

Transits of Saturn ask us to focus, work, and overcome our fears and obstacles in these areas of life. Each Saturn transit represents a significant developmental task. Often that means becoming aware of inhibitions, areas where we're challenged and immature. But the Saturn transit can teach us lessons that cause us to become more mature, more realistic in our appraisal of where we are in life, what our real talents, capacities, and limitations are, and what our responsibilities are. I'm not saying Saturn transits are rosy and easy; hard work is always involved. But work isn't as hard if you have focus and a sense of purpose. The transits of Saturn mean we have to face that area of life (house) or that part of ourselves (natal planet) with clarity and realism. The current transiting position of Saturn shows us where we need to get organized, focus on our responsibilities, and get things done. The cycle of Saturn delineates pivotal stages of our development. You should understand Saturn's four major phases— its conjunction, waxing square, opposition and waning square to its natal positions. Study Saturn's transits over the four angles and through the houses, and transiting Saturn's aspects to other planets. Saturn shows us areas where we need to work persistently to stabilize our lives.

Closely examine your experience of Saturn. Study what happened at each major phase of your Saturn cycle, the first quarter square at age 7–8, the opposition at age 14–15, the 3/4 square at age 21–22, the Saturn return at age 29–30, the square of your mid thirties (36–37), the opposition at age 43–45, and so forth. Consider each of these phases of life in terms of natal Saturn's sign and house position. For example, if you have natal Saturn in the 7th house, each major phase of the Saturn cycle describes a phase of your evolution in friendship, love, and interpersonal relationships. If you have Saturn in the 2nd house, each phase of Saturn's transit cycle will mark stages in your quest for financial stability and security. Saturn's natal placement tells us about areas of life where we feel blocked, inhibited, or fearful in youth, but where, through repeated experience, over time we can grow more confident. Also look ahead and anticipate what challenges and growth opportunities await you. If you haven't experienced your Saturn return or your Saturn opposition yet, predict or anticipate what issues may be most pressing at those times.

Study each Saturn transit with reference to transiting Saturn's current house position. For example, a woman named Frieda had Saturn transiting the first house opposite natal Mars in the 7th. This period featured conflict in relationships (7th house Mars) brought on by asserting herself more (Saturn in the 1st house). A man named John had transiting Saturn in the 4th house squaring Mars in the 7th house; he experienced relational conflict connected to issues with his parents (Mars in the 4th house) and stresses related to his home and living situation.

We need to master the lessons of Saturn to be successful human beings. Whenever I interpret a chart I carefully examine transits of Saturn through the houses and aspecting natal planets.

## URANUS TRANSITS

Transits of Uranus, Neptune, and Pluto are the hardest to predict because their effects are, to some degree, out of the control of the individual. These planets are conduits and symbols for transpersonal energies. They represent ways the universe moves us forward in our evolution, sometimes through unexpected changes that seem impelled by something bigger than we are, including forces of political change and social reorganization.

Uranus transits bring a feeling of change, excitement, restlessness, an interest in experimentation, trying something new in some area of life. If we're not ready for Uranus it can manifest as disruption, surprise, shock. These transits can bring sudden and unexpected changes. On the other hand, if we're living in alignment with our true selves, if we're individuating, then Uranus transits bring an air of excitement, freedom, exhilaration, and the feeling of sudden awakening, or being swept up in a wave, a strong wind, a ripple of change. Uranus is the catalyst of changes that thrust us into a new experience or a new attitude toward an area of life: Uranus-Mercury: change in how we think; Uranus-Moon: change in what we feel; Uranus-Venus: change in how we relate and with whom we interact. Uranus-Mars: change in how we assert ourselves or express our desires. Uranus transits to Mars transits usually bring an increase in energy, drive, motivation, anger, and libido.

Uranus transits highlight the importance of staying attuned to social, political, collective and technological trends. Recently, when transiting Uranus was about to turn stationary direct, my computer exhibited symptoms of extreme dementia and was clearly on its last legs. It was only four years old but it was quite out of date. The machine kept crashing and needed to be replaced. The universe was telling me to stay current and catch up with the next wave of technology.

Uranus can manifest as weird and unexpected events. A friend of mine had grown a thriving vegetable and herb garden for over twenty years. It was destroyed one night by a roaming pack of voracious wild pigs when transiting Uranus was exactly conjunct her Sun and opposite natal Pluto. Plant species—some of them quite rare—that she had been propagating for years were wiped out entirely in one night. Note the Pluto symbolism here, too: destruction, annihilation, being overwhelmed by a force greater than oneself. But there was another Uranian, unexpected development: A few days later, a man dressed in work clothes walked into a store where she worked. They struck up a conversation. He had recently relocated from another part of the country where he ran a pest eradication business. He had extensive prior experience with wild pigs!

Track the movement of Uranus through the houses of your chart, noting the connection to periods of change in that area of your life. Observe major contacts of Uranus to natal angles and natal planets. Pay special attention to the major phases of the Uranus transit cycle: the Uranus square (age 21), Uranus opposition (age 42), Uranus 3/4 square (age 63), and the Uranus return (age 84). Also note when Uranus is trine its natal position. Transiting Uranus contacting the natal angles is an especially potent symbol of change: Uranus conjunct Ascendant represents change in self, identity, demeanor, and appearance. Uranus conjunct Nadir portends change in location of home or office; relocation is possible. Uranus conjunct Descendant marks change in friendships and relationships; separation, endings of alliances or friendships, and beginnings of new alliances and friendships. Uranus conjunct Midheaven indicates change in occupation, social position, or professional objectives.


## Neptune Transits

Neptune is the most difficult planet to make accurate predictions about. Neptune transits are often periods of uncertainty, ungroundedness, or impracticality. They may bring feelings of transcendence and bliss, or of confusion, dissolution, and indecision. Transiting Neptune can cause inflation, grandiose and unrealistic expectations, or a highly expansive, imaginative, or spiritually uplifted expression of the planet involved. We may be totally up in the air about some area of life; things may feel utterly chaotic. When transiting Neptune was conjunct his Descendant, a real estate broker experienced the falling apart of his business, dissolving of associations with clients and several business partners. These transits require surrender and letting go. As Alexander Ruperti wrote,

> Neptune tends to unfocus whatever function of the body or psyche is represented by the sign and the planets involved. . . . [I]ts task is to dissolve the well-defined barriers established by Jupiter and Saturn. . . . Security and self-assuredness are undermined; irrational and unconscious elements in the personality invade the conscious ego, dissolving everything previously thought to be solid, reliable, and valid in one's life.[144]

When Neptune transits the natal Sun, we may experience a call to service or seek to surrender to the divine will. During Neptune-Moon transits we swim in deeper waters of emotional life, feelings of victimization, helplessness, self-pity, or abandonment often predominate; we may learn to express deep tenderness and nurturing. We may feel the peace and beauty of nature. Neptune transits to Mercury may manifest as indecision, lack of mental focus, or increase of imagination, attunement to hidden truths, secret knowledge, interest in metaphysics, religion, symbolism, myth; or we receive a stream of poetry or inspired ideas. Neptune transits to Venus teach us lessons of unconditional love, all-embracing compassion, expanded artistic or musical expression, and opening the heart. Neptune transits to natal Saturn may be destabilizing. Our established life structures become less compelling, resilient, or stable. We may experience a notable lack of focus or ambition; or we dream of more idealistic work. I became an astrologer when transiting Neptune was conjunct my natal Saturn. Neptune is the planet of deconditioning, so this is a time to suspend our assumptions or certainties about some area of life.

Study your past experiences of Neptune transits. Then contemplate upcoming Neptune transits. What effects do you anticipate? Actually, this is a trick question, because Neptune symbolizes the great unknown, those life lessons that expand our awareness only after leading us first into a situation of profound uncertainty. We have to enter the "cloud of unknowing" before the deepest spiritual realizations and inner redemption occur. The outcome of Neptune transits can be hard to predict. The greatest preparation for these transits is trust, faith, spirituality, meditation, prayer, receptivity, and openness to the unconscious and the guidance of dreams.

## Pluto Transits

Pluto acts as a cathartic agent. Its transits bring about a thorough reorganization and reexamination of an area of life. This can lead to empowerment and increased effectiveness, or we can be subjected to the power drives, hostility, or control of others. We meet our own shadow, or the shadow of others; we meet the shadow of humanity, the capacity, present in all of us, for cruelty, hurtfulness, negativity, and manipulative behavior. Pluto transits are often periods of testing. It may be a time of endings and new beginnings, crisis, catharsis, and release. No simple generalizations apply to Pluto, which encompasses the archetypes of death, rebirth, renewal, descent and resurfacing, our encounter with abusive or dictatorial power, hostility, negativity, and resentment, but also the coiled evolutionary power of the *kundalini shakti*. It's not easy to make clear predictions about the effects of Pluto transits in advance. These are long processes where the reflective astrologer makes observations and correlations while the transit is in progress.

Once I did a consultation with a well-known musician who was in hot water because of his multiple love affairs—ten over the past several years, he told me. He'd been keeping up appearances of being happily married until several of his lovers moved to the same town and they all became angry and jealous of one another. Now he was in real trouble. His wife was about to divorce him. He had progressed Venus-Sun conjunction in Aries in the 8<sup>th</sup> house. Transiting Saturn had recently been conjunct his natal Mars-South node at 21–24° of Taurus in the 9<sup>th</sup> house. His sense of identity and self-esteem were wrapped up with proving he was desirable to women. Solar arc Uranus was conjunct his Ascendant, signifying his urge for freedom and his defiance of tradition. Transiting Pluto was squaring his natal Moon in Pisces and his Descendant. Women were falling at his feet, very receptive to him: Moon in Pisces conjunct Descendant. With his Pisces Moon in the 7<sup>th</sup> house, he had no boundaries. His wife had been deeply devoted to him, but now she felt abandoned (Pisces Moon in the 7<sup>th</sup> house). And when she left him he felt abandoned, too. In fact, when she left he fell apart completely; he was a puddle of tears in my office. Pluto square his natal Moon corresponded to a period of emotional turbulence and intensity, and the realization that his actions were hurting others who were open and vulnerable to him. He was embodying the charisma and magnetism of Pluto, but he was abusing his fame and public influence.

A man with transiting Pluto conjunct his natal Mars in Sagittarius and square natal Saturn in Virgo grappled with his desire to make love with women other than his wife. He was going crazy with the urgent fire within him. He was able to restrain himself and rededicated his energies to his work in medical research (Saturn in Virgo). He embraced a fiery quest for deeper knowledge. This Pluto transit put him through a test about sexuality, trustworthiness, and commitment. A Pluto transit is a moment of truth, an evolutionary crossroads. One either takes a higher path or a lower one. It's for us to choose.

When it comes to lengthy Pluto transits remember the principle that we have to work with transits, not just dread them. Here's an example of a transit that might instill some concern or fear—a transit of Pluto to the natal Sun. For over a year Pluto was exactly semisquare my natal Sun in the 4<sup>th</sup> house. During that time my back yard was torn up completely. I removed eight old trees and replanted some new ones. I spent weeks digging out parasitic ivy and blackberry vines that were taking over everything. I spent days digging deep down into the earth to dig out some metal pipes and posts that had probably been there for about forty or fifty years. They were sticking out of the ground like an eyesore and I wanted to turn the soil over to prepare the yard, so I had to get those pipes out of there. There was something very mythic about digging so far into the earth, excavating. It was a time of endings and new beginnings, death and rebirth. Then I had to take care of some big drainage problems that caused water to back up during the winter rains and created a swamp. Pluto rules drainage, backup of water or sewage, release of pressure, and underground activity. That involved hiring some guys to dig tunnels and install underground pipes to route the water to the street. More Pluto! Also, I had a lot of intestinal upset, which meant that several times I had to fast for a day to clear out and let my cells breathe a little.

Then there was more 4th house drama. A Federal Express truck smashed through a redwood fence and ploughed through half of the front yard, destroying a garden, leaving a huge swath of plant debris and splintered wood. It took several months of haggling to reach a settlement with Fed Ex to cover the repairs. I replanted the garden. Here again, it was a time of crisis, endings, and new beginnings. With Pluto transits things happen that can't be changed. We may encounter powers bigger than ourselves, such as the impersonal machinations of a large organization, in this case the insurance company retained by Federal Express.

Another level of meaning of that Pluto-Sun transit was that it entailed a purification of some negative Sun tendencies: an unsatisfied need for attention, and an inflated sense of self-importance. Once I felt a lot of sadness about how modestly my book on *Spiritual Apprenticeship* had sold. These feelings came to a head one day at the university where I worked when John Robbins visited as a guest speaker. John Robbins is a popular writer about diet and nutrition who sold over a million copies of his book, *Diet for a New America*.[145] He showed up for his talk and he asked if a staff member would carry in a large carton of his books from his car in the parking lot. I thought to myself, "When I do a booksigning I carry my own books, dude." But as fate would have it I ended up having to do it, because it was my job. I had many strong emotions evoked by being the waterboy or "lackey" who got to carry books for the bestselling author. It was a humbling and ego-crunching experience, very appropriate for my Pluto-Sun transit! Later I was grateful for the experience because it flushed to the surface some unresolved woundedness about my self-esteem (Sun). It was only later that I was able to see how fortunate I was to have the chance to be in the presence of such an intelligent and inspiring person.

I experienced many Plutonian changes during this period, but they weren't so bad. I didn't die. A long Pluto transit isn't so much an event as a *process*. I can't guarantee that what I'm about to say always works, but I believe that through conscious attunement to the planetary archetype we can to some degree mitigate its less pleasant and desirable manifestations. Simplistic predictions will not do!

To conclude our discussion of transits, let's consider these words by Reinhold Ebertin:

> The effect of the cosmic constellations is dependent on the character and behavior of man himself. . . . If in the interpretation of transits we start from the assumption that an individual with his own will-power determines to a great extent the manifestation of the constellations and through the transits themselves is conscious of the potentialities and limits of a prognostication for the future in all circumstances, then this person, after a period of observation and experience, will be able to pilot his way through life with greater assurance and success. . . . The stars cannot be held accountable for the consequences of the improper use of astrology, only the individual himself is at fault.[146]

This is our goal: to use astrology to pilot our way through life successfully. Study of transits enables us to do exactly that.

Chapter 11

# *Secondary Progressions*

Secondary progressions measure how the birth chart unfolds in the days immediately after birth. Progressions show the progress and organic unfolding of the natal chart. In secondary progressions one day after birth is considered symbolically equivalent to one year of life. For example, the positions of the planets thirty-two days after birth help us understand the changes, growth, and evolution that have occurred within our inner structure by our thirty-second year. The birth chart is a snapshot of the sky frozen in time, showing the innate structure of the personality. Secondary progressions are like subsequent snapshots or subsequent frames of a moving picture, indicating the continuation, follow-through, and unfolding of the birth moment. Progressions show us how we evolve and change from within. This unfoldment occurs in a unique way for each person in the days after birth, due to the varying orbital speeds (and directions) of each planet. Thus, progressions show organic growth according to an individualized pattern of development. We examine aspects of progressed planets to natal planets and angles, aspects of two or more progressed planets, and aspects of progressed Ascendant and Midheaven to natal planets. We also observe progressed planets changing signs, contacting angles, or changing houses. One can immediately grasp the intuitive logic and organic reasoning of secondary progressions. This method is simple, basic, and powerful.

## LEARNING CHART CALCULATION

To understand how this method works it's helpful to understand how it's calculated. However, I recognize that some readers may be squeamish about math or uninterested in the technicalities. Therefore I have placed a brief tutorial in this footnote.[147] For an excellent text on chart calculation refer to Marion March and Joan McEvers, *The Only Way to Learn Astrology* (volume 2).[148] To progress the birth chart, we observe the movements of each planet in the days after birth, using an ephemeris. We carefully note how progressed planets change signs, contact chart angles, and form aspects to natal planets and other progressed planets. The progressed planets indicate the inner unfolding of the personality.

## PROGRESSED SUN

Begin by studying the progressed Sun. Identify what aspects the progressed Sun has made to your other natal planets and angles, from birth to the present. Using the ephemeris, determine how many days after birth these aspects occurred and thus in what year of life that progressed aspect occurred. When the progressed Sun aspects a planet, we absorb that planet fully; we integrate the internal function symbolized by the planet. Our whole life for that period is dominated by the experience of that planetary archetype. For example, when my progressed Sun was conjunct my Moon in the 4th house my family moved to a new home. When my progressed Sun was conjunct Venus in the 5th house at age 14, I performed in public, giving classical guitar concerts. When progressed Sun was conjunct Chiron (planet of the guru, the mentor) I met my guru, Swami Muktananda, and received *shaktipat* initiation. When the progressed Sun sextiled natal Saturn in Sagittarius I graduated from college. When progressed Sun trined natal Jupiter I received my M.A. in psychology (Jupiter: education). When progressed Sun trined Neptune I published a significant article on dreamwork[149] (Neptune) and made advances in my astrological teaching and writing.

Make similar observations about your own progressed Sun. Project forward into the future. What aspects will the progressed Sun make to other planets, and in what year? What do you anticipate?

## PROGRESSED MOON

Next, study the movement of the progressed Moon through the signs and houses of your natal chart. Follow your progressed Moon's passage through the twelve houses of your chart and sketch major life developments occurring at those times as they relate to the themes of that house and sign. For example, when the progressed Moon passed through my 4$^{th}$ house I got my own apartment, fixed it up, and spent all my time there. I learned to cook and take care of a household at that time. When the progressed Moon was in my 6$^{th}$ house I was involved in an intensive yoga teacher training and working on my health, and also working at several jobs. When the progressed Moon was in my 11$^{th}$ house I got involved in several organizations and conferences. When the progressed Moon entered my 12$^{th}$ house I began a period of seclusion and invisibility, focusing on my inner life, dreamwork, and personal therapy.

Note the progressed Moon's past contacts by conjunction, square or opposition to important points in your natal chart. Then project forward to future aspects of the progressed Moon. Periods when the progressed Moon is conjunct, square, or opposite natal planets bring heightened experience and expression of our natal planets.

Next, study the progressed lunation cycle, the ongoing cyclical relationship of the Sun and Moon in the days after birth. Track the progressed lunation cycle for your entire life, from birth up to now. I discussed this in Chapter 3.

## PROGRESSED MARS

Progressed Mars is a potent activator of natal planets. A man with natal Sun-Venus in Aries had experienced secondary progressed Mars conjunct Sun-Venus 7–12 years earlier. At that time, he fell deeply in love with a woman, they married, and the relationship lasted eight years. Now, several years after their divorce, he wondered why he couldn't seem to form an attachment to anyone else. He hadn't found anyone he "clicked" with in the same way. This progressed contact symbolized the most important love relationship of his lifetime. The fact was that he'd never gotten over this woman and was measuring all others in comparison to her. This is what would need to change before he'd be ready for a new love. He was astonished that astrology could indicate the timing of this relationship so precisely. Such is the magic of progressions.

When I met with a woman named Maggie I spent almost the entire hour of our consultation talking about one progressed aspect and the many life changes that it symbolized. Maggie's natal Sun was at 25° Aquarius 26', in the 5th house, directly opposite Uranus in Leo in the 11th house. Natal Mars at 23° Cap 52 progressed forward to conjunction with her natal Sun, at the same time that transiting Uranus was also conjunct her Sun in Aquarius. Maggie's life had changed recently when her boyfriend decided, solely on his own, to adopt a child. Maggie has Libra rising and Aries setting, thus Mars rules her 7th house: an action is initiated by the partner. Maggie had never planned on having children, but now she found herself this child's *de facto* foster-mother and she reacted by becoming enraged (Mars). She had to face her own hurt pride and egotism (Sun). Her Aquarius Sun opposite Uranus in Leo gave her personality an individualistic, rebellious, childish and childlike streak; she could be a little narcissistic. All of this was challenged by the demands of a child. With natal Moon in Virgo in the 12th house, Maggie was drawn to Buddhist meditation, introversion, and solitude, but these two contacts to her 5th house Sun brought the irresistible pull and demands of extraversion, people, children. Her Sun is dispositor of her 11th house and her life suddenly was focused around spending time with groups of children (11th house). Kids now became the focal point of her life. This example also illustrates the importance of assessing a planet's dispositorship in order to understand the meaning of a transiting or progressed planet.

Major progressed contacts color the entire period of life in which they occur. Let's look at the chart of a young woman named Liz (Chart 15). Several major developments in Liz's life were signified by progressed aspects. At age 7, Liz's natal Venus progressed to conjunction with Jupiter in Gemini on the 9th house cusp; she was in 2nd grade and she developed a talent for story telling and creative writing.

At age 18 her progressed Sun was conjunct Saturn in the 10th house. She got her first job and got more serious. Also, with natal Saturn in Leo, her father (Saturn) had heart problems (Leo rules the heart) at that time and she realized she needed to support her-

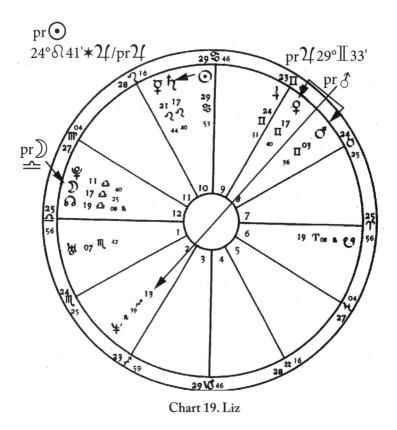

Chart 19. Liz

self and accomplish things; she became more serious and her ambitions began to form.

During Liz's college years she had progressed Mars opposite Neptune. She had very low self-esteem, used a lot of drugs, and was depressed. She got involved with a cult, which drained a lot of money from her bank account (Neptune in the 2nd house). "I felt like I was falling apart." It was a very Neptunian period. But at age 20, when her progressed Mars was conjunct natal Venus, Liz fell in love with the man she later married. The marriage occurred when the progressed Moon in Libra (love, marriage) was precisely conjunct her natal Moon and trine natal Venus.

At the time of consultation Liz had progressed Sun sextile natal Jupiter at ages 24–6 while she was studying for her Masters Degree, which she received when the progressed Sun was at 24° Leo 41. Note that natal Jupiter had progressed forward to 29° Gemini 33. Thus, the progressed Sun was also forming a sextile to *progressed* Jupiter. The entire period of time between progressed Sun sextile Jupiter and the progressed Sun-Jupiter sextile could be considered a Sun-Jupiter period, a period of growth and advancement through education. We determined that it would be a good time for Liz to continue graduate work toward her doctoral degree, and that is the path she followed. She also began teaching at a college during the same period. This is an example of how we use secondary progressions to project forward into the future. It isn't so much a matter of "prediction" but a matter of anticipation and capitalizing on our opportunities, in this case the opportunity to pursue higher education (Jupiter in the 9th house). The progressed planetary symbolism gave Liz confidence to move forward; it helped her formulate her goals and have faith in them.

Secondary progressions are an essential methodology for psychological astrologers, revealing the internal pattern of development that leads to maturation of personality and the evolution of consciousness.

# Chapter 12

## *Solar Arc Directions*

Solar arc directions are another powerful method of astrological prediction. This technique uses the motion of the progressed Sun to determine the rate by which to "direct" other planets forward. Secondary progressions examine the organic movement of planets in the days immediately after birth, with each planet moving at its own speed. The solar arc method directs all of the planets forward at the same rate of approximately 1° per year, which is the average daily motion of the Sun and the annual motion of the progressed Sun. The exact rate of the solar arc varies depending on the time of year of your birth. The Sun transits more slowly during the summer months, and thus, if your birthday is in the spring or summer, over time your accumulated solar arc will be slightly less than 1° per year. Nevertheless, we can begin with the assumption that all planets and angles are directed forward by approximately a degree per year of life, enabling us to anticipate the unfolding of our natal chart potentials. Using solar arcs we can reconstruct and anticipate the pivotal moments of a person's life at a glance, by visually projecting natal planets and angles forward to complete aspects to other planets or angles, and approximating the dates when these aspects will be in effect.

Look at Chart 16: Holly. Holly's natal Sun is at 17° Sagittarius 42' and Venus 24° Sag 09'. These two planets are separated by a distance of 6° 27'. This corresponds to age 6y 6 m. When solar arc Sun was conjunct Venus, Holly was in first grade, attending a very creative, artistic school; she adored her teacher and she had good friends.

Holly's Ascendant is 24° Virgo 25'. Natal Saturn is at 1° Libra 24'. Saturn is separated from the Ascendant by a distance of 6° 59', corresponding to almost exactly 7 years of age. Solar arc ASC was conjunct her natal Saturn at exactly age 7. At this time Holly entered second grade and she felt rejected by her peer group. She was traumatized in second grade, hated her teacher, and developed a weight problem and poor self-image (SA ASC conjunct Saturn).

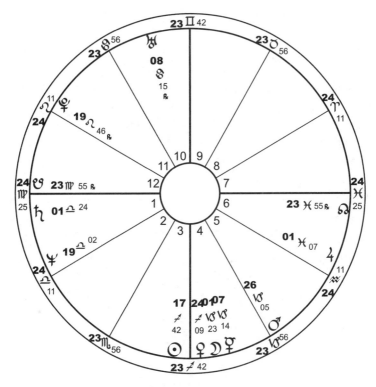

**Chart 20. Holly**

The distance between her MC (23° Gem 42') and opposition to natal Moon (1° Capricorn 23') was 7° 41', corresponding to age 7y 8m. At age 7y 8m, her SA Midheaven opposed her Moon. She had a better, more supportive third grade teacher, became closer to her mother, and met her best friend. She was healed by feminine energy (Moon).

At age 23y 3m, natal Jupiter at 1° Pisces 07' solar arced to conjunction with her DSC at 24° Pisces 25'. She started graduate school, and got a good job (natal Jupiter in 6th house). Here we refer back to the *natal placement* of the directed planet. She met an important professor (Jupiter) and had a five year personal relationship (DSC) with him.

Holly's natal ASC 24° Virgo 25' was separated from natal Neptune at 19° Libra 02' by a distance of 24° 37'. At age 24y 7m her solar arc ASC was conjunct Neptune: She was studying mysticism and religions at a university, doing astrology and Tarot readings. She accepted donations for readings but didn't charge money (Neptune: service, altruism). She had a powerful out-of-body dream of being admitted to a mystery school. She was richly living the archetypal symbolism of SA MC conjunct Neptune at this time.

Holly's MC at 23° Gem 42' was separated from opposition to natal Mars at 26° Cap 06' (in the 5th) by a distance of 32° 24', corresponding to 32y 5m of age. Thus, solar arc MC was opposite natal Mars in the 5th house at age 32y 5m. At this time she worked at a rock and roll radio station and was partying a lot (5th house), dating one of the disk jockeys, a man who was into cocaine and wild sex. Her life was focused on sex, drugs, and rock and roll. She was going out constantly to clubs and concerts (5th house Mars).

Natal Pluto at 19° Leo 46' (in the 11th house) was 35° 39' away from the ASC at 24° Virgo 25'. At age 35y 8m, when solar arc Pluto was conjunct her Ascendant, she bonded with her husband-to-be when his sister died suddenly. She learned wisdom through an encounter with death (Pluto). She lost a lot of weight at this time, transforming her body image: Pluto-Ascendant.

Now practice the solar arc method with your own chart. Using the average solar arc (1° per year) approximate when your natal planets will "direct" forward to form aspects to your natal planets and angles. Later you can go back and calculate precisely when the solar arc contacts occurred. Also clarify what solar arc contacts are upcoming in the future. What trends do you anticipate? The power of solar arc directions is that the symbolism is virtually certain to manifest visibly in our lives.

## CALCULATING SOLAR ARCS

To calculate your solar arc directions follow this procedure: Look up your birthday in the ephemeris. Determine your current age in years and months. Let's say that you're forty years and four months old. Count forty days after birth. This is the progressed date for your fortieth birthday. To account for the extra months since your birthday, multiply 4 months x 2 hours = 8 hours. Add 8 hours to your natal Greenwich Mean Time of birth. Let's review the logic of this. By progression, one day after birth (or twenty four hours) is symbolically equivalent to one year of life (twelve months), thus two hours after birth corresponds to one month of life.

Do the calculations for your current age. Find the progressed date and GMT corresponding to your current age in years and months. Now calculate the position of your progressed Sun. Find the distance in longitude between your natal Sun and progressed Sun. In our example, this distance will be approximately 40° 20'. This distance is called the *solar arc*. Now add this arc to each of your natal planets and natal angles (Ascendant, Descendant, Midheaven, and Nadir). These are your solar arc directed planets and angles. Note any current, upcoming, or recently completed contacts of solar arc planets to your natal planets or angles. Pay special attention to conjunctions, oppositions, squares, semi-squares (45° angle), and sesquiquadrate (135°) aspects, sometimes called the *kinetic* aspects because they're change-producing.[150] It's easy to locate the conjunction, square, and opposition. For example, progressed Moon at 18° Cancer is opposite Saturn at 18° Capricorn. But what's not so obvious at first is that Moon at 18° Cancer is also 45° (semi-square) to 3° Gemini and 3° Virgo, and it's also 135° (sesquiquadrate) from 3° Sagittarius and 3° Pisces. Thus any planet (or midpoint) placed on these degrees is receiving an aspect from the solar arc planet. To use solar arc directions you need to start paying attention to semisquare (45°) and sesquiquadrate (135°) aspects as well, which represent 1/8 and 3/8 of the circle. These aspects were emphasized by the great Reinhold Ebertin.[151]

Research past, current, and upcoming solar arc contacts to your chart. Note what happened, or what you predict may happen with upcoming contacts. Carefully study your natal chart's unfolding by solar arc direction from the beginning of your life. Start with planets near angles and consider the length of time it will take the natal planet to contact the angle, or the natal planet to reach the angle by solar arc. Note correlations between the planets and angles involved and estimate as closely as you can when this would have occurred. You can do this at a glance, noting the distance between the planets and between planets and angles. Approximate 5' of arc per month or

60' of arc per year. Note the solar arc movement of a planet such as Mars, Jupiter, or Saturn over another natal planet or cluster of planets. Try to recall if any events in your early life match the symbolism of the solar arc contact. Then go back and calculate the timing of these arcs precisely. Keep records of all your findings. This is the astrologer's alchemical laboratory procedure.

## Examples of Solar Arc Directions

To learn any predictive method we need to study retrospectively. We look backward into the past before we look forward into the future. We study events that have already occurred and find correlations between those events and planetary transits and progressions. We study our own charts in depth to see how we have responded to past planetary contacts. We also study life histories, to see how a person's natal structures, transits, and progressions have manifested. By studying past events we can anticipate the outcome of future transits and progressions; *we can predict*. We begin to discern how transits and progressions operate and how they correlate with real-life events. And we're alert for comparable occurrences in the future. This is the art of anticipation.

Sometimes in this chapter I cite some personal examples from my own life because I examine my own chart closely and keep a lot of detailed notes. In the process you'll learn a few details of my life, which is a typical life with various ups and downs, successes and failures, events both mundane and sublime that are indicated by planetary symbols. If you choose to try to figure out my chart, that's your prerogative. But I think your time is better spent applying these techniques to your own horoscope.

I have natal Sun in the 4th house square Jupiter. At age 12, when my solar arc Midheaven opposed my Sun and squared Jupiter, my family went on a trip to Africa. It was the voyage of a lifetime. It fulfilled the Jupiter symbolism of travel and adventure and the 4th house symbolism of family life experience.

When my solar arc Ascendant squared Venus I got involved in an important relationship. Some years later, when my solar arc

Midheaven opposed Venus I got involved in another important relationship.

When solar arc Saturn reached my 4th house cusp I had a reconciliation with my family (4th house), right before I moved across the country to live in the San Francisco Bay Area, where I have lived ever since. Solar arc contacts to the IC almost always signify important changes or developments regarding housing or relocation.

When solar arc Mars (ruler of my 7th house) was conjunct my 4th house cusp I had an intense relationship that ended when my girlfriend dumped me and began dating one of my coworkers, which caused me to become furiously jealous and enraged, a fiery Mars experience.

## An Example Combining Solar Arcs and Transits

Here's another example of a client's chart that vividly illustrates the power of solar arc directions. Look at Chart 17:

At age 6y 3m SA Saturn was conjunct Randi's Descendant: Her father, an undercover detective, disappeared suddenly and left the family for the first time. It was a time of sadness, fear, and social inhibitions for Anne. You couldn't have predicted her father leaving, but you would infer from Saturn's involvement there might be issues related to the father, and possible stresses or inhibitions in connecting to others. Now, note her natal Moon-Uranus conjunction in the 4th house. Some instability or change in the family home and environment was indicated. This came to fruition at age 8 when SA MC opposed Randi's Moon. At the same time, transiting Saturn was in Capricorn, opposite natal Moon-Uranus. Her family began moving constantly, living in a series of transient homes, causing Randi much emotional upset. At age 16–17, when the natal Sun progressed to conjunction with Venus, Randi fell in love for the first time. At the same age, SA Saturn was conjunct Neptune in the 7th house; it was a period of romantic illusions and disappointment, as her boyfriend was an alcoholic who lied to her. Note how the potentials of Neptune in the 7th house are brought vividly to life, including her ability to devote herself to somebody selflessly.

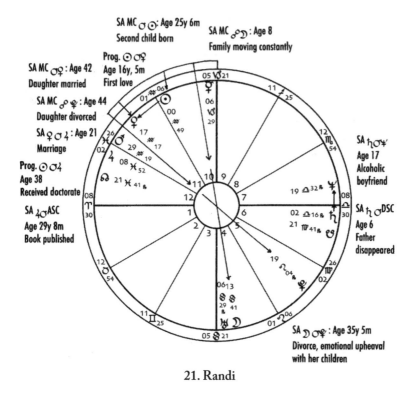

21. Randi

At age 21, when SA Venus (dispositor of the 7th house) was conjunct Jupiter she got married, and she and her husband relocated across country, bought a house, and had their first child; at the same time transiting Saturn in Cancer was conjunct Moon-Uranus in the 4th house. Saturn in the 4th house marked the beginning of family life. At age 25, when the SA Midheaven reached conjunction with her Aquarius Sun in the 11th house, Randi became a nationally recognized leader of an alternative, holistic health movement (11th house); she also joined a group healing arts clinic. Note that Randi's Sun rules her child-5th house. When SA MC was conjunct her Sun, Randi had her second child; the birth was timed exactly by transiting Saturn in Leo conjunct natal Pluto in the 5th house. However, soon thereafter Randi's husband started having an affair (transiting Saturn aspecting natal Venus opposite Pluto: relational complications, jealousy).

At age 30, during Randi's Saturn return (in the 7th house), she had serious marital problems, yet her professional practice with her husband was thriving. At the same time (age 30), SA Jupiter reached conjunction with Randi's Ascendant, and she had a book published that earned her lasting recognition in her field.

At age 35, when Randi had SA Mars square MC and SA Moon conjunct natal Pluto, she had an acrimonious divorce (Mars), emotional crisis (Moon-Pluto), and upheaval regarding her children (Pluto in Leo in the 5th house). She received her doctorate at age 38, when progressed Sun was conjunct Jupiter. It's astonishing how events unfold so closely linked to planetary symbolism.

When SA MC was conjunct natal Venus in the 11th house, Randi's daughter got married. Let's introduce a little derived house analysis—most often used in horary astrology but also very helpful in natal astrology. The 11th house is the 7th from the child-5th house; therefore it governs the child's relationship or marriage. Two years later, the SA MC opposed Pluto in the 5th house; her daughter divorced and became a single mother. When SA Venus reached conjunction with Randi's Ascendant, her daughter remarried, much more happily. Venus' meaning refers back to its natal placement in Randi's 11th house, the house of the child's marriage.

Randi remarried in the late 1980s when transiting Saturn in Capricorn squared natal Saturn and Neptune in the 7th house—that is, under a hard aspect of Saturn. Her second marriage is much better than her first. Saturn in the 7th house isn't a negative or malefic planetary influence. It indicates the potential for maturation and learning through experience in the domain of love and marriage.

Randi's Mercury in Capricorn conjunct the Midheaven is a potent force: she is a tremendous writer. She wrote all her major works during transits of Jupiter, Saturn, and Uranus to her natal Mercury. For the past few years her writing has been dormant. Randi was in mild despair; there seemed to be nothing else to say or write. But I noted transiting Saturn in Cancer opposite natal Mercury. Could it be that fairly soon Randi would once again be stirred to write? When Saturn turned retrograde and formed the second opposition to Mercury, she was contacted by a literary agent in New York about a book proposal. She threw herself into the new writing project with focus, energy, and enthusiasm.

These kinds of retrospective life studies teach us to assess planetary symbols and the developmental tasks and phases they indicate. And on this basis, it's possible to predict or anticipate future tasks and trends. These life studies teach us how astrology reveals the individual path of development and the timing of specific experiences.

## SOLAR ARCS AND MIDPOINTS

To gain a deeper understanding of solar arcs, we study contacts of solar arc planets to midpoints. This is the method taught in Ebertin's *Applied Cosmobiology*, and in Noel Tyl's *Prediction in Astrology*.[152] This is one of the most potent predictive methods in astrology. If you're new to astrology it's better to focus on solar arc planets contacting natal planets and angles. But if you're an experienced astrologer then try adding planetary midpoints to your study of solar arc directions,

Using your computer software, print a 90° midpoint sort. Then calculate your current solar arc planets. Suppose your SA Saturn is at 13° Virgo 51. Look at the 90° sort. 13° 51' of the four mutable signs (Gemini, Virgo, Sagittarius, and Pisces) is represented as 73°51' (30° of cardinal signs, plus 30° of fixed signs, plus 13°51' of mutable = 73° 51'). See if any natal midpoints fall near 73° 51'. If SA Saturn has just passed a midpoint, figure out how many months earlier the contact occurred. See if this corresponds to any events in recent memory. See if there are any current contacts. See if SA Saturn will contact any midpoints within the next twelve months. Note the midpoint contact, and look up this combination in Ebertin's book, *The Combination of Stellar Influences* (hereafter abbreviated as "COSI"). Leave room to make notes later on the actual events of this period. Also, check 45° and 135° aspects, as follows. Add one sign (30°) + 15°. 13° Virgo 51 + 45° = 28° Libra 51. Therefore, any planets or midpoints at 28° 51 of a cardinal sign are also activated by solar arc Saturn.

Rather than attempting a systematic presentation of solar arc contacts, I'm going to recount some personal anecdotes. Remember that we interpret solar arc contacts according to the meaning of both the SA planet and the natal planet.

Now I'll describe some personal examples beginning with solar arc planets contacting other planets or angles. Then I'll note examples involving midpoints. With midpoints the aspects used are the conjunction, semisquare, square, sesquiquadrate, and opposition. All of these aspects are considered equivalent, so if transiting or solar arc Uranus is aspecting Mars we say "Uranus = Mars"—regardless of the specific aspect involved.

When solar arc Saturn was conjunct my Moon in the 4th house my family was affected. My parents had to move out of their apartment after thirty five years and move into a new home. It was a very emotional time for all of us as we reviewed many years of memories (Moon). Because Moon rules my Cancer 10th house cusp, my career was also affected. I began taking my work more seriously. I joined a psychotherapy training group, and became more committed to being a therapist. Also when solar arc Saturn was conjunct Moon, I had to give a deposition regarding an auto accident I had been responsible for causing. According to Ebertin, the midpoint of Moon/Saturn represents "self control, . . . sense of duty, care, attention, . . . conscientiousness."[153] I interpreted it to mean "assuming responsibility," and that's exactly what I learned from this experience.

When my solar arc MC was conjunct Pluto in my 11th house I was asked to be a speaker at a national astrology conference (11th house). I had an article published in *Yoga Journal*, a publication with national readership, and I was hired to teach at a university. It was a time of empowerment and influence within several community and organizational settings. Ebertin says this of the contacts of Pluto/ MC: "The desire to become important. . . The power to attain success in life. . . . Authority. . . . The attainment of recognition and power."[154]

When I had SA Jupiter square MC I spoke at a national convention of the American Psychological Association, published an article on meditation and psychotherapy in *The American Journal of*

*Psychotherapy*, advanced to doctoral candidacy, wrote my dissertation, and published numerous astrological articles. Note how the Jupiter symbolism relates to developments in academic and intellectual pursuits.

When SA Mercury opposed my natal Uranus, and while SA Pluto squared natal Mercury I wrote my dissertation and completed my first book, *Astrology and Spiritual Awakening*. I experienced this as a time of innovative writing that occurred in a state of inspiration. The Pluto contact to Mercury brought the quality of in-depth research and analysis. I completed the final draft of my dissertation and busily forwarded copies to various professors when SA ASC formed a semisquare (45°) to Mercury. According to Ebertin, Mercury/ASC means "exchange of ideas and thoughts, . . . receiving documents, letters."[155]

When SA Moon semisquared Jupiter I bought a house: Ebertin says of Moon = Jupiter: "The feeling of happiness, . . . social successes, . . . attainment of material advantages."[156] Moon symbolizes a home.

When SA Jupiter was semisquare Jupiter, my book *Astrology and Meditation* was published, and I spoke at UAC, an international astrology conference.

Now I'll discuss some examples of solar arc planets contacting planetary midpoints. Once I had SA Uranus = Sun-Jupiter: "the expectation of good fortune, . . . sudden success."[157] At this time I got a good job as a psychotherapist at a family service agency.

When I had progressed Sun = Mars/Pluto I returned from a trip out of town to find out that while I was away my car had been smashed at the airport parking lot, by the driver of the airport shuttle bus! Ebertin says of Sun = Mars/Pluto: "Injury, accident, . . . an upset or shock caused by intervention of Higher Power."[158]

Once, when SA Uranus squared natal Saturn in Sagittarius, I was fired from a job. According to Ebertin, the midpoint of Saturn/Uranus denotes "unusual emotional tensions or strains, . . . emotional conflicts, rebellion, the urge for freedom, provocative conduct, . . . the overcoming of difficulties, . . . interventions in one's destiny."[159] Clearly this solar arc contact could herald career changes and upsets. At that time I also had transiting Pluto = Sun/MC, which implies death of the ego, a defeat. The MC governs one's image, how we're perceived by people, by the world. The Sun/MC midpoint signifies "individuality, the goal or object of life, consciousness of objective, . . . individual progress or advancement, the pursuit of one's objective."[160] Turning now to Pluto contacting this midpoint, Ebertin says of Pluto = Sun/MC: "A tragic destiny."[161] Being fired was definitely a setback.

When I had SA Neptune = Moon/Jupiter I had a slow month in my private practice and was quite discouraged. According to Ebertin, SA Neptune = Moon/Jupiter indicates "the tendency to abandon hope easily, bad social conditions, dwindling happiness."[162]

Once I had SA Sun = Moon/MC, which Ebertin describes as "a positive attitude to life, vigor, the spirit of enterprise."[163] I played a concert of original music, in collaboration with another musician. At the same time, I had SA Mars = Sun/Moon: "the urge to bring to fruition ideals and wishes, . . . the realization of joint objectives."[164] I also had SA Uranus = Sun/Venus, which I interpret as an unusual individual expression, an urge to create and express oneself musically.

I was watching closely when I had SA Pluto = Sun/Mars, about which Ebertin says: "fanaticism, . . . the overtaxing of one's strength, violence."[165] I didn't know what to predict, but I expected trouble of some kind. As the aspect became exact I developed an abessed tooth, which caused my face to become swollen, and I was rushed into emergency root canal surgery!

One day, while peacefully weeding my garden, I was stung by five yellow jackets, had an allergic reaction, and went into shock. I was rescued by paramedics and brought to the hospital. At that time I had SA Uranus = Mars/Pluto, which Ebertin interprets as indicating "cruelty, violence, brutality, sudden disasters or calamities of great consequence."[166]

One of the most significant solar arc contacts I've experienced was when SA Uranus = Sun/Moon, which indicates "the urge for freedom, the urge to act independently, . . . separation of the partners."[167] During this period I decided to self-publish my first book, after trying unsuccessfully for several years to find a publisher. I founded my own publishing company, feeling defiant toward friends who advised me not to do it.

I experienced some good fortune, being hired as a professor and graduate program director, and had an improvement in my income, when I had SA Moon = Sun/Jupiter: "A healthy soul in a healthy body, . . . a happy or wealthy person."[168]

At another time, I had SA Jupiter = Sun/MC. According to Ebertin this contact indicates a positive, optimistic attitude, "the attainment of one's objectives."[169] Noel Tyl interprets this contact as indicating optimism, publicity, fulfillment, ego recognition. At the time of this solar arc contact I sold out the first printing of one of my books.

Once I had SA Pluto = Sun/Saturn, which Ebertin describes as "Delicate health, a secluded, solitary way of life, [leading] a modest or simple life. . . . Developmental inhibitions owing to illness."[170] At the time, I had a bad cold, a car accident, and very little money. It was a solitary time.

I experienced power struggles and a major change in my job responsibilities against my will when I had solar arc Uranus = Pluto/MC. Ebertin describes this as "A sudden attainment of one's aim or aspirations with irresistible power. Sudden occupational changes."[171]

Many major events are portrayed through the symbolism of solar arc contacts. John F. Kennedy Jr. (born 11/25/1960 at 0:22 am EST, Washington, D.C.) was killed in a plane crash on July 18, 1999. At this time SA Mars (ruler of his Aries 8th house cusp) at 27° Leo 48' was exactly opposite his natal Moon at 27° AQ 25'. And his SA Midheaven at 18° Cancer 35' was precisely conjunct Mars, ruler of the 8th house. Also, he had transiting Pluto square natal Pluto, which was conjunct the Moon's nodes.

Solar arc directions are one of astrology's most potent and accurate predictive methods, an essential technique for the practitioner.

# PART SIX

# COUNSELING AT EVOLUTIONARY THRESHOLDS

*Man Contemplating the Sun Disk.* Babylonian cuneiform tablet[172]

# Chapter 13

## *Astrology and Crisis Counseling*

The great value of astrology is evident when we use it for guidance in crisis situations to help people in states of intense emotional upset. As guides to souls in the process of awakening, astrologers do a lot of crisis counseling and I expect we'll have an important role to play as we pass through our current world crisis—especially while the Uranus-Pluto square rocks our world for the next several years. I'll return to that in a moment. During tumultuous times it's important to remember that we're passing through a series of transitory states, none permanent. Changes keep coming, wave after wave. But planetary symbolism enables us to imagine future outcomes that give meaning to upheavals. We call upon the wisdom of astrology to shed light on some fairly difficult moments, and it can be effective spiritual medicine. Celestial patterns represent the person and pivotal phases of life in such a way that crisis periods can be put in perspective. Then we can transform within our situation, whatever the circumstances or difficulties. Then we can find our way through, walking on a narrow path.

The narrow path is the path for you. It's your way of harmony, your truth road, your path of individuation.[173] It's the way that's meant for you. It's the brightly lit path that opens where other roads are closed to you. It's the Tao, the clear way forward. Staying aligned to our own path of integrity and authenticity gives us the best chance to thrive during these uncertain times. We've all heard the prophecies and warnings. We can see the unsettled state of nature and feel this affecting us. During the unruly Uranus-Pluto square in effect between 2011–2015 (and for years beyond) we ought to be prepared for emergencies, storms, power outages, rising prices, food shortages, some chaos and social unrest. Many of our structures and certainties may be challenged and pressed upon. But if we stay on our own path and follow our celestial instructions, if we stay on our toes and focus on the here and now, we can step nimbly and act skillfully. The Hawaiian Huna teachings state, "Now is the moment of power. . . . Energy goes where attention flows." As astrologers, we feel our energy being expressed and distributed effectively in various directions, and can withdraw attention from areas not currently accentuated. We embrace the structures, limits, and tasks of the present moment, working steadily to enhance our situation. Understanding the cycles and rhythms of time and life's formative archetypes, we're prepared to look into the eye of the storm with clear vision.

Knowledge of astrology can't prevent us from having to go through a crisis but it helps us go through it with wisdom and courage. A man named Dilip was displaced from his home through foreclosure while transiting Pluto opposed his Moon in Cancer. Uprooted, he sold and gave away nearly everything he owned and moved onto a houseboat. Dilip lost fifty pounds and divested himself of much heavy sound equipment, furniture, and pack-rat collectibles. He survived and began a cycle of healthier living. It wasn't easy to downsize his life, yet it was reassuring for him to know that the symbolism of Pluto-Moon sometimes represents an unsettling experience affecting one's home environment. Many Pluto challenges involve some losses and endings and letting go. Knowing this allowed Dilip to go through it with open eyes, to let it happen. He could then embrace the process of setting up a new home base. In many instances, as one life gets torn down, we're presented with a fresh new beginning.

Joyce Jensen, the late astrologer, once told me this story. Apparently at one time Joyce was married to a man who was in the mafia. They enjoyed a materially prosperous existence through their involvement in the mob, and her husband bought her a pink Lincoln Continental with a pink steering wheel and pink leather bucket seats. During some transit involving Pluto and natal Mars the marriage became highly volatile, discordant, and unpleasant, and their arguments escalated to such a point that she decided to leave her husband. On the day she left him she was driving on the highway when suddenly steam started to come out of the hood. She pulled the car over to the side of the road and the next thing she knew, her pink Lincoln was going up in flames. This was an amazing synchronicity—the Pluto-Mars transit, the breakup, and the car's spontaneous combustion. She told me that was when she knew that stage of her life was really over. Joyce went on to found the Astrological Institute in Scottsdale, Arizona, the first accredited astrological school in the United States. That's a good example of rising from the ashes and creating a completely different life.

Author John Welwood speaks of allowing *the moment of world collapse*, encountering the truth of impermanence, vulnerability, and groundlessness.[174] Buddhist psychology teaches that we can enter deeply into spaciousness and non-solidity, and relax into gaps or open spaces, discovering the ground of awareness and fear in which grasping occurs, the open ground of our being. Through meditation, we learn to relax into the gaps and fall apart gracefully. "If we stay present and [do] not recoil from the emptiness when our familiar sense of self breaks down, we eventually discover a quality of presence that feels awake, alive, and liberating."[175] Contemplating astro-symbolism helps us stay in the fire, take a breath, face our situation squarely, and regain our ease of being.

## A RELATIONSHIP CRISIS

I often counsel clients in crisis about relationships. Lori was in an emotionally intense state while transiting Uranus in Pisces and transiting Saturn in Virgo squared her natal Moon-Mars-Neptune conjunction in Sagittarius in the 7th house. Lori was disillusioned with her boyfriend, Rolf, who wanted to be a rock star and a great writer, had a grandiose sense of mission, and felt that he was meant to be special. But Rolf was unproductive, and his efforts never seemed to go anywhere. He was unemployed, financially dependent, weak, whiny, and sexually dysfunctional. In all these ways, he embodied Lori's Mars-Neptune conjunction, going through cycles of creative inflation and enthusiasm, and darkly moody, deflated phases.

Lori was sick of Rolf's chaos and his dramas. She berated herself for being with a man her friends had described as a hopeless romantic, stoner space case, and needy child. She kept threatening to leave him, and he kept pleading for her to not be so angry. He himself was angry and felt misunderstood. Lori felt discouraged,

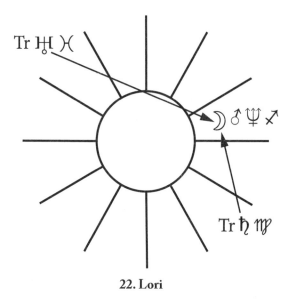

**22. Lori**

saying, "Every man I've been with has been a disappointment. They aren't well-adjusted people and they never have any money. They get so puffed up and preoccupied with their own trip that they emotionally wound and abandon me." Referring to the Mars-Neptune symbolism, I said, "So, they all see themselves as the great lover, or great seekers of truth and the great savior of the age, but they end up being weak, ineffectual and chronic depressives." Lori added: "Rolf kept saying he wanted to have this amazing, transcendent tantric sex with me, but then he couldn't perform." How very disappointing this was. Mars-Neptune energy stirs an urge for ecstasy and expanded consciousness but can also evoke sensitivity and vulnerability.

I wondered if perhaps this relationship was mirroring something unconscious and unrealized in Lori. She said she felt intellectually and spiritually lazy and admired how Rolf was always lit up by ideas and spiritual longing and had keen intuition and vivid imagination. I said, "With Mars-Neptune in the 7th house, you seek peace, bliss, and energetic awakening through sex and the intoxication of losing yourself in another person. You have huge expectations of a relationship and then titanic disappointments. I wonder if you feel this way about yourself too." "Oh yes," she said. "I'm always very disappointed in myself." I said, "I think you need to develop the qualities of a *bodhisattva* of compassion. That would be a broad-hearted expression of Moon-Mars-Neptune. You could be less hard on yourself, and maybe on Rolf. And it occurs to me that buddhas and bodhisattvas all wear a blissful, beatific smile, the sign of *maha-sukkha*, the great bliss. I think these transits to your Mars-Neptune are asking you to awaken your own bliss body and your own ecstasy through meditation, tantra, and mysticism. These planets say that you have this potential. And I sense that what you intend, and truly desire, is to invite Rolf to share this experience with you. Moon-Mars-Neptune in the 7th house suggests to me a need to transform anger, maybe to stop being so angry about everything, and as much as possible to cultivate spaciousness, stillness, peace and content-ment in your relationship." Lori realized that she'd been angry at Rolf for months (transits to Moon-Mars in 7th house), and saw how this fed his feelings of weakness, insecurity, and sexual performance anxiety. She softened a little bit as she told me how she would like to be more nurturing, validating his sexiness and sensitivity.

Lori renewed her faith in Rolf, and consciously chose to pre-serve and treasure this relationship. It's interesting as soon as she did this and got her heart right Rolf found a job editing and doing research at a university (Sagittarius), and began to develop his writ-ing. This conversation quelled the storm inside Lori. Her planetary symbolism affirmed how both of their emotional, intellectual, and energetic potentials were being awakened within this stormy and dynamic relationship.

### Transforming Through a Health Crisis

Some crises are built into our natal structure, and we have to bear them, and transform through them. A 25-year-old woman named Amber had natal Sun-Mercury-Venus in Cancer in the 12th house, opposite Jupiter and Neptune in Capricorn in the 6th house. Amber suffered from kidney disease and needed dialysis every night. This was an ordeal she suffered privately (12th house). It was her own form of personal religious martyrdom (Neptune opposite Sun).

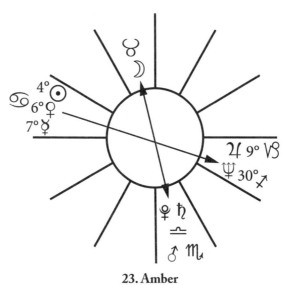

**23. Amber**

Amber spent a lot of time alone. She had a boyfriend, but none-theless she felt quite alone going through this nightly ordeal of plugging into the dialysis machine. This was a time each evening when she would have to grow quiet and pull her awareness inward (12<sup>th</sup> house planets, opposite Neptune). Sometimes she felt sorrow, sometimes deep serenity. Her medical condition was a spiritual trial and spiritual practice. Amber was quiet, sensitive. She was afraid that other people wouldn't like her because she had an illness, so she hid her condition from others (12<sup>th</sup> house Sun). She developed an interest in providing services to children with life-threatening illnesses. Who could better understand and express compassion for ailing children than someone with Sun-Venus in the 12<sup>th</sup> house (solitude, convalescence) opposite Jupiter-Neptune in the 6<sup>th</sup> house (illness and health). Having this vision of her future role made her situation feel more bearable. She'd gained wisdom she could share with others in pure service, to ease their suffering (Sun opposite Jupiter-Neptune in 6<sup>th</sup> house).

Amber's Moon in Taurus opposed a Mars-Saturn-Pluto con-junction in Scorpio in her 4<sup>th</sup> house. Her family was constantly in crisis, with people constantly getting angry and vicious with one another. She described it as a toxic environment where she felt under attack, and that her parents and siblings didn't take her illness seriously, sometimes treating her as if she was a bother. She was quietly seething with anger towards all of them. It seemed that the inflamed conditions of her family had started a war inside her psyche and her body that probably wasn't helpful to her physical condition. It was important for Amber to connect with this anger and to be aware of how it had emerged within this family. When transiting Jupiter in Leo squared her Mars-Saturn in Scorpio, Amber had a heated conversation with her father, expressing these long-buried resentments and grievances. In doing this, she felt a tangible surge of vitality, which helped her see the possibility of a path beyond helplessness and lonely feelings of martyrdom. To become whole, Amber needed to develop her fiery and willful core, to strengthen this foundation of assertive, aggressive energy.

## Transformation Through a Marital Crisis

Barry had Sun and Moon in Aries in the 7th house opposite Neptune in Libra, near his Libra Ascendant in the 12th house; and Mars-Saturn-Pluto in Leo, in the 10th house. Barry's life centered around his wife and three children, his marriage, career, and fatherhood. Note the Libra and 7th house relational emphasis, the 10th house professional emphasis, and also the powerful aspects involving Saturn in Leo (parenting and children). Barry was in the grips of a major depressive episode and was extremely unhappy in his marriage, experiencing lack of closeness, emotional alienation from his wife, dysthymia, loss of zest, and physical symptoms that seemed related to suppressed anger (high blood pressure, stomach ulcer, TMJ from grinding his teeth). As a child Barry felt oppressed by his mother's depression; in her childhood she suffered abandonment, neglect, and poverty (Moon-Neptune), and, as an adult, mother was typically in a depressed mood. Note how Barry's Sun is conjunct Moon in the 7th house; his identity centered around his relationship with his mother, and now his wife, Laxmi, caring for them and also identifying with their distressed emotional states.

Laxmi also struggled with depression. By derived house analysis, the 12th house is the 6th house from the 7th. So, with Neptune in

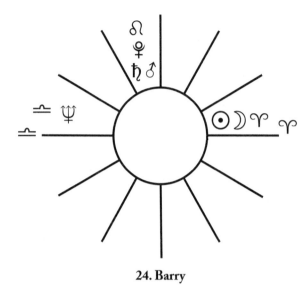

**24. Barry**

his 12ᵗʰ house, Barry's wife's work and health were major concerns. Laxmi was a social worker who encountered lots of suffering in her work, and she sacrificed herself for her work (Moon-Neptune), working long overtime hours on evenings and weekends. At work she was overwhelmed by the chaos and dysfunction, the constant budget crises. Looked at with some objectivity, Barry felt compassion and basic sympathy for her. Both of them were caring people who took on other people's pain. Barry said, "She's so busy taking care of other people she has nothing left over for me." With Sun conjunct Moon in the 7ᵗʰ house, Barry has enormous unmet needs for nurturing from his wife. Yet he was fully devoted to Laxmi. His Sun-Moon represented attunement to Laxmi's needs and allowing her to be securely attached to him, even though their connection was full of aggressive Aries barbs and disagreements of ego assertiveness. He recognized that, with the luminaries in willful Aries in the 7ᵗʰ house, both of them sometimes behaved unpleasantly. With Sun-Moon opposite Neptune, Barry is also selfless and service-oriented. I said, "It feeds you to give Laxmi support. Taking care of your wife and children is your path, your natural way of being. With Mars-Saturn-Pluto in Leo, parenting is a lot of work but you can feel proud of what you've created, and of the strong parental consistency, guidance, and leadership you've expressed, and your undying warmth." Barry felt relief hearing this affirmation of his internal conflict. His narrow path involved learning to gently but firmly assert himself within a situation of total commitment. It was a path of healing through tolerance, acceptance, and mutual recognition of needs. There was no place else to go. He was in this marriage, with all of its fiery sparks, for the long run.

## A YEAR OF RELATIONAL UPHEAVAL

A 38-year-old man named Jules became highly distraught while transiting Saturn was conjunct his natal Uranus and Pluto in the 8th house. During the first pass of this transit he caught his wife Ella in bed with one of her business associates. Ella became increasingly icy and distant and said she wanted to separate. Saturn's passage into Libra began with these relational challenges. After their divorce, Jules had many financial complications, declared bankruptcy, and began paying child support. Saturn's transit in the 8th house is often a period of interpersonal crisis and changes regarding shared finances and interpersonal agreements and commitments. Jules felt overwhelmed by his obligations, yet there was no avoiding them. Jules had natal Saturn in Taurus in the 4th house. First and foremost, he must be a provider for his family; he was a prodigious money-maker. In addition, note Mars in Aries in his 2nd house, Jules was highly energetic and motivated about making money. He felt tied down by job and wanted to do something else for a living, but he had to keep the money pouring in. Some things can't be changed. This was his responsibility, and he felt less depressed about his life the more he accepted this fact. With Saturn opposite Neptune at the Midheaven, Jules longed to be free, to travel and live freely, to explore his mystical side. The practical, grounded side of him co-existed with the dreamer who wanted to be a business entrepreneur and have his own company. With Sun in the 12th house and Neptune at the Midheaven, Jules was sustained by his spirituality and meditation practice, which helped him bear the need to work full-time to support two households.

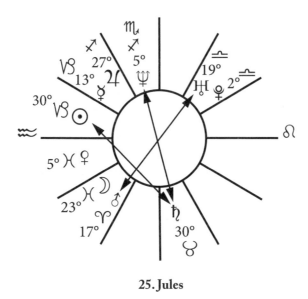

**25. Jules**

While transiting Saturn was conjunct his Pluto, the divorce got rather nasty and Jules felt betrayed and financially battered. He started dating and got into an intense relationship with a single mother named Helen, then got scared, withdrew, and broke up with her suddenly and somewhat insensitively. He started dating another woman, Tanya, who became important to him. They moved in together, then broke up, but continued living together as house-mates, hurting each other repeatedly when they'd bring home other sexual partners. Transiting Saturn conjunct Pluto in the 8th house evoked fierce jealousy, intense attraction and magnetism, followed by unpleasantness and hostility.

As Saturn turned direct in Libra, Jules made up his mind that Tanya was the person he loved and cared about, and he was deter-mined to win her back and to be with her. Several of his friends didn't like Tanya and warned him against her. But it was an irresist-ible attraction. They got back together in a molten sexual froth, a nuclear fusion that couldn't be denied or reasoned with (Pluto in 8th house). And Jules wanted to talk about joining their lives together. As a Capricorn he had a strong interest in settling down and having a respectable marriage. But Tanya felt smothered by Jules and didn't want to talk about commitment. While Saturn transited near natal Uranus there was no way for Jules to establish a traditional form or definition for this relationship. He and Tanya were lovers who enlivened one another, yet under the frenetic electricity of Uranus their connection couldn't be contained in vows and promises with permanence. Just before the final pass of transiting Saturn conjunct Uranus and opposite natal Mars, they broke up again abruptly, generating intense anger. Jules became fiercely jealous when Tanya started talking to her ex-boyfriend, and they broke things off with much iciness and acrimony. Abrupt separation is a typical manifestation of Uranus.

We have to live the truth of each moment as it is. The truth was that Jules needed freedom from bondage in the 8th house. He didn't know he wanted it. He *thought* he wanted a traditional marriage and family unit. Yet at some deeper level perhaps he didn't want it or need it. After all, he'd "written" a birth chart with Uranus in Libra in the 8th house. We experience liberation when we stop craving what cannot be and stop clinging too tightly to security, stability, and safety—when we embrace the excitement and free space of possibility. One can't underestimate the spiritual significance of assenting to this challenge. Rudhyar wrote:

Only that which has become empty of lower nature's contents can resonate to the voice of the Galaxy. This voice sounds continuously through every cell of our being. . . . But we cannot hear, as long as our attention is totally turned toward the Sun, our lord and master. To be able to gravitate toward our star, we have for an instant to neutralize solar gravitation. We need not go anywhere or generate any power. All the power we need is here. We have only to break our bondage to the lesser forms of gravitation terrestrial and solar. This means to stop believing in the inevitability of our subservience to these forms, to become inwardly still, and to let the vibrations of galactic space impress themselves upon our consciousness in their purity, their simplicity, their transcendence.

To let it happen: this is the key. We must let Uranus' invisible light become radiance within our silence. We must accept the discontinuity, the inconsistency, the paradoxes of spiritual existence.

346 PLANETS IN THERAPY

We must consent to be the "waterfalls," even though it means being deeply bruised by the rocks and the shock of plumbing into the depth, because what in us falls may be redeemed into light and illumine the minds of all men. Uranus demands of us the sacrifice of the waterfall, and we must let it happen. This is the supreme inconsistency; that the noise and passion of the waterfall is, to galactic ears, the silence that the divine can fecundate. At the core of the hurricane there is silence and stillness and so it is at the heart of all crises truly accepted and welcomed. [176]

Jules was emotionally exhausted from a year of relational upheavals. He began to let go of his expectations and to accept being a divorced and unmarried man. Then, at the final partile conjunction of Saturn conjunct Uranus, opposite Mars, something unexpected occurred: He called up Helen, humbly groveled and begged her to take him back, and they rekindled their romance, discovering a deep kinship. There was a release of Mars-Uranus energy that made Jules feel very sexually alive, but he felt no urgency to form a traditional marriage or domestic partnership. Helen wasn't inclined that way, was focused on her children, and didn't want them to live together. They saw each other once or twice a week and pursued their independent life goals. Jules felt grateful for the freedom this relationship afforded him (Uranus in Libra). Loving Helen worked out differently than he expected, yet it was wonderful. He also met one of Helen's friends, a vice president in a high-tech firm who offered Jules a lucrative business opportunity (Uranus: high-tech; 8th house: business, stock options). The changes during this Saturn transit were intense and unpredictable, but within one year Jules's life was totally transformed.

## A Case of Depression and Family Trauma

Tamara suffered from chronic depression. She had natal Pluto and Jupiter conjunct in Leo in her 4th house, square Sun-Saturn in Scorpio. Natal Pluto was exactly twelve degrees away from the IC, so I could see that her solar arc MC was opposite natal Pluto at age twelve. When I asked Tamara if there was any family trauma or loss

when she was twelve she said that her mother had committed suicide when she was eleven. After processing with her the impact of
that tragedy, I wondered aloud why the astrological measure was off
by a year. Perhaps, I wondered, her birth time was slightly inaccurate
and that would account for the discrepancy. Tamara replied that at
age 12 her father remarried and that she suddenly had to cope not
only with the loss of her mother but also the introduction of a new
woman into the family and household. That's when the emotional
impact of her mother's death really hit her. Solar arc MC opposite
Pluto in the 4th house represented trauma, death in the family, loss,
and the subtle power struggles she faced as an adolescent living
with a woman who replaced her mother in the home, before she'd
had a chance to mourn mother's death. This, she said, was when her
depression started. Tamara had always struggled to accept her stepmother, and to not feel guilty about having a relationship with her.
Tamara came to the realization that it was okay for her to have two
mothers, that it wasn't her fault that her mother died, and that she
had a stepmother. But many questions remained about her mother.
Who was she and what had she suffered? Now, while transiting
Saturn in Leo passed over natal Pluto, Tamara began a process of
grieving, redemption through suffering, and bringing closure to
these traumatic events.

Pluto in the 4th house can signify some highly charged issue or
trauma from the past, the family, one's ancestry. It occurred to me
that Tamara and her family, being Jewish, probably suffered from
trauma stemming from the Holocaust, with much intergenerational
transmission of stress, anxiety, and trauma. I wondered if perhaps
her mother's severe depression and eventual suicide were an expression of this. Tamara recalled that her father was profoundly traumatized by the Holocaust, having lost several relatives who died in
concentration camps. He was emotionally shut down and detached,
to the point of seeming somewhat numb. Her parents' marriage
wasn't a happy one. She recalled that her mother had been beaten
by her parents, whose families had been persecuted by Bolsheviks
in Russia. It wasn't unreasonable to ponder whether this history of
family trauma and domestic violence could have been a source of
her mother's despair and mental illness. All of this material came

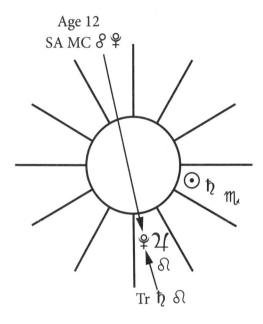

**26. Tamara**

to light while transiting Saturn was conjunct natal Pluto-Jupiter in Leo in her 4th house. The influence of Jupiter seemed to denote the magnitude of the family drama, trauma, and upheaval. Jupiter in Leo could also represent recovering a feeling of pride, dignity, and self-respect that her mother had lost touch with. Through remembrance and ritual, Tamara began to heal ancestral wounds of exile and persecution that were at the root of suffering and depression in her family and in her own psyche. Before this conversation, Tamara said, she'd never before made this connection between mother's suicide, intergenerational trauma, and her own depressed mood. Interpreting Pluto in the 4th house in this way had a powerful emotional impact.

## Death and Awakening

A crisis everyone will eventually face is experiencing the death of a loved one. My father died when transiting Pluto went stationary direct conjunct my natal Saturn. It was very sad, but necessary and inevitable. My father had natal Sun, Mars, Jupiter, and Saturn conjunct in Virgo. He was born the same week as Zipporah Dobyns and John Glenn. He was focused, educated, stern, analytical; he could be sharp and critical. He was a sociologist who studied the media and authored eleven books. He developed his natal potential admirably. He fell ill at the exact transit of Neptune opposite natal Neptune. In his final weeks and days he spent much of his time seemingly asleep but with his eyes wide open and looking upward toward his third eye. For ten weeks he appeared to be traveling in other worlds, gazing into realms beyond his physicality. Witnessing that during his Neptune transit was enlightening for me, and hopefully for him as well. He died October 15, 2005, during a lunar eclipse precisely at his Midheaven.

## HEALING EMOTIONAL TRAUMA

Kova came to see me in a state of emotional crisis and anguish. I immediately noticed she had natal Pluto closely square her Ascendant and opposite the Moon in Aquarius. Lunar aspects are always pivotal, and one shouldn't underestimate the importance of aspects to the Ascendant or Midheaven. Arguably Kova's entire story can be understood as an expression of Pluto opposite Moon and square Ascendant, aspects that suggest one could be touched by loss, trauma, or death. Kova informed me that, "My brother was killed as a young man in Vietnam. I was sexually abused by my uncle. I was date raped at 16. My father was bipolar, violent. I've had a lot of issues about judgment from women and feeling like women were trying to destroy me." These were manifestations of Pluto square Ascendant and opposite Moon. She'd been through hell. And there was much more.

At age 13, when solar arc Pluto reached conjunction to Kova's MC, there were several crucial events. "When I was 13, a girlfriend tried to strangle me because she was jealous about a boy who liked me. Soon thereafter I was diagnosed with lymphoma and underwent radiation, and surgery. Then during the second surgery I had a near-death experience. And if that wasn't enough, three weeks after my near-death experience my dad tried to assault me and my mother."

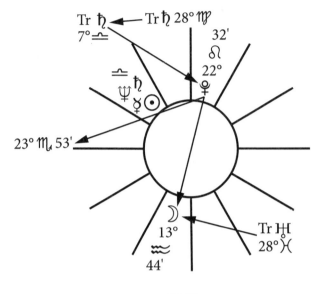

**27. Kova**

The highly evocative symbolism of astrology can spur spontaneous recovery of memories and healing from emotional trauma. Our discussion of this Pluto-Moon-Ascendant configuration gradually went deeper and closer to the original trauma of disturbances in the early mother-child relationship. Kova said, "My mother has always been hostile toward me. She wasn't safe and nurturing. I was born two months premature. I started out in an incubator for 6–8 weeks, with no touching, only bottle-fed. When I came out of the hospital we bonded poorly." The tearing apart of the primary attachment bond was signified by Moon opposite Pluto. At birth, Moon and Pluto were seven degrees apart, so by secondary progression this Moon-Pluto aspect would perfect in less than one year; that is, her Moon reached opposition to Pluto within one day after her birth, corresponding to her first year. And obviously her first year of life was very traumatic.

Kova's Sun was in the 11th house, the house corresponding to Aquarius, the eleventh sign. With her Libra Sun and Venus in the 11th house, Kova was a delightful, affable, beautiful, sweet person. She was deeply involved with her church and charitable organizations where she had many friends. She was deeply caring and emotionally involved with others, and a concerned, nurturing mother. Note that Kova's Moon is 21° 55' from the IC. She had her first child when her solar arc Moon was conjunct the IC, a few weeks before her 22nd birthday; she also had transiting Saturn in Cancer square Sun-Saturn in Libra (marriage and commitment).

In April 2010, Kova's mother had two strokes. Transiting Saturn and Uranus were at 28° Virgo/Pisces, in aspects of 45° and 135° to her natal Moon. Mother was now living with Kova and husband. At time of consultation (a few months later), transiting Saturn had moved into Libra, semisquare Pluto in Leo. I said, "It must be painful for you now that she's old and needy and you're caring for her. It must touch that part of you that was hurt by her refusal to validate you; I'm thinking here about Moon opposite Pluto in Leo as a symbol of narcissistic injuries." Kova said, "In my first two months, nobody held me or touched me. I was a hypersensitive, screaming baby. At my birth, mom didn't want to be married or pregnant and was in great emotional distress. I felt that she resented my existence." I said, "This the perfect time to deal with all these traumas and issues with your mother now that she's living with you and is at the end of her life. This Uranus transit to your Moon-Pluto brings an urge toward emotional closure and completion, which you're now achieving." Having this conversation over several sessions brought Kova some emotional relief. We could understand how these experiences had helped make her a fierce, loving, protective mother and grandmother, who was currently involved in helping her two daughters through their own marital problems. Saturn in Libra was transiting over her natal Libra planets in the 11th house, the relationship-7th house from the child-5th house. Kova had learned to face crisis and emotional ordeals with strength, determination, and unwavering love for her friends and family.

## The Astrology of Drugs and Substance Abuse

Some people deal with the stress of life and the world crisis by using lots of drugs—whether it is prescription pain medication, antidepressants, cocaine, or *ayahuasca*. I can't say enough bad about the abuse of speed, cocaine, and heroin. I've seen patients in my office strung out on crystal meth; these were some of the most extremely disordered, dysfunctional, and confused individuals I've ever met. The same is true of crack cocaine. I've never seen one good thing result from the use of these drugs. They cause gripping and disordering addictions.

Take the story of actor Charlie Sheen being fired from the TV sitcom "Two and a Half Men" after a drug-induced loss of judgment, during a transiting Neptune-Sun-Mars conjunction in Aquarius— a classic Neptune meltdown. Neptune rules drugs, addictions, delusions and grandiosity. Mars fuels Neptune's binges, inflation, impaired judgment and loss of self-control. Charlie bragged about how much crack he smoked and how his parties were trips to the Moon. Mars also lent a hostile, vituperative tone to Sheen's public comments about his producers and fellow cast members. During this time Sheen came across to the public as a completely bent and unhinged individual.

Then there's pot. So many people enjoy smoking weed and find that it enhances their creativity and sensory enjoyment of life. But I've also seen problems in people who use it constantly, especially health conditions such as asthma, bronchitis, throat and lung infections, dental plaque and gum disease, and negative impact on heart function. One client with Sun and Moon in Pisces was always telling me about his problems with asthma, and his need to use inhalers. Some months later he mentioned that every morning he liked to suck in a huge bong hit before he rolled out of bed. I said, "So you're giving yourself asthma." Any medicine can be overused and abused. A medicine should be a condiment of life, not the main course and the only nutrient. Certain entheogens or psychedelic plant medicines can be consciousness-enhancing and play an awakening role for some people at certain moments. For example, the famous Good Friday experiment at Marsh Chapel, Boston University, occurred on April 20, 1962 during a Full Moon in Scorpio conjunct Neptune. If you choose to use entheogens it's best to look for a moment that you'd like to imprint for some time to come. I know several people who journeyed on ayahuasca and had major healing experiences during the same Sun-Mars-Neptune transit that threw Charlie Sheen over the rails with crack cocaine.

But even entheogens can be abused. I know people who do journeys all the time. They take trips on Ecstasy, LSD, or mushrooms during some intense transit of Saturn or Mars, or when the Moon is in hard aspect to Saturn or Pluto or Mars. Then they feel bad, and get very emotionally distraught, depressed, or angry. An entheogen amplifies the inner space and circuitry of the psyche and the nervous system; it can amplify negative, aggressive, or traumatic material in the unconscious. So they may have a difficult time, getting stuck in states of Saturn despair or intense Mars rage. It surprises me that many people who take entheogens don't use astrology to time their journeys. They don't consider the transiting influences and at times they may act contrary to nature. It's like starting some big project on a void-of-course Moon or a waning Moon; this is counterintuitive for an astrologer.

A man named Wesley took an LSD journey on the day of a Moon-Saturn conjunction in Virgo. Most people feel a little depressed and anxious during a Moon-Saturn conjunction in Virgo. Wesley spent his whole trip in a state of emotional agony with self-critical voices telling him he was never good enough, in a state of intense anxiety. The drug just magnified the symbolism of the moment. I prefer to use that Virgo energy to clean my house and straighten up my desk, or work on my yoga poses and abdominal exercises. Another time Wesley took ayahuasca when the Moon was conjunct Pluto and he spent the entire time barfing. It was a total cleanse and emotional catharsis; and perhaps this needs to happen sometimes. But if you take a psychedelic journey presumably you want visions, expansion of perspective, lightness of being, so better to choose more favorable planetary aspects, for example transits involving Neptune-Sun, Neptune-Mercury, Neptune-Jupiter, or Neptune-Venus. These experiences need to happen at the right moment, with the right set and setting, the right intention and emotional readiness, and the right environment—safe, protected, in a place of natural beauty.

In April 1980, while my transiting Neptune was conjunct natal Saturn, I went to a spiritual retreat at the famous Indian Hot Springs in Eden, Arizona, near Safford. On the day of a Moon-

Neptune conjunction I was offered several fresh, juicy peyote cacti, which I chewed up and swallowed down with a mouthful of juice. I spent the day wandering around in the desert gazing at gorgeous blooming spring wildflowers and luminous hummingbirds hovering in eternity. My vibration was raised immensely and I ended the day sitting in lotus posture next to a hot mineral pool doing *bhastrika pranayama*, the Breath of Fire, and experienced myself transform into the plumed serpent Quetzalcoatl. As the sun set I felt the presence of the spirit of Peyote—father of visions, keeper of the door. This day is indelibly inscribed in my heart. It was a beautiful moment that's still alive for me. But I don't need to repeat that experience, because something different is happening now. Astrologers don't get hung up on the past or fixated on peak experiences. We keep growing and evolving.

## CULTURE, CRISIS, AND CREATIVITY

In the summer of 1983 I wrote to Rudhyar about his book *Culture, Crisis, and Creativity*, beginning a correspondence that lasted the final two years of his life. In that book, he considered how we can live creatively and meaningfully during our period of historical upheaval, with all its tumultuous social, economic, and environmental conditions, wars and geopolitical stresses, strange weather patterns, oil spills, nuclear emissions, rampant cancer, autism, and diabetes. In his view, we're living in the *autumnal phase* of the present culture cycle. Autumn is the season of decay, the moment of the seed falling into the ground, the withdrawing inward of life, the ending of a cycle. Then we face "the autumnal choice": to disintegrate with the falling leaves, oriented toward inevitable decay, or to participate in the formation of seeds, foundations for a future cycle of vegetation; seeds that are "oriented toward the sacrificial rite of germination, the rebirth of life forms. . . . Leaf decay and seed-rebirth. It is for human beings to choose the current to which they are drawn."[177] In making the autumnal choice we can accept autumnal decay while also looking forward to spring, birth, possibilities, the germination of seeds. We can become seed individuals discerning our role as agents of cultural rebirth and transformation. Our response to historical crisis can go beyond apocalyptic dread, beyond fundamentalism, indifference, or millennial hope, and beyond complacent individualism, to become expressions of a "culture-transcending hope."[178] Seed individuals focus their efforts on ventures and visions that will give birth to a new culture cycle, and live through discordant historical periods with grace and courage, serving as conduits of creative intelligence—of wholeness, love, and unity.

To do this requires attunement to the Spirit and conscious creativity. For Rudhyar, Spirit responds to a vital need and comes in answer, to fill a state of emptiness. Spirit always operates in relation to the requirements of a particular time and place. It wants to respond to us here and now, in our present conditions. Spirituality is a process of becoming a "focalizing lens" for responses of the Spirit. It's a "conscious release of power," expressing future-oriented, evolutionary impulses. Creativity is the ability to envision and act in behalf of the creation or inception of a new state of being:

> What is needed is the rapid. . . development and expansion of a
> consciousness enabling [us] to envision, feel, and become commit-
> ted in advance to an as-yet-unknown future, simply because [we]
> realize that this future is needed and (however delayed it may be)
> inevitable.[179]

This is how we are to use astrology—to envision the future that is needed. A person committed to manifesting a future envisioned state of being is what Rudhyar calls a "hierophanic artist." The term suggests that such a person is able to contain and focus a "hierophany," a manifestation of the Sacred, and is thus a "hierophant," an initiate. Whereas the path of the monk, priest, or ascetic was appropriate in earlier times, the hierophanic artist is Rudhyar's image of the heroic spiritual personage of our era. Hierophanic artists create "magical forms"—images, myths, creative works that exert a liberating, transformative influence, articulating the "seed forms" of a future cycle.[180]

Launching these seed forms could mean envisioning an urban community garden, a wind power business, a brilliant novel, film, or website. It could mean exploring cohousing, permaculture, or bio-dynamic gardening, joining a spiritual community or artist's collective, raising a strong family, playing in a band, or becoming an innovator in our field of study or employment. For me personally, it has taken the form of promoting the marriage of astrology and counseling psychology, to create therapeutic astrology. Whatever you feel to be your calling at this time will suffice. Pick a task, a contribution, a loving, spiritual labor and devote yourself to it. We are seeking to participate in "a purposeful release of focalized power through an effective form in answer to a need."[181] This release of power is impelled by a transformative purpose, not just by a desire to glorify the ego and talents of the creative personality (the goal of what Rudhyar calls "romantic art") or to produce sensual, emotional, or mental pleasures through enjoyment of artistic forms in themselves ("aesthetic art"). What we need is an *art of revelation*, which envisions the redemptive possibilities of this charged and pregnant moment of world crisis. Rudhyar writes:

Is it art's function only to reflect the vulgarization and decomposition of values and symbols of a slowly decaying culture-whole? Is it not rather to inspire, stimulate, arouse, and impregnate our . . . new generations with an eagerness to give up the role of decaying leaves and assume that of seed, pregnant with a living futurity? . . . There are autumnal moments in a culture when a cathartic type of art is meant either to force upon the people who can stand its tragic implications the realization that the culture-whole is nearing its crisis of death and rebirth, or to open the consciousness of a relatively few men and women to the presence and subtle impact of transcendent forces that summon to radical self-transformation and spiritual transmutation those who are ready, and assist those who are willing and able. . . . The magically oriented artist seeks . . . to fecundate open minds by projecting into them a vision and power of transformation.[182]

Several insights flow from this passage. Rudhyar instructs those committed to conscious response to planetary crisis to formulate a vision of our potential future and to remain open to the influence of "transcendent forces" summoning us to act on behalf of this future, through our creative gestures and transformative intentions. In his philosophy, each person's birth represents a potential answer to a need of a greater whole—the family, tribe, nation, humanity, our precious planet Earth, our intelligent solar system, and the galaxies beyond. As astrologers, we follow the discipline of the celestial order and strive to perform our role in planetary evolution, making our lives a performance of the spiritual archetypes represented in our birth maps. We're guided through various initiations and stages of development, and transform ourselves with devotion to each task, each phase of existence. The astrological life takes on the quality of a grand ceremonial. We engage both the peaceful and the wrathful deities, working with all of the energies.

Hierophanic artists create new myths and new visions to counteract the prevailing atmosphere of apocalyptic fear and confusion. This creation of new myths is the optimal response to "the entropic psalmody of the dying culture."[183]

> The myth-maker does not meet his crises in terms of strictly personal circumstances and idiosyncracies; he sees in them symbols; he expands their meaning until they begin not merely to reflect, but to bring to a sharp personal focus, the crisis of his culture and, perhaps, in a larger sense, of humanity. He lives a symbolic life. But it is the kind of symbolic life that fits in and gives meaning to a crisis situation; it is therefore a life of transformation, an alchemical life, a hierophanic life, revealing of the sacred nature of the world crisis.[184]

This is why we need astrology—to discover the myths of our lives so we can live a symbolic life and give meaning to our present crisis, so we can be conscious participants in the planetary rites of passage that are initiating humanity into a new level of consciousness. The current Uranus-Pluto square (2011–2015) is the crescendo and climax of history and the defining astrological event of our present lifetimes. We will surely experience how the power and intelligence of our universe is awake and at play in everything that happens. Now we need the wisdom of the waterfall, and to let the changes happen. If you use your study of astrology to prepare and refine yourself, to form your own vision and enact it, the power of transformation (Uranus-Pluto) can pour through you in the coming years and make something magical and hierophanic happen in your life. I hope that reading this book will help you do that.

## THE MAGNETISM OF THE CENTER

In the early afternoon of September 11, 2001 I was in England, standing inside the Rollright Stones, the oldest megalithic stone circle in Europe. I was transfixed at the center and experienced the focusing and intensification of space created by the circle of stone pillars. I sat in the middle and felt that I couldn't move from the spot. Upon returning to my car I felt a sudden urge to turn on the radio, where the first thing I heard was the announcement that the World Trade Center had been attacked by airplanes. Recalling that moment reminds me to always adhere to the center at the moment of crisis. Astrology is a path that conveys the magnetism of the center at every moment. That includes the difficult experiences too. Astrology is the distillation of meanings through the ordeals of a life constantly subject to the turbulent, sometimes paradoxically mismatched vibrational influences carried by the planets.

For example, my body took a pounding recently while transiting Saturn was conjunct my Ascendant. Two interconnected events occurred within 24 hours at the Full Moon in April 2011. One night, I was at a friend's birthday party. I reached down to pet his dog, who, apparently startled, bit me on the arm below my wrist. The following day was the Full Moon in Libra, conjunct Saturn, opposite Sun and Mars in Aries. Transiting Mars and Saturn were in exact opposition, with Saturn near my Ascendant and Mars conjunct my Descendant. I took my dog Kona for a walk in a local park. Suddenly Kona became aggressive toward another dog, snarling, showing her teeth, lunging, and running rapidly in circles. I tried to break up this fracas, but bearing my fresh bite wound I was somewhat tentative and frightened (Saturn-Ascendant), not commanding and confident and decisive. In the scuffle I fell to the ground and reached out my left arm to break my fall. Suddenly the other dog's owner intervened, pulling the dogs apart, but in doing so he hit the back of my arm, hyperextending the elbow, fracturing my radius and ulna. I had to postpone my usual handstands, headstands, and guitar playing for a number of months. But I gradually resumed running and swimming and getting lots of physical therapy and orthopedic massage. While transiting Saturn is near the Ascendant we have to come to terms with the life of the body. It's often a challenging time when one is bound to face some adversities, or stress involving the body. Astrology was so valuable to me during the weeks of recuperation with my arm in a splint and my ego totally crushed. It helped me understand the power of the moment of impact with the Saturnine Full Moon opposite Mars on my Descendant. I remembered Charles Carter's book on the astrology of accidents, which teaches us to contemplate and understand those intense moments in life when forces collide.[185]

Several people asked me whether, as an astrologer, I could have predicted these incidents. My answer is I couldn't have predicted it, but what's more important is the meaning I derive from the events once they've happened. For example, my transits suggested a need to encounter in others a strong measure of fierce, aggressive, impulsive, abrupt Aries energy (Mars in Aries conjunct Descendant).

My point in recounting this story is that each of us carries our own measure of *dukkha*; each of us is suffering something. This injury reminded me to soften, breathe, accept what is, and generate compassion. It made me want to pay more attention to what others are going through, and to extend the ray of my care and concern. This seems especially important right now with the passage of Neptune into Pisces. In 2011 there has been flooding in the Midwestern United States along the Mississippi river; mass displacement of Japanese residents in the vicinity of the Fukishima nuclear facilities after the recent tsunami; budgetary crises causing cuts in social programs and services and closing of state parks in California and elsewhere; melting of arctic glaciers; people affected by tornadoes, hurricanes, and flooding; the mortgage foreclosure crisis that has lowered housing prices and put many homeowners "under water"—

all of these are manifestations of Neptune in Pisces. This is a period to cultivate spirituality and stillness, to be liquid, fluid, yielding, the fish at one with the ocean.

Powerful forces are gathering in the next few years, especially the square of Uranus in Aries square Pluto in Capricorn, from 2011–2015 (especially in 2012). This potent alignment demands flexibility, adaptability, and composure in the face of intensifying social, economic, and environmental changes, social revolutions, and agitated forces of nature, such as earthquakes, volcanoes, tropical storms. As I write this (in late August 2011), Hurricane Irene is causing flooding and power outages along the east coast of the United States. In other U.S. regions drought and unprecedented heat are causing major crop damage. Just as the 1960s Uranus-Pluto conjunction was a historical watershed, the current Uranus-Pluto square marks a time of planetary change and awakening—a confluence of institutional stresses, reorganization of social and economic systems, global warming and climate disruption, shifting of tectonic plates, and a psychological tilting and recalibration of our axes. The earthquake, tsunami, and nuclear emergency in Japan that occurred on the day Uranus entered O° Aries (the "world point") may be viewed as harbingers events. Currently (in 2011) numerous European countries are on the brink of fiscal collapse, with the potential to create havoc in world financial markets. With Pluto in Capricorn we may see audacious assertions of the power of the ruling classes, corporations, the national security state, and increased social management and globalization of trade, finance, and government, while the Uranian forces of freedom, revolt, revolution, and progressive movements for social change will also be intensifying. Recent uprisings in Egypt, Libya, Syria, and Yemen are coinciding with ongoing or escalating sociopolitical conflicts involving nations such as Iraq, Iran, Afghanistan, Israel, Pakistan, China, India, and Kashmir. International relations are increasingly complex and volatile. And now the Occupy Wall Street movement has spread to cities throughout the United States and the world. Perhaps most pressing of all, our world must find innovative solutions (Uranus) to issues of energy production, resource conservation and recycling (Pluto).

It's important to note when Uranus and Pluto turn stationary retrograde and stationary direct in motion, so we can tune into these changes of planetary phase polarity. And within the long, extended tone of planetary transformation heralded by Uranus-Pluto, we can expect periodic waves, crescendos, and intensifications when planets such as Sun, Mars, Jupiter, and Saturn form aspects to the outer planet square. For example, note these periods:

- June 2012, Sun in Cancer opposite Pluto in Capricorn, square Uranus in Aries.
- July 2012 Mars in Libra opposite Uranus, square Pluto.
- September 2012: Sun in Libra opposite Uranus, square Pluto.
- November 2012: Mars conjunct Pluto in Capricorn, square Uranus.
- December 2012-January 2013: Sun-Pluto conjunction in Capricorn, square Uranus.
- March–April 2013: Sun-Venus-Mars-Uranus conjunction in Aries, square Pluto.
- November 2012-October 2013: Saturn in Scorpio quincunx Uranus in Aries, likely to be a notable historical defining moment corresponding to 2012 U.S. election.
- June–July 2013: Sun and Mars in Cancer, opposite Pluto, square Uranus.
- July 2013–May 2014: Jupiter in Cancer opposite Pluto, square Uranus. Sun and Mars also transit in Cancer, July–August 2013.
- January 2014: Sun-Pluto conjunction in Capricorn, square Mars in Libra.
- April 2014: Sun conjunct Uranus in Aries, square Pluto.
- June–July 2014: Sun in Cancer, Mars in Libra, aspecting Uranus and Pluto.
- November 2014: Mars conjunct Pluto in Capricorn, square Uranus.
- January 2015: Sun conjunct Pluto in Capricorn, square Uranus.
- July 2015: Sun and Mars in Cancer, opposite Pluto, square Uranus.

- January 2016: Sun-Pluto in Capricorn, square Uranus.
- October 2016: Mars-Pluto in Capricorn, square Jupiter in Libra, square Uranus.
- July 2017: Sun and Mars in Cancer, opposite Pluto in Capricorn, square Uranus.

In 2018–19 Saturn transits Capricorn, and is joined by Jupiter, forming a triple conjunction of Jupiter-Saturn-Pluto throughout 2020. Study how these planets in the final ten degrees of Capricorn activate your horoscope so you can be prepared to respond to the forces moving through you, and to meet this decade's challenges with Capricorn leadership, professionalism, and effective organizing skills.

Obviously many other things will be happening astrologically (for example, the Jupiter-Saturn square in August 2015 at 29° Leo-Scorpio), and yet these are the dominant structural influences of these years. I recommend that all astrologers keep a running scorecard of noteworthy personal and collective transformational events during these periods.

As we cross this threshold in history and the evolution of our planet, astrology helps keep us connected to our own center and to walk the true and narrow path with equanimity. With transiting Uranus in Aries from 2011 to 2018, soldiers and armies are engaged and emboldened. So must each individual be bold and heroic and true to our individual destinies and patterns of development. The Uranus-Pluto square signifies revolution, transformation, and reconstruction of paradigms, life structures, and social institutions. The Great Dragon of time and change is snapping its tail. Either we ride on the dragon's tail or we're cast aside with a swipe of its tail. Change is inevitable, but astrology can help us ride the wave, by understanding change. All we have to do is to take a breath and remain responsive to whatever the next transit and the next moment will call forth. And this reminds me of a final story.

On New Year's Eve, January 1, 1980 I sat by myself at midnight on a park bench in New York's Central Park. Snow was falling in blankets on my wool coat and long hair. I was feeling very alone and somewhat sad and afraid. I also felt expectant; I knew I was on a journey but the way forward in my life was shrouded in snowy darkness. I remember looking up at the sky and asking for some guidance on my path. After I sat out in the blizzard for a while I returned to my parent's apartment building at 135 Central Park West, where I was visiting. As I waited for the elevator to arrive an amazing thing happened. John Lennon entered the lobby and walked down the corridor directly towards me. Lennon lived in the Dakota, across the street, so it was not unusual to sight him in the neighborhood, but I'd never seen him so close, and there wasn't another soul around. As he walked past me to the staircase, John gave me a sincere and direct look that silently said hello. Respecting his privacy, I smiled and nodded back without words. It felt like it all happened in slow motion, like a dream. And this reminds me that sometimes, even at the moment of darkness, when we are feeling at our lowest, something totally unexpected and fantastic can happen! One week after seeing John Lennon I left on a road trip to the gentle forests of Oregon where I received the transmission of astrology from several wise teachers. Thirty-one years later, I'm still all lit up by astrology, whose celestial instructions nourish and guide us, helping each of us become a unified ray of the divine.

Appendix

# *Zodiacal Signs: The Pulse of Life*

Rudhyar's book *The Pulse of Life* offers beautiful descriptions of the twelve zodiacal signs.

In Aries, cosmic strength and the power of humanity are expressed through the individual. "Pride may roar through his ego. He may be arrogant."[186] Nevertheless, great force is at his command.

In Taurus, personality seeks to establish itself in a tangible manner. One seeks security and stabilization. Emotion is aroused by objects. This is the phase of coalescing action, functional, productive activity, possessiveness, as well as "determination, stubborn self-will and fixity of purpose."[187]

In Gemini, a person seeks "extension of the sphere of his experience."[188] This is the phase of thought, comparison, analysis, development of intellect, use of language, and craving for classification, logic, and complexity of experience. "There is so much that is felt, touched, dimly sensed."[189] Here one tries to find words "to help memorize the fragrance of fleeting experiences."[190]

In Cancer, we focus our life energies through our emotional attachment to others, and experience fulfillment as we establish a home and family. Here we feel "the need to assume responsibility toward one's fellow men [and women] and to participate consciously in the life of a social whole. . . . [We] limit, stabilize, and deepen each other within the social root pattern."[191]

In Leo, an inner power urges us "to create a progeny," to experience the integration of parents to children, of older to younger generations, "the responsibility of the present toward the future."[192] Here "individualization. . . grows through man's attempts at self-expression. . . . The personality at the Leo stage of experience overdoes everything."[193] The keynote is "dramatic exteriorization of personality in order to gain social recognition. . . . Leo likes to take risks, to make dramatic bids for leadership."[194] The Leo individual "gives generously of self and of life," but exhibits "an unyielding individualism" and "extremes of sensitiveness to anything that seems to challenge personal dignity and pride."[195]

In Virgo, we develop "the power of intellectual analysis and discrimination."[196] Here the focus is self-integrity, health and hygiene, learning in the role of an apprentice, eliminating impurities, and developing greater potency and skill through technique.

In Libra, we experience "the triumph of united action and social cooperation over individualistic self-expression and emotional self-centeredness"—making more tangible "the reality of human interchange, the reality of the community."[197] Libra, the time of the fall equinox and ascendancy of the Night force, denotes "the momentum of the social process."[198] We feel a new social eagerness, and seek love, harmony, and happiness in human relationships. Libra also represents physical attraction, beautiful form, charm, and aesthetic refinement, which causes us to evaluate things, people, and events by referring them to fixed social standards.[199]

Scorpio is the phase of hibernation, death, or regeneration. Here the reality of human interchange, living together, is vitalized, made poignant, dramatic, and inescapable, especially through experiencing sex, the builder of civilization.[200] Rudhyar describes Scorpio as the individual's urge "to merge in absolute union with other individuals in order to constitute together a greater organic whole…. [It is] "the need to be more than oneself…, to flow into others."[201] We experience sex as "a means to reach liberation from the narrow limits of self."[202] Scorpio can also be a phase of "greed for social power and lust" in which we misuse the products of social interchange.[203]

Sagittarius is the phase of "generalizations, or religion and philosophy, of abstraction and metaphysics."[204] Here "men lose the sense of the earth, the narrow feeling of self-preservation and security, the will to personal happiness—and soar on the wings of self-denial toward distant social or mystical ideas."[205] The Sagittarius Centaur symbol suggests that here we possess the horse's power, which we can mount and with which we can expand our range of activity. Thus, it denotes power that can be tamed and used. If Scorpio represents "The 'Two-as-One' realization produced by the ecstasy of sex fulfillment,"[206] then Sagittarius denotes power with "direction and purpose."[207] This may also be a phase of "fanaticism and intolerance

..., a stubborn and unyielding mentality;"[208] an obsession with ethics, codifying and interpreting doctrines of philosophy or religion.
But this may also be the phase of the planner, the prophet, or the
seer.

In Capricorn, the sign of Christmas, "the State rules supreme."
Its symbol of power is Caesar. Caesar and Christ both operate in
Capricorn. "Caesar is at the apex of his power; Christ is only a
hunted baby. Yet Caesar's empire will soon collapse and the power
of the Christos will wax ever stronger through Aquarius and Pisces.
... In Capricorn, the individual power of the individual personality
is seeking its way out, struggling from under the great weight of the
State."[209] In Capricorn, the Night force triumphs. Society and the
State dominate our lives. "Perceivers of the beyond are superceded
by organizers of empire."[210] Here the individual is consumed by
politics and the search for power in society. We assume a profession
and a particular social function. But this can also be the phase of the
yogi's control and mastery over self.

In Aquarius, we pursue social idealism and social reform, dissatisfied with the status quo. Aquarius is "constructive development of
the State and civilization through inventions, social improvements.
... It may also mean revolution and a complete upheaval of State
and civilization. . . . Aquarius represents civilization expanding or
reforming itself through its inventors, seers, and revolutionists. . . .
[We try] passionately to cease being a mere creature of the State"
and pour ourselves into "a specialized social group consecrated
to reform."[211] Here one may be a fanatic or an "inventive genius."
Aquarius denotes rebellion, eccentricity, allegiance to a group, and
dedication to the ideals of Democracy and human freedom.[212] This
is the sign of seed men and women who release "the 'Living Waters'
of the New Life."[213]

In Pisces, we experience "storms and disintegration, . . . purga-
tion. . . and repentance, the death of all established structures. . . .
Pisces is the mythical Deluge and the age of universal dissolution.
. . . [Here we] must cling to no stability or no past greatness. . . .
[We] must learn to give up [our] comfortable reliance upon the
structure of society. [We] must learn to stand alone and to rely only
upon [our] own inner voice, . . . and face the unknown with simple

faith."[214] Here we experience silence and nothingness. The Piscean's duty is "to serve God, . . . that which no revolution can disturb. . . . [It is] to renounce and transcend. . . . [We experience] the Eternal Feminine. . . [,] the eternal Crysalis, which is as nothing, yet contains all potencies of renewal."[215] Pisces is the sign of "metamorphosis, . . . psychic glamor[,]. . . rapture and. . . eternal mist; openness to God and mediumship."[216] There is violence and storm here. "Pisces is aroused depth," but also expectancy, pure compassion, the end of the cycle, "the promise of eternal rebirth."[217]

# Endnotes

1   S. Grof, *Beyond the Brain* (Albany, NY: State University of New York Press, 1985), pp. 393–94.

2   J. Hillman, Senex and Puer, in *The Puer Papers* (J. Hillman, Ed.) (Dallas, TX: Spring, 1979), p. 16.

3   C. G. Jung, A Study in the Process of Individuation, in *Mandala Symbolism* (Princeton, NJ: Bollingen, 1950/1972), pp. 59–60.

4   In an earlier work, I wrote: "Takra's Jupiter precisely opposed my Sun. He himself is a Jupiterian figure with Jupiter conjunct Pluto in Leo, square Mars. A scholar and world traveler, Andrés had served as Venezuelan ambassador to India, stationed for several years in New Delhi, where he hobnobbed with all the local yogis and *jyotishas* (astrologers). He had a vast library full of rare books on astrology, yoga, and mysticism, which I devoured hungrily. We spent days at a time hunkering down in the library of his opulent home in Boulder, Colorado, reading and discussing books on topics such as *vimsottari dasa* progressions in Hindu astrology, ... mythology of the sidereal zodiac .. , and how to rectify a birth time by examining the shape of a person's face. He fed me protein drinks and drove me around in his red Jaguar. With a 5th house Cancer Sun, Takra is a man of ease, comfort, and infectious warmth—a great mentor." G. Bogart, *Astrology and Meditation* (Bournemouth, U.K.: Wessex Astrologer, 2002), p. 34.

5   D. Rudhyar, *Person-Centered Astrology* (1976, Santa Fe, NM: Aurora Press), p. 81.

6   D. Rudhyar, *An Astrological Mandala* (New York: Vintage, 1973), pp. 13–5.

7   "Matthaus Merian originally made this engraving for J. D. Mylius's *Opus Medico-Chymicum* (1618). It was later used in the appendix to the *Musaeum Hermeticum* (1625). Merian presented all the components of the Great Work in a single great synthesis: a horizontal axis separates the sphere of the divine from the wheel of nature. . . . The dividing artist stands surrounded by a forest of metal, separating .. . chaotic matter into day and night, sun and moon, sulphur and mercury, fire and water. The great unification occurs at the centre of the wheel, the interesction of the axes, in the sign of the mercurial lapis. . . . The deer-headed figure . . . is the hunter Acteon, who espies nature (Diana/Luna) unclothed. For Giordano Bruno, he is a symbol of the fearless searcher after truth." A. Roob, *Alchemy and Mysticism: The Hermetic Museum* (New York: Taschen, 2001), p. 465.

Johannes Fabricius noted that this image depicts "mystical union at the still point of the turning world. . . . [A] symbol of totality is the star-studded hermaphrodite triumphing with his twin-bladed ax on the backs of two united lions and subsuming the cross-like division of the engraving, divided horizontally into heaven and earth, vertically into day and night. The lions are symbols of sulphur and mercury, emerging from the earth as a flame and a spring just behind the lions' tails. Also, they symbolize Sol and Luna, who appear as a naked man and woman. . . . Luna carries a bunch of grapes, the Milky Way springing from her breast of abundance; she stands in the Hermetic river, her beauty being admired by Actaeon, the mythical huntsman who for viewing naked Artemis bathing was changed into a stag as punishment. . . . Sol and Luna are chained to the revolving cosmos, which also appears as the wheeling crown of the sun-tree [on both sides of which] stretches the trees of the other planetary gods or metals. . . . Above the trees of the magical garden, the philosopher's egg wheels its way into the world. The entrance of the *ovum philosophorum* into the world of manifest existence takes places with its expulsion from the world of unmanifest existence (or "Paradise"). The chains of naked Adam and Eve show their intimate connection with this birthlike movement of the philosophical egg. . . .[T]heir chains tie them to the world of creation, duality, and sexual[ity]—a level of existence set apart from the world of uncreation, oneness, and spiritual bliss at the top of the engraving. This is the sphere of Paradise symbolized by the heavenly Kindergarten, or the philoso-phers' rose garden." J. Fabricius, *Alchemy: The Medieval Alchemists and their Royal Art* (London, Diamond Books, 1976), p. 161.

8    Angular relationships between planets based on dividing the sky by five (the quin-tile, 72°), and seven (septile, 51°25') are also important. See B. Tierney, *Dynamics of Aspect Analysis* (Sebastopol, CA: CRCS, 1983). Also see S. Arroyo, *Astrology, Karma, and Transformation* (Sebastopol, CA: CRCS, 1978), Chapter Six.

9    See R. Ebertin, *The Combination of Stellar Influences* (Aalen, Germany: Ebertin Verlag, 1972); R. Hand, *Horoscope Symbols* (Atgien, PA: Schiffer, 1981*)*, and C. Harvey, *Working with Astrology* (London: Penguin Arkana, 1990). For further study, read R. Ebertin, *Applied Cosmobiology* (Tempe, AZ: American Federation of Astrologers, 1972*)*; and E. Kimmel, *Cosmobiology for the 21ˢᵗ Century* (Tempe, AZ: American Federation of Astrologers, 2000).

10    I. Yalom, *Existential Psychotherapy* (New York: Basic Books, 1980).

11    N. Tyl, *The Missing Moon* (Minneapolis, Llewellyn, 1995); N. Tyl, *Analysis and Prediction* (St. Paul, MN: Llewellyn, 1974); N. Tyl, *Holistic Astrology: The Analysis of Inner and Outer Environments* (McLean, VA: TAI Books, 1980); N. Tyl, *Prediction in Astrology* (St. Paul, MN: Llewellyn, 1991). Also see Tyl's, *The Expanded Present* (St. Paul, MN: Llewellyn, 1976), an excellent book on secondary progressions.

12    "Bohme called [Saturn] 'the cold, sharp and string, astringent ruler,' who cre-ated the material skeleton of the world. The influences of this planet were held responsible for all kinds of poverty and misery. For the Neoplatonists, however, he rose to become the most sublime figure in a philosophically interpreted pantheon. According to Plotinus, he symbolizes the pure spirit, and Agrippa . . . referred to him as 'a great, wise and understanding lord, the begetter of silent contemplation' and a 'keeper and discoverer of mysteries.' In this way [Saturn] rose to become the patron of the alchemists, their central role model." A. Roob, *The Hermetic Museum: Alchemy and Mysticism*, op cit., p. 189.

13    D. Levinson, *The Seasons of a Man's Life* (New York: Ballantine, 1978).

14    H. Gadamer, *Dialogue and Dialectic* (New Haven, CT: Yale University Press, 1983). Also see P. Ricoeur, *The Conflict of Interpretations: Essays in Hermeneutics* (Evanston, IL: Northwestern University Press, 2007).

15   C. Taylor, *Human Agency and Language* (Boston: Cambridge University Press, 1985).

16   B. Schermer, *Astrology Alive: A Guide to Experiential Astrology and the Healing Arts* (New York: Crossing Press, 1998).

17   G. Bogart, *Dreamwork and Self-Healing* (London: Karnac, 2009).

18   D. Rudhyar, *An Astrological Mandala* (New York: Vintage, 1973), p. 385.

19   A. Ruperti, *Cycles of Becoming* (Sebastopol, CA: CRCS, 1978), p. 7.

20   D. Rudhyar, *The Practice of Astrology as a Technique of Human Understanding* (Baltimore, MD: Penguin, 1968), p. 8.

21   D. Rudhyar, *Person-Centered Astrology* (Santa FE, NM: Aurora Press, 1976), pp. 78, 81, 95, 100, 102.

22   D. Rudhyar, *Astrological Signs: The Pulse of Life* (Boulder, CO: Shambhala, 1976), pp. 12, 15.

23   D. Rudhyar, *The Lunation Cycle* (Santa Fe, NM: Aurora Press, 1967), p. 33.

24   Ibid, p. 32.

25   Ibid, p. 31.

26   Rudhyar says the Third Quarter phase is a "crisis in the formulation and the sharing of meaning and value with other human beings." Ibid, p. 33.

27   Rudhyar, in collaboration with artist Anthony Milner, developed a diagram called the Phase Mandala is a way of visually depicting the major phases of the progressed lunation cycle so they may be viewed as an organic whole. You can find an explanation of the Phase Mandala in Aurora Press' current edition of *The Lunation Cycle*.

28   D. Rudhyar, *The Lunation Cycle*, op cit., pp. 34–5.

29   Summarized from Dane Rudhyar and Leyla Rael, *Astrological Aspects*, op cit.

30   B. Tierney, *Dynamics of Aspect Analysis* (Sebastopol, CA: CRCS, 1983).

31   D. Rudhyar, *The Practice of Astrology as a Technique of Human Understanding*, op cit., p. 65.

32   Ibid, p. 64.

33   See G. Bogart, *Astrology and Meditation* (Bournemouth, U.K.: Wessex Astrologer, 2002) for discussion of these Venus cycles, and the Jupiter-Saturn cycle.

34   A. Ruperti, *Cycles of Becoming* (Sebastopol, CA: CRCS, 1978).

35   Rudhyar wrote, "He who does not really 'transcend' time, but rather includes in his greatly extended perceptions of the whole of his cycle of living as a person… has developed *eonic* consciousness. He understands the meanings of and the unfolding interconnections between all the phases of his evolution as a center of consciousness and of power." D. Rudhyar, *An Astrological Mandala*, op cit., p. 378.

36   Ibid, p. 234. On January 2, 2002, while writing this chapter, I meditated with Rudhyar's picture and asked his spirit to guide me to a theme he would like expressed in this presentation of his work. I drew a Sabian Symbol using the

oracular technique described in *An Astrological Mandala*, using a deck of cards. I drew the Sabian Symbol for 8° Capricorn.

37   G. Bogart, *Finding Your Life's Calling: Spiritual Dimensions of Vocational Choice* (Berkeley, CA: Dawn Mountain Press, 1995).

38   D. Rudhyar, *The Astrology of Transformation* (Wheaton, IL: Quest Books, 1980), p. 65.

39   D. Rudhyar, *The Sun is Also a Star* (Santa Fe, NM: Aurora Press, 1975), p. 53.

40   D. Rudhyar, *Beyond Individualism* (Wheaton, IL: Quest Books, 1979), p. 14.

41   Ibid, p. 142.

42   D. Rudhyar, *The Astrology of Transformation*, op cit., p. 83.

43   Ibid, p. 130.

44   Ibid, pp. 130–31, 136.

45   G. Bogart, *Culture, Crisis, and Creativity: Rudhyar's Prophetic Vision* (Berkeley, CA: Dawn Mountain Press, 1985).

46   D. Rudhyar, *The Sun is Also a Star*, op cit., p. 41.

47   D. Rudhyar, *Beyond Individualism*, op cit., pp. 70–1.

48   Ibid, p. 74.

49   L. T. Yeshe, "Bodhicitta: The Perfection of Dharma." See www.lamayeshe.org. For this discussion I also referred to "Engendering Bodhicitta" by the Venerable Kalu Rinpoche (www.kagyu.org).

50   Because I am power that is total, / I desire nothing./ How could I? / To desire / is to admit lack of power. / But to him that is power as destiny, / death is open. / He marches into it / towards the Soul. / I am marching on, my friends, into my space and my silence. / It is as if I were all open, / open like an ever-receding sky. / It is so quiet / I can sense the heart beats / of multitudes of destinies. / I am poised in all destinies." D. Rudhyar, "23," cited in L. Rael, *The Essential Rudhyar* (Palo Alto, CA: Rudhyar Institute for Transpersonal Activity, 1983), p. 65.

51   D. Rudhyar, *Beyond Individualism*, op cit., p. 74.

52   D. Rudhyar, *An Astrological Mandala*, op cit., p. 288.

53   G. Bogart, *Astrology and Meditation*, op cit.

54   D. Rudhyar, *Beyond Personhood* (Palo Alto, CA: Rudhyar Institute for Transpersonal Activity, 1982), pp. 33, 37.

55   Ibid, p. 38.

56   D. Rudhyar, *The Astrology of Transformation*, op cit., p. 97.

57   D. Rudhyar, *The Sun is Also a Star*, op cit., p. 42.

58   Ibid, p. 79.

59   Ibid, p. 69.

60   In Rudhyar's words, "Pluto refers to the power generated by true occult concentration. . . . It focuses all the energies of the living organism upon a center of immoveable consciousness. At this center, the power of the galactic center—the divine within, yet beyond us—can be experienced." Ibid, p. 43.

61   D. Rudhyar, *Occult Preparations for a New Age* (Wheaton, IL: Quest Books, 1975), pp. 225–6, 234, 250.

62   See Chapter 13 of this volume.

63   D. Rudhyar, *Beyond Individualism*, op cit., p. 74.

64   D. Rudhyar, *Beyond Personhood*, op cit., pp. 7, 12, 20.

65   G. Bogart, *The Nine Stages of Spiritual Apprenticeship* (Berkeley, CA: Dawn Mountain Press, 1997).

66   D. Rudhyar, *Rhythm of Wholeness* (Wheaton, IL: Quest Books, 1983), pp. 159–60.

67   M. Eliade, *The Sacred and the Profane* (New York: Harcourt Brace Jovanovich, 1987).

68   These insights came to me on May 13, 2002, with transiting Mercury and Moon conjunct the exact degree of Rudhyar's natal Pluto.

69   D. Rudhyar, *An Astrological Mandala*, op cit., p. 385.

70   "On this bas-relief from 9th-century BC Nimrud, a scene of homage and reverence takes place under the protection of the sun-disk, here winged, and its consort the moon, a conjunction of pure light and its dark reflection." Commentary from J. C. Cooper, *An Illustrated Encyclopaedia of Traditional Symbols* (London: Thames & Hudson, 1978), p. 53.

71   D. Rudhyar, *Person Centered Astrology*, op cit.

72   C. G. Jung, On Synchronicity. *Collected Works, Volume 8* (Princeton, NJ: Bollingen, 1951).

73   G. Bogart, Vocational Astrology Simplified. *The Mountain Astrologer* (April/May 2012). This is an abridged version of *Vocational Astrology Simplified*, published by Dawn Mountain Press in 2005.

74   The researches of Michel Gauquelin and Cyril Fagan showed that planets placed in the "foreground" of the chart—within ten to fifteen degrees (on either side) of the Ascendant, Descendant, MC, or IC—are accentuated and play a central role in shaping the individual's life and character.

75   G. Hill, *Masculine and Feminine* (Boston: Shambhala, 1992).

76   Z. Dobyns, *Expanding Astrology's Universe* (San Diego, CA: ACS, 1982).

77   N. Tyl (Ed.), *How to Use Vocational Astrology for Success in the Workplace* (St. Paul, MN: Llewellyn, 1992).

78   D. Rudhyar, *An Astrological Mandala*, op cit., pp. 379 ff.

79   G. Bogart, *Dreamwork and Self-Healing*, op cit. In this work I present a complete method for self-unfolding through the yoga of dreams.

80   R. Moore, Ritual Process, Initiation, and Contemporary Religion, in M. Stein & R. L. Moore (Eds.), *Jung's Challenge to Contemporary Religion* (Wilmette, IL: Chiron, 1987).

81   A. Bharati, *The Tantric Tradition* (New York: Anchor Books, 1965).

82  This process is detailed in G. Bogart, *Astrology and Spiritual Awakening* (Richmond, CA: Dawn Mountain Press, 1994.

83  See *Astrology and Spiritual Awakening* for an in-depth discussion of this process.

84  D. Rudhyar, *An Astrological Mandala*, op cit., p. 385.

85  "The inscription on the meditational image urges saturnine self-knowledge. 'Visit the interior of the earth and through rectification (purification through repeated distillation) you will find the hidden stone.' The number seven of the sublimations—Blake speaks of seven ovens of the soul—was assigned to Saturn as the seventh planet in the cosmological system." A. Roob, *Alchemy and Mysticism*, op cit., p. 189.

86  Zipporah Dobyns, personal communication.

87  E. M. Hallowell & J. J. Ratey, *Driven to Distraction: Recognizing and Coping with Attention Deficit Disorder* (Revised edition) (New York: Anchor, 2011).

88  R. D. Stolorow & F. M. Lachmann, Transference: The Future of an Illusion. *The Annual of Psychoanalysis*, volumes 12–13 (New York: International Universities Press, 1985).

89  See "Conscious Suffering" in *Astrology and Meditation*, op cit., pp. 98–103.

90  J. Gottman, *Seven Principles for Making Marriage Work* (New York: Orion, 2000).

91  R. Kegan, *The Evolving Self* (Cambridge, MA: Harvard University Press, 1982).

92  H. Kohut & E. S. Wolf, Disorders of the Self and their Treatment. *International Journal of Psychoanalysis* (59, 1978).

93  E. Edinger, *Anatomy of the Psyche* (La Salle, IL: Open Court, 1985), p. 19.

94  E. Edinger, *The Mystery of the Coniunctio* (Toronto: Inner City, 1994), p. 47.

95  Ibid.

96  G. Bogart, *The Nine Stages of Spiritual Apprenticeship* (Richmond, CA: Dawn Mountain Press, 1997).

97  Edinger wrote, "Psychic growth involves a series of inflated or heroic acts. These provoke rejection, and are followed by alienation, repentance, restitution and renewed inflation. This cyclic process repeats itself again and again. . . ." E. Edinger, *Ego and Archetype* (Boston: Shambala, 1992), p. 42.

98  E. Edinger, *Anatomy of the Psyche* (Wilmette, IL: Open Court, 1985), p. 52.

99  The term "holding environment" was coined by Donald Winnicott. See D. W. Winnicott, *The Child, the Family, and the Outside World* (New York: Perseus, 1992).

100  J. Holmes, *John Bowlby and Attachment Theory* (New York: Routledge, 1993).

101  J. Piaget & B. Inhelder, *The Psychology of the Child* (New York: Basic Books, 1969).

102  L. Kohlberg, *Collected Papers on Moral Development and Moral Education* (Cambridge, MA: Center for Moral Education).

103  See N. Tyl (Ed.), *Sexuality in the Horoscope* (Minnepolis: Llewellyn, 1995).

104    G. Vaillant, *Adaptation to Life* (Boston: Little, Brown, 1977); G. Vaillant, *Aging Well: Surprising Guideposts to a Happier Life from the Landmark Harvard Study* (Boston: Little, Brown, 2002).

105    E. Erikson, *Identity and the Life Cycle* (New York: W.W. Norton, 1994).

106    D. Levinson, *The Seasons of a Man's Life*, op cit.

107    S. Arroyo, *Astrology, Karma, and Transformation* (Sebastopol, CA: CRCS, 1978), Chapter Five; and A. Ruperti, *Cycles of Becoming*, op cit., Chapter Six.

108    D. Rudhyar, Great Turning Points in a Human Life. In *Astrology and the Modern Psyche* (Sebastopol, CA: CRCS, 1976), pp. 159–61.

109    D. Levinson, *The Seasons of a Man's Life*, op cit.

110    M. Lachman, Development in Midlife. *Annual Review of Psychology* (55, 2004), pp. 305–31.

111    A. Ruperti, *Cycles of Becoming*, op cit., Chapter Six.

112    D. Rudhyar, Great Turning Points in a Human Life, op cit.

113    M. Starck, Challenges of Aging. *The Mountain Astrologer* (Dec 2009/Jan 2010), p. 76.

114    Ibid.

115    Ibid, p. 77.

116    E. Cumming & W. Henry, *Growing Old: The Process of Disengagement* (New York: Basic Books, 1961).

117    L. Corbet, Transformation of the image of God leading to self-initiation into old age. In L.C. Mahdi, S. Foster, & M. Little, (Eds.), *Betwixt and between* (LaSalle, IL: Open Court, 1987), pp. 371–88.

118    R. Havighurst, B. Neugarten, & S. Tobin, Disengagement, Personality, and Life Satisfaction in the Later Years. In D. Neugarten (Ed.), *The Meanings of Age: Selected Papers of Bernice L. Neugarten* (Chicago: University of Chicago Press, 1996), pp. 281–87.

119    R. Atchley, *Continuity and Adaptation in Aging: Creating Positive Experiences* (Belmont, CA: Wadsworth, 1999). Also see, P. Kolb, Developmental Theories of Aging. In S. G. Austrian (Ed.), *Developmental Theories Through the Life Cycle* (New York: Columbia University Press, 2002), pp. 264–324.

120    M. Starck, Challenges of Aging, op cit., p. 78.

121    G. Bogart, *Dreamwork and Self-Healing*, op cit.

122    C. G. Jung, *Memories, Dreams, Reflections* (New York: Vintage, 1961), Chapter 6.

123    S. Hoeller, *The Gnostic Jung and the Seven Sermons to the Dead* (Wheaton, IL: Quest Books, 1982).

124    My account of Bleuler's work is adapted from H. Ellenberger (1970). *The discovery of the unconscious: The history and evolution of dynamic psychiatry*. New York: Basic Books.

125  For a riveting account see J. Kerr, *A Most Dangerous Method: The Story of Jung,
     Freud, and Sabina Spielrein* (New York, Vintage, 1994). According to Kerr, Otto
     was the son of Hanns Gross, a prominent professor, considered the founder of
     criminology and "a force in European sociology.... Gross was in no little conflict
     with his ... father. Alarmed at his son's behavior, which was passing beyond eccen-
     tricity into his own special area of competency, outright criminality, Gross senior
     had been trying for months, for everyone's protection, to get his son committed
     to a hospital." Jung was assigned to his case. Gross was described by Ernest Jones
     as 'a genius' with 'penetrating powers of divining the inner thoughts of others.'
     "An extremely brilliant man, Gross never lacked for influential followers through-
     out his short life. His novel psychiatric and psychological theories were debated
     by the best intellects of his day. He ... appeared as a character in a half-dozen
     novels. In Munich he split his time between Kraepelin's clinic, where he had one
     of the prized assistantships, and the cafes of the Schwabing district, Munich's
     answer to Greenwich Village, where he conducted impromptu psychoanalyses
     into the night.... Gross wanted a world where monogamy did not exist, where
     all patriarchal authority had been overthrown [in favor of] communal living and
     self-exploration" (pp. 186–87). He was in trouble over several scandals involving
     female patients, one of whom committed suicide. Also, "Gross was addicted to
     both cocaine and morphine.... [T]he erosion of Gross' personality had only just
     begun and his intellect and charm were still intact. It could have been said about
     him as it was once said of Lord Byron: he was mad, bad, and dangerous to know.
     Gross and Jung hit it off famously right from the start." Jung saw Gross as his
     psychic "twin brother" and dedicated himself to analyzing and curing this impor-
     tant new patient. "Jung devoted every free hour and then some to the care of this
     intriguing man. At one point they stayed up analyzing continuously for twelve
     hours" (p. 187). Eventually, "Gross was able to turn the tables so that what trans-
     pired was equally an analysis of Jung" (p. 188). Sabina Speilrein wrote this about
     Jung in one of her letter-drafts of spring 1909: "Now he arrives, beaming with
     pleasure, and tells me with strong emotion about Gross, about the great insight he
     has just received (i.e., about polygamy); he no longer wants to suppress his feeling
     for me, he admitted that I was his first, dearest friend, etc., etc. (his wife of course
     excepted), and that he wants to tell me everything about himself" (pp. 191–92).
     In all of this, one sees expressions of transiting Uranus opposite Jung's Venus and
     Mercury.

126  See H. Ellenberger, *The discovery of the unconscious*, op cit.; and M. Goldwert,
     "Jung's breakdown." In *Wounded healers* (New York: University Press of America,
     1992), pp. 81–91.

127  C. G. Jung, *Memories, Dreams, Reflections* (New York, Vintage, 1963), p. 175.

128  See my discussion of the archetypes in *Dreamwork and Self-Healing*, op cit.

129  D. Bair, *Jung: A Biography* (New York: Little Brown, 2003).

130  E. Edinger, *Ego and Archetype*, op cit.

131  I. Hickey, *Astrology: A Cosmic Science* (2nd edition) (Sebastopol, CA: CRCS,
     1992), pp. 285, 287, 292.

132   The Dalai Lama, born July 6, 1935 6:00 am TLT, GMT: July 5, 1935 at 11:15, Tangster, Tsinghai Province, Tibet, 36 N 32, 101E12. Source: Lois Rodden, *Astrodata II*. The Dalai Lama's birth date and time are disputed. Lois Rodden (astrology's leading authority on the accuracy of birth data) used data cited in a letter from the office of his Holiness, the Dalai Lama, and also cited in his Autobiography, *Freedom From Exile*. Other birth dates for the Dalai Lama that have been offered are July 6, 1933 and December 18, 1933. The birth data used here, July 6, 1935 at 6 AM, is from L. Rodden, *Astrodata II* (Tempe, AZ: American Federation of Astrologers, 1993).

133   D. W. Sue, C. M. Capodilupo, G. Y. Torino, J. M. Bucceri, A. M. Holder, K. L. Nadal, & M. Esquilin (2007). Racial microaggressions in everyday life: Implications for clinical practice. *American Psychologist*, 62 (4), 271–86.

134   S. Aurobindo, *Bhagavad Gita and its Message* (A. Roy, transl.) (Twin Lakes, WI: Lotus Press, 1995), pp. 44–6, 80, 94, 96, 103, 196-97. Gita passages are from chapter and verse II-61, IV-21 & 22, V-23, and VI-7.

135   H. I. Khan, *The Complete Sayings of Hazrat Inayat Khan* (Rhinebeck, NY: Sufi Order Publications).

136   "More than 23 symbols . . . are in this illustration from *Microcosmos Hypochondriacus*, a 17th century alchemical text. Besides the familiar symbols, such as Sun, Triangle, Eagle, Lion, Dove, and Lamb, the picture also contains the Peacock, Pelican, Forge, Caduceus, Goose, Ship, and many other symbolic allusions to the transformative steps and processes of alchemy." J. C. Cooper, *An Illustrated Encyclopaedia of Traditional Symbols*, op cit., p. 2.

137   J. Gottman, *Seven Principles for Making Marriage Work*, op cit.

138   See L. Spoto, *Jung's Typology* (Wilmette, IL: Chiron, 1995).

139   E. Edinger, *The Mystery of the Conuiunctio* (Toronto: Inner City Books, 1994).

140   L. Sargent, *How To Handle your Human Relations* (Tempe, AZ: American Federation of Astrologers, 1958), p. 66.

141   D. Rudhyar, *The Practice of Astrology*, op cit., p. 16.

142   G. Bogart & T. Tarriktar, An Introduction to Minor Progressions. *The Mountain Astrologer*, October/November 1991.

143   A. Ruperti, *Cycles of Becoming*, op cit., pp. 8–9.

144   Ibid, p. 213.

145   J. Robbins, *Diet for a New America* (Tiburon, CA: H.J. Kramer, 1998).

146   R. Ebertin, *Transits* (Aalen, Germany: Ebertin Verlag, 1971), pp. 29, 33.

147   Let's take a few moments to learn how to calculate progressions using an ephemeris, a calculator, and a little basic math. I know that computers can do this for us now, but gaining familiarity with these basic procedures expands our under-standing of astrological techniques and timing. Recall that all the great ancient and medieval astrologers were astronomers and mathematicians.

To progress the birth chart, we observe the movements of each planet in the days after birth, using an ephemeris, and we measure their positions using the same procedures as in calculating natal planets. Let's look at an example. Please follow along with a calculator. A woman named Debbie was born January 31, 1942 at 7:40 am in Miami, Florida. Look up this date in your ephemeris. First we need to check whether Daylight Savings Time or War Time was in effect. As this was a winter birth, Daylight Savings Time was not in effect. However, I note that this birthday occurred during the period of World War II so it's possible War Time was in effect. Using the American Atlas we look up this date and find that War Time began on February 9, 1942, nine days after the native's birth; thus War Time was not in effect. Thus, 7:40 is the birth time; no adjustment is required. Miami is 5 hours west of Greenwich, England, so add 5 hours to the birth time. 7:40 + 5 = 12:40 GMT. The Greenwich Mean Time (GMT) of birth is 12:40, or 12.66 hours. We'll use this GMT to calculate Debbie's natal planets. On midnight January 31 the Sun was placed at 10° Aquarius 29. On the following midnight, February 1, Sun was at 11° Aquarius 30. Thus, in 24 hours Sun moved 1° 1', or 61' of arc. If the Sun moved 61' in 24 hours, then how far did it move in 12.66 hours? We can represent this in this ratio: 61 / 24 = $n$ / 12.66. To calculate $n$, cross-multiply: 61 x 12.66 = 772.26. Divide 772.26 by 24. 772.26÷24 = 32; $n$ = 32'. *In 12.66 hours the Sun moved 32'.* Add 32' to the Sun's first position of 10° Aquarius 29'. 10° 29' + 32'= 10° Aquarius 61'. Subtract 60. The natal Sun is at 11° Aquarius 01'.

Now let's calculate her natal Moon. On midnight January 31 Moon was at 24° Cancer 28'. On midnight, February 1, Moon was at 7° Leo 01'. Thus, in 24 hours Moon moved 12° 33', or 753' of arc. If Moon moved 753' in 24 hours, then how far did it move in 12.66 hours? Set up this ratio: 753 / 24 = $n$ / 12.66. Cross-multiply: 753 x 12.66 = 9532.98. Divide 9532.98 by 24. 9532.98÷24 = 397. In 12.66 hours Moon moved 397' or 6° 37'. Add 6° 37' to Moon's first midnight position of 24° Cancer 28'. 24° Cancer 28' + 6° 37'= 1° Leo 05'. This is the position of the natal Moon. Calculate the other planets in a similar manner.

Now let's calculate Deb's progressed planets for October 31, 2003, when she is 61 years and 9 months old. Count 61 days forward in the ephemeris: April 4, 1942. If we calculate the planets for 12.66 hours we will know where her progressed planets are on her 61st birthday, January 31, 2003. We now correct the GMT to account for the extra 9 months. If 1 year (or 12 months) is equivalent to 24 hours after birth, then each month equals 2 hours of GMT. Multiply 2 hours x 9 months = 18 hours. 12h 40m GMT + 18 h = 30h 40m GMT, or 6:40 (6.66) on the following day, April 5, 1942. This is the date and time we use to calculate her progressed Sun. At midnight April 5, the Sun was at 14° Aries 34,' and the following midnight it was 15° Aries 33'. The Sun moved 59' in that 24 hour period, so how far did it travel in 6.66 hours? Cross-multiply using this ratio: 59 / 24 = $n$ / 6.66 ; 59 x 6.66 = 392.94 ; 392.94 ÷ 24 = 16. 14° Aries 34' + 16'= 14° Aries 50'. This is Deb's progressed Sun for October 31, 2003.

Now, using your ephemeris progress your own birth planets. Using this method, you can look deeply into your future potentials, understanding the internal evolution of the birth moment.

148    M. March & F McEvers, *The Only Way to Learn Astrology, Volume 2: Math & Interpretation Techniques* (San Diego, CA: ACS, 1983).

149    G. Bogart, Seven Dreams in a Case of Childhood Sexual Abuse. *Dreaming: Journal of the Society for the Study of Dreams* (Vol. 3, 3, 1993).

150 See S. Arroyo, *Astrology, Karma, and Transformation*, op cit., Chapter 6.

151 R. Ebertin, *Applied Cosmobiology*, op cit.

152 N. Tyl, *Prediction in Astrology*, op cit.

153 R. Ebertin, *The Combination of Stellar Influences*, op cit., p. 102.

154 Ibid, p. 218.

155 Ibid, p. 132.

156 Ibid, p. 100.

157 Ibid, p. 74.

158 Ibid, p. 163.

159 Ibid, p. 184.

160 Ibid, p. 92.

161 Ibid, p. 93.

162 Ibid, p. 101.

163 Ibid, p. 115.

164 Ibid, p. 71.

165 Ibid, p. 77.

166 Ibid, p. 163.

167 Ibid, p. 71.

168 Ibid, p. 79.

169 Ibid, p. 93.

170 Ibid, pp. 81–2.

171 Ibid, p. 219.

172 "A 9th century cuneiform tablet records the refoundation of the temple of the sun by the Babylonian ruler Nabu-apal-iddina, who sits in reverence beside the rayed disk symbolic of the sun's presence." Commentary from J. C. Cooper, *An Illustrated Encyclopaedia of Traditional Symbols* (London: Thames & Hudson, 1978), p. 163. The image is described thus by the British Museum catalogue: "Nabu-aplu-iddina being led by the priest Nabu-nadin-shum and the goddess Aa into the presence of the Sun-god, who is seated within Ebabbara. Before the god is the solar disc, resting upon an altar which is supported by ropes held by attendant deities, whose bodies spring from the roof of the shrine. In the field above the Sun-god . . . are a lunar disc, a solar disc and an eight-pointed star, the symbols of Sin, Shamash and Ishtar. The god wears a horned headdress and carries the ringed rod in his right hand. The shrine is represented as resting on the heavenly ocean."

173 G. Bogart, *Finding Your Life's Calling* (Berkeley, CA: Dawn Mountain Press, 1995).

174 J. Welwood, *Toward a Psychology of Awakening* (Boston, Shambhala, 2002).

175 Ibid, p. 157.

176 D. Rudhyar, *The Sun is also a Star*, op cit., p. 54.

177   D. Rudhyar, *Culture, Crisis, and Creativity* (Wheaton, IL: Quest Books, 1977), pp. 20, 65.

178   Ibid, p. 145.

179   Ibid, p. 65.

180   Leyla Rael wrote: "Seed forms are the bare, spare, essentialized and condensed expressions of the end of a cycle. They at once recapitulate the ancient yet eternal past in which the cycle was rooted, pose the unsolved problems of the present, and anticipate as yet unknown and unknowable future solutions. They are conveyors— "evocateurs"—of understanding and visions rather than concrete forms serving utilitarian purposes. They may be philosophical or psychological systems, or symbolic and evocative works of art. Whatever they are, they are geared to a future of which their creator can only see the structural outline or prenatal glow." D. Rudhyar & L. Rael, *Astrological Aspects* (Santa Fe, NM: Aurora Press, 1980), p. 79.

181   D. Rudhyar, *Culture, Crisis, and Creativity*, op cit., p. 171.

182   Ibid, pp. 100, 84, 101.

183   D. Rudhyar, *Culture, Crisis, and Creativity*, op cit., p. 149.

184   Ibid, pp. 183–184.

185   C. E. O. Carter, *The Astrology of Accidents* (Bel Air, MD: Astrology Classics, 2010).

186   D. Rudhyar, *Astrological Signs: The Pulse of Life* (Boulder, CO: Shambhala, 1976), p. 31.

187   Ibid, p. 41.

188   Ibid, p. 44.

189   Ibid, p. 46.

190   Ibid, p. 46.

191   Ibid, p. 60.

192   Ibid, p. 61.

193   Ibid, pp. 62, 64–5.

194   Ibid, p. 65.

195   Ibid, p. 68.

196   Ibid, p. 64.

197   Ibid, pp. 80–1.

198   Ibid, p. 81.

199   Ibid, p. 86.

200   Ibid, pp. 88–9.

201   Ibid, p. 90.

202   Ibid, p. 91.

203   Ibid, p. 93.

204   Ibid, p. 96.

205   Ibid, p. 97.
206   Ibid, p. 98.
207   Ibid, p. 100.
208   Ibid, pp. 97, 101.
209   Ibid, p. 107.
210   Ibid, p. 107.
211   Ibid, p. 116.
212   Ibid, p. 118.
213   Ibid, p. 123.
214   Ibid, pp. 124–26.
215   Ibid, pp. 126–27, 129.
216   Ibid, p. 130.
217   Ibid, p. 133.

# *About the Author*

Greg Bogart, Ph.D, MFT is a psychotherapist and astrologer in the San Francisco Bay Area. He teaches in the Counseling Psychology and East-West Psychology programs at the California Institute of Integral Studies, and also teaches developmental psychology at Sonoma State University. Greg is a licensed Marriage and Family Therapist and a board certified professional counselor. He is certified as an astrological counselor by NCGR (National Council for Geocosmic Research) and ISAR (International Society for Astrological Research). Websites: www.gregbogart.net, www.dawnmountain.com.